Be Reasonable

Selected Quotations for Inquiring Minds

Laird Wilcox & John George

Prometheus Books

59 John Glenn Drive
Buffalo, New York 14228-2197

Published 1994 by Prometheus Books

98 97 96 95 94   5 4 3 2 1

Library of Congress Cataloging-in-Publication Data

Be reasonable : selected quotations for inquiring minds : an authoritative reference guide / [edited by] Laird Wilcox and John George.
       p.   cm.
   Includes index.
   ISBN 0-87975-867-8
   1. Rationalism—Quotations, maxims, etc. I. Wilcox, Laird M. II. George, John H.
BL2747.B4   1994
149′.7—dc20   93-34704
                                                                CIP

Printed in the United States of America on acid-free paper.

Contents

Preface

The basic purpose of this collection is to present ideas and points of view to readers, which, we hope, will goad them into some serious considerations (or reconsiderations) of their own values, opinions, and beliefs. We tended to pick viewpoints that were disquieting, skeptical, sometimes cynical, but always thought-provoking.

In the course of various research projects over the past twenty-five years or so, I have collected quotations on subjects of personal interest. Numerous friends also supplied me with a steady stream of material, which was dutifully written down on file cards and in several notebooks. In 1987 I privately published a collection of about five hundred of my favorite examples, and I have also incorporated a large number of relevant quotations in my series of research guides on political and metaphysical movements.[1] John George has also maintained a long-time professional interest in quotations, particularly those that are bogus, fake, and misattributed. He co-authored (with Paul Boller) a detailed study of fake and misleading quotations.[2]

John and I met in 1985 at a lecture he was giving on political extremism at the University of Missouri at Kansas City; from 1989 to 1992 we collaborated on a study of extremist political movements.[3] Being incorrigible skeptics and freethinkers, as well as strong civil libertarians and First Amendment champions, we have found that further collaboration was an easy and natural thing for us, hence this book.

PRINCIPLES OF SELECTION

While much of this material comes from individuals who are widely quoted and represented in other compilations, we attempted to include a fair number of quotations from lesser known sources. We have made a sincere commitment to accuracy and we think we have largely succeeded. However, given the wide range of sources consulted, both primary and secondary, some errors and inaccuracies are almost inevitable. Although we believe that the great majority of these quotations are original to the authors to whom they are attributed, we cannot state unequivocally that this is so in every case. We checked a large number of problematic quotations and ended up discarding several of them. We would be interested in learning of any errors so that we may correct them in a future edition.

We have made an effort to provide a wide variety of material along our lines of interest. Often, for the sake of balance, we chose quotations that we did not agree with ourselves, but which we felt were appropriate for inclusion.

The bias of this collection lies both in its subject matter and in our approach to it. We have purposefully sought quotations that are unconventional, provocative, and iconoclastic. We have a certain disdain for rigid ideological formulations, for mindless causes and crusades, and for fanatics and true believers, as well as for those who would oppress them. We feel that the way to "truth," or any approximation of it, lies in hard, honest thinking, experimentation, and playing around with ideas, including those that are potentially wrong or harmful. John and I are particularly fond of a quotation by the late U.S. Supreme Court Justice William O. Douglas:

> A function of free speech under our system of government is to invite dispute. It may indeed best serve its high purpose when it induces a condition of unrest, creates dissatisfaction with conditions as they are, or even stirs people to anger. Speech is often provocative and challenging. It may strike at prejudices and preconceptions and have profound, unsettling effects as it presses for acceptance of an idea.

CONTEXT

It must be remembered that quotations are, almost by definition, statements removed from their original context. It is not difficult to find contradictory statements in the writings of many individuals, and some writers may be surprisingly ambivalent about an issue. Some civil libertarians, for example, wax eloquent when defending the rights of those with whom they agree, and then attach qualifiers and reservations to the statements of those whom they disagree with or hate. In general, however, we eliminated quotations where there were serious questions about context.

The choice of subject headings is somewhat arbitrary. There were several choices for each subject heading, and we chose the one that we felt was most inclusive.

ACKNOWLEDGMENTS

Both John George and I express our great appreciation to the many people who have sent us materials over the years, and to Eugene O'Connor, our editor at Prometheus Books, whose suggestions and editing have proved invaluable.

Laird Wilcox

NOTES

1. Laird Wilcox, *Guide to the American Right: Directory and Bibliography* (Kansas City: Editorial Research Service, 1969–93); *Guide to the American Left: Directory and Bibliography* (Kansas City: Editorial Research Service, 1970–93); *Guide to the American Occult: Directory and Bibliography* (Kansas City: Editorial Research Service, 1980–91).

2. Paul F. Boller, Jr., and John George, *They Never Said It: A Book of Fake Quotes, Misquotes, and Misleading Attributions* (New York: Oxford University Press, 1989).

3. John George and Laird Wilcox, *Nazis, Communists, Klansmen, and Others on the Fringe: Political Extremism in America* (Buffalo, N.Y.: Prometheus Books, 1992).

Civil Liberties

Law is merely the expression of the will of the strongest for the time being, and therefore laws have no fixity, but shift from generation to generation. BROOKS ADAMS (1848–1927), *The Law of Civilization and Decay,* 1896.

A lawyer's primer: if you don't have the law, you argue the facts; if you don't have the facts, you argue the law; if you have neither the facts for the law, then you argue the constitution. ANONYMOUS.

It makes no difference whether a good man has defrauded a bad man or a bad man defrauded a good man, or whether a good or a bad man has committed adultery: the law can look only to the amount of damage done. ARISTOTLE (384–322 B.C.), *The Nicomachean Ethics,* 340 B.C.

It is part of the function of "law" to give recognition to ideas representing the exact opposite of established conduct. Most of the complications arising from the necessity of pretending to do one thing, while actually doing another. THURMAN ARNOLD (1891–1969), *The Symbols of Government,* 1935.

One of the Seven [wise men of Greece] was wont to say: That laws were like cobwebs, where the small flies are caught, and the great break through. SIR FRANCIS BACON (1561–1626), *Apophthegms,* 1625.

Persecution in intellectual countries produces a superficial conformity, but also underneath an intense, incessant, implacable doubt. WALTER BAGEHOT (1826–1877), *Contemporary Review,* April 1874.

Can any of you seriously say the Bill of Rights could get through Congress today? It wouldn't even get out of committee. F. LEE BAILEY, *Newsweek,* April 17, 1967.

The right to unite freely and to separate freely is the first and most important of all political rights. MIKHAIL A. BAKUNIN (1814–1876), *Proposition Motivée,* 1868.

There is in all of us a strong disposition to believe that anything lawful is also legitimate. This belief is so widespread that many persons have erroneously held that things are "just" because law makes them so. CLAUDE-FRÉDÉRIC BASTIAT (1801–1850), *The Law,* 1850.

The punishment of death is the war of a nation against a citizen whose destruction it judges to be necessary or useful. CESARE BECCARIA (1738–1794), *On Crimes and Punishments,* 1764.

For a punishment to be just it should consist of only such gradations of intensity as suffice to deter men from committing crimes. CESARE BECCARIA (1738–1794), *On Crimes and Punishments,* 1764.

Liberty is the soul's right to breathe, and, when it cannot take a long breath, laws are girdled too tight. HENRY WARD BEECHER (1813–1887), *Proverbs From Plymouth Pulpit,* 1887.

There shall be no differences, save by merit of character, by merit of ability, by merit of service to country. Those are the true tests of value of any man or woman, white or colored. ANNIE WOOD BESANT (1847–1933), *Wake Up India,* 1913.

It is my belief that there are "absolutes" in our Bill of Rights, and that they were put there on purpose by men who knew what words meant and meant their prohibitions to be "absolutes." HUGO L. BLACK (1886–1971), U.S. Supreme Court Justice, 1962.

The layman's constitutional view is that what he likes is constitutional and that which he doesn't like is unconstitutional. HUGO L. BLACK (1886–1971), U.S. Supreme Court Justice, *New York Times,* February 26, 1971.

It is better ten guilty persons escape than one innocent suffer. SIR WILLIAM BLACKSTONE (1723–1780), *Commentaries on the Laws Of England,* 1765.

The public good is in nothing more essentially interested, than in the protection of every individual's private rights. WILLIAM BLACKSTONE (1723–1780), *Commentaries on the Laws of England,* 1783.

In the whole history of law and order, the biggest step was taken by primitive man when . . . the tribe sat in a circle and allowed only one man to speak at a time. An accused who is shouted down has no rights whatever. CURTIS BOK (1897–1962), *Saturday Review,* 1954.

At the foundation of our civil liberty lies the principle that denies to government official an exceptional position before the law and which subjects them to the same rules of conduct that are commands to the citizen. LOUIS B. BRANDEIS (1856–1941), U.S. Supreme Court Justice, *Burdeau* v. *McDowell,* 1921.

To declare that in the administration of criminal law the end justifies the means—to declare that the Government may commit crimes in order to secure conviction of a private criminal—would bring terrible retribution. LOUIS B. BRANDEIS (1856–1941), U.S. Supreme Court Justice, 1912.

We are so concerned to flatter the majority that we lose sight of how every so often it is necessary in order to preserve freedom for the minority, let alone for the individual, to face that majority down. WILLIAM F. BUCKLEY, JR., *The Jeweler's Eye,* 1968.

Judges . . . rule on the basis of law, not public opinion, and they should be totally indifferent to the pressures of the times. WARREN E. BURGER, Chief Justice, U.S. Supreme Court, *Christian Science Monitor,* February 11, 1987.

Today, the grand jury is the total captive of the prosecutor who, if he is candid, will concede that he can indict anybody, at any time, for almost anything, before any grand jury. WILLIAM J. CAMPBELL, Judge, U.S. District Court, *Newsweek,* August 22, 1977.

The verdict of capital punishment destroys the only indisputable human community there is, the community in the face of death. . . . Religious values . . . are the only ones on which the death penalty can be based, since according to their own logic they prevent that penalty from being final and irreparable: it is justified only insofar as it is not supreme. ALBERT CAMUS (1913–1960), *Evergreen Review,* 1962.

It is for ordinary minds, and not for psychoanalysts, that our rules of evidence are framed. They have their source very often in considerations of administrative convenience, or practical expediency, and not in the rules of logic. BENJAMIN N. CARDOZO (1870–1938), U.S. Supreme Court Justice, *Shepard* v. *United States,* 1933.

The law is not the private property of lawyers, nor is justice the exclusive province of judges and juries. In the final analysis, true justice is not a matter of courts and law books, but of a commitment in each of us to liberty and mutual respect. JAMES EARL CARTER, U.S. President, *Dallas Times-Herald,* April 26, 1978.

Any one of the strange laws we suffer is a compromise between a fad and a vested interest. GILBERT KEITH CHESTERTON (1874–1936), *Saint Thomas Aquinas,* 1933.

Nothing can be more abhorrent to democracy than to imprison a person or keep him in prison because he is unpopular. This is really the test of civilization. WINSTON CHURCHILL (1874–1965), Letter, November 21, 1943.

There is nothing that can help you understand your beliefs more than trying to explain them to an inquisitor. FRANK CLARK, *Reader's Digest,* July, 1978.

Our history shows that the death penalty has been unjustly imposed, innocents have been killed by the state, effective rehabilitation has been impaired, judicial administration has suffered. It is the poor, the weak, the ignorant, the hated who are executed [and] racial discrimination occurs in the administration of capital punishment. RAMSEY CLARK, U.S. Attorney General, *New York Times,* July 3, 1968.

It is not uncommon for ignorant and corrupt men to falsely charge others with doing what they imagine that they themselves, in their narrow minds and experience, would have done under the circumstances. JOHN H. CLARKE, American Jurist, *Valdez* v. *United States,* 1917.

The Bill of Rights is a born rebel. It reeks with sedition. In every clause it shakes its fist in the face of constituted authority. . . . It is the one guarantee of human freedom to the American people. FRANK I. COBB (1869–1923), *LaFollette's Magazine,* January, 1920.

There is revolution in reaction, as well as in radicalism, and Toryism speaking a jargon of law and order may often be a graver menace to liberty than radicalism bellowing the empty phrases of the soapbox demagogue. FRANK I. COBB (1869–1923), *LaFollette's Magazine,* January, 1920.

The victim to too severe a law is considered as a martyr rather than a criminal. CHARLES CALEB COLTON (1780–1832), *Lacon,* 1825.

No person shall be held to answer for a capital, or otherwise infamous crime, unless on a presentment or indictment of a Grand Jury, . . . nor shall any person be subject for the same offense to be twice put in jeopardy of life or limb; nor shall be compelled in any Criminal Case to be a witness against himself, nor be deprived of life, liberty, or property, without due process of law; nor shall private property be taken for public use, without just compensation. CONSTITUTION OF THE UNITED STATES, Fifth Amendment, 1791.

Things in law tend to be black and white. But we all know that some people are a little bit guilty, while other people are guilty as hell. However, once you get into the courtroom, you are doomed to do battle: then it becomes yes or no, guilty or not guilty. You cannot bring in a verdict that the defendant is a little bit guilty. DONALD R. CRESSEY, Professor of Law, *Center Magazine,* May–June 1978.

It will be found an unjust and unwise jealousy to deprive a man of his natural liberty upon the supposition he may abuse it. OLIVER CROMWELL (1599–1658), Address, First Protectorate Parliament, 1654.

When law enforcers are shown to have such unswerving integrity, only the most churlish among us would question the methods they use to "get their man," though these methods often involve violations of citizens constitutional rights. . . . Constitutional guarantees are regarded as bothersome "technicalities" that impede honest law enforcers in the performance of their duties. If such methods are shown to be acceptable police procedure, what safeguards are left for someone who is not undeniably guilty but actually innocent. DONNA WOOLFOLK CROSS, *Media-Speak: How Television Makes Up Your Mind,* 1983.

The court should be a place where anybody can come—whatever they have in their pocket—and be able to file a complaint in a simple fashion and at least have somebody give consideration to it and give them an opportunity to be heard. JUDGE THOMAS B. CURTIN, *New York Times,* October 7, 1971.

I hear much of people's calling out to punish the guilty, but very few are concerned to clear the innocent. DANIEL DEFOE (1660–1731), *An Appeal to Honor and Justice,* 1715.

A people who extend civil liberties only to preferred groups start down the path either to dictatorship of the right or the left. WILLIAM O. DOUGLAS (1898–1980), U.S. Supreme Court Justice, quoted in *New York Times* obituary, January 20, 1980.

The Fifth Amendment is an old friend and a good friend. It is one of the great landmarks in men's struggle to be free of tyranny, to be decent and civilized. WILLIAM O. DOUGLAS (1898–1980), U.S. Supreme Court Justice, *An Almanac of Liberty,* 1954.

It is better, so the Fourth Amendment teaches us, that the guilty sometimes go free than the citizens be subject to easy arrest. WILLIAM O. DOUGLAS (1898–1980), U.S. Supreme Court Justice, *Henry* v. *United States,* 1959.

Any time we deny any citizen the full exercise of his constitutional rights, we are weakening our own claim to them. DWIGHT D. EISENHOWER (1890–1969), U.S. President, *Reader's Digest,* December 1963.

Good men must not obey the laws too well. RALPH WALDO EMERSON (1803–1882), *Essays,* 1844.

What is the fairest fruit of the English Tree of Liberty? The security of our rights and of the law, and that no man shall be brought to trial where there is a prejudice against him. THOMAS ERSKINE (1750–1823), *Defense of Thomas Paine,* December 20, 1792.

There is no zeal blinder than that which is inspired with a love of justice against offenders. HENRY FIELDING (1707–1754).

A criminal trial is not a search for truth. It is much too circumscribed for that. Rather, a trial is a formalized contest for the hearts and minds of a panel of twelve. It is a quest for a verdict in which information is selected and screened (we can almost say "processed") before it is allowed to reach jurors. PHILLIP FINCH, *Fatal Flaw,* 1992.

In a civilized society, all crimes are likely to be sins, but most sins are not and ought not to be treated as crimes. GEOFFREY FISHER, Archbishop of Canterbury, *Look* magazine, March 17, 1959.

Procedure is the bone structure of a democratic society. Our scheme of law affords great latitude for dissent and opposition. It compels wide tolerance not only for their expression but also for the organization of people and forces to bring about the acceptance of the dissenter's claim. Both our institutions and the characteristics of our national behavior make it possible for opposition to be translated into policy, for dissent to prevail. We have alternatives to violence. ABE FORTAS, *Concerning Dissent and Civil Disobedience,* 1968.

I should, indeed, prefer twenty men to escape death through mercy, than one innocent to be condemned unjustly. SIR JOHN FORTESCUE, English Jurist, *De Laudibus Legum Angliae,* 1740.

The law, in its majestic equality, forbids all men to sleep under bridges, to beg in the streets, and to steal bread—the rich as well as the poor. ANATOLE FRANCE (1844–1924), *Crainquebille,* 1902.

Ours is an accusatorial and not an inquisitorial system—a system in which the state must establish guilt by evidence independently and freely secured and may not by coercion prove its charge against an accused out of his own mouth. FELIX FRANKFURTER (1882–1965), U.S. Supreme Court Justice, 1961.

It is not only under Nazi rule that police excesses are inimical to freedom. It is easy to make light of insistence on scrupulous regard for the safeguards of civil liberties when invoked on behalf of the unworthy. History bears testimony that by such disregard are the rights of liberty extinguished, heedlessly, at first, then stealthily, and brazenly in the end. FELIX FRANKFURTER (1882–1965), U.S. Supreme Court Justice, *David* v. *United States,* 1946.

The history of liberty has largely been the history of the observance of procedural safeguards. FELIX FRANKFURTER (1882–1965), U.S. Supreme Court Justice, *McNabb* v. *United States,* 1943.

A court which yields to the popular will thereby licenses itself to practice despotism, for there can be no assurance that it will not on another occasion indulge its own will. FELIX FRANKFURTER (1882–1965), U.S. Supreme Court Justice, *A.F.L.* v. *American Sash & Door,* 1949.

That it is better one hundred guilty persons should escape than that one innocent person should suffer, is a maxim that has been long and generally approved. BENJAMIN FRANKLIN (1706–1790), Letter, March 14, 1785.

Nobody wants literate people to go to prison—they have a distressing way of revealing what it's actually like and destroying our illusions about training and rehabilitation with nasty stories about sadism and futility and buckets of stale urine. DAVID FROST and ANTHONY JAY, *The English,* 1968.

When public men indulge themselves in abuse, when they deny others a fair trial, when they resort to innuendo and insinuation, to libel, scandal, and suspicion, then our democratic society is outraged, and democracy is baffled. It has no apparatus to deal with the boor, the lout, and the anti-democrat in general. J. WILLIAM FULBRIGHT, Speech, February 2, 1954.

The more laws the more offenders. THOMAS FULLER (1608–1661), *Gnomologia,* 1732.

The equal right of all men to the use of land is as clear as their equal right to breathe the air—it is a right proclaimed by the fact of their existence. For we cannot suppose that some men have a right to be in this world and others have no right. HENRY GEORGE (1839–1897), *Progress and Poverty,* 1879.

Humanity's most valuable assets have been the non-conformists. Were it not for the non-conformists, he who refuses to be satisfied to go along with the continuance of things as they are, and insists upon attempting to find new ways of bettering things, the world would have known little progress, indeed. JOSIAH WILLIAM GITT (1884–1973), *Gazette and Daily,* February 2, 1957.

In our own lifetime we have seen how essential fair trials are to civilization. The establishment of the modern dictatorships was not the result of a failure of democracy, it was due to a failure of law. There is no "trying" choice between fair trials and free speech, because free speech itself will die if there are no fair trials. For that matter it is almost always the first victim. ARTHUR L. GOODHART, *New York Law Journal,* 1964.

I know of no method to secure the repeal of bad or obnoxious laws so effective as their stringent execution. ULYSSES S. GRANT (1822–1885), Inaugural Address, March 4, 1869.

There can be no truer principle than this—that every individual of the community at large has an equal right to the protection of government. ALEXANDER HAMILTON (1757–1804), Speech, June 29, 1787.

In a free government the security for civil rights must be the same as that for religious rights. It consists in the one case in the multiplicity of interests, and in the other in the multiplicity of sects. ALEXANDER HAMILTON (1757–1804), *The Federalist,* 1788.

I had rather take my chance that some traitors will escape detection than spread abroad a spirit of general suspicion and distrust, which accepts rumor and gossip in place of undismayed and unintimidated inquiry. I believe that the community is already in process of dissolution where each man begins to eye his neighbor as a possible enemy, where non-conformity with the accepted creed, political as well as religious, is mark of disaffection; where denunciation, without specification or backing, takes the place of evidence; where orthodoxy chokes freedom of dissent; where faith in the eventual supremacy of reason has become so timid that we dare not enter our convictions in the open lists, to win or lose. LEARNED HAND (1972–1961), Judge, U.S. Court of Appeals, Address, New York University, October 24, 1952.

What seems fair enough against a squalid huckster of bad liquor may take on a different face, if used by a government determined to suppress political opposition under the guise of sedition. LEARNED HAND (1872–1961), Judge, U.S. Court of Appeals, *United States* v. *Kirschenblatt,* 1926.

Heretics have been hated from the beginning of recorded time; they have been ostracized, exiled, tortured, maimed and butchered; but it has generally proved impossible to smother them; and when it has not, the society that has succeeded has always declined. LEARNED HAND (1872–1961), Judge, U.S. Court of Appeals, Speech, 1955.

The Constitution is not a panacea for every blot upon the public welfare. Nor should the Court, ordained as a judicial body, be thought of as a general haven for reform movements. JOHN MARSHALL HARLAN (1833–1911), U.S. Supreme Court Justice, 1964.

In view of the Constitution, in the eye of the law, there is in this country no superior, dominant, ruling class of citizens. There is no caste here. Our Constitution is colorblind, and neither knows nor tolerates classes among citizens. JOHN MARSHALL HARLAN (1833–1911), U.S. Supreme Court Justice, *Plessy* v. *Ferguson,* 1896.

The convoluted wording of legalisms grew up around the necessity to hide from ourselves the violence we intend toward each other. Between depriving a man of one hour from his life and depriving him of his life there exists only a difference of degree. You have done violence to him, consumed his energy. FRANK HERBERT, *Dune,* 1965.

What is hateful to you, do not to your fellow: that is the whole Law: all the rest is interpretation. HILLEL (30 B.C.–10 A.D.), *Talmud.*

Whatever disagreement there may be as to the scope of the phrase "due process of law" there can be no doubt that it embraces the fundamental conception of a fair trial, with opportunity to be heard. OLIVER WENDELL HOLMES, JR. (1841–1935), *Frank* v. *Mangum,* 1915.

Great cases like hard cases make bad law. For great cases are called great, not by reason of their real importance in shaping the law of the future, but because of some accident of immediate overwhelming interest which appeals to the feelings and distorts the judgement. OLIVER WENDELL HOLMES, JR. (1841–1935), *Northern Securities* v. *United States,* 1904.

For my part I think it a less evil that some criminals should escape, than that the government should play an ignoble part. OLIVER WENDELL HOLMES, JR. (1841–1935), *Olmstead* v. *United States,* 1928.

The Fourteenth Amendment was adopted with a view to the protection of the colored race, but has been found to be equally important in its application to the rights of all. OLIVER WENDELL HOLMES, JR. (1841–1935), *United States* v. *Olmstead,* 1928.

So long as governments set the example of killing their enemies, private individuals will occasionally kill theirs. ELBERT G. HUBBARD (1856–1915), *Contemplations,* 1902.

It is the essence of the institutions of liberty that it be recognized that guilt is personal and cannot be attributed to the holding of opinions or to mere intent in the absence of overt acts. CHARLES EVANS HUGHES (1862–1948), U.S. Supreme Court Justice, *Harvard Law Review,* April 1948.

As long as our government is administered for the good of the people, and is regulated by their will; as long as it secures to us the rights of persons and of property, liberty of conscience and of the press, it will be worth defending. ANDREW JACKSON (1767–1845), First Inaugural Address, March 4, 1829.

If there is any fixed star in our constitutional constellation, it is that no official, high or petty, can prescribe what shall be orthodox in politics, nationalism, religion, or other matters of opinion or force citizens to confess by word or act their faith therein. ROBERT H. JACKSON (1892–1954), U.S. Supreme Court Justice, *West Virginia Board of Education* v. *Barnette,* 1943.

Our protection against all kinds of fanatics and extremists, none of whom can be trusted with unlimited power over others, lies not in their forebearance but in the limitations of our constitution. ROBERT H. JACKSON (1892–1954), U.S. Supreme Court Justice, *American Communications Assn* v. *Douds,* 1950.

I cannot say that our country could have no secret police without becoming totalitarian, but I can say with great conviction that it cannot become totalitarian without a centralized national police. ROBERT H. JACKSON, U.S. Supreme Court Justice, *The Supreme Court in the American System of Government,* 1955.

To compel a man to furnish contributions of money for the propagation of opinions which he disbelieves and abhors, is sinful and tyrannical. THOMAS JEFFERSON (1743–1826), *Virginia Statutes of Religious Freedom,* 1779.

A bill of rights is what the people are entitled to against every government on earth, general or particular and what no just government should refuse to rest on inference. THOMAS JEFFERSON (1743–1826), 1787.

The sword of the law should never fall but on those whose guilt is so apparent as to be pronounced by their friends as well as foes. THOMAS JEFFERSON (1743–1826), Letter, 1801.

It is not only vain, but wicked, in a legislator to frame laws in opposition to the laws of nature, and to arm them with the terrors of death. This is truly creating crimes in order to punish them. THOMAS JEFFERSON (1743–1826), *Note on the Crimes Bill,* 1779.

It is more dangerous that even a guilty person should be punished without the forms of law than that he should escape. THOMAS JEFFERSON (1743–1826), Letter to William Carmichael, May 27, 1788.

Every man should know that his conversations, his correspondence, and his personal life are private. LYNDON B. JOHNSON, Remarks, March 10, 1967.

There are some acts of justice which corrupt those who perform them. JOSEPH JOUBERT (1754–1824), *Pensées,* 1842.

I submit that an individual who breaks a law that conscience tells him is unjust, and who unwillingly accepts the penalty of imprisonment in order to rouse the conscience of the community over its injustice, is in reality expressing the highest respect for the law. MARTIN LUTHER KING, JR. (1929–1968), *Why We Can't Wait,* 1964.

In the ideological fight for dominion over people's minds, the courts are agencies closely connected with public affairs. At least in nontotalitarian countries they remain outside the direct control of the executive establishment. Yet their particular public position of trust has made the courts' conduct of politically tinged trials a crucial element in the political process. OTTO KIRCHHEIMER, *Political Justice,* 1961.

The grand paradox of our society is this: we magnify man's rights but we minimize his capacities. JOSEPH W. KRUTCH (1893–1970), *The Measure of Man,* 1954.

A guilty man is punished as an example for the mob; an innocent man convicted is the business of every honest person. JEAN de LA BRUYÈRE (1645–1696), *Les Caractères,* 1688.

Let no man think we can deny civil liberty to others and retain it for ourselves. When zealous agents of the Government arrest suspected "radicals" without warrant, hold them without prompt trial, deny them access to counsel and admission of bail . . . we have shorn the Bill of Rights of its sanctity. . . . ROBERT M. LAFOLLETTE, SR. (1855–1925), *The Progressive,* March 1920.

Many laws as certainly make bad men, as bad men make many laws. WALTER SAVAGE LANDOR (1775–1864), *Imaginary Conversations,* 1901.

All free constitutions are formed with two views—to deter the governed from crime, and the governors from tyranny. JOHN LANSING, JR. (1754–1829), Debate, Constitutional Convention, 1787.

Love of justice in the generality of men is only the fear of suffering from injustice. FRANÇOIS, DUC de LA ROCHEFOUCAULD (1613–1680), *Maxims,* 1665.

No citizen enjoys genuine freedom of religious conviction until the state is indifferent to every form of religious outlook from Atheism to Zoroastrianism. HAROLD J. LASKI (1893–1950), *Grammar of Politics,* 1925.

If by the mere force of numbers a majority should deprive a minority of any clearly written constitutional right, it might, in a moral point of view, justify revolution. ABRAHAM LINCOLN (1809–1865), First Inaugural Address, March 4, 1861.

Freedom for supporters of the government only, for the members of one party only—no matter how big its membership may be—is no freedom at all. Freedom is always freedom for the man who thinks differently. ROSA LUXEMBURG (1880–1919).

To argue against any breach of liberty from the ill use that may be made of it, is to argue against liberty itself, since all is capable of being abused. LORD GEORGE LYTTLETON (1709–1773).

To punish a man because we infer from the nature of some doctrine which he holds, or from the conduct of other persons who hold the same doctrines with him, that he will commit a crime, is persecution, and is, in every case, foolish and wicked. THOMAS BABINGTON MACAULAY (1800–1859), *Hallam,* 1828.

The legal code can never be identified with the code of morals. It is no more the function of government to impose a moral code than to impose a religious code. And for the same reason. ROBERT M. MACIVER, *The Web of Government,* 1947.

Agents provocateurs are more powerful than ordinary malefactors. They have more means at their disposal because they enjoy a special immunity. The struggle against such sophisticated forms of temptation is especialy difficult for the victim. The marked person is a priori in an unfavorable position. MIESZYSLAW MANELI, *Freedom and Tolerance,* 1984.

All men are created equally free and independent, and have certain inherent rights, of which they cannot, by any compact, deprive or divest their posterity; among which are the enjoyment of life and liberty, with the means of acquiring and possessing property, and pursuing the obtaining of happiness and safety. GEORGE MASON (1725–1792), First Draft, *Virginia Declaration of Rights.*

We need criminals to identify ourselves with, to secretly envy and to stoutly punish. They do for us the forbidden, illegal things we wish to. KARL A. MENNINGER, *The Crime of Punishment,* 1968.

Psychologically, it is important to understand that the simple fact of being interviewed and investigated has a coercive influence. As soon as a man is under cross-examination, he may become paralyzed by the procedure and find himself confessing to deeds he never did. In a country where the urge to investigate spreads, suspicion and insecurity grow. JOOST A. MERLOO, *The Rape of the Mind,* 1956.

May God prevent us from becoming "right-thinking men"—that is to say men who agree perfectly with their own police. THOMAS MERTON (1915–1968), *New York Times,* December 11, 1968.

Repression occurs when agents of social control use force to prevent movement organizations from functioning or prevent people from joining movement organizations. The variety of repressive tactics includes indicting activists on criminal charges, using infiltrators to spy on or disrupt groups, physically attacking members and offices, harassing members and potential recruits by threatening their access to jobs and schools, spreading false information about groups and people, and anything else that makes it more difficult for the movement to put its views before relevant audiences. FREDERICK D. MILLER, in *Social Movements of the Sixties and Seventies* (Jo Freeman, ed.), 1983.

Laws are maintained in credit, not because they are essentially just, but because they are laws. It is the mystical foundation of their authority; they have none other. MICHEL de MONTAIGNE (1532–1592), *Essays.*

There is no crueler tyranny than that which *is* perpetrated under the shield of law and in the name of Justice. CHARLES-LOUIS de SECONDAT, BARON de MONTESQUIEU (1689–1755), *The Spirit of the Laws,* 1748.

There is no liberty if the judiciary power be not separated from the legislative and executive. CHARLES-LOUIS de SECONDAT, BARON de MONTESQUIEU (1689–1755), *The Spirit of the Laws,* 1748.

We ought to be very cautious in the prosecution of magic and heresy. The attempt to put down these two crimes may be extremely perilous to liberty, and may be the origin of a number of petty acts of tyranny if the legislator be not on his guard; for as such an accusation does not bear directly on the overt acts of a citizen, but refers to the idea we entertain of his character. CHARLES-LOUIS de SECONDAT, BARON de MONTESQUIEU (1689–1755), *The Spirit of the Laws*, 1748.

Commitment to the religion clauses of the Constitution is a moral commitment to them as articles of peace in a pluralistic society. JOHN COURTNEY MURRAY, *We Hold These Truths*, 1960.

Speaking generally, punishment hardens and numbs, it produces obstinacy, it sharpens the sense of alienation and strengthens the power of resistance. FRIEDRICH NIETZSCHE (1844–1900), *The Genealogy of Morals*, 1887.

A prohibition whose reason we do not understand or admit is not only for the obstinate man but also for the man thirsty for knowledge almost the injunction: let us put it to the test, so as to learn why this prohibition exists. FRIEDRICH NIETZSCHE (1844–1900), *The Wanderer and His Shadow*, 1880.

The number of laws is constantly growing in all countries and, owing to this, what is called crime is very often not a crime at all, for it contains no element of violence or harm. P. D. OUSPENSKY (1878–1947), *A New Model of the Universe*, 1931.

In existing criminology there are concepts: a criminal man, a criminal profession, a criminal society, a criminal sect, a criminal cast and a criminal tribe, but there is no concept of a criminal state, or a criminal government, or criminal legislation. Consequently the biggest crimes actually escape being called crimes. P. D. OUSPENSKY (1878–1947), *A New Model of the Universe*, 1931.

As to religion, I hold it to be the indispensable duty of all government to protect all conscientious professors thereof, and I know of no other business which government hath to do therewith. THOMAS PAINE (1737–1809), *Age of Reason*, 1793.

The first maxim of a free state is that the laws be made by one set of men, and administered by another; in other words, that the legislative and judicial characters are kept separate. WILLIAM PALEY (1743–1805), *The Principles of Moral and Political Philosophy*, 1785.

The proper end of punishment is not the satisfaction of justice, but the prevention of crime. WILLIAM PALEY (1743–1805), *The Principles of Moral and Political Philosophy*, 1785.

Justice without force is impotent, force without justice is tyranny. Unable to make what is just strong, we have made what is strong just. BLAISE PASCAL (1623–1662), *Pensées*.

The guarantee of equal protection cannot mean one thing when applied to one individual and something else when applied to a person of another color. If both are not accorded the same protection, then it is not equal. LEWIS F. POWELL, JR., U.S. Supreme Court Justice, *University of California* v. *Bakke*, 1978.

Lawyers [are] operators of the toll bridge across which anyone in search of justice has to pass. JANE BRYANT QUINN, *Newsweek,* October 9, 1975.

The reformative effect of punishment is a belief that dies hard, chiefly, I think, because it [punishment] is so satisfying to our sadistic impulses. BERTRAND RUSSELL (1872–1970), *Ideas That Have Harmed Mankind,* 1946.

Stupid men—you would believe in laws which punish murder by murder. GEORGE SAND (1804–1876), *Intimate Journal,* 1837.

If the prisoner should ask the judge whether he would be content to be hanged, were he in his case, he would answer no. Then, says the prisoner, do as you would be done to. JOHN SELDEN (1584–1654), *Table-Talk,* 1689.

It is the deed that teaches, not the name we give it. Murder and capital punishment are not opposites that cancel one another, but similars that breed their own kind. GEORGE BERNARD SHAW (1856–1950), quoted in *Amnesty Update,* January/February 1990.

Assassination on the scaffold is the worst form of assassination, because there it is invested with the approval of society. GEORGE BERNARD SHAW (1856–1950), *Maxims For Revolutionaries,* 1903.

It is the right of our people to organize to oppose any law and any part of the constitution with which they are not in sympathy. ALFRED E. SMITH (1873–1944), Speech, League of Women Voters, 1927.

Vices are simply the errors which a man makes in his search after his own happiness. Unlike crimes, they imply no malice toward others, and no interference with their persons or property. In vices, the very essense of crime—that is, the design to injure the person or property of another—is wanting. It is a maxim of the law that there can be no crime without a criminal intent. . . . LYSANDER SPOONER (1808–1887), 1875.

The right to defy an unconstitutional statute is basic in our scheme. Even when an ordinance requires a permit to make a speech, to deliver a sermon, to picket, to parade, or to assemble, it need not be honored when it's invalid on its face. POTTER STEWART (1915–1985), U.S. Supreme Court Justice, *Walker* v. *Birmingham,* 1967.

The Fourth Amendment and the personal rights it secures have a long history. At the very core stands the right of a man to retreat into his own home and there be free from unreasonable governmental intrusion. POTTER STEWART (1915–1985), U.S. Supreme Court Justice, *Bartkus* v. *Illinois,* March 5, 1961.

The right to enjoy property without unlawful deprivation, no less than the right to speak out or the right to travel is, in truth, a "personal" right. POTTER STEWART (1915–1985), U.S. Supreme Court Justice, *Lynch* v. *Household Finance Corporation,* 1972.

It is a maxim among lawyers that whatever hath been done before may be done again, and therefore they take special care to record all the decisions formerly made against common justice and the general reason of mankind. These, under the name of precedents, they produce as authorities to justify the most iniquitous opinions; and the judges never fail of directing them accordingly. JONATHAN SWIFT (1667–1745), *Gulliver's Travels,* 1726.

Laws are like cobwebs, which may catch small flies, but let wasps and hornets break through. JONATHAN SWIFT (1667–1745), *Gullivers Travels,* 1726.

Men are rewarded and punished not for what they do, but rather for how their acts are defined. This is why men are more interested in better justifying themselves than in better behaving themselves. THOMAS SZASZ, *The Second Sin,* 1973.

The more corrupt the state, the more numerous the laws. CORNELIUS TACITUS (55–117 A.D.).

Constitutions are checks upon the hasty action of the majority. They are the self-imposed restraints of a whole people upon a majority of them to secure sober action and a respect for the rights of the minority. WILLIAM HOWARD TAFT (1857–1930), U.S. President, Veto Message, Arizong Enabling Act, 1911.

No doctrine involving more pernicious consequences was ever invented by the wit of man than that any [constitutional] provisions can be suspended during any of the great exigencies of government. ROGER B. TANEY (1777–1864), U.S. Supreme Court Justice, *Ex parte Milligan,* 1866.

Laws are rules established by men who are in control of organized violence for the nonfulfillment of which those who do not fulfill them are subjected to personal injuries, the loss of liberty, and even capital punishment. In this definition is contained the answer to the question as to which gives men the power to establish laws. What gives them the power to establish laws is the same thing which secures obedience to them: organized violence. LEO TOLSTOY (1828–1910), *The Slavery of Our Times.*

We enact many laws that manufacture criminals, and then a few that punish them. BENJAMIN R. TUCKER (1854–1939), *Instead of a Book,* 1893.

Everyone has the right to freedom of thought, conscience and religion; this right includes freedom to change his religion or belief, and freedom, either alone or in community with others, and in public or in private, to manifest his religion or belief in teaching, practice, worship and observance. UNITED NATIONS UNIVERSAL DECLARATION OF HUMAN RIGHTS, Article 18, 1948.

All men have equal rights to liberty, to their property, and to the protection of the laws. VOLTAIRE (1694–1778), *Essay on Manners,* 1756.

It is better to risk saving a guilty man than to condemn an innocent one. VOLTAIRE (1694–1778), *Zadig,* 1747.

The tyranny of the many would be when one body takes over the rights of others, and then exercises its power to change the laws in its favor. VOLTAIRE (1694–1778), *Philosophical Dictionary,* 1764.

No man shall twice be sentenced by Civil Justice for one and the same crime, offence, or trespass. NATHANIEL WARD (1578-1652), *The Massachusetts Body of Liberties,* 1641.

Life and liberty can be as much endangered from illegal methods used to convict those thought to be criminals as from the actual criminals themselves. EARL WARREN (1891-1974), Chief Justice, U.S. Supreme Court, 1959.

To require conformity in the appreciation of sentiments or the interpretation of language, or uniformity of thought, feeling, or action, is a fundamental error in human legislation—a madness which would be only equalled by requiring all to possess the same countenance, the same voice or the same stature. JOSIAH WARREN (1798-1874), *Equitable Commerce,* 1855.

Whatever government is not a government of laws, is a despotism, let it be called what it may. DANIEL WEBSTER (1782-1852), Speech, August 25, 1825.

Lawyers have been known to wrest from reluctant juries triumphant verdicts of acquittal for their clients, even when those clients, as often happens, were clearly and unmistakably innocent. OSCAR WILDE (1854-1900), *The Decay of Lying,* 1889.

The rights of all persons are wrapped in the same constitutional bundle as those of the most hated member of the community. A. L. WIRIN, *Time,* February 10, 1978.

Envy, Resentment, and Egalitarianism

Few men have the strength of character to rejoice in a friend's success without a touch of envy. AESCHYLUS (525–456 B.C.), *Agamemnon,* 490 B.C.

The dog with the bone is always in danger. AMERICAN PROVERB.

As iron is eaten away by rust, so the envious are consumed by their own passion. ANTISTHENES (5th–4th c. B.C.).

Equality . . . is the result of human organization. We are not born equal. HANNAH ARENDT (1906–1975), *The Origins of Totalitarianism,* 1951.

Democracy arose from men thinking that if they were equal in any respect they are equal in all respects. ARISTOTLE (384–322 B.C.), *Politics,* 322 B.C.

Inferiors revolt in order that they may be equal, and equals that they may be superior. Such is the state of mind which creates revolutions. ARISTOTLE (384–322 B.C.), *Politics,* 322 B.C.

He who cannot possibly mend his own case, will do what he can to impair others. SIR FRANCIS BACON (1561–1626), *Essays,* 1625.

Envy is a gadding passion, and walketh the streets, and doth not keep home. SIR FRANCIS BACON (1561–1626), *Essays,* 1625.

Power frustrates; absolute powerlessness frustrates absolutely. Absolute frustration is a dangerous emotion to run the world with. RUSSELL BAKER, *New York Times,* May 1, 1969.

Equality may perhaps be a right, but no power on earth can ever turn into a fact. HONORÉ de BALZAC (1799–1850), *La Duchesse de Langeais.*

The hardest sentiment to tolerate is pity, especially when it's deserved. Hatred is a tonic, it vitalizes us, it inspires vengeance, but pity deadens, it makes our weakness weaker. HONORÉ de BALZAC (1799–1850), *La Peau de Chagrin,* 1831.

Envy is the most stupid of vices, for there is no single advantage to be gained from it. HONORÉ de BALZAC (1799–1850), *La Peau de Chagrin,* 1831.

[Envy is] the most corroding of the vices and also the greatest power in any land. JAMES M. BARRIE (1860–1937).

The creative person is both more primitive and more cultivated, more destructive and more constructive, a lot madder and a lot saner, than the average person. DR. FRANK BARRON, *Think,* November 1962.

Hatred rarely does any harm to its object. It is the hater who suffers. His soul is warped and his life poisoned by dwelling on past injuries or projecting schemes of revenge. Rancor in the bosom is the foe of personal happiness. LORD BEAVERBROOK (1878–1964), *The Divine Propagandist.*

The sadist cannot stand the separation of the public and the private; nor can he grant to others the mystery of their personality, the validity of their inner self . . . in order for him to feel his maximum power, he wants the world to be peopled with concrete manipulable objects. ERNEST BECKER, *The Structure of Evil,* 1968.

The defect of equality is that we only desire it with our superiors. HENRY-FRANÇOIS BECQUE (1837–1899), *Querelles Littéraires,* 1890.

The dullard's envy of brilliant men is always assuaged by the suspicion that they will come to a bad end. MAX BEERBOHM (1872–1956), *Zuleika Dobson,* 1911.

Envy is a state of exquisite tension, torment and ill will provoked by an overwhelming sense of inferiority, impotence, and worthlessness. It begins in the eye of the beholder and is so painful to the mind that the envious person will go to almost any lengths to diminish, if not destroy, whatever or whoever may have aroused it. JOSEPH H. BERKE, *The Tyranny of Malice,* 1988.

Ultimately egalitarianism leads to the idealization of the State. The contradiction is that when people try to solve the problems of life by imbuing the State or party or collective with omnipotent maternal (and paternal) powers, their greed and envy tend to turn toward these entities, too. JOSEPH H. BERKE, *The Tyranny of Malice,* 1988.

We know well enough when we're being unjust or despicable. But we don't restrain ourselves because we experience a certain pleasure, a primitive sort of satisfaction in moments like that. UGO BETTI (1892–1953), *Landslide,* 1936.

Envy and hatred are always united. They gather strength from each other by being engaged upon the same object. JEAN de LA BRUYÈRE (1645–1696), *Les Caractères,* 1688.

Is it really surprising that whenever you get striving for equality and fraternity, the guillotine appears on the scene. VLADIMIR BUKOVSKY, *To Build a Castle,* 1978.

The dearest ambition of a slave is not liberty, but to have a slave of his own. SIR RICHARD BURTON (1821–1890).

They are proud in humility; proud that they are not proud. ROBERT BURTON (1577–1640), *Anatomy of Melancholy,* 1621.

Every other sin hath some pleasure annexed to it, or will admit of an excuse: envy alone wants both. ROBERT BURTON (1577–1640), *The Anatomy of Melancholy*, 1621.

The slave begins by demanding justice and ends by wanting to wear a crown. He must dominate in turn. ALBERT CAMUS (1913–1960), *The Rebel*, 1951.

Psychoanalytic theory holds that by attributing his own consciously unacceptable motives to others, the individual is able to avoid perceiving them as belonging to himself. ARTHUR R. COHEN, *Attitude Change and Social Influence*, 1964.

For one man who sincerely pities our misfortunes, there are a thousand who sincerely hate our success. CHARLES CALEB COLTON (1780–1832), *Lacon*, 1825.

If you want enemies, excel others; if you want friends, let others excel you. CHARLES CALEB COLTON (1780–1832), *Lacon*, 1820.

Destroy him as you will, the bourgeois always bounces up. Execute him, expropriate him, starve him out en masse, and he reappears in your children. CYRIL CONNOLLY (1903–1975), 1937.

Equality may be divided into that of condition and rights. Equality of condition is incompatible with civilization, and is found only to exist in those communities that are but slightly removed from the savage state. In practice, it can only mean a common misery. JAMES FENIMORE COOPER (1789–1851), *The American Democrat*, 1838.

All men have an equal right to the free development of their faculties; they have an equal right to the impartial protection of the state; but it is not true, it is against all the laws of reason and equity . . . that the indolent man and the laborious man, the spendthrift and the economic, the imprudent and the wise, should obtain and enjoy an equal amount of goods. VICTOR COUSIN (1792–1867), *Justice and Charity*, 1848.

Every member of the society spies on the rest, and it is his duty to inform against them. All are slaves and equal in their slavery. . . . The great thing about it is equality. . . . Slaves are bound to be equal. FYODOR DOSTOEVSKY (1821–1881), *The Possessed*.

Couldn't we even argue that it is because men are unequal that they have that much more need to be brothers. CHARLES DU BOS (1882–1939), *Journal intime*, February 27, 1918.

To speak ill of others is a dishonest way of praising ourselves; let us be above such transparent egotism. WILL DURANT (1885–1981), *New York World-Telegram*, June 6, 1958.

Nature smiles at the union of freedom and equality in our utopias. For freedom and equality are sworn and everlasting enemies, and where one prevails the other dies. Leave men free, and their natural inequalities will multiply almost geometrically. WILL DURANT (1885–1981) and ARIEL DURANT (1898–1981), *The Lessons of History*, 1968.

Inequality is not only natural and inborn, it grows with the complexity of civilization. Hereditary inequalities breed social and artificial inequalities; every invention or discovery is made or seized by the exceptional individual, and makes the strong stronger, the weak relatively weaker than before. Economic development specializes functions, differentiates abilities, and makes men unequally valuable to their group. WILL DURANT (1885–1981) and ARIEL DURANT (1898–1981), *The Lessons of History,* 1968.

The experience of the past leaves little doubt that every economic system must sooner or later rely upon some form of the profit motive to stir individuals and groups to productivity. Substitutes like slavery, police supervision, or ideological enthusiasm prove too unproductive, too expensive, or too transient. WILL DURANT (1885–1981) and ARIEL DURANT (1898–1981), *The Lessons of History,* 1968.

The phenomenon [*sic*] of authoritarianism, violence and domination have yet other psychological explanations. Sometimes they are due to compensation for individual failures. The weak, the stupid and the failure try to assert themselves by humiliating those who are superior to them, by trying to bring others down below their own level. MAURICE DUVERGER, *The Idea of Politics,* 1964.

Half of the harm that is done in the world is due to people who want to feel important. T. S. ELIOT (1888–1965).

Envy is the tax which all distinctions must pay. RALPH WALDO EMERSON (1803–1882), *Journals,* 1824.

The hater of property and of government takes care to have his warranty deed recorded, and the book written against fame and learning has the author's name on the title page. RALPH WALDO EMERSON (1803–1882), *Journals,* 1831.

We do not quite forgive a giver. The hand that feeds us in in some danger of being bitten. RALPH WALDO EMERSON (1803–1882), *Second Series,* 1844.

He who despises his own life is soon master of another's. ENGLISH PROVERB.

Envy is the adversary of the fortunate. EPICTETUS (ca. 55–135 A.D.), *Enchiridion,* 110 A.D.

[Envy is] an exquisitely irrational phenomenon, insofar as it pursues no other serviceable end than that of attacking what is valuable in the other, including his capacity of giving it to us. R. ETCHEGOYEN et al., *International Journal of Psycho-Analysis,* 68:49–61, 1987.

There is a fatal socialism that merely wishes to pull a few people down, rather than pull a large number up; and although throughout its history it has seldom come fully to grips with the envy that the leveling impulse will always too easily incite. HENRY FAIRLIE, *The Seven Deadly Sins Today,* 1978.

We even envy someone who is good! We will not believe that they are good, or that they are as good as they seem, or that they are good for the right reasons. If they are not simply hypocritical, there must be an ulterior motice, or some psychological complex. HENRY FAIRLIE, *The Seven Deadly Sins Today,* 1978.

The wholesale, utopian, social engineer determined to impose his long-term policies no matter what the immediate discontents, is by his cloth precluded from learning from his mistakes. Nor can he take account of the insight that there will always be unintended consequences, whether good, bad, or mixed. ANTONY FLEW, *The Politics of Procrustes,* 1981.

If . . . it is imperative that "life-chances" be equalized through an equalization of wealth and income, then we may ask to be told whether the same imperative also requires such measures as are implemented in the nightmare worlds of L. P. Hartley and Kurt Vonnegut; and if not, why not. (The former, in "Facial Justice," tells of the pretty undergoing plastic surgery to remove their envy-provoking excesses of appeal. In the story "Harrison Bergeron," the latter described those with talents above average being implanted physiologically with anti-pacesetters, curbing them down to the level of the rest). ANTONY FLEW, *The Politics of Procrustes,* 1981.

But in recognizing envy in himself, a person is acknowledging inferiority with respect to another; he measures himself against someone else, and finds himself wanting. It is, I think, this implied admission of inferiority, rather than the admission of envy, that is so difficult for us to accept. GEORGE FOSTER, *Current Anthropology,* April 1972.

Men are entitled to equal rights—but to equal rights to unequal things. CHARLES JAMES FOX (1749–1806).

It is a wise man who said that there is no greater inequality than the equal treatment of unequals. FELIX FRANKFURTER (1882–1965), U.S. Supreme Court Justice, *Dennis* v. *United States,* 1949.

There is perhaps no phenomenon which contains so much destructive feeling as "moral indignation," which permits envy or hate to be acted out under the guise of virtue. ERIC FROMM (1900–1980), *Man for Himself,* 1947.

Nothing sharpens sight like envy. THOMAS FULLER (1654–1734), *Gnomologia,* 1732.

Legislators and revolutionaries who promise liberty and equality at the same time are either psychopaths or mountebanks. JOHANN WOLFGANG von GOETHE (1749–1832), *Maxims and Reflections,* no. 953.

The envious die not once, but as often as the envied win applause. BALTASAR GRACIAN (1601–1658), *The Art of Worldly Wisdom,* 1647.

When you cannot get a thing, then is the time to have contempt for it. BALTASAR GRACIAN (1601–1658), *The Art of Worldly Wisdom,* 1647.

Perhaps the greatest consolation of the oppressed is to consider themselves superior to their tyrants. JULIEN GREEN, *Adrienne Mesurat,* 1927.

You have a right to nothing that is liable to cause envy in the heart of a fellow-delinquent [citizen]. Our constitution and way of life are based on it. L. P. HARTLEY (1895–1972), *Facial Justice*, 1960.

Envy is a littleness of soul, which cannot see beyond a certain point, and if it does not occupy the whole space feels itself excluded. WILLIAM HAZLITT (1778–1830), *Characteristics*, 1823.

Those who are fond of setting to rights have no great objection to seeing them wrong. There is often a great deal of spleen at the bottom of benevolence. WILLIAM HAZLITT (1778–1830), *Characteristics*, 1823.

Envy, among other ingredients, has a mixture of the love of justice in it. We are more angry at undeserved that at deserved good fortune. WILLIAM HAZLITT (1778–1830), *Characteristics*, 1823.

Envy and anger shorten life. HEBREW PROVERB.

We clamor for equality chiefly in matters in which we ourselves cannot hope to obtain excellence. ERIC HOFFER (1902–1983), *The Passionate State of Mind*, 1954.

The sense of inferiority inherent in the act of imitation breeds resentment. The impulse of imitators is to overcome the model they imitate. ERIC HOFFER (1902–1983), *The Ordeal of Change*, 1964.

I doubt if the oppressed ever fight for freedom. They fight for pride and for power—power to oppress others. The oppressed want above all to imitate their oppressors; they want to retaliate. ERIC HOFFER (1902–1983), quoted in Calvin Tompkins, *Eric Hoffer: An American Odyssey*, 1968.

There is probably an element of malice in the readiness to overestimate people; we are laying up for ourselves the pleasure of later cutting them down to size. ERIC HOFFER (1902–1983), *New York Times Magazine*, April 25, 1971.

The self-despisers are less intent on their own increase than on the diminution of others. Where self-esteem is unobtainable, envy takes the place of greed. ERIC HOFFER (1902–1983), *The Passionate State of Mind*, 1954.

Those who see their lives as spoiled and wasted crave equality and fraternity more than they do freedom. If they clamor for freedom, it is but freedom to establish equality and uniformity. ERIC HOFFER (1902–1983), *The True Believer*, 1951.

Whereas envy leads to a hateful attitude toward those who have what is believed to be unavailable to the self, it also leads to attitudes that keep that which is envied unavailable. ALTHEA HORNER, *The Wish for Power and the Fear of Having It*, 1989.

Compensatory power makes up for feelings of shame or humiliation usually associated with being powerless. Defensive power protects the person from anxiety-provoking dangers that accompany the lack of power in interpersonal situations. ALTHEA HORNER, *The Wish for Power and the Fear of Having It*, 1989.

That at the core of every idealist there reigns a demon of cruelty, a monster thirsty for blood—no one must admit this as a universal law, else Time, that suave imposter, could not go on. . . . ELBERT HUBBARD (1856–1915), *The Philistine.*

Even in envy may be discerned something of an instinct for justice, something of a wish to see fair play, and things on a level. LEIGH HUNT (1784–1859), *The Indicator,* 1821.

That all men are equal is a proposition to which, in ordinary times, no sane individual has ever given his assent. ALDOUS HUXLEY (1894–1963), *Proper Studies.*

The doctrine that all men are, in any sense, or have been, at any time, free and equal, is an utterly baseless fiction. THOMAS HENRY HUXLEY (1825–1895), *On the Natural Inequality of Man,* 1890.

Such seems to be the disposition of man, that whatever makes a distinction produces rivalry. SAMUEL JOHNSON (1709–1784) Boswell's *Life of Johnson,* 1791.

It is better that some should be unhappy than that none should be happy, which would be the case in a general state of equality. SAMUEL JOHNSON (1709–1784), Boswell's *Life of Johnson,* 1791.

[Envy is] almost the only vice which is practicable at all times, and in every place; the only passion which can never lie quiet from want of irritation. SAMUEL JOHNSON (1709–1784), Boswell's *Life of Johnson,* 1791.

Your levellers wish to level down as far as themselves; but they cannot bear levelling up to themselves. SAMUEL JOHNSON (1709–1784), Boswell's *Life of Johnson,* 1791.

Most of the misery which the defamation of blameless actions or the obstruction of honest endeavors brings upon the world is inflicted by men that propose no advantage to themselves but the satisfaction of poisoning the banquet which they cannot taste, and blasting the harvest which they have no right to reap. SAMUEL JOHNSON (1709–1784), *The Rambler,* 1751.

The impulse for envy is thus inherent in the nature of man, and only its manifestation makes of it an abominable vice, a passion not only distressing and tormenting to the subject, but intent on the destruction of happiness of others. IMMANUEL KANT (1724–1804), *The Metaphysic of Morals,* 1797.

The impulse to mar and to destroy is an ancient and almost as nearly universal as the impulse to create. The one is an easier way than the other of demonstrating power. JOSEPH WOOD KRUTCH (1893–1970), *The Best of Two Worlds.*

There is a dull, animalistic leaning towards social conformity (identity) as well as a programmatic, fanatical drive in that direction . . . its driving motor is fear, formed by an inferiority complex and engendering hatred, with envy as its blood brother. . . . The demand for equality and identity arises precisely in order to avoid that fear, that feeling of inferiority. Nobody is better, nobody is superior, nobody feels challenged, everybody is "safe." ERIK von KUEHNELT-LEDDIHN, *Leftism Revisited,* 1990.

All men are created equal—until they prove otherwise. BEN KUROKI, *New York Herald Tribune,* November 4, 1945.

To the schizophrenic, liking someone equals being like that person; being like a person is equated with being the same as that person, hence with losing identity. Hating and being hated may therefore be felt to threaten loss of identity less than do loving and being loved. R. D. LAING, *The Divided Self,* 1950.

Those who speak against the great do not usually speak from morality, but from envy. WALTER SAVAGE LANDOR (1775–1864), *Imaginary Conversations.*

Envy is not an original temper, but the natural, necessary and unavoidable effect of emulation, or a desire for glory. WILLIAM LAW (1686–1761), 1728.

No man who says "I am as good as you" believes it. The claim to equality is made only by those who feel themselves to be in some way inferior. C. S. LEWIS (1898–1963), *Screwtape Proposes a Toast.*

Envy, like flame, soars upward. LIVY (59 B.C.–17 A.D.), *History of Rome.*

[Envy is] uneasiness of the mind, caused by the consideration of a good we desire, obtained by one we think should not have it before us. JOHN LOCKE (1632–1704).

The puritan hated bear-baiting, not because it gave pain to the bear, but because it gave pleasure to the spectators. THOMAS BABINGTON MACAULAY (1800–1859), *History of England,* 1849.

I am Envy. I cannot read and therefore wish all books were burnt. I am lean with seeing others eat. CHRISTOPHER MARLOWE (1564–1593), *Doctor Faustus,* 1604.

Man loves malice, but not against one-eyed men nor the unfortunate, but against the fortunate and proud. MARTIAL (42–102 A.D.), *Epigrams,* 86 A.D.

Equality of opportunity means equal opportunity to be unequal. IAN MACLEOD (1913–1970).

Failure makes people bitter and cruel. Success improves the character of man. W. SOMERSET MAUGHAM (1874–1965), *The Summing Up,* 1938.

[Puritanism is] the haunting fear that someone, somewhere may be happy. H. L. MENCKEN (1880–1956), *A Book of Burlesques,* 1920.

If on the sudden he begins to rise; No man that lives can count his enemies. THOMAS MIDDLETON (d. 1627), *A Trick to Catch the Old One,* 1608.

It is the American vice, the democratic disease which expresses its tyranny by reducing everything unique to the level of the herd. HENRY MILLER (1891–1980), *Wisdom of the Heart,* 1941.

The envious will die, but envy never. MOLIÈRE (1622–1673), *Tartuffe,* 1667.

Passion for equality blinds the utopian to the fact that society, as a whole, is based on inequality of men in two respects: the inventor, the innovator, the exceptional man creates something new and insures continuous progress; the others emulate his work or merely improve their own lot by benefiting from his creativity. THOMAS MOLNAR, *Utopia: The Perennial Heresy,* 1967.

Since we cannot attain to greatness, let us revenge ourselves by railing against it. MICHEL de MONTAIGNE (1533–1592), *Essays,* 1588.

If we only wanted to be happy it would be easy; but we want to be happier than other people, which is almost always difficult, since we think them happier than they are. CHARLES-LOUIS de SECONDAT, BARON de MONTESQUIEU (1689–1755), *Pensées,* 1750.

Whenever I encounter envy I always try to provoke it: before an envious man I always praise those who make him turn pale. CHARLES-LOUIS de SECONDAT, BARON de MONTESQUIEU (1689–1755), *Pensées,* 1750.

Whoever is dissatisfied with himself is continually ready for revenge, and we others will have to be his victims. FRIEDRICH NIETZSCHE (1844–1900), *Human All Too Human,* 1878.

He that humbleth himself wishes to be exalted. FRIEDRICH NIETZSCHE (1844–1900), *Human All Too Human,* 1878.

The envious man is susceptible to every sign of individual superiority to the common herd, and wishes to depress everyone once more to the level—or raise himself to the superior place. FRIEDRICH NIETZSCHE (1844–1900), *Human All Too Human,* 1878.

Nothing on earth consumes a man more quickly than the passion of resentment. FRIEDRICH NIETZSCHE (1844–1900), *Ecce Homo,* 1888.

Envy is a compound of covetousness, felt impotence, and nihilistic resentment of anything and everything that is honored in a culture. ROBERT NISBET, *Prejudices: A Philosophical Dictionary,* 1982.

Equality feeds on itself as no other single social value does. It is not long before it becomes more than a value. It takes on the overtones of redemptiveness and becomes a religious rather than a secular idea. ROBERT NISBET, *Twilight of Authority,* 1981.

In the past, unifying ideas tended to be religious in substance. There are certain signs that equality is taking on a sacred aspect among many minds today, that it is rapidly acquiring dogmatic status, at least among a great many philosophers and social scientists. ROBERT NISBET, *The Public Interest,* 1974.

Equality has a built-in revolutionary force lacking in such ideas as justice or liberty. For once the ideal of equality becomes uppermost it can become insatiable in its demands. In this respect it resembles some of the religious ideals or passions which offer, just by virtue of the impossibility of ever giving them adequate representation in the actual world, almost unlimited potentialities for continuous onslaught against institutions. ROBERT NISBET, *The Twilight of Authority,* 1981.

Egalitarianism seems to require a political system in which the state is able to hold in check those . . . groups which, by virtue of skills or education or personal attributes, might otherwise attempt to stake claims to a disproportionate share of society's rewards. The most effective way of holding such groups in check is by denying them the right to organize politically, or in other ways, to undermine social equality. FRANK PARKIN, *Class Inequality and Political Order,* 1972.

The more intelligence one has the more people one finds original. Commonplace people see no difference between men. BLAISE PASCAL (1623–1662), *Pensées.*

It is a nobler fate to be envied than to be pitied. PINDAR (522–438 B.C.), *Pythian Odes,* 475 B.C.

The doctrine of equality seldom embraces those who are worse off than its exponents. R. A. PIDDINGTON, *The Next British Empire,* 1938.

We ought to be guarded against every appearance of envy, as a passion that always implies inferiority wherever it resides. PLINY THE ELDER (23–79 A.D.).

To vilify a great man is the readiest way in which a little man can himself attain greatness. EDGAR ALLAN POE (1809–1849), *Marginalia,* 1844–49.

Envy, to which the ignoble mind's a slave/ Is emulation in the learned or brave. ALEXANDER POPE (1688–1744), *An Essay on Man,* 1732.

"Equality before the law" is not a fact but a political demand based upon a moral decision; and it is quite independent of the theory—which is probably false—that "all men are born equal." SIR KARL POPPER, *The Open Society and Its Enemies,* 1962.

Every major horror of history was committed in the name of an altruistic motive. AYN RAND (1905–1982), *The Fountainhead,* 1943.

Do not fool yourself by thinking that altruists are motivated by compassion for the suffering; they are motivated by hatred for the successful. AYN RAND (1905–1982), Attributed, 1982.

We hate to see people standing too much above ourselves; we never endure it patiently. In practical life we never submit to it. We either grow up to the advanced people, or we pull the advanced people down. THOMAS BRACKETT REED (1839–1902), Speech, 1891.

In the misfortune of our best friends, we always find something which is not displeasing to us. FRANÇOIS, DUC de LA ROCHEFOUCAULD (1613–1680), *Maxims,* 1665.

We would frequently be ashamed of our good deeds if people saw all the motives that produced them. FRANÇOIS, DUC de LA ROCHEFOUCAULD (1613–1680), *Maxims,* 1665.

Envy is more irreconciliable than hatred. FRANÇOIS, DUC de LA ROCHEFOUCAULD (1613–1680), *Maxims, 1665.*

The nature of things continually tends to the destruction of equality. JEAN-JACQUES ROUSSEAU (1712–1778), *The Social Contract, 1762.*

Since unhappiness excites interest, many, in order to render themselves interesting, feign unhappiness. JOSEPH ROUX (1834–1905), *Reflections of a Parish Priest, 1886.*

If there were in the world today any large number of people who desired their own happiness more than they desired the unhappiness of others, we could have a paradise in a few years. BERTRAND RUSSELL (1872–1970), *New York Times,* May 18, 1961.

Envy . . . is one form of a vice, partly moral, partly intellectual, which consists in seeing things never in themselves but only in their relations. BERTRAND RUSSELL (1872–1970), *The Conquest of Happiness, 1930.*

One cannot exaggerate the importance of . . . aggressor identification in political life. . . . If all human societies, up until today, have persevered in the necessity of having victims, it can only be that those who control societies are so deeply frightened that they can only feel better by seeing that others are brought down. ELI SAGAN, *At The Dawn of Tyranny, 1985.*

The dignity of the individual requires that he not be reduced to vassalage by the largesse of others. ANTOINE de SAINT-EXUPÉRY (1900–1944), *Flight to Arras, 1942.*

The apparently innocuous demand for equality—of whatever kind, whether sexual, social, political, religious or material—in fact conceals only the desire for the demotion, in accordance with a selected scale of values, of those having more assets. . . . Only the one who fears he will lose, demands it as a universal principle. MAX SCHELER (1874–1928), *Ressentiment, 1961.*

When hatred does not dare come out in the open it can be easily expressed in the form of ostensible love—love for something which has features that are the opposite of those of the hated object. This can happen in such a way that the hatred remains secret. MAX SCHELER (1874–1928), *Ressentiment, 1961.*

True education makes for inequality; the inequality of individuality, the inequality of success; the glorious inequality of talent, of genius; for inequality, not mediocrity, individual superiority, not standardization, is the measure of progress in the world. FELIX F. SCHELLING (1858–1945), *Pedagogically Speaking, 1929.*

Ressentiment begins with perceived injury that may have a basis in fact, but more often it is occasioned by envy for the possessions or qualities possessed by another person. This phenomenon differs from mere envy or resentment because it is not content to suffer quietly but has a festering quality that seeks outlet in doing harm to its object. HERBERT SCHLOSSBERG, *Idols for Destruction, 1990.*

The leveling movement has nothing to do with justice, because its impulse is not to raise those who are down but to topple those who are up; ressentiment is the motive. HERBERT SCHLOSSBERG, *Idols for Destruction,* 1990.

To claim "humanitarian motives," when the true motive is envy and its supposed appeasement, is a favorite rhetorical device of politicians today, and has been for at least a hundred and fifty years. HELMUT SCHOECK, *Envy: A Theory of Social Behavior,* 1966.

We are thus confronted by an antinomy, an irreconcilable contradiction: envy is an extremely antisocial and destructive emotional state, but it is, at the same time, the most completely socially oriented. HELMUT SCHOECK, *Envy: A Theory of Social Behavior,* 1966.

Much modern egalitarianism seems to stem not from universalist doctrines about rights so much as a nihilistic disbelief in them. If there are no rights, no obligations, no values, but only subjective preferences, then no one has the right to anything. From which it follows that no one has the right to any more of anything than anybody else. ROGER SCRUTON, *A Dictionary of Political Thought,* 1982.

People are always blaming their circumstances for what they are. I don't believe in circumstances. The people who get on in this world are the people who get up and look for the circumstances they want, and, if they can't find them, make them. GEORGE BERNARD SHAW (1856–1950), *Mrs. Warren's Profession,* 1893.

Democracy substitutes election by the incompetent many for appointment by the corrupt few. GEORGE BERNARD SHAW (1856–1950), *Maxims for Revolutionists.*

The fact that children of the lower classes are bombarded with lower-class values every day of their lives suffices to explain why so few of them ever accomplish anything. The powerful resentments within the lower classes, which punish deviation from norms with not only verbal abuse but frequently with physical violence, act as exceedingly powerful deterrents to upward mobility. ROBERT SHEAFFER, *Resentment against Achievement,* 1988.

Resentment must wear masks when it appears in public. It is sometimes disguised as the pursuit of "social justice," or the "class struggle," or perhaps "divine morality"—all lofty sounding terms invented to mask the ugly reality of a mob outraged by the wealth earned by others. Hence, resentment must remain a covert revengefulness at least until it is firmly in control. ROBERT SHEAFFER, *Resentment against Achievement,* 1988.

Jealousy is the fear or apprehension of superiority; Envy our uneasiness under it. WILLIAM SHENSTONE (1714–1763), *Essays on Men and Manners,* 1764.

After this Teseus killed a man called Procrustes, who lived in what was known as Corydallus in Attica. This person forced passing travelers to lie down on a bed, and if they were too long for the bed he lopped off those parts of their bodies which protruded, while racking out the legs of the ones who were too short. This was why he was given the name of Procrustes (The Racker). DIODORUS SICULUS (1st c. B.C.), *The Library of History.*

We pay close attention to unpredictable persons who seem to have a great deal of freedom. We admire them, fear them, attempt to win their approval, or if all else fails, try to stay out of their reach. Because we are prone to ingratiate ourselves with people who seem free, we make them powerful. IVAN STEINER, *Psychology Today,* August 1973.

The only shape in which equality is really connected with justice is this—justice presupposes general rules. If these general rules are to be maintained at all, it is obvious that they must be applied equally to every case which satisfies their terms. JAMES FITZJAMES STEPHEN (1829–1894), *Liberty, Equality and Fraternity,* 1873.

We must recover the element of quality in our traditional pursuit of equality. We must not, in opening our schools to everyone, confuse the idea that all should have an equal chance with the notion that all have equal endowments. ADLAI E. STEVENSON (1900–1965), *New York Times,* April 6, 1958.

Let our children grow tall, and some taller than others if they have it in them to do so. MARGARET THATCHER, British Prime Minister, Speech, 1975.

Base envy withers at another's joy, and hates that excellence it cannot reach. JAMES B. V. THOMSON (1834–1882), *The Seasons.*

The foremost or indeed the sole condition required in order to succeed in centralizing the supreme power in a democratic community is to love equality or to get men to believe you love it. Thus, the science of despotism, which was once so complex, has been simplified and reduced, as it were, to a single principle. ALEXIS de TOCQUEVILLE (1805–1859), *Democracy in America,* 1835.

Whatever may be the general endeavor of a community to render its members equal and alike, the personal pride of individuals will always seek to rise above the line, and to form somewhere an inequality to their own advantage. ALEXIS de TOCQUEVILLE (1805–1859), *Democracy in America,* 1835.

Every central power which follows its natural tendencies courts and encourages the principle of equality; for equality singularly facilitates, extends, and secures the influence of a central power. ALEXIS de TOCQUEVILLE (1805–1859), *Democracy in America,* 1935.

Americans are so enamored of quality that they would rather be equal in slavery than unequal in freedom. ALEXIS de TOCQUEVILLE (1805–1859), *Democracy in America,* 1835.

Latent in every man is a venom of amazing bitterness, a black resentment; something that curses and loathes life, a feeling of being trapped, of having trusted and been fooled, of being the helpless prey of impotent rage. . . . PAUL VALÉRY (1871–1945), *Mauvaises pensées et autres,* 1942.

It is not true that equality is a law of nature. Nature knows no equality. Its sovereign law is subordination and dependence. MARQUIS de LUC de VAUVENARGUES (1715–1747), *Réflexions et Maximes,* 1740.

We are obsessed with an enemy presence, and we seek information about it more often at the dictates of our unconscious processes than in recognition of real circumstances. Such preoccupation often characterizes the weaker of two parties, no doubt being fed by envy. VAMIK D. VOLKAN, *The Need to Have Enemies and Allies,* 1988.

Moral indignation is jealousy with a halo. H. G. WELLS (1866–1946), *The Wife of Sir Isaac Harman,* 1914.

Equality cannot really be imposed. If any authority is strong enough to level people, it is also strong enough to create special privileges for itself. That is, in a complex society the great equalizers do not include themselves among those to be equalized. Political inequality in turn is convertible, and is habitually converted, into social and economic equality. ROBERT WESSON, *Politics: Individual and State,* 1988.

Many who are deeply attached in theory to principles of equality uphold and esteem in practice their own distinctiveness. Reformers or radicals devoted to the cause of the poor commonly shrink from mingling socially with them, as though the disease of poverty were contagious. ROBERT WESSON, *Politics: Individual and State,* 1988.

Fanatics and True Believers

I have noted that persons with bad judgment are most insistent that we do what they think best. LIONEL ABEL, *Important Nonsense,* 1986.

Patriotism is in political life what faith is in religion, and it stands to the domestic feelings and to homesickness as faith to fanaticism and to superstition. LORD ACTON (1834–1902), *The Home and Foreign Review,* July 1932.

Ambition raises a secret tumult in the soul; it inflames the mind, and pits it into a violent hurry of thought. JOSEPH ADDISON (1672–1719), *The Spectator,* December 24, 1711.

Man tends to treat all of his opinions as principles. HERBERT AGAR, *A Time for Greatness,* 1942.

Nothing is more dangerous than an idea, when a man has only one idea. ALAIN (1868–1951), *Propos sur la religion,* 1938.

Action and faith enslave thought. Both of them in order not to be troubled by reflection, criticism and doubt. HENRI FRÉDÉRIC AMIEL (1821–1881), *Journal intime.*

There is an illusion of central position, justifying one's own purposes as right and everybody else's as wrong, and providing a proper degree of paranoia. Righteous ends, thus approved, absolve of guilt the most violent means. ROBERT ARDREY

Angry men are blind and foolish, for reason at such a time takes flight and, in her absence, wrath plunders all the riches of the intellect, while the judgment remains the prisoner of its own pride. PIETRO ARETINO (1492–1556), Letter, 1537.

Agitators are like those who fish for eels. When the water is tranquil they catch nothing, but if they stir up the mud they make a haul. ARISTOPHANES (455–380 B.C.).

Some men are just as sure of the truth of their opinions as others are of what they know. ARISTOTLE (384–322 B.C.), *Nichomachean Ethics,* 340 B.C.

We praise a man who is angry on the right grounds, against the right persons, in the right manner, at the right moment, and for the right length of time. ARISTOTLE (384–322 B.C.), *Nichomachean Ethics,* 340 B.C.

It is easy to fly into a passion—anybody can do that—but to be angry with the right persons to the right extent and at the right time and with the right object and in the right way—that is not easy, and it is not everybody who can do it. ARISTOTLE (384–322 B.C.), *Nicomachean Ethics,* 340 B.C.

The demagogue . . . is a good showman, whether at Nuremberg before a youth conference, or in Georgia at a political barbeque. He knows the tricks of the ham actor, the gestures, the tones of voice that can arouse passions. ELLIS G. ARNALL, *The Shore Dimly Seen,* 1946.

Fanaticism is a more powerful combatant than avarice. GERTRUDE ATHERTON (1857–1948), *Doomswoman,* 1892.

I dreamt a line that would make a motto for sober philosophy: Neither a be-all nor an end-all be. J. L. AUSTIN (1916–1960), *Philosophical Papers,* 1961.

So long as there are ernest believers in the world, they will always wish to punish opinions, even if their judgment tells them it is unwise, and their conscience it is wrong. WALTER BAGEHOT (1826–1877), *Literary Studies,* 1879.

Usually, terrible things that are done with the excuse that progress requires them are not really progress at all, but just terrible things. RUSSELL BAKER.

It is unfortunate, considering that enthusiasm moves the world, that so few enthusiasts can be trusted to speak the truth. ARTHUR BALFOUR (1848–1930), 1918.

Until now all human history has been only a perpetual and blood immolation of millions of poor human beings in honor of some pitiless abstraction—God, country, power of State, national honor, historical, judicial rights, political liberty, public welfare. MIKHAIL A. BAKUNIN (1814–1876), *God and State.*

A strong sense of identity gives man an idea he can do no wrong; too little accomplishes the same. DJUNA BARNES, *Nightwood,* 1937.

[Fanaticism is] that which is founded on pride and which glories in persecution. CESARE BECCARIA (1738–1794), *On Crimes and Punishments,* 1764.

Doctrine is nothing but the skin of truth set up and stuffed. HENRY WARD BEECHER (1813–1887), *Life Thoughts.*

A great deal of intelligence can be invested in ignorance when the need for illusion is deep. SAUL BELLOW.

There are few catastrophes so great and irremediable as those that follow an excess of zeal. R. H. BENSON (1871–1914).

When a man speaks of the need for realism one may be sure that this is always the prelude to some bloody deed. SIR ISAIAH BERLIN, quoted in the *London Times,* 1981.

The first sign of corruption in a society that is still alive is that the end justifies the means. GEORGES BERNANOS (1888–1948), *Last Essays,* 1955.

"Mad" is a term we use to describe a man who is obsessed with one idea and nothing else. UGO BETTI (1892–1953), *Struggle till Dawn*, 1949.

You rebel—and yet you want them: those obligations, those penalties, those debts!—Man wants to serve! UGO BETTI (1892–1953), *The Fugitive*, 1953.

Rebel: A proponent of a new misrule who has failed to establish it. AMBROSE BIERCE (1842–1914), *The Devil's Dictionary*, 1881–1911.

Ambition: An overmastering desire to be vilified by enemies while living and made ridiculous by friends when dead. AMBROSE BIERCE (1842–1914), *The Devil's Dictionary*, 1881–1911.

The true fanatic is a theocrat, someone who sees himself as acting on behalf of some superpersonal force: the Race, the Party, History, the proletariat, the Poor, and so on. These absolve him from evil, hence he may safely do anything in their service. LLOYD BILLINGSLEY, *Religion's Rebel Son: Fanaticism in Our Time*, 1986.

I must create a system or be enslaved by another man's. WILLIAM BLAKE (1757–1827), *The Marriage of Heaven and Hell*, 1790.

A belief is not merely an idea the mind possesses; it is an idea that possesses the mind. ROBERT BOLTON (1814–1877).

The essence of a heretic, that is, of some one who has a particular opinion, is that he clings to his own ideas. JACQUES-BÉNIGNE BOSSUET (1627–1704), *Histoire de variations*.

A heretic . . . is a fellow who disagrees with you regarding something that neither one of you knows anything about. WILLIAM COWPER BRANN (1855–1898).

Vain are the thousand creeds that move men's hearts: unutterably vain; Worthless as wither'd weeds. EMILY BRONTË (1818–1848), *Last Lines*.

Just as every conviction begins as a whim so does every emancipator serve his apprenticeship as a crank. A fanatic is a great leader who is just entering the room. HEYWOOD BROUN (1888–1939), 1928.

Yea, even amongst the wider militants, how many wounds have been given, and credits slain, for the poor victory of an opinion, or the beggarly conquest of a distinction. SIR THOMAS BROWNE (1605–1682), *Religio Medici*, 1642.

A good cause needs not be patroned by passion, but can sustain itself upon a temperate dispute. SIR THOMAS BROWNE (1605–1682), *Religio Medici*, 1642.

[A fanatic is] one compelled to action by the need to find a strong meaning in life. The fanatic determines for himself what role he is to play in life, and his intense devotion to a cause is the means. EUGENE E. BRUSSELL.

[A demagogue is] one who maximizes his appeal to the frustrated, to the dispossessed of the earth. He offers vivid and dramatic, simplistic solutions to all of life's problems. EUGENE E. BRUSSELL.

In the manifest failure of their abilities, they take credit for their intentions. EDMUND BURKE (1729–1797), *Observations,* 1769.

It is a general error to imagine the loudest complainers for the public to be the most anxious for its welfare. EDMUND BURKE (1729–1797), *Observations,* 1769.

People crushed by law have no hope but from power. If laws are their enemies, they will be enemies to laws; and those who have much to hope and nothing to lose will always be dangerous, more or less. EDMUND BURKE (1729–1797), Letter to the Hon. C. J. Fox, October 8, 1777.

O wad some pow'r the giftie gie us, / To see ourselves as others see us! / It would frae many a blunder frae is, / And foolish notion. ROBERT BURNS (1756–1796).

It is always easier to believe than to deny. Our minds are naturally affirmative. JOHN BURROUGHS (1837–1921), *The Light of Day,* 1900.

It is in the uncompromisingness with which dogma is held and not in the dogma, or want of dogma, that the danger lies. SAMUEL BUTLER (1835–1902), *The Way of All Flesh* (1903).

Some men delight in things for no reason but because they are ugly and infamous. SAMUEL BUTLER (1835–1902), *Prose Observations,* 1860–80.

The interval between the decay of the old and the formation and the establishment of the new, constitutes a period of transition, which must always necessarily be one of uncertainty, confusion, error, and wild and fierce fanaticism. JOHN C. CALHOUN (1782–1850), *A Disquisition on Government,* 1850.

The prophet and the martyr do not see the hooting of the throng. Their eyes are fixed on the eternities. BENJAMIN N. CARDOZO (1870–1938), U.S. Supreme Court Justice, *Law and Literature,* 1931.

All extremes are error. The reverse of error is not truth, but error still. Truth lies between these extremes. WILLIAM CECIL (1520–1598).

Man as an individual is a genius. But men in the mass form the Headless Monster, a great, brutish idiot that goes where prodded. CHARLES CHAPLIN (1889–1977).

Your noblest natures are most credulous. GEORGE CHAPMAN (1559–1634), *Bussy d'Ambois,* 1604.

In a martial age the reformer is called a mollycoddle; in a commercial age, an incompetent, a disturber of values; in a fanatical age, a heretic. If an agitator is not reviled, he is a quack. JOHN JAY CHAPMAN (1862–1933), *Practical Agitation,* 1900.

Materialists and madmen never have doubts. GILBERT KEITH CHESTERTON (1874–1936), *Orthodoxy,* 1909.

There are two kinds of people in the world: the conscious and the unconscious dogmatists. I have always found myself that the unconscious dogmatists were by far the most dogmatic. GILBERT KEITH CHESTERTON (1874–1936), *Generally Speaking,* 1928.

The true way to overcome the evil in class distinctions is not to denounce them as revolutionists denounce them, but to ignore them as children ignore them. GILBERT KEITH CHESTERTON (1874–1936), *Charles Dickens: Last of the Great Men.*

Each generation of rebels in turn is remembered by the next, not as the pioneers who began the march, or started to break away from the old conventions; but as the old convention from which only the very latest rebels have dared to break. GILBERT KEITH CHESTERTON (1874–1936), *All I Survey,* 1934.

When a man fights it means that a fool has lost his argument. CHINESE PROVERB.

It is said that famous men are usually the product of an unhappy childhood. The stern compression of circumstances, the twinges of adversity, the spur of slights and taunts in early years, are needed to evoke that ruthless fixity of purpose and tenacious mother-wit without which great actions are seldom accomplished. SIR WINSTON CHURCHILL (1874–1965), *Marlborough, His Life and Times,* 1933–38.

Although the force of fanatical passion is far greater than that exerted by any philosophical belief, its sanction is just the same. It gives men something which they think is sublime to fight for. WINSTON CHURCHILL (1874–1965), *The River War,* 1899.

The history of ideas is the history of the grudges of solitary men. E. MICHEL CIORAN.

Persecution is a very easy form of virtue. JOHN DUKE COLERIDGE (1820–1884), English Jurist, *Reg.* v. *Ramsey,* 1883.

Every reform, however necessary, will by weak minds be carried to an excess which will itself need reforming. SAMUEL TAYLOR COLERIDGE (1772–1834).

The wise only possess ideas; the greater part of mankind are possessed by them. SAMUEL TAYLOR COLERIDGE (1772–1834), *Daniel Defoe,* 1820.

He that dies a martyr proves that he was not a knave, but by no means that he was not a fool. CHARLES CALEB COLTON (1790–1832), *Lacon,* 1820.

What are the triumphs of war, planned by ambition, executed by violence, and consummated by devestation? The means are the sacrifice of many, the end the bloated aggrandizement of the few. CHARLES CALEB COLTON (1790–1832), *Lacon,* 1825.

If a cause be good, the most violent attack of its enemies will not injure it so much as an injudicious defense of it by its friends. WALTER COLTON.

We must select the illusion which appeals to our temperment, and embrace it with passion if we want to be happy. CYRIL CONNOLLY (1903–1974).

To have his path made clear to him is the aspiration of every human being in our beclouded and tempestuous existence. JOSEPH CONRAD (1857–1924), *The Mirror of the Sea,* 1906.

Action is consolatory. It is the enemy of thought and the friend of illusions. JOSEPH CONRAD (1857–1924), 1904.

All ambitions are lawful except those which climb upward on the miseries or credulities of mankind. JOSEPH CONRAD (1857–1924), *A Personal Record,* 1912.

The demagogue is one who advances his own interests by affecting a deep devotion to the interests of the people. JAMES FENIMORE COOPER (1759–1851), *On Demagogues.*

To have a grievance is to have a purpose in life. ALAN COREN, *The Sanity Inspector,* 1974.

Real rebels are rarely anything but second rate outside their rebellion; the drain of time and temper is ruinous to any other accomplishment. JAMES GOULD COZZENS, *Children and Others,* 1964.

The definition of the Left is a group of people who will never be happy unless they can convince themselves that they are about to be betrayed by their leaders. R. H. S. CROSSMAN (1907–1974), *Diary,* July 3, 1959.

My advice to a young man seeking deathless fame would be espouse an unpopular cause and devote his life to it. GEORGE W. CURTISS (1824–1892).

The worst atrocities are probably committed by those who are most afraid. LORD D'ABERNON (1857–1941).

The world is made up for the most part of morons and natural tyrants, sure of themselves, strong in their own opinions, never doubting anything. CLARENCE S. DARROW (1857–1938), *Personal Liberty,* 1928.

Fanaticism is . . . overcompensation for doubt. ROBERTSON DAVIES, *The Manticore,* 1972.

We believe whatever we want to believe. DEMOSTHENES (384-322 B.C.), *Third Olynthiac,* 348 B.C.

Fanaticism is just one step away from barbarism. DENIS DIDEROT (1713–1784), 1760.

Demagogues and agitators are very unpleasant, but they are incidents to a free and constitutional country, and you must put up with these inconveniences or do without many important advantages. BENJAMIN DISRAELI (1804–1881), Speech, 1867.

Sincerity is all that counts. It's a widespread modern heresy. Think again. Bolsheviks are sincere. Fascists are sincere. Lunatics are sincere. People who believe the earth is flat are sincere. They can't all be right. Better make certain first you've got something to be sincere about and with. TOM DRIBERT (1905–1976), 1937.

A fanatic is a man that does what he things th' Lord wud do if He knew th' facts iv th' case. FINLEY PETER DUNNE (1867–1936), *Mr. Dooley's Philosophy,* 1900.

No one can go on being a rebel too long without turning into an autocrat. LAWRENCE DURRELL, *Balthazar,* 1958.

They shield themselves from facts, I suppose, by a biased selection of books and newspapers to read. Many violent conflicts of opinion come down to a difference in reading matter. MAX EASTMAN (1883–1969), *Reflections on the Failure of Socialism,* 1962.

Man is ready to die for an idea, provided that idea is not quite clear to him. PAUL ELDRIDGE.

It is by no means self-evident that human beings are most real when most violently excited; violent physical passions do not in themselves differentiate men from each other, but rather tend to reduce them to the same state. T. S. ELIOT (1888–1965), *After Strange Gods,* 1934.

Half of the harm that is done in this world is due to people who want to feel important. T. S. ELIOT (1888–1965).

We are reformers in spring and summer, in autumn and winter we stand by the old; reformers in the morning, conservatives at night. Reform is affirmative; conservatism goes for comfort, reform for truth. RALPH WALDO EMERSON (1803–1882).

A sect or party is an elegant incognito devised to save man from the vexation of thinking. RALPH WALDO EMERSON (1803–1882), *Journals,* 1831.

If a man fasten his attention on a single aspect of truth and apply himself to that alone for a long time, the truth becomes distorted and not itself but falsehood. RALPH WALDO EMERSON (1803–1882), *Essays: First Series,* 1841.

He who despises his own life is soon master of another's. ENGLISH PROVERB.

It is not the suffering but the cause which makes the martyr. ENGLISH PROVERB.

Why, do you not know, then that the origin of all human evils, of the baseness and cowardice, is not death, but rather the fear of death. EPICTETUS (ca. 55–135 A.D.), *Discourses.*

There are some passions so close to virtues that there is danger least we be deceived by the doubtful distinction between them. DESIDERIUS ERASMUS (1466–1536), *Enchiridion,* 1501.

A wise fellow who is also worthless always charms the rabble. EURIPIDES (480–405 B.C.), *Hippolytus,* 428 B.C.

The demagogue, puffing up the people with words, sways them to his interest. When calamity follows he escapes from justice. EURIPIDES (480–405 B.C.), *The Suppliant Woman,* 421 B.C..

A man is a lion in his own cause. DAVID FERGUSSON, *Scottish Proverbs,* 1641.

My generation of radicals and breakers-down never found anything to take the place of the old virtues of work and courage and the old graces of courtesy and politeness. F. SCOTT FITZGERALD (1896–1940), *Letters,* 1963.

Fanaticism is faith, the essence of faith, active faith, the faith that works miricles. GUSTAVE FLAUBERT (1821–1880), *Letters.*

Nothing great is ever done without fanaticism. Fanaticism is religion; and the eighteenth-century *philosophes* who decried the former actually overthrew the latter. GUSTAVE FLAUBERT (1821–1880), *Letters.*

Fanaticism is the child of false zeal and of superstition, the father of intolerance and of persecution. JOHN WILLIAM FLETCHER (1729–1789).

There lies at the back of every creed something terrible and hard for which the worshiper may one day be required to suffer. E. M. FORSTER (1879–1970), *Two Cheers for Democracy,* 1951.

To die for an idea is to set a rather high price upon conjecture. ANATOLE FRANCE (1844–1924), *The Revolt of the Angels,* 1914.

A man in a passion rides a mad horse. BENJAMIN FRANKLIN (1706–1790), *Poor Richard's Almanac,* 1749.

We know the crimes that fanaticism in religion has caused; let us be careful not to introduce fanaticism in philosophy. FREDERICK THE GREAT (1712–1786), Letter to Voltaire, 1775.

Every man has a wild animal within him. FREDERICK THE GREAT (1712–1786), Letter to Voltaire, 1775.

The aim of sadism is to transform a man into a thing, something animate into something inanimate, since by complete and absolute control the living loses one essential quality of life—freedom. ERICH FROMM (1900–1980), *Escape from Freedom,* 1941.

The people I am most scared of are the people who are scared of me. ROBERT FROST (1874–1963).

It is a curiosity of human nature that lack of self-assurance seems to breed an exaggerated sense of power and mission. J. WILLIAM FULBRIGHT, *The Arrogance of Power,* 1966.

The weakest and most timorous are the most revengeful and implacable. THOMAS FULLER (1654–1734), 1732.

Zeal without knowledge is fire without light. THOMAS FULLER (1654–1734), 1732

I don't mind martyrdom for a policy in which I believe, but I object to being burnt for someone else's principles. JOHN GALSWORTHY (1867–1933).

Political extremism involves two prime ingredients: an excessively simple diagnosis of the world's ills and a conviction that there are identifiable villains back of it all. JOHN W. GARDNER, *No Easy Victories*, 1968.

There are those who lust for the simple answers of doctrine or decree. They are on the left and right. They are not confined to a single part of our society. They are the terrorists of the mind. A. BARTLETT GIAMATTI (1938–1989), Baccalaureate Address, Yale University, May 26, 1986.

Isn't your life extremely flat / With nothing to grumble at?" WILLIAM S. GILBERT (1836–1911).

All ideologies are relative; the only absolute is the torment men inflict on each other. YEVGENIA GINSBERG.

Never contend with a man who has nothing to lose. BALTASAR GRACIAN (1601–1658), *The Art of Worldly Wisdom*, 1647.

Movements born in hatred very quickly take on the characteristics of the thing they oppose. J. S. HABGOOD, Archbishop of York, 1986.

There is an accumulative cruelty in a number of men, though none in particular are ill-natured. GEORGE SAVILLE, MARQUIS of HALIFAX, *Political Thoughts and Reflections*, 17th c.

Among men who have overturned the liberties of republics, the greatest number have begun by paying obsequious court to the people; commencing demagogues, and ending tyrants. ALEXANDER HAMILTON (1757–1805), *The Federalist*, 1787.

Perseverence is the most overrated of traits, if it is unaccompanied by talent. SYDNEY J. HARRIS, *Chicago Daily News*, January 9, 1958.

One cannot look too closely at and weigh in too golden scales the acts of men hot in their political excitement. SIR HENRY HAWKINS (1817–1907), English Jurist, *Ex Parte Castioni*, 1890.

The world owes all its onward impulses to men ill at ease. The happy man inevitably confines himself within ancient limits. NATHANIEL HAWTHORNE (1804–1864), *The House of the Seven Gables*, 1851.

The extraordinary persistence of the fanatical discourse, not only in tone and gesture, is the expression of a dualist division of the world into good and evil. ANDRE HAYNAL et al., *Fanaticism: A Historical and Psychoanalytical Study*, 1983.

Fanaticism can be found in either or both camps in the struggles pitting one party against the other, but it is always to be found wherever the cause takes precedence over the human person, blind devotion over free well, obsession over discernment. ANDRE HAYNAL et al., *Fanaticism: A Historical and Psychoanalytical Study,* 1983.

"He who is not with us is against us" is a principle basic to all fanaticism. ANDRE HAYNAL et al., *Fanaticism: A Historical and Psychoanalytical Study,* 1983.

Violent antipathies are always suspicious, and betray a secret affinity. WILLIAM HAZLITT (1778–1830), *Characteristics,* 1823.

Demagogy, the Holy Alliance of the Peoples. HEINRICH HEINE (1797–1856).

When religion and politics travel in the same cart, the riders believe nothing can stand in their way. FRANK HERBERT, *Dune,* 1965.

Membership in a conspiracy, as in an army, frees people from the sense of personal responsibility. FRANK HERBERT, *Dune,* 1965.

One of the most dangerous things in the universe is ignorant people with real grievances. That is nowhere near as dangerous, however, as an informed and intelligent society with grievances. The damage that vengeful intelligence can wreak, you cannot even imagine. FRANK HERBERT, *Dune,* 1965.

The greatness of every mighty organization embodying an idea in this world lies in the religious fanaticism and intolerance with which, fanatically convinced of his own right, intolerantly imposes its will against others. ADOLPH HITLER (1889–1945), *Mein Kampf,* 1925–27.

To have a grievance is to have ? purpose in life. ERIC HOFFER (1902–1983), *The Passionate State of Mind,* 1954.

Vehemence is the expression of a blind effort to support and uphold something that can never stand on its own. Whether it is our own meaningless self we are upholding, or some doctrine devoid of evidence, we can do it only in a frenzy of faith. ERIC HOFFER (1902–1983), *The Passionate State of Mind,* 1954.

Mass movements can rise and spread without a belief in God, but never without a belief in a devil. ERIC HOFFER (1902–1983), *The True Believer,* 1951.

It is to escape the responsibility for failure that the weak so eagerly throw themselves into grandiose undertakings. ERIC HOFFER (1902–1983), *The True Believer,* 1951.

You can discover what your enemy fears most by observing the means he uses to frighten you. ERIC HOFFER (1902–1983), *The True Believer,* 1951.

If there is anything more dangerous to the life of the mind than having no independent commitment to ideas, it is having an excess commitment to some special or constricting idea. RICHARD HOFSTADTER (1916–1970), *Anti-Intellectualism in American Life,* 1963.

Martyrs and persecutors are the same type of man. As to which is the persecutor and which the martyr, this is only a question of transient power. ELBERT HUBBARD (1856–1915), *The Note Book,* 1927.

There is a Set of Men lately sprung up amongst us, who endeavor to distinguish themselves by ridiculing every Thing, that has hitherto appeared sacred and venerable in the eyes of Mankind. Reason, Sobriety, Honor, Friendship, Marriage, are the perpetual Subjects of their insipid Raillery. Were the Schemes of these Anti-reformers to take Place, all the Bonds of Society must be broken. DAVID HUME (1711–1776), *Of Moral Prejudices.*

Nothing else in the world . . . not all the armies . . . is so powerful as an idea whose time has come. VICTOR HUGO (1802–1885), *The Future of Man.*

The consistent thinker, the consistently moral man, is either a walking mummy or else, if he has not succeeded in stifling all his vitality, a fanatical monomaniac. ALDOUS HUXLEY (1894–1963), *Do What You Will,* 1929.

Sons have always had a rebellious wish to be disillusioned by that which charmed their fathers. ALDOUS HUXLEY (1894–1963), *Music at Night,* 1931.

The end cannot justify the means for the simple and obvious reason that the means employed determine the nature of the ends produced. ALDOUS HUXLEY (1894–1963), *Ends and Means,* 1937.

The surest way to work up a crusade in favor of some good cause is to promise people they will have a chance of maltreating someone. To be able to destroy with good conscience, to be able to behave badly and call your bad behavior "righteous indignation"—this is the height of psychological luxury, the most delicious of moral treats. ALDOUS HUXLEY (1894–1963), *Crome Yellow,* 1921.

Every crusader is apt to go mad. He is haunted by the wickedness which he attributes to his enemies; it becomes in some sort a part of him. ALDOUS HUXLEY (1894–1963), *The Devils of Louden,* 1952.

Every institution not only carries within it the seeds of its own dissolution, but prepares the way for its most hated rival. WILLIAM RALPH INGE (1860–1954), *Outspoken Essays: Second Series,* 1922.

The greatest obstacle to progress is not man's inherited pugnacity, but his incorrigible tendency to parasitism. WILLIAM RALPH INGE (1860–1954), *Outspoken Essays: First Series,* 1919.

Every man who attacks my belief diminishes in some degree my confidence in it, and therefore makes me uneasy, and I am angry with him who makes me uneasy. SAMUEL JOHNSON (1709–1784), *Boswell's Life of Johnson,* 1791.

That fellow seems to me to possess but one idea, and that a wrong one. SAMUEL JOHNSON (1709–1784), *Boswell's Life of Johnson,* 1791.

It is very natural for young men to be vehement, acrimonious and severe. For as they seldom comprehend at once all the consequences of a position, or perceive the difficulties by which cooler and more experienced reasoners are restrained from confidence, they . . . are inclined to impute uncertainty and hesitation to want of honesty, rather than of knowledge. SAMUEL JOHNSON (1709–1784), *The Rambler,* 1751.

Passions are spiritual rebels and raise sedition against the understanding. BEN JONSON (1573–1637), *Timber,* 1640.

The man who promises everything is sure to fulfil nothing, and everyone who promises too much is in danger of using evil means in order to carry out his promises, and is already on the road to perdition. CARL GUSTAV JUNG (1875–1961).

Two deputies, one of whom is a radical, have more in common than two radicals, one of whom is a deputy. ROBERT de JOUVENEL, *La République des camarades,* 1914.

When once a man is determined to believe, the very absurdity of the doctrine does but confirm him in his faith. JUNIUS (1740–1818), *Letters.*

There is holy mistaken zeal in politics as well as religion. By persuading others, we convince ourselves. JUNIUS (1740–1818), *Letters.*

Liberty in the wild and freakish hands of fanatics has once more, as frequently in the past, proved the effective helpmate of autocracy and the twin brother of tyranny. OTTO KAHN (1867–1934), Speech, University of Wisconsin, 1918.

It's much easier to do and die than it is to reason why. G. A. STUDDERT KENNEDY.

The ultimate weakness of violence is that it is a descending spiral, begetting the very thing it seeks to destroy. Instead of diminishing evil, it multiplies it. Through violence you may murder the liar, but you cannot murder the lie, nor establish the truth. Through violence you may murder the hater, but you do not murder hate. In fact, violence merely increases hate. MARTIN LUTHER KING (1929–1968), *Where Do We Go from Here,* 1967.

Those who wallow in the imperfections of their society or turn them into an excuse for a nihilistic orgy usually end up by eroding all social and oral restraints; eventually in their pitiless assault on all beliefs they multiply suffering. HENRY KISSINGER, *The White House Years,* 1979.

Every crusade tends, by the very difficulty of its struggle and the fervor of its hope, to develop overdrive—a determination that may go too far. ORRIN E. KLAPP, *Collective Search for Identity,* 1969.

The goal of a crusade is to defeat an evil, not merely to solve a problem. This gives it the sense of righteousness. The crusader may think of himself as a hero and his opponents as villains. Indeed, the crusade classifies as a kind of villifying movement. ORRIN E. KLAPP, *Collective Search for Identity,* 1969.

The absolute morality of a crusade . . . leads easily to authoritarianism; indeed, the ideal crusader is close to a fanatic. A crusading movement is basically a political sect. ORRIN E. KLAPP, *Collective Search for Identity,* 1969.

To say that one has "seen the light" is a poor description of the mental rapture which only the convert knows. . . . There is now an answer to every question, doubts and conflicts are a matter of the tortured past. ARTHUR KOESTLER (1904–1983), *The God That Failed,* 1949.

Violence in word and deed is the hallmark of the mass movement uncommitted to institutional means. Mass behavior, then, involves direct, activist modes of response to remote symbols. WILLIAM KORNHAUSER, *The Politics of Mass Society,* 1959.

One of the saddest things about conformity is the ghastly sort of nonconformity it breeds: the noisy protesting, the aggressive rebelliousness, the rigid counter-fetishism. LOUIS KRONENBERGER (1904–1980), *Company Manners,* 1954.

The impulse to mar and to destroy is almost as nearly universal as the impulse to create. The one is an easier way than the other of demonstrating power. JOSEPH WOOD KRUTCH (1893–1970), *The Best of Two Worlds,* 1950.

Everyone believes very easily whatever he fears or desires. JEAN de LA FON-TAINE (1621–1695), *Fables,* 1671.

Man is so made that when anything fires his soul impossibilities vanish. JEAN de LA FONTAINE (1621–1695), *Fables,* 1671.

A man can compromise to gain a point. . . . Remember this . . . even a rebel grows old, and sometimes wiser. He finds the things he rebelled against are now the things he must defend against newer rebels. LOUIS L'AMOUR (1908–1988), *The Walking Drum,* 1984.

To die for what one believes is all very well for those so inclined, but it has always seemed to me the most vain of solutions. There is no cause worth dying for that is not better served by living. LOUIS L'AMOUR (1908–1988), *The Walking Drum,* 1984.

To what excesses will men not go to for the sake of a religion in which they believed so little and which they practice so imperfectly. JEAN de LA BRUYÈRE (1645–1696), *Les Caractères,* 1688.

A man who cannot find tranquility within himself will search for it in vain elsewhere. FRANÇOIS, DUC de LA ROUCHEFOUCAULD (1613–1689), *Maxims,* 1665.

When our hatred is too keen it puts us beneath those whom we hate. FRANÇOIS, DUC de LA ROCHEFOUCAULD (1613–1689), *Maxims,* 1665.

The renown of great men should always be measured by the means which they have used to acquire it. FRANÇOIS, DUC de LA ROCHEFOUCAULD (1613–1689), *Maxims,* 1665.

It is a fact of history that in every age of transition men are never so firmly bound to one way of life as when they are about to abandon it, so their fanaticism and intolerance reach their most intense forms just before tolerance and mutual acceptance come to be the natural order of things. BERNARD LEVIN, *The Pendulum Years,* 1971.

With most men, unbelief in one thing springs from blind belief in another. GEORGE CHRISTOPH LICHTENBERG (1742–1799), *Reflections,* 1799.

Ambition and suspicion always go together. GEORGE CHRISTOPH LICHTEN-BERG (1742–1799), *Reflections,* 1799.

There is no arguing with the pretenders to a divine knowledge and to a divine mission. They are possessed with the sin of pride, they have yielded to the perennial temptation. WALTER LIPPMANN (1889–1974), *The Public Philosophy,* 1955.

The demagogue, whether of the Right or Left, is an undetected liar. WALTER LIPPMANN (1889–1974), *Atlantic Monthly,* 1939.

The gradual realization that extremist and intolerant movements in modern society are more likely to be based on the lower classes than on the middle and upper classes has posed a tragic dilemma for those intellectuals of the democratic left who once believed the proletariat necessarily to be a force for liberty, racial equality, and social progress. SEYMOUR MARTIN LIPSET, *Political Man,* 1960.

I know that a creed is the shell of a lie. AMY LOWELL (1874–1925), *What's O'Clock,* 1925.

When I am angry I can write, pray, and preach well, for then my whole temperament is quickened, my understanding sharpened, and all mundane vexations and temptations gone. MARTIN LUTHER (1483–1546).

In every age the vilest specimens of human nature are to be found among demagogues. THOMAS BABINGTON MACAULAY (1800–1859), *History of England.*

A radical may be many things and he may be moved by complex motives, but in the last analysis he is an idealist who feels compelled to right existing wrongs. His rebelliousness may be a form of compensation for suffering from authority or poverty, from thwarted ambition or personal maladjustment. The radical is driven by a messianic urge to remake the world. CHARLES A. MADISON, *Critics and Crusaders,* 1947.

In all humanism there is an element of weakness, which in some circumstances may be its ruin, connected with its contempt of fanaticism, its patience, its love of skepticism. THOMAS MANN (1875–1955), 1950.

If you are possessed by an idea, you will find it expressed everywhere, you even smell it. THOMAS MANN (1875–1955), 1903.

A demagogue is a person with whom we disagree as to which gang should mismanage the country. DON MARQUIS (1878–1937).

An idea isn't responsible for the people who believe in it. DON MARQUIS (1878–1937).

The demagogue is one who preaches doctrines he knows to be untrue to men he knows to be idiots. H. L. MENCKEN (1880–1956).

A sense of humor always withers in the presence of the messianic delusion, like justice and truth in front of patriotic passion. H. L. MENCKEN (1880–1956), *Prejudices.*

Life has to be given a meaning because of the obvious fact that it has no meaning. HENRY MILLER (1891–1980), *The Wisdom of the Heart,* 1941.

How strange it is to see with how much passion / People see things only in their own fashion! MOLIÈRE (1622–1673), *School for Wives,* 1662.

We believe nothing so firmly as what we least know. MICHEL de MONTAIGNE (1533–1592), *Essays,* 1580.

Men are tormented by the opinions they have of things, not by the things themselves. MICHEL de MONTAIGNE (1533–1592), *Essays,* 1580.

Faith, fanatic faith, once wedded fast / To some dear falsehood, hugs it to the last. THOMAS MOORE (1779–1852), *Lalla Rookh,* 1817.

The size of a man can be measured by the size of the thing that makes him angry. J. KENFIELD MORLEY, *Some Things I Believe,* 1937.

What matters most about political ideas is the underlying emotions, the music, to which ideas are a mere libretto, often of very inferior quality. SIR LEWIS NAMIER (1888–1960), *Personalities and Powers,* 1955.

The chief use to which we put our love of the truth is in persuading ourselves that the we we love is true. PIERRE NICOLE (1625–1695), *Essay on Morals.*

With all great deceivers there is a noteworthy occurrence to which they owe their power. In the actual act of deception they are overcome by belief in themselves: it is this which then speaks miraculously and compellingly to those who surround them. FRIEDRICH NIETZSCHE (1844–1900), 1878.

Whoever fights monsters should see to it that in the process he does not become a monster. And if you gaze long enough into an abyss, the abyss will gaze back into you. FRIEDRICH NIETZSCHE (1844–1900), *Beyond Good and Evil,* 1886.

Mistrust those in whom the impulse to punish is strong. FRIEDRICH NIETZSCHE (1844–1900).

The value of a thing lies not in what one attains with it, but in what one pays for it—what it costs us. FRIEDRICH NIETZSCHE (1844–1900), *Twilight of the Idols,* 1889.

The beating of drums, which delights young writers who serve a party, sounds to him who does not belong to the party like a rattling of chains, and excites sympathy rather than admiration. FRIEDRICH NIETZSCHE (1844–1900), *Miscellaneous Maxims and Opinions,* 1879.

Madness is rare in individuals—but in groups, political parties, nations, and eras it's the rule. FRIEDRICH NIETZSCHE (1844–1900), *Beyond Good and Evil,* 1886.

Men of fixed convictions do not count when it comes to determining what is fundamental in values and lack of values. Men of convictions are prisoners. FRIEDRICH NIETZSCHE (1844–1900), *The Antichrist,* 1888.

Disloyalty, however picayune, is unforgivable to the fanatic. Even the appearance of disloyalty is sufficient for banishment of the offender, no matter how many years of unquestioning devotion have been given; they are as nothing compared to the enormity of the moment. ROBERT NISBET, *Prejudices: A Philosophical Dictionary,* 1982.

The fanatic has the gift of hate in superlative intensity. Most human beings are unable to sustain hatred for more than a short time . . . but the fanatic can hate for a lifetime. . . . The fanatic forgets nothing; no detail is too small not to remember for decades and to nourish constantly by the acids of hate. ROBERT NISBET, *Prejudices: A Philosophical Dictionary,* 1982.

I know of no higher fortitude than stubborness in the face of overwhelming odds. LOUIS NIZER, *My Life in Court,* 1962.

Oh, to grasp this sorry scheme of things entire, shatter it to bits, and remold it nearer to the heart's desire. OMAR KHAYYAM (1048–1131), *The Rubiayat.*

Hatred is a feeling which leads to the extinction of values. JOSÉ ORTEGA y GASSET (1883–1955), *Meditations on Quixote,* 1914.

One defeats a fanatic precisely by not being a fanatic oneself, but on the contrary by using one's intelligence. GEORGE ORWELL (1903–1950), 1949.

Fortunately for themselves and the world, nearly all men are cowards and dare not act on what they believe. Nearly all of our disasters come of a few fools having the "courage of their convictions." COVENTRY PATMORE (1823–1896).

Force empowers its own adversaries. It raises up its own destruction. It engenders its own destruction. ROY PEARSON, *The Dilemma of Force,* 1968.

Passion is a sort of Fever in the Mind, which ever leaves us weaker than it found us. . . . It may be termed, the Mob of the Man, that commits a Riot upon his Reason. WILLIAM PENN (1644–1718), *Some Fruits of Solitude,* 1693.

They all want the truth—a truth that is: something specific; something concrete! They don't care what it is. All they want is something categorical, something that speaks plainly! LUIGI PIRANDELLO (1867–1936), *It Is So! (If You Think So),* 1917.

To live only for some future goal is shallow. It's the sides of the mountain that sustain life, not the top. ROBERT M. PIRSIG, *Zen and the Art of Motorcycle Maintenance,* 1974.

[When reason] is asleep, then the wild beast within us, gorged with meat or drink, starts up and having shaken off sleep, goes forth to satisfy his desires; and there is no conceivable folly or crime it won't commit. PLATO (428–347 B.C.).

All seems infected that the infected spy / As all looks yellow to the jaundiced eye. ALEXANDER POPE (1688–1744), *An Essay on Criticism,* 1711.

The ruling passion, be what it will. The ruling passion conquers reason still. ALEXANDER POPE (1688–1744), *Moral Essays.*

The same ambition can destroy or save, And makes a Patriot as it makes a knave. ALEXANDER POPE (1688–1744), *An Essay on Man,* 1732.

I do not wish to imply that conspiracies never happen. On the contrary, they are typical social phenomena. They become important, for example, whenever people who believe in the conspiracy theory get into power. And people who sincerely believe that they know how to make heaven on earth are most likely to adopt the conspiracy theory, and to get into a counterconspiracy against nonexisting conspirators. . . . SIR KARL POPPER, *The Open Society and Its Enemies,* 1962.

Creeds are devices to keep heretics out rather than draw people in. GERALD PRIESTLAND, *Something Understood.*

It is desire that engenders belief and if we fail as a rule to take this into account, it is because most of the desires that create beliefs end . . . only with our own life. MARCEL PROUST (1871–1922), *Remembrance of Things Past,* 1913–26.

He who is feared by many must fear many. PUBLILIUS SYRUS (1st c. B.C.), *Sententiae,* 50 B.C.

Man makes holy what he believes, as he makes beautiful what he loves. ERNEST RENAN (1823–1892), 1857.

Men are suffering from the fever of violent emotion, and so they make a philosophy of it. S. RADHAKRISHNAN (1888–1975), *The Reign of Religion in Philosophy,* 1922.

Oh liberty! Oh liberty! What crimes are committed in thy name. MADAME ROLAND (1754–1793).

You sometimes find something good in the lunatic fringe. In fact, we have got as part of our social and economic government today a whole lot of things which in my boyhood were considered lunatic fringe, and yet they are now part of everyday life. FRANKLIN D. ROOSEVELT (1882–1945), U.S. President, Press Conference, May 30, 1944.

The less reasonable a cult is, the more men seek to establish it by force. JEAN-JACQUES ROUSSEAU (1712–1778).

Fanaticism is a camouflage for cruelty. Fanatics are seldom humane, and those who sincerely dread cruelty will be slow to adapt to a fanatical creed. BERTRAND RUSSELL (1872–1970), *Theory and Practice of Bolshevism,* 1920.

Belief in a Divine Mission is one of the many forms of certainty that have afflicted the human race. BERTRAND RUSSELL (1872–1970), *Unpopular Essays,* 1950.

The opinions that are held with passion are always those for which no good ground exists; indeed the passion is the measure of the holder's lack of rational conviction. Opinions in politics and religion are almost always held passionately. BERTRAND RUSSELL (1872–1970), *Skeptical Essays,* 1961.

The twin concepts of sin and vindictive punishment seem to be at the root of much that is most vigorous, both in religion and politics. BERTRAND RUSSELL (1872–1970), *Unpopular Essays,* 1950.

Most of the greatest evils that man has inflicted upon man have come through people feeling quite certain about something which, in fact, was false. BERTRAND RUSSELL (1872–1970), *Ideas That Have Harmed Mankind,* 1946.

Demagoguery enters at the moment when, for want of a common denominator, the principle of equality degenerates into the principle of identity. ANTOINE de SAINT-EXUPÉRY (1900–1944), *Flight to Arras,* 1942.

New truths are always being prepared in the cellars of violence. ANTOINE de SAINT-EXUPÉRY (1900–1944).

What sets us against one another is not our aims—they all come to the same thing—but our methods, which are the fruit of our varied reasoning. ANTOINE de SAINT-EXUPÉRY (1900–1944), *Wind, Sand and Stars,* 1939.

The meaning of things lies not in the things themselves but in our attitude towards them. ANTOINE de SAINT-EXUPÉRY (1900–1944), *The Wisdom of the Sands.*

Even the heretics and atheists, if they had profundity, turn out after a while to be forerunners of some new orthodoxy. What they rebel against is a religion alien to their nature; they are atheists only by accident, and relatively to the convention which inwardly offends them. GEORGE SANTAYANA (1863–1952), *Reason in Religion.*

Fanaticism consists in redoubling your effort when you have forgotten your aim. GEORGE SANTAYANA (1863–1952), *The Life of Reason,* 1905.

There is nobody as enslaved as the fanatic, the person in whom one impulse, one value, has assumed ascendency over all others. MILTON R. SAPERSTEIN, *Paradoxes of Everyday Life,* 1955.

The man who fears nothing is as powerful as he who is feared by everybody. FRIEDRICH von SCHILLER (1759–1805), *The Robbers,* 1781.

Martyrdom has always been a proof of the intensity, never of the correctness, of a belief. ARTHUR SCHNITZLER (1862–1951).

A man of correct insight among those who are duped and deluded resembles one whose watch is right while all the clocks in the town give the wrong time. He alone knows the correct time, but of what use is this to him? The whole world is guided by the clocks that show the wrong time. ARTHUR SCHOPENHAUER (1783–1860), *Parerga and Paralipomena*, 1851.

Every miserable fool who has nothing at all of which he can be proud, adopts as a last resource pride in the nation to which he belongs; he is ready and happy to defend all of its faults and follies tooth and nail, thus reimbursing himself for his own inferiority. ARTHUR SCHOPENHAUER (1783–1860), *Parerga and Paralipomena*, 1851.

Extremism: Vague term, which can mean: 1. Taking a political idea to its limits, regardless of "unfortunate" repercussions, impracticalities, arguments, and feelings to the contrary, and with the intention not only to confront, but also to eliminate opposition. 2. Intolerance towards all views other than one's own. 3. Adoption of means to political ends which show disregard for the life, liberty and human rights of others. ROGER SCRUTON, *A Dictionary of Political Thought*, 1982.

One can always legislate against specific acts of human wickedness: but one can never legislate against the irrational itself. MORTON SEIDEN, *A Paradox of Hate: A Study in Ritual Murder*, 1967.

What nature requires is obtainable, and within easy reach. It's for the superfluous we sweat. LUCIUS ANNAEUS SENECA (4 B.C.–65 A.D.), *Epistles.*

And so, to the end of history, murder shall breed murder, always in the name of right and honor and peace, until the gods are tired of blood and create a race that can understand. GEORGE BERNARD SHAW (1858–1950), *Caesar and Cleopatra*, 1900.

Martyrdom is the only way in which a man can become famous without ability. GEORGE BERNARD SHAW (1858–1950).

What a man believes may be ascertained, not from his creed, but from the assumptions on which he habitually acts. GEORGE BERNARD SHAW (1856–1950).

Belief is a passion, or involuntary operation of the mind, and like other passions, its intensity is precisely proportionate to the degree of excitment. PERCY BYSSHE SHELLEY (1792–1822), 1813.

The whole fabric of society presents a most threatening aspect. What is most ominous of an approaching change is the strength which the popular party has suddenly acquired, and the importance which the violence of the demagogues has assumed. PERCY BYSSHE SHELLEY (1792–1822), *Letter to Byron*, November 20, 1816.

To praise oneself is considered improper, immodest; to praise one's own sect, one's own philosophy, is considered the highest duty. LEO SHESTOV (1866–1938), *All Things Are Possible,* 1905.

Ideological extremism is the enemy of the privacy and publicity which support our liberties. EDWARD A. SHILS, *The Torment of Secrecy,* 1956.

Every communist has a fascist frown, every fascist a communist smile. MURIEL SPARK, *Girls of Slender Means,* 1982.

The mark of the immature man is that he wants to die nobly for a cause, while the mark of the mature man is that he wants to live humbly for one. WILHELM STEKEL (1868–1940).

'Tis known by the name of perseverance in a good cause, and obstinacy in a bad one. LAURENCE STERNE (1713–1768).

If you want a war, nourish a doctrine. Doctrines are the most frightful tyrants to which men are ever subject, because doctrines get inside a man's reason and betray him against himself. Civilized men have done their fiercest fighting for doctrines. WILLIAM GRAHAM SUMNER (1840–1910), *Essays.*

The thirst for glory is an epidemic which robs a people of their judgment, seduces their vanity, cheats them of their interests, and corrupts their consciences. WILLIAM GRAHAM SUMNER (1840–1910), 1899.

The most positive men are the most credulous. JONATHAN SWIFT (1667–1745), *Thoughts on Various Subjects.*

Ambition often puts men upon doing the meanest offices; so climbing is performed in the same posture with creeping. JONATHAN SWIFT (1667–1745), *Thoughts on Various Subjects.*

Where the true believer speaks metaphorically but claims that he asserts literal truths. Heresy may consist of no more than insisting that a metaphorical truth may be a literal falsehood. THOMAS SZASZ, *Heresies,* 1976.

Every creed, philosophy, political system that prescribes how people should live is bound to be wrong—in the sense that it sets itself against the fundamental human needs for autonomy and diversity. THOMAS SZASZ, *The Untamed Tongue,* 1990.

There is a sort of man who goes through the world in a succession of quarrels, always able to make out that he is in the right, although he never ceases to put other men in the wrong. SIR HENRY TAYLOR (1810–1886), *The Statesman,* 1836.

The weakness of the fanatic is that those whom he fights have a secret hold upon him, and to this weakness he and his groups will finally succumb. PAUL TILLICH (1886–1965).

The basis of fascism is blind belief and a contempt for reason. Fascism exploits the fear of reason which lives secretly in the conscious and subconscious minds of many people. Reason means facing life and facts. ERNST TOLLER (1883–1939).

If there were more extremists in evolutionary periods, there would no revolutionary periods. BENJAMIN R. TUCKER (1854–1939), *Instead of a Book,* 1893.

A nihilist is a man who bows down to no authority, and takes no principle on faith. IVAN S. TURGENEV (1818–1883), *Fathers and Sons,* 1862.

At the extreme, the process of stereotyping eventuates in dehumanization: the enemy is judged to be so inhumanly evil or contemptible that anything may be done to "it" without subjectively compromising one's own humanity and sense of morality. AUSTIN J. TURK, *Political Criminality,* 1982.

The radical invents the views. When he has worn them out, the conservative adopts them. MARK TWAIN (1835–1910), *Notebooks.*

An attitude of permanent indignation signifies great mental poverty. Politics compels its votaries to take that line and you see their minds growing more and more impoverished every day, from one burst of righteous anger to the next. PAUL VALÉRY (1871–1945), *Tel Quel,* 1941–43.

Human beings are perhaps never more frightening than when they are convinced beyond doubt that they are right. LAURENS van der POST, *The Lost World of the Kalahari,* 1958.

There have been quite as many martyrs for bad causes as for good ones. HENDRICK van LOON (1882–1944).

No one is more liable to make mistakes than the man who acts only on reflection. MARQUIS de VAUVENARGUES (1715–1747), *Reflections and Maxims,* 1746.

[Fanaticism is] the effect of a false conscience, which makes religion subservient to the caprices of the imagination, and the excesses of the passions. VOLTAIRE (1694–1778), *Philosophical Dictionary,* 1764.

What is more dangerous, fanaticism or atheism? Fanaticism is certainly a thousand times more deadly; for atheism inspires no bloody passion, whereas fanaticism does; it is not opposed to crime, but fanaticism causes crimes to be committed. VOLTAIRE (1694–1778), *Philosophical Dictionary,* 1764.

A firm and vibrant political idea requires a strong sense of shared endeavor, without which no organizational devices can keep people firmly united. ROBERT WESSON, *Politics: Individual and State,* 1988.

The pseudo-conscience demands not obedience to the inner law of our being, but conformity to superimposed convention. FRANCIS G. WICKES (1875–1967), *The Creative Process,* 1948.

The worst vice of the fanatic is his sincerity. OSCAR WILDE (1854–1900).

The nihilist, that strange martyr who has no faith, who goes to the stake without enthusiasm, and dies for what he does not believe, is a purely literary product.

He was invented by Turgenev, and completed by Dostoyevsky. OSCAR WILDE (1854–1900), *The Decay of Lying,* 1891.

The value of an idea has nothing whatsoever to do with the sincerity of the man who expresses it. OSCAR WILDE (1854–1900).

All fanaticism is a strategy to prevent doubt from becoming conscious. H. A. WILLIAMS, *The True Wilderness,* 1965.

In times of disorder and stress, the fanatics play a prominent role; in times of peace, the critics. Both are shot after the revolution. EDMUND WILSON (1895–1972), *Memoirs of Hecate County,* 1949.

Generally young men are regarded as radicals. This is a popular misconception. The most conservative persons I ever met are college undergraduates. WOODROW WILSON (1856–1924), U.S. President.

No people are more conservative than liberals in their liberalism and revolutionaries in their revolutions. LEONARD WOOLF (1880–1969), *After the Deluge,* 1931.

[A believer is] one in whom persuasion and belief had ripened into faith and faith became a passionate intuition. WILLIAM WORDSWORTH (1770–1850), *The Excursion,* 1814.

Things fall apart / the centre cannot hold / Mere anarchy is loosed upon the world / The blood-dimmed tide is loosed, and everywhere the ceremony of innocence is drowned / The best lack all conviction, while the worst are full of passionate intensity. WILLIAM BUTLER YEATS (1865–1939), *The Second Coming,* 1921.

All empty souls tend to extreme opinion. It is only in those who have built up a rich world of memories and habits of thought that extreme opinions affront the sense of probability. WILLIAM BUTLER YEATS (1865–1939), *Autobiography.*

[The fanatic is] the insecure person anywhere, at any time, who gives himself without reservation to any movement that promises him meaning through action. ROBERT ZWICKEY.

Freedom of Speech and of the Press

I had rather starve and rot and keep the privilege of speaking the truth as I see it, than of holding all the offices that capital has to give from the presidency down. BROOKS ADAMS (1848–1927), *The Degradation of the Democratic Dogma.*

The jaws of power are always open to devour, and her arm is always stretched out, if possible, to destroy the freedom of thinking, speaking, and writing. JOHN ADAMS (1735–1826), 1765.

Civil liberty can be established on no foundation of human reason which will not at the same time demonstrate the right to religious freedom. JOHN QUINCY ADAMS (1767–1848), Letter, 1823.

The truth that makes men free is for the most part the truth which men prefer not to hear. HERBERT SEBASTIEN AGAR (1897–1980), *A Time for Greatness,* 1942.

Freedom of thought and freedom of speech in our great institutions are absolutely necessary for the preservation of our country. The moment either is restricted, liberty begins to wither and die. . . . JOHN PETER ATGELD (1847–1902), 1897.

Liberty of speech inviteth and provoketh liberty to be used again, and so bringeth much to a man's knowledge. SIR FRANCIS BACON (1561–1626), *The Advancement of Learning,* 1605.

A forbidden writing is thought to be a certain spark of truth, that flies up in the face of them who seek to tread it out. SIR FRANCIS BACON (1561–1626), *The Advancement of Learning,* 1605.

Letting a maximum number of views be heard regularly is not just a nice philosophical notion. It is the best way any society has yet discovered to detect maladjustments quickly, to correct injustices, and to discover new ways to meet the continuing stream of novel problems that rise in a changing environment. BEN BAGDIKIAN.

The oppression of any people for opinion's sake has rarely had any other effect than to fix those opinions deeper, and render them more important. HOSEA BALLOU (1771–1852).

Thought that is silenced is always rebellious. Majorities, of course, are often mistaken. This is why the silencing of minorities is necessarily dangerous. Criticism and dissent are the indispensable antidote to major delusions. ALAN BARTH, *The Loyalty of Free Men,* 1951.

One of the best ways to get yourself a reputation as a dangerous citizen these days is to go about repeating the very phrases which our founding fathers used in the great struggle for independence. CHARLES A. BEARD (1874–1948), 1935.

No great advance has ever been made in science, politics, or religion, without controversy. LYMAN BEECHER (1775–1863).

There is tonic in the things that men do not love to hear. Free speech is to a great people what the winds are to oceans . . . and where free speech is stopped miasma is bred, and death comes fast. HENRY WARD BEECHER (1813–1887).

In order to get the truth, conflicting arguments and expressions must be allowed. There can be no freedom without choice, no sound choice without knowledge. DAVID K. BERNINGHAUSEN, *Arrogance of the Censor,* 1982.

Anonymous pamphlets, leaflets, brochures and even books have played an important role in the progress of mankind. Persecuted groups and sects from time to time throughout history have been able to criticize oppressive practices and laws either anonymously or not at all. . . . It is plain that anonymity has sometimes been assumed for the most constructive purposes. HUGO L. BLACK (1886–1971), U.S. Supreme Court Justice, *Talley* v. *California,* 1960.

Freedom to publish means freedom for all and not for some. Freedom to publish is guaranteed by the constitution but freedom to continue to prevent others from publishing is not. HUGO L. BLACK (1886–1971), U.S. Supreme Court Justice, *One Man's Stand for Freedom,* 1963.

Freedom of speech means that you shall not do something to people either for the views they have, or the views they express, or the words they speak or write. HUGO L. BLACK (1886–1971), U.S. Supreme Court Justice, *One Man's Stand for Freedom,* 1963.

An unconditional right to say what one pleases about public affairs is what I consider to be the minimum guarantee of the First Amendment. HUGO L. BLACK (1886–1971), U.S. Supreme Court Justice, *New York Time Company* v. *Sullivan,* 1964.

Criticism of government finds sanctuary in several portions of the First Amendment. It is part of the right of free speech. It embraces freedom of the press. HUGO L. BLACK (1886–1791), U.S. Supreme Court Justice, 1961.

The interest of the people lies in being able to join organizations, advocate causes, and make political "mistakes" without being subjected to governmental penalties. HUGO L. BLACK (1886–1971), U.S. Supreme Court Justice, 1959.

Compelling a man by law to pay his money to elect candidates or advocate laws or doctrines he is against differs only in degree, if at all, from compelling him by law to speak for a candidate, a party, or a cause he is against. The very reason for the First Amendment is to make the people of this country free to think, speak, write and worship as they wish, not as the Government commands. HUGO L. BLACK (1886–1971), U.S. Supreme Court Justice, *IAM* v. *Street,* 367 U.S., 1961.

By placing discretion in the hands of an official to grant or deny a license, such a statute creates a threat of censorship that by its very existence chills free speech. HARRY A. BLACKMUN, U.S. Supreme Court Justice, *Roe* v. *Wade,* 1973.

Freedom of the mind requires not only, or not even especially, the absence of legal constraints but the presence of alternative thoughts. The most successful tyranny is not the one that uses force to assure uniformity, but the one that removes the awareness of other possibilities. ALAN BLOOM (1930–1992), *The Closing of the American Mind,* 1987.

No more fatuous chimera ever infested the brain than that you can control opinions by law or direct belief by statute, and no more pernicious sentiment ever tormented the human heart than the barbarous desire to do so. The field of inquiry should remain open, and the right of debate must be regarded as a sacred right. WILLIAM E. BORAH (1865–1940), U.S. Senator, 1917.

Without an unfettered press, without liberty of speech, all the outward forms and structures of free institutions are a sham, a pretense—the sheerest mockery. If the press is not free; if speech is not independent and untrammelled; if the mind is shackled or made impotent through fear, it makes no difference under what form of government you live, you are a subject and not a citizen. WILLIAM E. BORAH (1865–1940), U.S. Senator, Remarks to the Senate, April 19, 1917.

The American press is extraordinarily free and vigorous, as it should be. It should be, not because it is free of inaccuracy, oversimplification and bias, but because the alternative to that freedom is worse than those failings. ROBERT BORK, Judge, U.S. Court of Appeals, *New York Times,* 1985.

Without free speech no search for truth is possible . . . no discovery of truth is useful. CHARLES BRADLAUGH (1833–1891), Speech, 1890.

If special honor is claimed for any, then heresy should have it as the truest servitor of human kind. CHARLES BRADLAUGH (1833–1891), Speech, 1881.

Fear of serious injury cannot alone justify the oppression of free speech and assembly. Men feared witches and burnt women. . . . To justify suppression of free speech there must be reasonable ground to fear that serious evil will result if free speech is practiced. There must be reasonable ground to believe that the danger apprehended is imminent. There must be reasonable ground to believe that the evil to be prevented is a serious one. . . . [N]o danger flowing from speech can be deemed clear and present, unless the incidence of the evil apprehended is so imminent that it may befall before there is an opportunity for full discussion. Only an emergency can justify repression. Such must be the rule if authority is to be reconciled with freedom. LOUIS B. BRANDEIS (1865–1941), U.S. Supreme Court Justice, *Whitney* v. *California,* 1927.

If there be time to expose through discussion the falsehood and fallacies, to avert the evil by the process of education, the remedy to be applied is more speech, not enforced silence. LOUIS B. BRANDEIS (1865–1941), U.S. Supreme Court Justice, *Whitney* v. *California,* 1927.

All ideas having even the slightest redeeming social importance—unorthodox ideas, controversial idea, even ideas hateful to the prevailing climate of opinion— have the full protection of the guaranties. . . . WILLIAM J. BRENNAN, U.S. Supreme Court Justice, *Roth* v. *U.S.,* 1957.

Free speech is about as good a cause as the world has ever known. But it . . . gets shoved aside in favor of things which seem at a given moment more vital . . . everybody favors free speech in the slack moments when no axes are being ground. HEYWOOD BROUN (1888–1939), 1926.

The right to discuss freely and openly, by speech, by the pen, by the press, all political questions, and to examine and animadvert upon all political institutions is a right so clear and certain, so interwoven with our other liberties, so necessary, in fact, to their existence, that without it we must fall into despotism and anarchy. WILLIAM CULLEN BRYANT (1794–1878), *New York Evening Post,* November 18, 1837.

Universities should be safe havens where ruthless examination of realities will not be distorted by the aim to please or inhibited by the risk of displeasure. KINGMAN BREWSTER, President, Yale University, April 11, 1964.

The censor believes that he can hold back the mighty traffic of life with a tin whistle and a raised right hand. For after all, it is life with which he quarrels. HEYWOOD BROUN (1888–1939), in *The Fifty Year Decline and Fall of Hollywood* (E. Goodman), 1961.

Free speech is about as good a cause as the world has ever known. But, like the poor, it is always with us and gets shoved aside in favor of things more vital. HEYWOOD BROUN (1888–1939), *New York World,* October 23, 1926.

The more unpopular an opinion is, the more necessary is it that the holder should be somewhat punctilious in his observance of conventionalities generally. SAMUEL BUTLER (1835–1902), Notebooks, 1912.

Freedom of the press is perhaps the freedom that has suffered the most from the gradual degradation of the idea of liberty. ALBERT CAMUS (1913–1960), *Resistance, Rebellion and Death.*

Of freedom of thought and speech . . . one may say that it is the matrix, the indispensable condition, of nearly every other form of freedom. BENJAMIN CARDOZO (1870–1938), U.S. Supreme Court Justice, *Palko* v. *Connecticut,* 1937.

The freedom to express varying and often opposing ideas is essential to a variety of conceptions of democracy. If democracy is viewed as essentially a process—a way in which collective decisions for a society are made—free expression is crucial to the openness of the process and to such characteristics as elections, representation of interests, and the like. JONATHAN D. CASPER, *The Politics of Civil Liberties,* 1972.

The majority of us are for free speech when it deals with subjects concerning which we have no intense feelings. EDMUND B. CHAFFEE (1887–1936).

The real value of freedom is not to the minority that wants to talk, but to the majority, that does not want to listen. ZECHARIAH CHAFFEE, JR. (1885–1957), *The Blessings of Liberty.*

You make men love their government and their country by giving them the kind of government and the kind of country that inspire respect and love: a country that is free and unafraid, that lets the discontented talk in order to learn the causes of their discontent and end those causes, that refuses to impel men to spy on their neighbors, that protects its citizens vigorously from harmful acts while it leaves the remedies for objectionable ideas to counterargument and time. ZECHARIAH CHAFEE, JR. (1885–1957), *Free Speech in the United States,* 1942.

Forms of expression always appear turgid to those who do not share the emotions they represent. GILBERT KEITH CHESTERTON (1874–1936), *A Handful of Authors.*

The theory of free speech, that truth is so much larger and stranger and more many-sided than we know of, that it is very much better at all costs to hear every one's account of it, is a theory which has been justified on the whole by experiment, but which remains a very daring and even a very surprising theory. It is really one of the great discoveries of the modern time. GILBERT KEITH CHESTERTON (1974–1936), *Robert Browning,* 1914.

From a comparative perspective, the United States is unusual if not unique in the lack of restraints on freedom of expression. It is also unusual in the range and effectiveness of methods employed to restrain freedom of thought. . . . Where the voice of the people is heard, elite groups must insure their voice says the right things. NOAM CHOMSKY, *Index on Censorship,* July/August 1986.

Everybody is in favor of free speech. Hardly a day passes without its being extolled, but some people's idea of it is that they are free to say what they like, but if anyone says anything back, that is an outrage. WINSTON CHURCHILL (1874–1965), Speech, House of Commons, 1943.

From the standpoint of freedom of speech and the press, it is enough to point out that the state has no legitimate interest in protecting any or all religions from views distasteful to them. . . . It is not the business of government to suppress real or imagined attacks upon a particular religious doctrine. TOM C. CLARK (1899–1977), U.S. Supreme Court Justice, *Burstyn* v. *Wilson,* 1952.

Make no laws whatever concerning speech, and speech will be free; so soon as you make a declaration on paper that speech shall be free, you will have a hundred lawyers proving that "freedom does not mean abuse, nor liberty license," and they will define and define freedom out of existence. VOLTARINE de CLEYRE (1866–1912), in *The Cry for Justice* (Upton Sinclair).

Censorship always defeats its own purpose, for it creates, in the end, the kind of society that is incapable of exercising real discretion. . . . In the long run it will create a generation incapable of appreciating the difference between independence of thought and subservience. HENRY STEELE COMMAGER, *Freedom, Loyalty and Dissent,* 1954.

Our tradition is one of protest and revolt, and it is stultifying to celebrate the rebels of the past while we silence the rebels of the present. HENRY STEELE COMMAGER (1902–1984), *Freedom, Loyalty and Dissent,* 1954.

The justification and the purpose of freedom of speech is not to indulge those who want to speak their minds. It is to prevent error and discover truth. There may be other ways of detecting error and discovering truth than that of free discussion, but so far we have not found them. HENRY STEELE COMMAGER (1902–1984), *Freedom and Order,* 1966.

Diversity of opinion within the framework of loyalty to our free society is not only basic to a university but to the entire nation. JAMES BRYANT CONANT (1893–1978), *Education in a Divided World,* 1948.

Congress shall make no law respecting an establishment of religion, or prohibiting the free exercise thereof; or abridging the freedom of speech, or of the press; or the right of the people peaceably to assemble, and to petition the Government for a redress of grievances. CONSTITUTION OF THE UNITED STATES, First Amendment, 1791.

Every politician, every member of the clerical profession, ought to incur the reasonable suspicion of being an interested supporter of false doctrines who becomes angry at opposition, and endeavors to cast an odium on free inquiry. Fraud and falsehood demand examination. THOMAS COOPER (1759–1839).

The objector and the rebel who raises his voice against what he believes to be the injustice of the present and the wrongs of the past is the one who hunches the world along. CLARENCE S. DARROW (1857–1938), Communist Trial, 1920.

The Constitution is a delusion and a snare if the weakest and humblest man in the land cannot be defended in his right to speak and his right to think as much as the strongest in the land. CLARENCE S. DARROW (1857–1938), Communist Trial, 1920.

False facts are highly injurious to the progress of science, for they often endure long; but false views, if supported by some evidence, do little harm, for everyone takes a salutary pleasure in proving their falseness; and when this is done, one path towards error is closed and the road to truth is often at the same time opened. CHARLES DARWIN (1809–1882), *The Descent of Man.*

This nation was conceived in liberty and dedicated to the principle—among others—that honest men may honestly disagree; that if they all say what they think, a majority of the people will be able to distinguish truth from error; that in the competition of the market place of ideas, the sounder ideas will in the long run win out. ELMER DAVIS (1890–1958), *But We Were Born Free,* 1954.

I think that the influence towards suppression of minority views—towards orthodoxy in thinking about public issues—has been more subconscious than unconscious, stemming to a very great extent from the tendency of Americans to conform . . . not to deviate or depart from an orthodox point of view. WILLIAM O. DOUGLAS (1898–1980), U.S. Supreme Court Justice, 1958.

Where suspicion fills the air and holds scholars in line for fear of their jobs, there can be no exercise of the free intellect. Supineness and dogmatism take the place of inquiry. . . . A problem can no longer be pursued to its edges . . . discussion often leaves off where it should begin. WILLIAM O. DOUGLAS (1898–1980), U.S. Supreme Court Justice, 1952.

The struggle is always between the individual and his sacred right to express himself and . . . the power structure that seeks conformity, suppression and obedience. WILLIAM O. DOUGLAS (1898–1980), U.S. Supreme Court Justice.

Restriction of free thought and free speech is the most dangerous of all subversions. It is the one un-American act that could most easily defeat us. WILLIAM O. DOUGLAS (1898–1980), U.S. Supreme Court Justice.

It is our attitude toward free thought and free expression that will determine our fate. There must be no limit on the range of temperate discussion, no limits on thought. No subject must be taboo. No censor must preside at our assemblies. WILLIAM O. DOUGLAS (1898–1980), U.S. Supreme Court Justice. Address, Author's Guild, 1952.

[A] function of free speech under our system of government is to invite dispute. It may indeed best serve its high purpose when it induces a condition of unrest, creates dissatisfaction with conditions as they are, or even stirs people to anger. Speech is often provocative and challenging. It may strike at prejudices and preconceptions and have profound unsettling effects as it presses for acceptance of an idea. WILLIAM O. DOUGLAS (1898–1980), U.S. Supreme Court Justice, *Terminiello* v. *Chicago,* 337 U.S., 1949.

Laws alone cannot secure freedom of expression; in order that every man present his views without penalty there must be a spirit of tolerance in the entire population. ALBERT EINSTEIN (1879–1955), *Out of My Later Years,* 1950.

By academic freedom I understand the right to search for truth and to publish and teach what one holds to be true. This right implies also a duty: one must not conceal any part of what one has recognized to be true. ALBERT EINSTEIN (1879–1955), Letter on his seventy-fifth birthday, 1954.

Here in America we are descended in spirit from revolutionists and rebels—men and women who dare to dissent from accepted doctrine. DWIGHT D. EISENHOWER (1890–1969), U.S. President, Speech, Columbia University, 1954.

Don't join the book burners. Don't think you are going to conceal faults by concealing evidence that they ever existed. DWIGHT D. EISENHOWER (1890–1969), U.S. President, Speech, Dartmouth College, 1953.

It is frequently said that speech that is intentionally provocative and therefore invites physical retaliation, can be punished or suppressed. Yet plainly no such general proposition can be sustained. Quite the contrary. . . . The provocative nature of the communication does not make it any the less expression. Indeed, the whole theory of free expression contemplates that expression will in many circumstances be provocative and arouse hostility. The audience, just as the speaker, has an obligation to maintain physical restraint. THOMAS I. EMERSON, *The System of Freedom of Expression,* 1970.

The right to freedom of expression is justified first of all as the right of an individual purely in his capacity as an individual. It derives from the widely accepted premise of Western thought that the proper end of man is the realization of his character and potentialities as a human being. THOMAS I. EMERSON, *Yale Law Journal,* 1963.

Suppression of expression conceals the real problems confronting a society and diverts public attention from the critical issues. It is likely to result in neglect of the grievances which are the actual basis of the unrest, and thus prevent their correction. THOMAS I. EMERSON, *Yale Law Journal,* 1963.

The right of all members of society to form their own beliefs and communicate them freely to others must be regarded as an essential principle of a democratically organized society. THOMAS I. EMERSON, Toward a General Theory of the First Amendment, 1966.

The freedom of speech, and debates or proceedings in Parliament, ought not to be impeached or questioned in any court or place out of Parliament. THE ENGLISH BILL OF RIGHTS, December 1689.

The beginning of philosophy is the recognition of the conflict between opinions. EPICTETUS (ca. 55–135 A.D.), *Discourses,* ca. 110 A.D.

The American feels so rich in his opportunities for free expression that he often no longer knows what he is free from. Neither does he know where he is not free; he does not recognize his native autocrats when he sees them. ERIK H. ERIKSON, *Childhood and Society,* 1950.

When men can freely communicate their thoughts and their sufferings, real or imagined, their passions spend themselves in air, like gunpowder scattered upon the surface—but pent up by terrors, they work unseen, burst forth in a moment, and destroy everything in their course. Let reason be opposed to reason, and argument to argument, and every good government will be safe. THOMAS ERSKINE (1750–1823), Lord Chancellor of England.

The liberty of the press would be an empty sound, and no man would venture to write on any subject, however pure his purpose, without an attorney at one elbow and a counsel at the other. From minds thus subdued by the fear of punishment, there could issue no works of genius to expand the empire of human reason. THOMAS ERSKINE (1750–1823), Lord Chancellor of England, Trial of John Stockdale, December 9, 1789.

If you admit that to silence your opponent by force is to win an intellectual argument, then you admit the right to silence people by force. HANS EYSENCK.

Censorship, in any form, represents a lack of trust in the judgment of the individual. The passage of time provides the best perspective for sorting the wheat from the chaff. BRUCE E. FLEURY, 1982.

We are willing enough to praise freedom when it is safely tucked away in the past and cannot be a nuisance. In the present, amidst dangers whose outcome we cannot foresee, we get nervous about her, and admit censorship. E. M. FORSTER (1879–1970), *Two Cheers for Democracy,* 1951.

Dissent and dissenters have no monopoly on freedom. They must tolerate opposition. They must accept dissent from their dissent. And they must give it the respect and the lattitude which they claim for themselves. ABE FORTAS, U.S. Supreme Court Justice, *New York Times Magazine,* May 12, 1968.

Opinions become dangerous to a state only when persecution makes it necessary for the people to communicate their ideas under the bond of secrecy. CHARLES JAMES FOX (1749–1806), Speech, House of Commons, 1797.

Every attempt to gage the free expression of thought is an unsocial act against society. That is why judges and juries who try to enforce such laws make themselves ridiculous. JAY FOX, in *Liberty and the Great Libertarians* (Charles Spradling).

Liberty of thought soon shrivels without freedom of expression. Nor can truth be pursued in an atmosphere hostile to the endeavor or under dangers which are hazarded only by heroes. FELIX FRANKFURTER (1882–1965), U.S. Supreme Court Justice, Concurring Opinion, *Dennis et al.* v. *United States,* 1951.

Freedom of expression is the wellspring of our civilization. . . . Therefore the liberty of man to search for truth ought not to be fettered, no matter what orthodoxies he may challenge. FELIX FRANKFURTER (1882–1965), U.S. Supreme Court Justice.

Without freedom of thought there can be no such thing as wisdom; and no such thing as public liberty without freedom of speech. BENJAMIN FRANKLIN (1706–1790), *The New England Courant,* July 9, 1722.

We must dare to think "unthinkable" thoughts. . . . We must learn to welcome and not to fear the voices of dissent. . . . Because when things become unthinkable, thinking stops and action becomes mindless. J. WILLIAM FULBRIGHT, Speech, U.S. Senate, March 27, 1964.

I know of no inquiry which the impulses of man suggests that is forbidden to the resolution of man to pursue. MARGARET FULLER (1810–1850), *Summer on the Lakes,* 1844.

The very act of labeling some item as pornographic or obscene creates a social response very close to that brought on by pornography itself. The act of labeling often generates social anticipation. . . . JOHN H. GAGNON and WILLIAM SIMON, *Trans-Action,* July–August, 1967.

Under the privilege of the First Amendment many, many ridiculous things are said. JOHN KENNETH GALBRAITH, PBS "Firing Line," December 9, 1989.

The freedom of speech and the freedom of the press have not been granted to the people in order that they may say things which please, and which are based upon accepted thought, but the right to say the things which displease, the right to say the things which convey the new and yet unexpected thoughts, the right to say things, even though they do a wrong. SAMUEL GOMPERS (1850–1924), *Seventy Years of Life and Labor,* 1925.

Heresy is only another word for freedom of thought. GRAHAM GREENE (1904–1991).

Books won't stay banned. They won't burn. Ideas won't go to jail. In the long run of history, the censor and the inquisitor have always lost. The only sure weapon against bad ideas is better ideas. The source of better ideas is wisdom. A. WHITNEY GRISWOLD (1909–1963), *Atlantic Monthly,* November 1952.

The freedom of thought and speech arising from and privileged by our constitution gives force and poignancy to the expressions of our common people. FRANCIS GROSE (1731–1791), *Classical Dictionary of the Vulgar Tongue,* 1785.

To render the magistrate a judge of truth, and engage his authority in the suppression of opinions, shews an inattention to the nature and designs of political liberty. ROBERT HALL (1764–1831), *An Apology for the Liberty of the Press,* 1793.

All discussion, all debate, all dissidence tends to question and in consequence, to upset existing convictions; that is precisely its purpose and its justification. LEARNED HAND (1872–1961), Judge, U.S. Court of Appeals.

Political agitation, by the passions it arouses or the convictions it engenders, may in fact stimulate men to the violation of the law. Detestation of existing politics is easily transformed into forcible resistance of the authority which puts them in execution, and it would be folly to disregard the causal relation between the two. Yet to assimilate agitation, legimate as such, with the direct incitement to violent resistance, is to disregard the tolerance of all methods of political agitation which in normal times is a safeguard of free government. LEARNED HAND (1872–1961), Judge, U.S. Court of Appeals, *Masses Pub Co.* v. *Patten,* 1917.

In the end it is worse to suppress dissent than to run the risk of heresy. LEARNED HAND (1872–1961), Judge, U.S. Court of Appeals, Speech, Harvard University, 1958.

I cannot assent to the view, if it be meant that the legislature may impair or abridge the rights of a free press and of free speech whenever it thinks that the public welfare requires that it be done. The public welfare cannot override constitutional privilege. JOHN MARSHALL HARLAN (1833–1911), U.S. Supreme Court Justice, *Patterson* v. *Chicago.*

When free discussion is denied, hardening of the arteries of democracy has set in, free institutions are but a lifeless form, and the death of the republic is at hand. WILLIAM RANDOLPH HEARST (1863–1951), June 13, 1941.

We hold that no person or set of persons can properly establish a standard of expression for others. WILLIAM RANDOLPH HEARST (1863–1951), Independence League Platform, 1924.

We hold that the greatest right in the world is the right to be wrong, that in the exercise thereof people have an inviolable right to express their unbridled thoughts on all topics and personalities. WILLIAM RANDOLPH HEARST (1863–1951), *New York Journal,* February 1, 1924.

Fraud may consist as well in the suppression of what is true as in the representation of what is false. JUSTICE HEATH, English Jurist, *Tapp* v. *Lee,* 1803.

Whenever books are burned men also in the end are burned. HEINRICH HEINE (1797–1856), *Almansor: A Tragedy,* 1823.

To limit the press is to insult a nation; to prohibit reading of certain books is to declare the inhabitants to be either fools or knaves. CLAUDE-ADRIEN HELVETIUS (1715–1771), *On The Mind.*

The sooner we all learn to make a decision between disapproval and censorship, the better off society will be. . . . Censorship cannot get at the real evil, and it is an evil in itself. GRANVILLE HICKS.

Where men cannot freely convey their thoughts to one another, no other liberty is secure. WILLIAM E. HOCKING (1873–1966), *Freedom of the Press,* 1947.

Another perceived attribute of intellectuals that needs rethinking and revision: the assumption that they are deeply and unequivocally committed to personal, political and intellectual freedom and especially free expression . . . many Western intellectuals' commitment to intellectual freedom is selective at best. PAUL HOLLANDER, *Society,* July–August 1983.

I think we should be eternally vigilant against attempts to check the expression of opinions that we loathe and believe to be fraught with death, unless they imminently threaten interference with the . . . pressing purposes of the law that an immediate check is required to save the country. OLIVER WENDELL HOLMES, JR. (1841–1935), U.S. Supreme Court Justice.

Every idea is an incitement. It offers itself for belief, and if believed it is acted on unless some other belief outweighs it or some failure of energy stifles the movement at its birth. The only difference between the expression of an opinion and an incitement is the speaker's enthusiasm for the result. OLIVER WENDELL HOLMES, JR. (1841–1935), U.S. Supreme Court Justice, *Gitlow* v. *N.Y.,* 1922.

But when men have realized that time has upset many fighting faiths, they may come to believe . . . that the best test of truth is the power of the thought to get itself accepted in the competition of the market. . . . That at any rate is the theory of our Constitution. OLIVER WENDELL HOLMES, JR. (1841– 1935), U.S. Supreme Court Justice, *Abrams* v. *U.S.,* 1919.

If there is any principle of the Constitution that more imperatively calls for attachment than any other it is the principle of free thought—not freedom for those who agree with us but freedom for the thought we hate. OLIVER WENDELL HOLMES, JR. (1841–1935), U.S. Supreme Court Justice, *U.S.* v. *Schwimmer.*

The very aim and end of our institutions is just this: that we may think what we like and say what we think. OLIVER WENDELL HOLMES, SR. (1809– 1894), *The Professor at the Breakfast Table,* 1860.

It [freedom] is a thing of the spirit. Men must be free to worship, to think, to hold opinions, to speak without fear. They must be free to challenge wrong and oppression with the surity of justice. HERBERT CLARK HOOVER (1874– 1964), U.S. President, *Addresses on the American Road.*

The freedom of the press is one of the great bulwarks of liberty, and can never be restrained but by despotic government. EDGAR WATSON HOWE (1853–1937), *Country Town Sayings,* 1911.

I express many absurd opinions. But I am not the first man to do it; American freedom consists largely in talking nonsense. EDGAR WATSON HOWE (1853– 1937), *Preaching from the Audience,* 1926.

The greater the importance to safeguarding the community from incitements to the overthrow of our institutions by force and violence, the more imperative is the need to preserve the constitutional rights of free speech, free press and free assembly in order to maintain the opportunity for free political discussion. CHARLES EVANS HUGHES (1862–1948), U.S. Supreme Court Justice, *DeJonge* v. *Oregon,* 1937.

The liberty of the press is not confined to newspapers and periodicals. It necessarily embraces pamphlets and leaflets. These indeed have been historic weapons in the defense of liberty, as the pamphlets of Thomas Paine and others in our own history abundantly attest. CHARLES EVANS HUGHES (1862– 1948), U.S. Supreme Court Justice, *Lovell* v. *City of Griffin,* 1938.

Our institutions were not devised to bring about uniformity of opinion; if they had been we might well abandon hope. It is important to remember, as has well been said, "the essential characteristic of true liberty is that under its shelter many different types of life and character and opinion and belief can develop unmolested and unobstructed." CHARLES EVANS HUGHES (1862–1948), U.S. Supreme Court Justice, in *Forbes* magazine, November 1, 1957.

The right to comment freely and criticize the action, opinions, and judgment of courts is of primary importance to the public generally. Not only is it good for the public, but it has a salutary effect on courts and judges as well. JAMES P. HUGHES, U.S. Supreme Court Justice, *State* v. *Nixon,* 1935.

The right to be heard does not automatically include the right to be taken seriously. HUBERT HUMPHREY (1911–1978), U.S. Vice President, Speech, 1965.

None of us would trade freedom of expression for the narrowness of the public censor. America is a free market for people who have something to say, and need not fear to say it. HUBERT H. HUMPHREY (1911–1978), U.S. Vice President, *New York Times,* March 9, 1967.

The policy of the repression of ideas cannot work and never has worked. The alternative to it is the long, difficult road of education. To this the American people have been committed. ROBERT M. HUTCHINS (1899–1977), 1949.

A civilization in which there is not a continuous controversy about important issues . . . is on the way to totalitarianism and death. ROBERT M. HUTCHINS (1899–1977), *The University of Utopia,* 1953.

Free speech is meaningless unless it tolerates the speech that we hate. HENRY J. HYDE, U.S. Congressman, Speech, May 3, 1991.

Did you ever hear anyone say "That work had better be banned because I might read it and it might be very damaging to me"? JOSEPH HENRY JACKSON (1894–1955).

Those who begin coercive elimination of dissent soon find themselves exterminating dissenters. Compulsory unification of opinion achieves only a unanimity at the graveyard. ROBERT H. JACKSON (1892–1954), U.S. Supreme Court Justice.

Freedom to differ is not limited to things that do not matter much. That would be a mere shadow of freedom. The test of its substance is the right to differ as to things that touch the heart of the existing order. ROBERT H. JACKSON (1892–1954), U.S. Supreme Court Justice, *West Virginia State Board of Education* v. *Varnette,* 1943.

The very purpose of a Bill of Rights was to withdraw certain subjects from the vicissitudes of political controversy, to place them beyond the reach of majorities and officials and to establish them as legal principles to be applied by the courts. One's right to life, liberty, and property, to free speech, a free press, freedom of worship and assembly, and other fundamental rights may not be submitted to a vote: they depend upon the outcome of no elections. ROBERT H. JACKSON (1892–1954), U.S. Supreme Court Justice, *West Virginia State Board of Education* v. *Barnette,* 1943.

Thought control is a copyright of totalitarianism, and we have no claim to it. It is not the function of our government to keep the citizen from falling in error; it is the function of the citizen to keep the government from falling into error. ROBERT H. JACKSON (1892–1954), U.S. Supreme Court Justice, *American Communications Assn.* v. *Douds,* 1950

Our forefathers found the evils of free thinking more to be endured than the evils of inquest or suppression. This is because thoughtful, bold and independent minds are essential to the wise and considered self-government. ROBERT H. JACKSON (1892–1954), U.S. Supreme Court Justice, *Atlantic Monthly,* January 1955.

The price of freedom of religion, or of speech, or of the press, is that we must put up with, and even pay for, a good deal of rubbish. ROBERT H. JACKSON (1892–1954), U.S. Supreme Court Justice.

The day that this country ceases to be free for irreligion, it will cease to be free for religion. ROBERT H. JACKSON (1892–1954), *Zorach* v. *Clausor,* 1952.

In our country are evangelists and zealots of many different political, economic and religious persuasions whose fanatical conviction is that all thought is divinely classified into two kinds—that which is their own and that which is false and dangerous. ROBERT H. JACKSON (1892–1954), U.S. Supreme Court Justice, 1950.

Error of opinion may be tolerated where reason is left free to combat it. THOMAS JEFFERSON (1743–1813), U.S. President, *Notes on the State of Virginia,* 1785.

The only security of all is in a free press. The force of public opinion cannot be resisted, when permitted freely to be expressed. The agitation it produces must be submitted to. THOMAS JEFFERSON (1743–1813), U.S. President, Letter to Marquis de LaFayette, 1823.

It is error alone which needs the support of government. Truth can stand by itself. THOMAS JEFFERSON (1743–1826), U.S. President, *Notes on the State of Virginia,* 1785.

The will of the people is the only legitimate foundation of any government, and to protect its free expression should be our first object. THOMAS JEFFERSON (1743–1826), U.S. President, First Inaugural Address, March 4, 1801.

And, finally, that truth is great and will prevail if left to herself: that she is the proper and sufficient antagonist to error, and has nothing to fear from the conflict unless by human interposition disarmed of her natural weapons, free argument and debate; errors ceasing to be dangerous when it is permitted freely to contradict them. THOMAS JEFFERSON (1743–1826), U.S. President, Virginia Act for Religious Freedom, 1786.

Freedom of religion, freedom of the press, freedom of person under the protection of habeas corpus; and trial by juries impartially selected—these principles form the bright constellation which has gone before us. THOMAS JEFFERSON (1743–1826), U.S. President, First Inaugural Address, March 4, 1801.

In the most civilized and progressive countries freedom of discussion is recognized as a fundamental principle. C. E. M. JOAD (1891–1953), *The Recovery of Belief,* 1952.

Free speech, free press, free religion, the right of free assembly, yes, the right of petition . . . well, they are still radical ideas. LYNDON B. JOHNSON (1908–1973), U.S. President, Speech, August 3, 1965.

In order that all men may be taught to speak truth, it is necessary that all likewise should learn to hear it. SAMUEL JOHNSON (1709–1784), *The Rambler,* 1750–52.

[Censors are] people with secret attractions to various temptations. . . . They are defending themselves under the pretext of defending others, because at heart they fear their own weaknesses. ERNEST JONES (1879–1958).

Persecution is the first law of society because it is always easier to suppress criticism than to meet it. HOWARD MUMFORD JONES, *Primer of Intellectual Freedom,* 1949.

The Liberty of the press is the Palladium of all the civil, political and religious rights of an Englishman. JUNIUS, 1769.

Academic freedom really means freedom of inquiry. To be able to probe according to one's own interest, knowledge and conscience is the most important freedom the scholar has, and an undissociable part of that process is to state its results. DONALD KENNEDY, President, Stanford University, 1986.

We are not afraid to entrust the American people with unpleasant facts, foreign ideas, alien philosophies, and competitive values. For a nation that is afraid to let its people judge the truth and falsehood in an open market is afraid of its people. JOHN FITZGERALD KENNEDY (1917–1963), U.S. President.

In a free society art is not a weapon. . . . Artists are not engineers of the soul. JOHN FITZGERALD KENNEDY (1917–1963), U.S. President, 1963.

People hardly ever make use of the freedom they have, for example, freedom of thought; instead they demand freedom of speech as a compensation. SØREN KIERKEGAARD (1813–1855).

Freedom of the press, freedom of association, the inviolablity of domicile, and all the rest of the rights of man are respected so long as no one tries to use them against the privileged class. On the day they are launched against the privileged they are thrown overboard. PRINCE PETER KROPOTKIN (1842–1921).

Free inquiry entails recognition of civil liberties as integral to its pursuit, that is, a free press, freedom of communication, the right to organize opposition parties and to join voluntary associations, and freedom to cultivate and publish the fruits of scientific, philosophical, artistic, literary, moral and religious freedom. Free inquiry requires that we tolerate diversity of opinion and that we respect the right of individuals to express their beliefs, however unpopular they may be, without social or legal prohibition or fear of success. PAUL KURTZ, "A Secular Humanist Declaration," in *On the Barricades,* 1989.

The principle of free speech is no new doctrine born of the constitution of the United States. It is a heritage of English-speaking peoples, which has been won by incalculable sacrifice, and which they must preserve so long as they hope to live as free men. ROBERT M. LaFOLLETTE (1855–1925), U.S. Senator, Speech, October 6, 1917.

No citizen enjoys genuine freedom of religious conviction until the state is indifferent to every form of religious outlook from atheism to Zoroastrianism. HAROLD J. LASKI (1893–1950), *Grammar of Politics,* 1925.

The bourgeoisie is many times stronger than we. To give it the weapon of freedom of the press is to ease the enemy's cause, to help the class enemy. We do not desire to end in suicide, so we will not do this. V. I. LENIN (1870–1924), *Pravda,* 1912.

Books of apostates, heretics, schismatics, and all other writers defending heresy or schism or in any attacking the foundations of religion, are altogether prohibited. POPE LEO XIII (1810–1903), *General Decrees concerning the Prohibition and Censorship of Books,* January 25, 1897.

The liberty of thinking and publishing whatsoever each one likes, without any hindrances, is not in itself an advantage over which society can wisely rejoice. On the contrary, it is the fountainhead and origin of many evils. POPE LEO XIII (1810–1903), *Immortale Dei.*

The problem of freedom in America is that of maintaining a competition of ideas, and you do not achieve that by silencing one brand of idea. MAX LERNER, *Actions and Passions,* 1949.

Every compulsion is put upon writers to become safe, polite, obedient, and sterile. In protest, I declined election to the National Institute of Arts and Letters some years ago, and now I must decline the Pulitzer Prize. SINCLAIR LEWIS (1885–1951), 1926.

The burning of an author's books, imprisonment for opinion's sake, has always been the tribute that an ignorant age pays to the genius of its time. JOSEPH LEWIS (1889–1968), *Voltaire: The Incomparable Infidel.*

Freedom of the press is guaranteed only to those who own one. A. J. LIEBLING (1904–1963).

For in the absence of debate unrestricted utterance leads to the degradation of opinion. By a kind of Gresham's law the more rational is overcome by the less rational, and the opinions that will prevail will be those which are held most ardently by those with the most passionate will. WALTER LIPPMANN (1889–1974), *Essays in the Public Philosophy,* 1955.

I honor the man who is willing to sink, / Half his present repute for the freedom to think, / And when he has thought, be his cause strong or weak, / Will risk t'other half for the freedom to speak. JAMES RUSSELL LOWELL (1819–1891), *A Fable for Critics,* 1848.

Toward no crimes have men shown themselves so cold-bloodedly cruel as in punishing differences of opinion. JAMES RUSSELL LOWELL (1819–1891), *Literary Essays.*

Once you permit those who are convinced of their own superior rightness to censor and silence and suppress those who hold contrary opinions, just at that moment the citadel has been surrendered. ARCHIBALD MACLEISH (1892–1982), *Saturday Review,* May 12, 1979.

Whilst we assert a freedom to embrace, to profess, and to observe the Religion which we believe to be of divine origin, we cannot deny an equal freedom to those whose minds have not yet yielded to the evidence which has convinced us. JAMES MADISON (1751–1836), *Memorials and Remonstrances, 1785.*

It is impossible for ideas to compete in the marketplace if no forum for their presentation is provided or available. THOMAS MANN (1875–1955)

If the First Amendment means anything, it means that a state has no business telling a man, sitting alone in his own house, what books he may read or what films he may watch. THURGOOD MARSHALL (1908–1993), U.S. Supreme Court Justice, 1969.

The freedom of the press is one of the great bulwarks of liberty, and can never be restrained but by despotic governments. GEORGE MASON (1725–1792), Virginia Bill of Rights, June 12, 1776.

If all mankind minus one were of one opinion and only one person were of the contrary opinion, mankind would be no more justified in silencing that person than he, if he had the power, would be justified in silencing mankind. . . . If the opinion is right, they are deprived of the opportunity of exchanging error for truth; if wrong, they lose, what is almost as great a benefit, the clearer perception and livelier impression of truth, produced by its collision with error. JOHN STUART MILL (1806–1873), *On Liberty,* 1859.

We can never be sure that the opinion we are endeavoring to stifle is a false opinion; and if we were sure, stifling it would be an evil still. JOHN STUART MILL (1806–1873), *On Liberty,* 1859.

If any opinion be compelled to silence, that opinion may, for aught we can certainly know, be true. To deny this is to assume our own infallibility. JOHN STUART MILL (1806–1873), *On Liberty,* 1859.

Give me liberty to know, to utter, and to argue freely according to conscience, above all liberties. JOHN MILTON (1608–1674), *Areopagitica,* 1644.

Never in the world were any two opinions alike, any more than any two hairs or grains of sand. Their most universal quality is diversity. MICHEL de MONTAIGNE (1532–1592), *Essays,* 1580.

Where it is a duty to worship the sun it is pretty sure to be a crime to examine the laws of heat. JOHN MORLEY (1838–1923), *Voltaire,* 1872.

You have not converted a man because you have silenced him. JOHN MORELY (1838–1923).

We owe to democracy, at least in part, the regime of discussion in which we live; we owe it the principal modern liberties: those of thought, press and association. And the regime of free discussion is the only one which permits the ruling class to renew itself . . . which eliminates that class quasiautomatically when it no longer corresponds to the interests of the country. GAETANO MOSCA, *Partiti e Sindacata nella crisi del regime parlamentare,* 1961.

If you think there is freedom of the press in the United States, I tell you there is no freedom of the press. . . . They come out with the cheap shot. The press should be ashamed of itself. They should come to both sides of the issue and hear both sides and let the American people make up their minds. BILL MOYERS, *Columbia Journalism Review,* March/April 1982.

Freedom of speech, freedom of the press, and freedom of religion all have a double aspect—freedom of thought and freedom of action. FRANK MURPHY (1890–1959), U.S. Supreme Court Justice, *Jones* v. *Opelika,* 1941.

Very commonly in ages when civil rights of one kind are in evidence—those pertaining to freedom of speech and thought in, say, theater, press, and forum, with obscenity and libel laws correspondingly loosened—very real constrictions of individual liberty take place in other, more vital, areas: political organization, voluntary association, property, and the right to hold jobs, for example. ROBERT NISBIT, *Twilight of Authority,* 1981.

The only way to make sure people you agree with can speak is to support the rights of people you don't agree with. ELEANOR HOLMES NORTON, *The New York Post,* March 28, 1970.

There must be no barriers for freedom in inquiry. There is no place for dogma in science. The scientist is free, and must be free to ask any question, to doubt any assertion, to seek for any evidence, to correct any errors. J. ROBERT OPPENHEIMER (1904–1967), *Life* magazine, October 10, 1949.

If liberty means anything at all, it means the right to tell people what they do not want to hear. GEORGE ORWELL (1903–1950), *Animal Farm,* 1945.

At any given moment there is an orthodoxy, a body of ideas which it is assumed all right-thinking people will accept without question. It is not exactly forbidden to state this or that or the other, but it is "not done." . . . Anyone who challenges the prevailing orthodoxy finds himself silenced with surprising effectiveness. A genuinely unfashionable opinion is almost never given a fair hearing, either in the popular press or in the highbrow periodicals. GEORGE ORWELL (1903–1950).

I have always strenuously supported the right of every man to his opinion, however different that opinion might be to mine. He who denies to another this right, makes a slave of himself to his present opinion, because he precludes himself the right of changing it. THOMAS PAINE (1737–1809), *The Age of Reason.*

He that would make his own liberty secure, must guard even his enemy from oppression; for if he violates this duty, he establishes a precedent that will reach to himself. THOMAS PAINE (1737–1809), *Dissertations on First Principles of Government,* 1795.

The writer is the Faust of modern society, the only surviving individualist in a mass age. To his orthodox contemporaries he seems a semi-madman. BORIS PASTERNAK (1890–1960), *London Observer,* December 20, 1959.

One has the right to be wrong in a democracy. CLAUDE PEPPER, 1946.

No matter whose lips that would speak, they must be free and ungagged. The community which dares not protect its humblest and most hated member in the free utterance of his opinions, no matter how false or hateful, is only a gang of slaves. If there is anything in the universe that can't stand discussion, let it crack. . . . Let us always remember that he does not really believe his own opinions, who dares not give free scope to his opponent. WENDELL PHILLIPS (1811–1884), Speech, 1863.

The legislature of the United States shall pass no law on the subject of religion nor touching or abridging the liberty of the press. CHARLES PINCKNEY (1757–1824), Resolution offered in the Constitutional Convention, 1787.

There is no inherent misdirection in holding unorthodox views. Indeed, the autonomous individual, free from compulsive conformance and unquestioned assumptions, is likely to be unorthodox. . . . They stimulate the climate of controversy without which political democracy becomes an empty formalism. SNELL PUTNEY and GAIL PUTNEY, *The Adjusted American,* 1964.

Heresy hunters are intolerant not only of unorthodox ideas;. . . . they are intolerant of any ideas which are really alive and not empty cocoons. PHILIP LEE RALPH, *Story of Civilization,* 1954.

The nation relies upon public discussion as one of the indispensable means to attain correct solutions to problems of social welfare. Curtailment of free speech limits this open discussion. Our whole history teaches that adjustment of social relations through reason is possible when free speech is maintained. STANLEY F. REED (1884–1980), U.S. Supreme Court Justice, 312 U.S. at 319–320.

To be able to think freely, a man must be certain that no consequences will follow whatever he writes. ERNEST RENAN (1823–1892), 1879.

We all know that books burn—yet we have the greater knowledge that books cannot be killed by fire. People die, but books never die. No man and no force can abolish memory. . . . FRANKLIN D. ROOSEVELT (1882–1945), U.S. President, 1942.

The truth is found when men are free to pursue it. FRANKLIN D. ROOSEVELT (1882–1945), U.S. President, Speech, Temple University, February 22, 1936.

If the fires of freedom and civil liberties burn low in other lands, they must be made brighter in our own. If in other lands the press and books and literature of all kinds are censored, we must redouble our efforts here to keep them free. If in other lands the eternal truths of the past are threatened by intolerance we must provide a safe place for their perception. FRANKLIN D. ROOSEVELT (1882–1945), U.S. President, Speech, June 30, 1938.

Wide differences of opinion in matters of religious, political and social belief must exist if conscience and intellect alike are not to be stunted. THEODORE ROOSEVELT (1858–1919), U.S. President, Speech, April 23, 1910.

Free speech, exercised both individually and through a free press, is a necessity in any country where people are themselves free. THEODORE ROOSEVELT (1858–1919), U.S. President, *Kiplinger Washington Letter,* April 23, 1918.

Heretical views arise when the truth is uncertain, and it is only when the truth is uncertain that censorship is invoked. BERTRAND RUSSELL (1872–1970), *The Value of Free Thought.*

It was not by accident or coincidence that the rights to freedom in speech and press were coupled in a single guaranty with the rights of the people peacably to assemble and to petition for redress of grievances. All these, though not identical, are inseparable. They are cognate rights, and therefore are united in the first Article's assurance. Judge WILEY B. RUTLEDGE, *Thomas* v. *Collins,* 1944.

Freedom of thought is the only guarantee against an infection of people by mass myths, which, in the hands of treacherous hypocrites and demagogues, can be transformed into bloody dictatorships. ANDREI SAKHAROV (1921–1989), *Progress, Coexistence and Intellectual Freedom,* 1968.

Surely a large part of the zealous repression of radical protest in America has its roots in the fact that millions of men who are apparently "insiders" know how vulnerable the system is because they know how ambiguous their own attachments to it are. The slightest challenge exposes the fragile foundations of legitimacy of the state. JOHN SCHARR, *Power and Community,* 1970.

Unto the lewd all things are lewd, and their profession of much purity is a mask for much lewdness. . . . I know and am persuaded that there is nothing unclean in itself, but to him that esteemeth anything to be unclean, well it showeth him to be obsessed by his own lewdness. THEODORE SCHROEDER (1864–1940), *A Challenge to the Sex Censors,* 1938.

Tocqueville saw the brute repression of deviants as a necessity if men were to keep convincing themselves of their collective dignity through their collective sameness. The "poets of society," the men who challenged the norms, would have to be silenced so that sameness could be maintained. RICHARD SENNETT, *The Uses of Disorder: Personal Identity and City Life,* 1970.

All great truths begin as blasphemies. GEORGE BERNARD SHAW (1856–1950), *Annajanska,* 1919.

Assassination is the extreme form of censorship. GEORGE BERNARD SHAW (1856–1950).

Truth generally lies in the coordination of antagonistic opinions. HERBERT SPENCER (1820–1903), *Autobiography.*

The most tyrannical governments are those which make crimes of opinions, for everyone has an inalienable right to his own thoughts. BARUCH SPINOZA (1632–1677), *Tractatus Theologico-Politicus,* 1670.

Laws which prescribe what everyone must believe, and forbid men to say or write anything against this or that opinion, are often passed to gratify, or rather to appease the anger of those who cannot abide independent minds. BARUCH SPINOZA (1632–1677), *Tractatus Theologico-Politicus,* 1670.

Laws directed against opinions affect the generous-minded rather than the wicked, and are adapted less for coercing criminals than for irritating the upright. BARUCH SPINOZA (1632–1677), cited in *Atlantic Monthly,* January 1955.

Every man who says frankly and fully what he thinks is so far doing a public service. We should be grateful to him for attacking most unsparingly our most cherished opinions. SIR LESLIE STEPHEN (1832–1904), *The Suppression of Poisonous Opinions,* 1883.

The government must pursue a course of complete neutrality toward religion. JOHN PAUL STEVENS, U.S. Supreme Court Justice, 1985.

We in America today would limit our freedom of expression and of conscience. In the name of unity, they would impose a narrow conformity of ideas and opinion. . . . Only a government which fights for civil liberties and equal rights for its own people can stand for freedom in the rest of the world. ADLAI E. STEVENSON (1900–1965), February 14, 1953.

The sound of tireless voices is the price we pay for the right to hear the music of our own opinions. ADLAI E. STEVENSON (1900–1965), Speech, August 28, 1952.

It is a common heresy and its graves are to be found all over the earth. It is the heresy that says you can kill an idea by killing a man, defeat a principle by defeating a person, bury truth by burying its vehicle. ADLAI E. STEVENSON (1900–1965), November 9, 1952.

The first principle of a free society is an untrammeled flow of words in an open forum. ADLAI E. STEVENSON (1900–1965), *New York Times,* January 19, 1962.

Do the people of this land . . . desire to preserve those [liberties] protected by the First Amendment. . . . If so, let them withstand all beginnings of encroachment. For the saddest epitaph which can be carved in memory of a vanquished liberty is that it was lost because its posessors failed to stretch forth a saving hand while yet there was time. GEORGE SUTHERLAND (1862–1942), U.S. Supreme Court Justice, *Associated Press* v. *National Labor Relations Board,* 1937.

A free press stands as one of the great interpreters between the government and the people. To allow it to be fettered is to fetter ourselves. GEORGE SUTHERLAND (1862–1942), U.S. Supreme Court Justice, *Grosjean* v. *American Press Co.,* 1936.

Liberty of conscience is nowadays only understood to be the liberty of believing what men please, but also of endeavoring to propagate that belief as much as they can. JONATHAN SWIFT (1667–1745), 1715.

Dissent . . . is a right essential to any concept of the dignity and freedom of the individual; it is essential to the search for truth in a world wherein no authority is infallible. NORMAN THOMAS (1884–1968), *New York Times Magazine,* 1959

Man's drive for self-expression, which over the centuries has built his monuments, does not stay within set bounds; the creations which yesterday were detested and the obscene become the classics of today. MATTHEW TOBRINER, Justice, California State Supreme Court, *Wall Street Journal,* February 3, 1964.

There is no more fundamental axiom of American freedom than the familiar statement: In a free country we punish men for the crimes they commit but never for the opinions they have. HARRY S. TRUMAN (1884–1972), U.S. President, Message, Veto of the McCarran Act, September 22, 1950.

Once a government is committed to the principle of silencing the voice of opposition, it has only one way to go, and that is down the path of increasingly repressive measures, until it becomes a source of terror to all its citizens and creates a country where everyone lives in fear. HARRY S. TRUMAN (1884–1972), U.S. President, 1950.

Irreverence is the champion of liberty, and its only sure defense. MARK TWAIN (1835–1910), Notebook.

It were not best that we should all think alike; it is difference of opinion that makes horseraces. MARK TWAIN (1835–1910), *Pudd'nhead Wilson.*

Everyone has the right . . . to hold opinions without interference and to seek, receive and impart information and ideas through any media regardless of frontiers. UNIVERSAL DECLARATION OF HUMAN RIGHTS, Article 19, 1948.

The basis of the First Amendment is the hypothesis that speech can rebut speech, propaganda will answer propaganda, free debate of ideas will result in the wisest governmental policies. FREDERICK M. VINSON (1890–1953), U.S. Supreme Court Justice, *Dennis* v. *United States,* 1951.

The censor's sword pierces deeply into the heart of free expression. EARL WARREN (1891–1974), U.S. Supreme Court Justice, *Times Film Corp* v. *City of Chicago,* January 23, 1961.

If men are to be precluded from offering their sentiments on a matter which may involve the most serious and alarming consequences that can invite the consideration of mankind, reason is of no use; the freedom of speech may be taken away, and dumb and silent we may be led, like sheep to the slaughter. GEORGE WASHINGTON (1732–1799), U.S. President, 1783.

Freedom of communion means, clearly and unquestionably, freedom to speak, debate, and write in privacy; to share confidence with intimates and confidants, and to prepare positions in groups and institutions for presentation to the public at a later point. ALAN WESTIN, *Privacy and Freedom,* 1967.

A despot doesn't fear eloquent writers preaching freedom—he fears a drunken poet who may crack a joke that will take hold. E. B. WHITE (1899–1985).

You say that freedom of utterance is not for time of stress, and I reply with the sad truth that only in time of stress is freedom of utterance in danger. . . . Only when free utterance is suppressed is it needed, and when it is needed it is most vital to justice. WILLIAM ALLEN WHITE (1868–1944), *The Editor and His People,* 1924.

[Freethinking is when] men can speak in whatever way given them to utter what their hearts hold—by voice, by posted card, by letter or by press. WILLIAM ALLEN WHITE (1868–1944).

You can have no wise laws nor free enforcement of wise laws unless there is free expression of the wisdom of the people—and, alas, their folly with it. But if there is freedom, folly will die of its own poison, and the wisdom will survice. WILLIAM ALLEN WHITE (1868–1944), *The Editor and His People,* 1924.

I have always been among those who believe that the greatest freedom of speech was the greatest safety, because if a man is a fool the best thing to do is to encourage him to advertise the fact by speaking. WOODROW WILSON (1856–1924), U.S. President, Address at the Institute of Paris, May 10, 1919.

Since direct political discussion was prohibited, all literature tended to become a criticism of Russian life, and literary criticism but another form of social criticism. . . . If the censor forbade explicit statement, he was skillfully eluded by indirection—by innocent seeming tales of other lands or times, by complicated parables, animal fables, double meanings, overtones, by investing apparently trivial events with the pent-up energies possessing the writer, so that the reader became compelled to dwell upon them until their hidden meanings became manifest. BERTRAM WOLFE (1896–1977), *Three Who Made a Revolution,* 1964.

The history of intellectual growth and discovery clearly demonstrates the need for unfettered freedom, the right to think the unthinkable, discuss the un-mentionable, and challenge the unchallengeable. C. VAN WOODWARD, Report on Free Speech, *New York Times,* January 28, 1975.

An opinion, right or wrong, can never constitute a moral offense, nor be in itself a moral obligation. It may be mistaken; it may involve an absurdity, or a contradiction. It is a truth, or it is an error; it can never be a crime or a virtue. FRANCIS WRIGHT (1795–1852), *A Few Days in Athens.*

Academic freedom means the right, long accepted in the academic world, to study, discuss, and write about facts and ideas without restrictions, other than those imposed by conscience and morality. Report, YALE UNIVERSITY, *New York Times,* February 18, 1952.

The loss of liberty in general would soon follow the suppression of the liberty of the press; for it is an essential branch of liberty, so perhaps it is the best preservative of the whole. JOHN PETER ZENGER (1697–1746), 1733.

Government and Politics

When a man you like switches from what he said a year ago, or four years ago, he is a broad-minded person who has courage enough to change his mind with changing conditions. When a man you don't like does it, he is a liar who has broken his promise. FRANKLIN P. ADAMS (1881–1960).

Modern politics is, at bottom, a struggle not of men but of forces. The men become every year more and more creatures of force, massed around central powerhouses. HENRY BROOKS ADAMS (1838–1918), *The Education of Henry Adams,* 1907.

Politics, as a practice, whatever its professions, has always been the systematic organization of hatreds. HENRY BROOKS ADAMS (1838–1918), *The Education of Henry Adams,* 1907

It is weakness rather than wickedness which renders men unfit to be trusted with unlimited power. JOHN ADAMS (1735–1826), U.S. President, 1788.

A power in the individuals who compose legislatures, to fish up wealth from the people, by nets of their own weaving . . . will corrupt legislative, executive, and judicial public servants. JOHN ADAMS (1735–1826), U.S. President, 1811.

Man tends to treat all of his opinions as principles. HERBERT AGAR (1897–1980), *A Time for Greatness.*

Establishment: An exclusive group of powerful people who rule a government or society by means of private agreements or decisions. *American Heritage Dictionary.*

Politics is the gentle art of getting votes from the poor and campaign funds from the rich, by promising to protect each from the other. OSCAR AMERINGER (1870–1943), *The American Guardian.*

The test of every religious, political or educational system, is the man it forms. HENRI FRÉDÉRIC AMIEL (1821–1881), *Journal intime,* June 17, 1852.

Growing older, I have lost the need to be political, which means, in this country, the need to be left. I am driven into grudging toleration of the Conservative party because it is the party of nonpolitics, of resistance to politics. KINGSLEY AMIS.

Let men be on their guard against those who flatter and mislead the multitude: their actions prove what sort of men they are. Of the tyrant, spies and informers are their principal instruments. War is his favorite occupation, for the sake of engrossing the attention of the people, and making himself necessary to have as their leader. ARISTOTLE (384–322 B.C.) *Politics.*

The liberal is accustomed to appearing radical to conservatives, counter-revolutionary to radicals, and as a fink to activists of all persuasions. HARRY S. ASHMORE.

The perfect bureaucrat everywhere is the man who manages to make no decisions and escapes all responsibility. BROOKS ATKINSON, *Once around the Sun,* 1951.

To exploit and to govern mean the same thing. Exploitation and government are two inseparable expressions of what is called politics. MIKHAIL A. BAKUNIN (1814–1876), *The Knouto-Germanic Empire and the Social Revolution,* 1871.

The state is force incarnate, its essence is command and compulsion. MIKHAIL A. BAKUNIN (1814–1876), *God and the State,* 1882.

In any assembly the simplest way to stop the transaction of business and split the ranks is to appeal to a principle. JACQUES BARZUN, *The House of Intellect,* 1959.

Among the several cloudy appellatives which have been commonly employed as cloaks for misgovernment, there is none more conspicuous in this atmosphere of illusion than the word Order. JEREMY BENTHAM (1748–1832), *The Book of Fallacies,* 1824.

Politics, n. A strife of interests masquerading as a contest of principles. AMBROSE BIERCE (1842–1914), *The Devil's Dictionary,* 1881–1911.

Conservative, n. A statesman who is enamoured of existing evils, as distinguished from the liberal, who wishes to replace them with others. AMBROSE BIERCE (1842–1914), *The Devil's Dictionary,* 1881–1911.

The marvel of all history is the patience with which men and women submit to burdens unnecessarily laid upon them by their governments. WILLIAM E. BORAH (1865–1940).

The chief characteristic of the [liberal] attitude are human sympathy, a receptivity to change, and a scientific willingness to follow reason rather than faith. CHESTER BOWLES, *The New Republic,* July 22, 1946.

Experience should teach us to be most on guard to protect liberty when the government's purposes are beneficent. Men born to freedom are naturally alert to repel invasion of their liberty by evil-minded rulers. The greatest dangers to our liberty lurk in insidious encroachment by men of zeal, well-meaning but without understanding. LOUIS B. BRANDEIS (1856–1941), U.S. Supreme Court Justice, *Olmstead* v. *United States,* 1928.

There exists a "fear of freedom" of selfhood, which makes people want to submerge themselves in the mass and confession is one of the obvious means by which they can do so, for thereby they lose those traits which cause them to feel separate. The other, of course, is to lose one's sense of personal identity by submerging it in the collective behavior of a crowd. JAMES A. C. BROWN (1911–1964), *Techniques of Persuasion,* 1963.

It is proof of a base and low mind for one to think with the masses or majority, merely because the majority is the majority. Truth does not change because it is, or is not, believed by a majority of people. GIORDANO BRUNO (1544–1600).

All government, indeed every human benefit and enjoyment, every virtue, and every prudent act, is founded on compromise and barter. EDMUND BURKE (1729–1797), *Speech on Conciliation with America,* March 22, 1975.

In a democracy the majority of citizens is capable of exercising the most cruel oppressions upon the minority . . . and that oppression of the minority will extend to far greater numbers, and will be carried on with much greater fury, than can almost ever be apprehended. EDMUND BURKE (1729–1797), *Reflections on the Revolution in France,* 1790.

Those who are subjected to wrong under multitudes are deprived of all external consolations. They seem deserted by mankind; overpowered by a conspiracy of their whole species. EDMUND BURKE (1729–1797), *Reflections on the Revolution in France,* 1790.

When bad men combine, the good must associate; else they will fall, one by one, an unpitied sacrifice in a contemptible struggle. EDMUND BURKE (1729–1797), *Thoughts on the Cause of the Present Discontents,* 1770.

Modern liberalism, for most liberals, is not a consciously understood set of rational beliefs, but a bundle of unexamined prejudices and conjoined sentiments. The basic ideas and beliefs seem more satisfactory when they are not made fully explicit, when they merely lurk rather obscurely in the background, coloring the rhetoric and adding a certain emotive glow. JAMES BURNHAM (1905–1987), *Suicide of the West,* 1964.

Government has no right to control individual liberty beyond what is neccessary to the safety and well-being of society. Such is the boundary which separates the power of the government and the liberty of the citizen or subject in the political state. JOHN C. CALHOUN (1782–1850), Speech, 1848.

Politics and the fate of mankind are shaped by men without ideals and without greatness. Men who have greatness within them don't go in for politics. ALBERT CAMUS (1913–1960), *Notebooks,* 1962.

The office of government is not to confer happiness, but to give men opportunity to work out happiness for themselves. WILLIAM ELLERY CHANNING (1780–1842), 1827.

There are [so] few wise [men]. Every aristocracy that has ever existed has behaved, in all essential points, exactly like a small mob. GILBERT KEITH CHESTERTON (1874–1936), *Heretics,* 1905.

It is muddleheaded to say, I am in favor of this kind of political regime rather than that: what one really means is, I prefer this kind of police. E. MICHEL CIORAN.

War is regarded as nothing but the continuation of state policy with other means. KARL von CLAUSEWITZ (1780–1831), *On War,* 1833.

As in political so in literary action a man wins friends for himself by the passion of his prejudices and by the consistent narrowness of his outlook. JOSEPH CONRAD (1857–1924), *A Personal Record,* 1912.

The main task of a free society is to civilize the struggle for power. Slavery of the acquiescent majority to the ruthless few is the hereditary state of mankind; freedom a rarely acquired characteristic. R. H. S. CROSSMAN (1907–1974).

The danger is not that a particular hand is unfit to govern. Every class is unfit to govern. JOHN DAHLBERG, LORD ACTON (1843–1902), Letter to Mary Gladstone, April 24, 1881.

The one pervading evil of democracy is the tyranny of the majority. JOHN DAHLBERG, LORD ACTON (1834–1902), Lecture, 1877.

Liberty is not a means to a higher political end. It is itself the highest political end. JOHN DAHLBERG, LORD ACTON (1834–1902), *Lectures on Modern History,* 1906.

There is one safeguard known generally to all the wise, which is an advantage and security to all, but especially to democracies as against despots. What is it? Distrust. DEMOSTHENES (384–322 B.C.), *Philippics.*

Government is everywhere to a great extent controlled by powerful minorities, with an interest distinct from the mass of the people. GOLDSWORTHY LOWES DICKINSON (1862–1932), *The Choice before Us,* 1917.

Government has hardened into a tyrannical monopoly, and the human race in general becomes as absolutely property as beasts in the plow. JOHN DICKINSON (1732–1808), Letter, 1802.

Who are a free people? Not those over whom government is reasonably exercised, but those who live under a government so constitutionally checked and controlled that proper provision is made against its being otherwise exercised. JOHN DICKINSON (1732–1808), *Farmer's Letters,* 1767.

Watch out for the fellow who talks about putting things in order! Putting things in order always means getting other people under your control. DENIS DIDEROT (1713–1784), 1796.

The Constitution is not neutral. It was designed to take the government off the backs of people. WILLIAM O. DOUGLAS (1898–1980), U.S. Supreme Court Justice, *The Court Years: 1939–1975,* 1980.

Those in power need checks and restraints lest they come to identify the common good with their own tastes and desires, and their continuation in office as essential to the preservation of the nation. WILLIAM O. DOUGLAS (1898–1980), U.S. Supreme Court Justice, *We The Judges,* 1956.

Nor is the peoples judgement always true; / the most may err as grossly as the few. JOHN DRYDEN (1631–1700), *Absalom and Achitophel,* 1681.

A great civilization is not conquered from without until it has destroyed itself within. The essential cause of Rome's decline lay in her people, her morals, her class struggle, her failing trade, her bureaucratic despotism, her stifling taxes, her consuming wars. WILL DURANT (1885–1981), *Caesar and Christ,* 1944.

Why do people speak of great men in terms of nationality? Great Germans, great Englishmen? Goethe always protested against being called a German poet. Great men are simply men. ALBERT EINSTEIN (1879–1955), *New York Times,* 1926.

I suspect that in our loathing of totalitarianism, there is infused a good deal of admiration for its efficiency. T. S. ELIOT (1888–1965), 1939.

The less government we have, the better—the fewer laws, and the less confided power. RALPH WALDO EMERSON (1803–1882), *Essays,* 1844.

Democracy becomes a government of bullies tempered by editors. RALPH WALDO EMERSON (1803–1882), *Journals,* 1846.

There is less intention in history than we ascribe to it. We impute far-sighted plans to Caesar and Napoleon; but the best of their power was in nature, not in them. RALPH WALDO EMERSON (1803–1882), *Spiritual Laws.*

There is no necessary connection between the desire to lead and the ability to lead, and even less the ability to lead somewhere that will be to the advantage of the led. BERGEN EVANS, *The Spoor of Spooks and Other Nonsense,* 1954.

No human government has a right to inquire into private opinions. . . . Men are the best judges of the consequences of their own opinions, and how far they are likely to influence their actions; and it is most unnatural and tyrannical to say, "As you think, so must you act. I will collect the evidence of your future conduct from what I know of your opinions." CHARLES JAMES FOX (1749–1806), Speech, House of Commons, May 8, 1789.

A people living under the . . . threat of war and invasion is very easy to govern. It demands no social reform. It does not haggle over armaments and military expenditures. It pays without discussion, it ruins itself, and that is a fine thing for the financiers and manufacturers for whom patriotic terrors are an abundant source of gain. ANATOLE FRANCE (1844–1924), *Penguin Island,* 1908.

The heart of the liberal philosophy is a belief in the dignity of the individual, in his freedom to make the most of his capacities and opportunities according to his own lights. . . . This implies a belief in the equality of men in one sense; in their inequality in another. MILTON FRIEDMAN, *Capitalism and Freedom*, 1962.

The lust for freedom is not rooted in strength but in weakness. ERICH FROMM (1900–1980), *Escape from Freedom*, 1941.

Few things are as immutable as the addiction of political groups to the ideas by which they have won office. JOHN KENNETH GALBRAITH, *The Affluent Society*, 1958.

The conservative is led by disposition, not unmixed with pecuniary self-interest, to adhere to the familiar and established. JOHN KENNETH GALBRAITH, *The Affluent Society*, 1958.

Let us not fall into the . . . pernicious error that multitude is divine because it is multitude. JAMES A. GARFIELD (1831–1881), U.S. President, speech at Hudson College, July 2, 1873.

Truth no more relies for success on ballot boxes than it does on cartridge boxes. Political action is not moral action. WILLIAM LLOYD GARRISON (1805–1879), *The Liberator*, March 13, 1846.

Since government, even in its best state is an evil, the object principally to be aimed at is that we should have as little of it as the general peace of human society will permit. WILLIAM GODWIN (1756–1836), *An Enquiry concerning Political Justice*, 1793.

Whenever government assumes to deliver us from the trouble of thinking for ourselves, the only consequences it produces are those of torpor and imbecility. WILLIAM GODWIN (1756–1836), *An Enquiry concerning Political Justice*, 1793.

Which is the best government? That which teaches us to govern ourselves. JOHANN WOLFGANG von GOETHE (1749–1832), *Maxims and Reflections.*

There is no greater fallacy than the belief that aims and purposes are one thing, while methods and tactics are another. This conception is a potent menace to social regeneration. All human experience teaches that methods and means cannot be separated from the ultimate aim. EMMA GOLDMAN (1869–1940), *My Disillusionment in Russia*, 1923.

Political repression consists of government action which grossly discriminates against persons or organizations viewed as presenting a fundamental challenge to existing power relationships or key governmental policies, because of their perceived political beliefs. ROBERT JUSTIN GOLDSTEIN, *Political Repression in Modern America*, 1968.

Certain things we cannot accomplish . . . by any process of government. We cannot legislate intelligence. We cannot legislate morality. No, and we cannot legislate loyalty, for loyalty is a kind of morality. A. WHITNEY GRISWOLD (1909–1963), *Essays on Education,* 1954.

The conservative errs in regarding man as though he were a wolf, the liberal errs in regarding man as though he were a lamb; neither will concede that he is both in nearly equal proportion. SIDNEY J. HARRIS, 1980.

Treason doth never prosper: what's the reason! For if it prosper, none dare call it treason. SIR JOHN HARRINGTON (1770–1831), *Epigrams.*

There have existed, in every age and every country, two distinct orders of men—the lovers of freedom and the devoted advocates of power. ROBERT Y. HAYNES, Speech, U.S. Senate, January 21, 1830

The majority, compose them how you will, are a herd, and not a very nice one. WILLIAM HAZLITT (1778–1830), *The Atlas,* February 8, 1829

What experience and history teach is this—that people and governments never have learned anything from history, or acted on principles deduced from it. GEORG WILHELM FRIEDRICH HEGEL (1770–1831), *The Philosophy of History.*

The police force and the ranks of prison officers attract many aberrant characters because they afford legal channels for pain-inflicting, power-wielding behavior, and because these very positions confer upon their holders a large degree of immunity. H. von HENTIG, *The Criminal and His Victim.*

Governments, if they endure, always tend increasingly toward aristocratic forms. No government in history has been known to evade this pattern. And as the aristocracy develops, government tends more and more to act exclusively in the interests of the ruling class—whether that class be hereditary royalty, oligarchs of financial empires, or entrenched bureaucracies. FRANK HERBERT, *Dune,* 1965.

A great politician has to bother himself less with means than with goals. ADOLPH HITLER (1889–1945), *Mein Kampf.*

There are very few so foolish that they had not rather govern themselves than be governed by others. THOMAS HOBBES (1588–1679), *Leviathan,* 1651.

No matter how noble the objectives of a government, if it blurs decency and kindness, cheapens human life, and breeds ill will and suspicion—it is an evil government. ERIC HOFFER (1902–1983), *The Passionate State of Mind,* 1954.

By most indications we have been made a more docile, tamer, and timid people who think and act in approved ways, not by threats of jail, but because we want to please those above us or because it is enough to know that the government has our number, usually our social security number, and has put it into a computer. NICHOLAS von HOFFMAN, *Washington Post,* July 9, 1975.

Scholars know that the processes of politics normally involve exaggeration, myth making, and fierce animosities. RICHARD HOFSTADTER (1916–1970), *The American Political Tradition,* 1948.

One of the central assumptions of the concept of democracy, perhaps its most central assumption, is that by and large human beings are better judges of their own interests. . . . The operating maxim of the democratic ideology is, "Whoever wears the shoe knows best where it pinches." From this most of the other attributes essential to a democracy follow, most notably the legal right of opposition and the power of majorities to change political shoes in the light of experience. SIDNEY HOOK (1902–1989), *Political Power and Personal Freedom,* 1959.

Liberalism is a force truly of the spirit proceeding from the deep realization that economic freedom cannot be sacrificed if political freedom is to be preserved. HERBERT CLARK HOOVER (1874–1964), U.S. President, Speech, October 21, 1932.

Nothing appears more surprising to those who consider human affairs with a philosophical eye, than the ease with which the many are governed by the few. DAVID HUME (1711–1766), *First Principles of Government,* 1742.

"And that," put in the Director sententiously, "that is the secret of happiness and virtue—liking what you've got to do. All conditioning aims at that: making people like their unescapable social destiny." ALDOUS HUXLEY (1894–1963), *Brave New World,* 1932.

The most shocking fact about war is that its victims and its instruments are human beings, and that these individual beings are condemned by the monstrous conventions of politics to murder or be murdered in quarrels not their own. ALDOUS HUXLEY (1894–1963), *The Olive Tree,* 1937.

The results of political changes are hardly ever those which their friends hope or their foes fear. THOMAS HENRY HUXLEY (1825–1895), *Government,* 1890.

Democracy is only an experiment in government, and it has the obvious disadvantage of counting votes instead of weighing them. WILLIAM RALPH INGE (1860–1965), *Possible Recovery?*

A wise and frugal government, which shall restrain men from injuring one another, shall leave them otherwise free to regulate their own pursuits of industry and improvement, and shall not take from the mouth of labor the bread it has earned—this is the sum of good government. THOMAS JEFFERSON (1743–1826), U.S. President, First Inaugural Address, March 4, 1801.

A conservative is a man who will not look at the new moon out of respect for that "ancient institution," the old one. DOUGLAS JERROLD (1803–1857).

Power is always gradually stealing away from the many to the few, because the few are more vigilant and consistent. SAMUEL JOHNSON (1709–1784), *The Adventurer.*

The tragedy of all political action is that some problems have no solution; none of the alternatives are intellectually consistent or morally uncompromising; and whatever decision is taken will harm somebody. JAMES JOLL, *Three Intellectuals in Politics,* 1960.

Act in such a way that you always treat humanity, whether in your own person or in the person of another, never simply as a means but always at the same time as an end. IMMANUEL KANT (1724–1804).

The enjoyment of power inevitably corrupts the judgment of reason, and perverts its liberty. IMMANUEL KANT (1724–1804), *Perpetual Peace,* 1795.

Every social war is a battle between the very few on both sides who care and who fire their shots across a crowd of spectators. MURRAY KEMPTON, *Part of Our Time,* 1955.

One of the most curious things about politics in America is the extraordinary lack of knowledge concerning its practice and principles, not only on the part of the people as a whole but of the practitioners themselves. FRANK R. KENT (1877–1958), *Political Behavior,* 1928.

Reward and punishment are the twin instruments of power in the state; they must not be revealed to anyone. LAO-TZU (604–531 B.C.), *Tao Te Ching.*

A slave has but one master; an ambitious man has as many masters as there are people who may be useful in bettering his position. JEAN de LA BRUYÈRE (1645–1696), *Les Caractères,* 1688.

Men would not live long in society if they were not the dupes of each other. FRANÇOIS, DUC de LA ROCHEFOUCAULD (1613–1680), *Maxims,* 1665.

[A power seeker is a person who] pursues power as a means of compensation against deprivation. Power is expected to overcome low estimates of the self, by changing either the traits of the self or the environment in which it functions. HAROLD D. LASWELL, *Power and Personality,* 1948.

Whatever has been a ruling power in the world, whether it be ideas or men, has in the main enforced its authority by means of the irresistible force expressed by the word "prestige." GUSTAVE LE BON (1841–1931), *The Crowd,* 1922.

A democracy is a state which recognizes the subjugation of the minority to the majority, that is, an organization for the systematic use of violence by one class against the other, by one part of the population against another. V. I. LENIN (1870–1924), *The State and Revolution.*

Men have always found it easy to be governed. What is hard is for them to govern themselves. MAX LERNER.

No man is good enough to govern another man without that man's consent. ABRAHAM LINCOLN (1809–1865), U.S. President, Speech, 1854.

In a democracy, the opposition is not only tolerated as constitutional, but must be maintained because it is indispensable. WALTER LIPPMANN (1889–1974), *Atlantic Monthly,* August 1939.

A good statesman, like any other sensible human being, always learns more from his opponents than from his fervent supporters. WALTER LIPPMANN (1889–1974), *Atlantic Monthly,* August 1939.

Successful . . . politicians are insecure and intimidated men. They advance politically only as they placate, appease, bribe, seduce, bamboozle or otherwise manage to manipulate the demanding and threatening elements of their constituencies. WALTER LIPPMANN (1889–1974), *The Public Philosophy,* 1955.

When philosophers try to be politicians they generally cease to be philosophers. WALTER LIPPMAN (1889–1974), *A Preface To Politics,* 1914.

This is one of the paradoxes of the democratic movement—that it loves a crowd and fears the individuals who compose it—that the religion of humanity should have no faith in human beings. WALTER LIPPMANN (1889–1974), *A Preface To Politics,* 1914.

Freedom of men under a government is to have a standing rule to live by, common to every one of that society, and made by the legislative power vested in it. JOHN LOCKE (1632–1704), *Two Treatises on Government,* 1690.

There is no nation on earth so dangerous as a nation fully armed, and bankrupt at home. HENRY CABOT LODGE (1850–1924), Speech, 1916.

The people are no more capable of organizing and acting to attain and guard their general interests by sound political action than they are of achieving immortality by incantation and prayer. Unless saved by forces outside themselves they are perpetually doomed to be victims of their own ineptitude or of their shrewd exploiters. FERDINAND LUNDBERG, *Scoundrels All,* 1968.

A coup consists of the infiltration of a small but critical segment of the state apparatus, which is then used to displace the government from its control of the remainder. EDWARD LUTTWAK, *Coup d'État,* 1968.

The only thing that saves us from the bureaucracy is inefficiency. An efficient bureaucracy is the greatest threat to liberty. EUGENE McCARTHY, *Time* magazine, February 12, 1979.

Bureaucracy, the rule of no one, has become the modern form of despotism. MARY McCARTHY, *The New Yorker,* October 18, 1958.

Nothing is so galling to a people, not broken in from birth, as a paternal, or, in other words, a meddling government, a government which tells them what to read, and say, and eat, and drink, and wear. THOMAS BABINGTON MACAULAY (1800–1859), *Southey's Colloquies,* 1830.

Many politicians . . . are in the habit of laying it down as a self-evident proposition, that no people ought to be free till they are fit to use their freedom. The maxim is worthy of the fool . . . who resolved not to go into the water till he had learned to swim. THOMAS BABINGTON MACAULAY (1800–1859).

There is a change in society. There must be a corresponding change in the government. We are not, we cannot, in the nature of things, be what our fathers were. THOMAS BABINGTON MACAULAY (1800–1859), 1831.

I have not the slightest doubt that, if we had a purely democratic government . . . either the poor would plunder the rich, and civilization would perish, or order and property would be saved by a strong military government, and liberty would perish. THOMAS BABINGTON MACAULAY (1800–1859), Letter, 1857.

Every political sect has its esoteric and its exoteric school, its abstract doctrines for the initiated, its visible symbols, its imposing forms, its mythological fables for the vulgar. It has its altars and its deified heroes, its relics and pilgrimages, its canonized martyrs and confessors, its festivals and legendary miracles. THOMAS BABINGTON MACAULAY (1800–1859), *Edinburgh Review,* September 1828.

Many consider that a wise prince, when he has the opportunity, ought with craft to foster some animosity against himself so that, having crushed it, his renown may rise higher. NICCOLO MACHIAVELLI (1469–1527), *The Prince,* 1513.

Because conspiracies rarely succeed, they most often bring about the ruin of those who plan them, and they bring greatness to those against whom they are directed. NICCOLO MACHIAVELLI (1469–1527), *History of Florence, 1525.*

He who desires or attempts to reform the government of a state, and wishes to have it accepted and capable of maintaining itself to the satisfaction of everybody, must at least retain the semblance of the old forms; so that it may seem to the people that there has been no change in the institutions, even though in fact they are entirely different from the old ones. NICCOLO MACHIAVELLI (1469–1527), *Discourses on the First Ten Books of Livy,* 1517.

All well-governed states and wise princes have taken care not to reduce the nobility to despair, nor the people to discontent. NICCOLO MACHIAVELLI (1469–1527), *The Prince,* 1513.

There is no maxim, in my opinion, which is more liable to be misapplied, and which, therefore, more needs elucidation, than the current, that the interest of the majority is the political standard of right and wrong. JAMES MADISON (1751–1836), U.S. President, 1786.

The two points of difference between a democracy and a republic are: first, the delegation of the government, in the latter, to a small number of citizens, elected by the rest; secondly, the greater number of citizens, and greater sphere of country, over which the latter may be extended. JAMES MADISON (1751–1836), U.S. President, *The Federalist,* #10.

The government is the aggregate of the governors, and the governors . . . are those who have the power to make laws regulating the relations between men, and to force obedience to these laws. . . . Why abdicate one's own liberty, one's own initiative in favor of other individuals? Why give them the power to be the masters, with or against the wish of each, to dispose of the forces of all in their own way? ERRICO MALATESTA (1853–1932), *Anarchy.*

The first rudiments of morality, broached by skillful politicians, to render men useful to each other as well as tractable, were chiefly contrived that the ambitious might reap the more benefit from and govern vast numbers of them with the greatest ease and security. BERNARD de MANDEVILLE (1670–1733), *An Inquiry into the Origin of Moral Virtue,* 1723.

The classical liberal understanding of freedom is this: every individual should care for his own interests and mind his own business. . . . Every individual is a world unto himself, is a being in himself and is presupposed to be the best judge of his own affairs; everyone should respect the wishes, beliefs, and way of life of others. MIECZYSLAW MANELI, *Freedom and Tolerance,* 1987.

Politics is the art of looking for trouble, finding it everywhere, diagnosing it incorrectly, and applying the wrong remedies. GROUCHO MARX (1891–1977).

Political power, properly so called, is merely the organized power of one class for suppressing another. KARL MARX (1818–1883), *The Communist Manifesto,* 1848.

Men may be without restraints in their liberty; they may pass to and fro at pleasure; but if their steps are tracked by spies and informers, their words noted down for crimination, their associates watched as conspirators—who shall say that they are free. SIR THOMAS MAY (1815–1886), *Constitutional History of England,* 1863.

Democracy is the theory that the common people know what they want, and deserve to get it good and hard. H. L. MENCKEN (1880–1956), *A Book of Burlesques,* 1920.

The most dangerous man, to any government, is the man who is able to think things out for himself, without regard to the prevailing superstition and taboo. H. L. MENCKEN (1880–1956).

The worst government is the most moral. One composed of cynics is often very tolerant and humane. But when fanatics are on top there is no limit to oppression. H. L. MENCKEN (1880–1956), *Minority Report.*

Politics, as hopeful men practice it in the world, consists mainly of the delusion that a change in form is a change in substance. H. L. MENCKEN (1880–1956), *Prejudices,* 1924.

The whole aim of practical politics is to keep the populace alarmed (and hence clamorous to be led to safety) by menacing it with an endless series of hobgoblins, all of them imaginary. H. L. MENCKEN (1880–1956), *The Smart Set,* December 1921.

A democratic constitution, not supported by democratic institutions in detail, but confined to the central government, not only is not political freedom, but often creates a spirit precisely the reverse, carrying down to the lowest grade in society the desire and ambition of political domination. JOHN STUART MILL (1806–1873), *Principles of Political Economy,* 1848.

The worth of a State, in the long run, is the worth of the individuals composing it. JOHN STUART MILL (1806–1873), *On Liberty,* 1859.

In its narrowest acceptation, order means obedience. A government is said to preserve order if it succeeds in getting itself obeyed. JOHN STUART MILL (1806–1873), *Considerations on Representative Government,* 1861.

There is a movement from widely scattered little powers to concentrate powers and the attempt at monopoly control from powerful centers, which, being partly hidden, are centers of manipulation as well as of authority. C. WRIGHT MILLS (1916–1962), *The Power Elite,* 1956.

When complaints are freely heard, deeply considered, and speedily reformed, then is the utmost bound of civil liberty obtained that wise men look for. JOHN MILTON (1608–1674), *Aeropagitica,* 1644.

The deterioration of every government begins with the decay of the principles on which it was founded. CHARLES-LOUIS de SECONDAT, BARON de MONTESQUIEU (1689–1755), *The Spirit of the Laws,* 1748.

In constitutional states liberty is but a compensation for the heaviness of taxation. In despotic states the equivalent for liberty is the lightness of taxation. CHARLES-LOUIS de SECONDAT, BARON de MONTESQUIEU (1689–1755), *The Spirit of the Laws,* 1748.

What the individual is not allowed to want for himself, he is encouraged to seek for the legal fiction called "the state." . . . By transferring his egotism and power impulses to the nation, the individual gives his uninhibited aspirations not only a vicarious satisfaction . . . while society puts liabilities upon aspirations for individual power, it places contributions to the collective power of the state at the top of the hierarchy of values. HANS MORGANTHAU, *Ethics,* October 1945.

All human society amounts to manipulation of human beings by each other. Everything depends upon who is doing the manipulating and for what purpose. BARRINGTON MOORE, JR., *Injustice: The Social Basis of Obedience and Revolt,* 1973.

A politician is . . . trained in the art of inexactitude. His words tend to be blunt or rounded, because if they have a cutting edge they may return to wound him. EDWARD R. MORROW (1908–1965), Speech, 1959.

Whoever took part in an election knows perfectly well that the representative is not elected by the voters but . . . has himself elected by them. Or, if that sounds too unpleasant . . . his friends have him elected. In any case, a candidacy is always the work of a group of people united for a common purpose, an organized minority which inevitably forces its will upon the disorganized majority. GAETANO MOSCA, *Partiti e Sindicati nelli crisi del regime parlamentare,* 1949.

Citizen participation is a device whereby public officials induce nonpublic individuals to act in a way the officials desire. DANIEL PATRICK MOYNIHAN, *The Public Interest,* Fall 1969.

My program is simple. I want to govern. BENITO MUSSOLINI (1883–1945), *My Autobiography.*

There are two levers for moving men—interest and fear. NAPOLEON BONAPARTE (1769–1821).

Politics is the diversion of trivial men who, when they succeed at it, become important in the eyes of more trivial men. GEORGE JEAN NATHAN (1882–1958), 1954.

The whole art of politics consists in directing rationally the irrationalities of men. REINHOLD NIEBUHR (1892–1971), Obituary, *New York Times,* June 2, 1971.

Morality is the best of all devices for leading mankind by the nose. FRIEDRICH NIETZSCHE (1844–1900), *The Anti-Christ,* 1895.

Few men are placed in such fortunate circumstances as to be able to gain office, or to keep it for any length of time, without misleading or bamboozling the people. FREDERICK SCOTT OLIVER (1864–1934), *Politics and Politicians,* 1934.

Men who are engaged in public life must necessarily aim at reducing opposition to a minimum, and one of the most obvious means to that end is by misrepresenting, discrediting or ruining their opponents. FREDERICK SCOTT OLIVER (1864–1934), *Politics and Politicians,* 1934.

What mattered were individual relationships. . . . The proles, it occurred to him, had remained in this condition. They were not loyal to a party or to a country or to an idea, they were loyal to one another. . . . The proles had stayed human. GEORGE ORWELL (1903–1950), *Nineteen Eighty-Four,* 1949.

Though the "informed citizen" is often claimed to be a necessary ingredient of democratic government, most citizens in our society are not very well-informed. STUART OSKAMP, *Attitudes and Opinions,* 1977.

There is a passion in the human heart stronger than the desire to be free from injustice and wrong, and that is the desire to inflict injustice and wrong upon others, and men resent more keenly an attempt to prevent them from oppressing other people than they do the oppression from which they themselves suffer. LORD PALMERSTON (1784–1865), Letter, 1859.

Government, even in its best state, is but a necessary evil, in its worst state, an intolerable one. THOMAS PAINE (1737–1809), *Common Sense,* 1776.

Now the sole remedy for the abuse of political power is to limit it; but when politics corrupt business, modern reformers invariably demand the enlargement of the political power. ISABEL PATERSON, *The God of the Machine.*

Let the people think they govern and they will be governed. WILLIAM PENN (1644–1718), *Reflections and Maxims,* 1693.

The makers of laws are the majority who are weak; they make laws and distribute praises and censures with a view to themselves and to their own interests; and they terrify the stronger sort of men, and those who are able to get the better of them, in order that they may not get the better of them. PLATO (428–347 B.C.), *Gorgias,* 360 B.C.

The politician who curries favor with the citizens and indulges them and fawns upon them and has a presentiment of their wishes, and is skilled at gratifying them, is esteemed as a great statesman. PLATO (428–347 B.C.), *The Republic,* 400 B.C.

Democracy is a charming form of government, full of variety and disorder, and dispensing a sort of equality to equals and unequals alike. PLATO (428–347), *The Republic,* 400 B.C.

Party-spirit at best is but the madness of many for the gain of a few. ALEXANDER POPE (1688–1744), Letter, 1714.

There is no doubt that the doctrine of the chosen people grew out of the tribal form of social life. Tribalism, i.e., the emphasis on the supreme importance of the tribe without which the individual is nothing at all, is an element which we shall find in many forms of historicist theories. Other forms which are no longer tribalist may still retain an element of collectivism; they may still emphasize the significance of some group or collective—for example, a class— without which the individual is nothing at all. SIR KARL POPPER, *The Open Society and Its Enemies,* 1966.

What we need and what we want is to moralize politics, and not to politicize morals. SIR KARL POPPER, *The Open Society and Its Enemies,* 1966.

There is a political maxim that all government tends to despotism, and like the human frame brings at its birth the latent seed which finally shall destroy the constitution. This is a melancholy truth—which is the lot of humanity. JOSIAH QUINCY, JR. (1744–1775), Letter, *Boston Gazette,* 1767.

Morality, including political morality, has to do with the definition of right conduct, and this is not simply by way of the ends of action. How we do what we do is as important as our goals. PAUL RAMSEY, *War and the Christian Conscience,* 1961.

A resolute minority has usually prevailed over an easygoing or wobbly majority whose prime purpose was to be left alone. JAMES RESTON, *Sketches in The Sand,* 1967.

Democracy tends to ignore, even deny, threats to its existence because it loathes doing what is needed to counter them. It awakens only when the danger becomes deadly, imminent, evident. By then, either there is too little time left for it to save itself, or the price of survival has become crushingly high. JEAN-FRAN-ÇOIS REVEL, *How Democracies Perish,* 1983.

The issues can be stated very briefly: Who will be controlled? Who will exercise control? What type of control will be exercised? Most important of all, toward what end or purpose, or in the pursuit of what value, will control be exercised. CARL ROGERS (1902–1987).

Kill a man, you are a murderer. Kill millions of men, and you are a conqueror. Kill everyone and you are a God. JEAN ROSTAND (1894–1977), *Thoughts of a Biologist,* 1955.

The problem is to find a form of association which will defend and protect with the whole common force the person and goods of each associate, and in which each, while uniting himself with all, may still obey himself alone, and remain as free as before. JEAN-JACQUES ROUSSEAU (1712–1778), *The Social Contract,* 1762.

The State is a collection of officials, different for different purposes, drawing comfortable incomes so long as the status quo is preserved. The only alteration they are likely to desire in the status quo is an increase of bureaucracy and of the power of bureaucrats. BERTRAND RUSSELL (1872–1970).

In a social system in which power is open to all, the posts which confer power will, as a rule, be occupied by men who differ from the average in being exceptionally power-loving. BERTRAND RUSSELL (1872–1970), *Power,* 1938.

When the state intervenes to insure the indoctrination of some doctrine, it does so because there is no conclusive evidence in favor of that doctrine. BERTRAND RUSSELL (1872–1970), 1928.

There is no nonsense so arrant that it cannot be made the creed of a vast majority by adequate government action. BERTRAND RUSSELL (1872–1970), *Unpopular Essays,* 1950

The working of great institutions is mainly the result of a vast mass of routine, petty malice, self-interest, and sheer mistake. GEORGE SANTAYANA (1863–1952), *The Crime of Galileo.*

The voice of the majority is no proof of justice. FRIEDRICH von SCHILLER (1758–1805), *Mary Stuart,* 1800.

Every miserable fool who has nothing at all of which he can be proud, adopts, as a last resource, pride in the nation to which he belongs; he is ready and glad to defend all its faults and follies tooth and nail, thus reimbursing himself for his own inferiority. ARTHUR SCHOPENHAUER (1788–1860).

Every institution is a racket. Whether we are considering political, religious, economic, ideological, or educational institutions, each is a formal, elaborate system designed for one purpose: to control people. Each seeks to persuade or compel individuals to divert their energies from the pursuit of private, personal objectives, and to dedicate themselves to organizational purposes. BUTLER D. SHAFFER, *Calculated Chaos,* 1985.

Institutions are the principle means by which conflict is produced and managed in society. Peace is incompatible with institutional activity. Stated another way, the success of institutions depends upon the creation of those conditions in which personal and social conflict will flourish. BUTLER D. SHAFFER, *Calculated Chaos*, 1985.

When a stupid man is doing something he is ashamed of, he always declares that it is his duty. GEORGE BERNARD SHAW (1856–1950), *Caesar and Cleopatra*, 1900.

A government that robs Peter to pay Paul can always depend upon the support of Paul. GEORGE BERNARD SHAW (1856–1950), *Everybody's Political What's What*, 1944.

Patriotism is your conviction that this country is superior to all others because you were born in it. GEORGE BERNARD SHAW (1856–1950).

The more democratic a government is the more authoritative it is, for with the people behind it, it can push its authority further than any Tsar or foreign despot dare do. GEORGE BERNARD SHAW (1856–1950), *The New Republic*, April 14, 1937.

Derived from the cult of state, of party, of power, politics are always sacrificing the interests and aspirations of man for a multi-headed monster, for an idol. IGNAZIO SILONE (1900–1978), *New York Times Book Review*, August 31, 1958.

It should be possible to design a world in which behavior likely to be punished seldom or never occurs. B. F. SKINNER, *Beyond Freedom and Dignity*, 1971

Two features of autonomous man—his freedom and dignity—are particularly troublesome. B. F. SKINNER, *Psychology Today*, August 1971.

There are signs of emotional instability in those who are deeply affected by the literature of freedom. B. F. SKINNER, *Psychology Today*, August 1971.

There is no art which one government sooner learns of another than that of draining money from the pockets of the people. ADAM SMITH (1723–1790), *Wealth of Nations*, 1776.

The thing we have to fear in this country, to my way of thinking, is the influence of the organized minorities, because somehow or other the great majority does not seem to organize. They seem to feel that they are going to be effective because of their known strength. ALFRED E. SMITH (1873–1944), Speech at Harvard University, June 22, 1933.

The words men fight and die for are the coins of politics, where by much usage they are soiled and by much manipulating debased. That has evidently been the fate of the word "democracy." It has come to mean whatever anyone wants it to mean. BERNARD SMITH, *The American Spirit*, 1941.

The war system makes the stable government of societies possible. It does this essentially by providing an external necessity for a society to accept political rule. In so doing, it establishes the basis for nationhood and the authority of government to control its constituents. SPECIAL STUDY GROUP, *Report from Iron Mountain*, 1967.

The basic authority of a modern state over its people resides in its war powers. . . . On a day-to-day basis, it is represented by the institution of police, armed organizations charged expressly with dealing with "internal enemies" in a military manner. SPECIAL STUDY GROUP, *Report from Iron Mountain,* 1967.

The following substitute institutions, among others, have been proposed for consideration as replacements for the nonmilitary functions of war . . . a) An omnipresent, virtually omnipotent international police force. b) An established and recognized extraterrestrial menace. c) Massive global environmental pollution. d) Fictitious alternate enemies. SPECIAL STUDY GROUP, *Report from Iron Mountain,* 1967.

By no process can coercion be made equitable. The freest form of government is only the least objectionable form. The rule of the many by the few, we call tyranny. The rule of the few by the many (Democracy) is tyranny also, only of a less intense kind. "You shall do as we will, not as you will," is in either case the declaration. HERBERT SPENCER (1820–1903), *The Right to Ignore the State.*

The fact disclosed by a survey of the past that majorities have been wrong, must not blind us to the complementary fact that majorities have usually not been entirely wrong. HERBERT SPENCER (1820–1903), *First Principles,* 1862.

In the first place, the difference between a "democratic" and an "authoritarian" personality is sometimes not in how he behaves but in how he is treated. DAVID SPITZ (1916–1979), *American Political Science Review,* vol. 52, 1958.

Constitutions are utterly worthless to restrain the tyranny of governments, unless it be understood that the people will by force compel the government to keep within constitutional limits. Practically speaking, no government knows any limits to its power except the endurance of the people. LYSANDER SPOONER (1808–1887), *Trial by Jury.*

All governments, the worst on earth and the most tyrannical on earth, are free governments to that portion of the people who voluntarily support them. LYSANDER SPOONER (1808–1887), *Trial by Jury.*

The power to command and the weakness to obey are the essence of government and the quintessence of slavery. CHARLES T. SPRADLING, *Liberty and the Great Libertarians.*

Governments cannot accept liberty as their fundamental basis for justice, because governments rest upon authority and not upon liberty. To accept liberty as the fundamental basis is to discard authority; that is, to discard government itself. CHARLES T. SPRADLING, *Liberty and the Great Libertarians.*

We no longer believe that it is just for one man to govern two men, but we have yet to outgrow the absurd belief that it is just for two men to govern one man. CHARLES T. SPRADLING, *Liberty and the Great Libertarians.*

The freedom of a government does not depend upon the quality of its laws, but upon the power that has the right to create them. THADDEUS STEVENS (1792–1868), Speech, U.S. House of Representatives, January 3, 1867.

Politics is perhaps the only profession for which no preparation is thought necessary. ROBERT LOUIS STEVENSON (1850–1894), *Familiar Studies of Men and Books.*

The object of the state is always the same: to limit the individual, to tame him, to subordinate him, to subjugate him. MAX STIRNER (1806–1856), *The Ego and His Own,* 1845.

A new race of men is springing up to govern the nation; they are hunters after popularity, men of ambition, not of the honor so much as the profits of an office . . . whose principles hang laxly upon them, and who follow not so much what is right as what leads them to a temporary vulgar applause. JOSEPH STORY (1779–1845).

When all the fine phrases are stripped away, it appears that the state is only a group of men with human interests, passions, and desires or, worse yet . . . an obscure clerk hidden in some corner of a governmental bureau. In either case the assumption of superhuman wisdom and virtue is proved false. WILLIAM GRAHAM SUMNER (1840–1910), *Commercial Crises,* 1879.

The more corrupt the State the more numerous the laws. CORNELIUS TACITUS (55–117 A.D.), *Annals.*

Far from establishing liberty throughout the world, war has actually encouraged and built up the development of dictatorships and has only restored liberty in limited areas at the cost of untold hardship, of human suffering, of death and destruction beyond the conception of our fathers. ROBERT A. TAFT (1889–1953), *A Foreign Policy for Americans,* 1951.

An important art of politicians is to find new names for institutions which under old names have become odious to the public. CHARLES-MAURICE TALLEYRAND (1754–1838).

Political principles resemble military tactics; they are usually designed for a war which is over. R. H. TAWNEY (1880–1962), *Equality,* 1931.

A government in which the majority rule in all cases cannot be based on justice, even as far as men understand it. HENRY DAVID THOREAU (1817–1862), *An Essay on Civil Disobedience,* 1849.

To render a people obedient and to keep them so, savage laws inefficiently enforced are less effective than mild laws enforced by an efficient administration regularly, automatically, as it were, every day and on all alike. ALEXIS de TOCQUEVILLE (1805–1859).

In politics a community of hatred is almost the foundation of friendship. ALEXIS de TOCQUEVILLE (1805–1859).

There has long existed and still exists a terrible superstition, which has done more harm, perhaps, than the most awful religious superstitions. It consists in the affirmation that, besides the duties of man to man, there are still more important obligations to an imaginary being . . . in political sciences this . . . being is government. LEO N. TOLSTOY (1828–1910).

Civilization consists in teaching men to govern themselves. BENJAMIN TUCKER (1854–1939), *Instead of A Book*, 1893.

Politics is the art of preventing people from taking part in affairs which properly concern them. PAUL VALÉRY (1871–1945), *Tel quel.*

The nation, being in effect a licensed predatory concern, is not bound by the decencies of that code of law and morals that governs private conduct. THORSTEIN VEBLEN (1857–1929), *Absentee Ownership*, 1923.

The spirit of nationalism has never ceased to bend human institutions to the service of dissension and distress. THORSTEIN VEBLEN (1857–1929), *Absentee Ownership*, 1923.

Patriotism may be defined as a sense of partisan solidarity in respect of prestige. THORSTEIN VEBLEN (1857–1929), *The Nature of Peace*, 1919.

In general, the art of government consists of taking as much money from one class of citizens to give to the other. VOLTAIRE (1694–1778), *Philosophical Dictionary*, 1764.

There has never been a perfect government, because men have passions; and if they did not have passions, there would be no need for government. VOLTAIRE (1694–1778), *Politics and Legislation: Republican Ideas.*

The wise and clever politician makes the passions and prejudices of his constituents one of his principle assets. Nearly all people vote not according to the best interests of the community, or even according to their own best interests as decided by calm and logical reasoning, but according to their passions and prejudices. J. H. WALLIS, *The Politician*, 1935.

Our supreme governors, the mob. HORACE WALPOLE (1717–1797), Letter to Horace Mann, September 7, 1743.

Conflict cannot be excluded from social life. "Peace" is nothing more than a change in the form of conflict or in the antagonists or in the objects of the conflict, or finally in the chances of selection. MAX WEBER (1864–1920), *The Methodology of the Social Sciences.*

Whether the mask is labeled Fascism, Democracy, or Dictatorship of the Proletariat, our great adversary remains the Apparatus—the bureaucracy, the police, the military. Not the one facing us across the frontier or the battlelines, which is not so much our enemy as our brother's enemy, but the one that calls itself our protector and makes it us slaves. SIMONE WEIL (1909–1943), *Politics*, Spring 1945.

Nationalism is a heretical religion based on the erroneous doctrine that nations have a soul and that this soul is more permanent, more "eternal," so to speak, than the soul of an individual. FRANZ WERFEL (1890–1945), *Between Heaven and Earth,* 1944.

The strife of politics tends to unsettle the calmest understanding, and ulcerate the most benevolent heart. There are no bigotries or absurdities too gross for parties to create or adopt under the stimulus of political passions. EDWIN PERCY WHIPPLE (1819–1886).

Governments are best classified by considering who are the "somebodies" they are in fact trying to satisfy. ALFRED NORTH WHITEHEAD (1861–1947), *Adventures in Ideas,* 1933.

As long as war is regarded as wicked, it will always have its fascination. When it is looked upon as vulgar it will cease to be popular. OSCAR WILDE (1854–1900), *The Critic as Artist,* 1891.

All modes of government are failures. Despotism is unjust to everybody, including the despot, who was probably made for better things. . . . High hopes were once formed of democracy; but democracy means simply the bludgeoning of the people by the people for the people. OSCAR WILDE (1854–1900), *The Soul of Man under Socialism,* 1881.

Crimes against the state and against officers of the state! History informs us that more wrong may be done on this subject than on any other whatsoever. JAMES WILSON (1742–1798), 1788.

Government should not be made an end in itself; it is a means only, a means to be freely adapted to advance the best interests of the social organism. The State exists for the sake of Society, not Society for the sake of the State. WOODROW WILSON (1856–1924), U.S. President, *The State: Elements of Historical and Practical Politics,* 1911.

Ideologies and Ideologues

Government by idea tends to take in everything, to make the whole of society obedient to the idea. Spaces not so governed are unconquered, beyond the border, unconverted, unconvinced, a future danger. LORD ACTON (1834–1902).

What all ideologies do claim is that at least their basic doctrines have the status of academic knowledge, that is, of demonstratable objective truth. Liberals, for example, claim to base their principles upon pure philosophy; Marxists claim that their analysis of society is fully scientific; Nazis claim their theory of universal struggle between Aryan and Jew to demonstratable historical truth; and so on. IAN ADAMS, *The Logic of Political Belief,* 1989.

To be possessed of a set of political beliefs, an ideology, is to understand the world in a certain way. And to have an understanding is to be master of a vocabulary, to be able to apply it appropriately. Each of the various sets of political beliefs—Liberalism, Nazism, Marxism and the rest—has a distinctive vocabulary of its own. IAN ADAMS, *The Logic of Political Belief,* 1989.

Ideologists do not speak of themselves as developing doctrine or dogma; for one of the rules of the game, so to speak, is the presentation of belief as objective knowledge where demonstration is adequate and faith unnecessary. But ideologists do develop doctrine just as theologists do, only they call it "theory." IAN ADAMS, *The Logic of Political Belief,* 1989.

From a "pragmatic" point of view, political philosophy is a monster, and wherever it has been taken seriously, the consequence, almost invariably, has been revolution, war, and eventually, the police state. HENRY DAVID AIKEN, *Commentary,* April 1964.

The presence of fear mixed with hatred animates the followers of all ideologies and totalizing theories. Thematic hostility toward those outside the ideology is justified on the grounds of self-preservation. All outsiders are seen as potential enemies. WAYNE ALLEN, *The World & I,* November, 1989.

In order to understand "ideological thinking," we must first grasp the importance of the ideology's claim to "knowledge." The fear of moving into an unknown future forms the attraction to the ideology. . . . [The prime function of] an ideology . . . is to explain every thing and every occurance by deducing it from the premise of the ideology. It seeks to make itself the method for knowing the world. There is a magnetic claim to "knowledge" which attracts the individual because the ideology makes thinking unnecessary. WAYNE ALLEN, *The World & I*, November 1989.

The myth of the Revolution serves as a refuge for utopian intellectuals; it becomes the mysterious, unpredictable intercessor between the real and the ideal. RAYMOND ARON (1905–1983), *The Great Debate*, 1965.

The intellectual who no longer feels attached to anything is not satisfied with opinion merely; he wants certainty, he wants a system. The revolution provides him with his opium. RAYMOND ARON (1905–1983), *The Great Debate*, 1965.

Intellectuals cannot tolerate the chance event, the unintelligible: they have a nostalgia for the absolute, for a universally comprehensive scheme. RAYMOND ARON (1905–1983), *The Great Debate*, 1965.

The whole history of civilization is strewn with creeds and institutions that were invaluable at first, and deadly afterward. WALTER BAGEHOT (1826–1877), *Physics and Politics*, 1869.

A total ideology is an all-inclusive system of comprehensive reality, it is a set of beliefs, infused with passion, and seeks to transform the whole of a way of life. This commitment to ideology—the yearning for a "cause," or the satisfaction of deep moral feelings—is not necessarily the reflection of interests in the shape of ideas. Ideology, in this sense, and in the sense that we use it here, is a secular religion. DANIEL BELL, *The End of Ideology*, 1960.

What gives ideology its force is its passion. Abstract philosophical inquiry has always sought to eliminate passion. . . . For the ideologue, truth arises in action, and meaning is given to experience by the "transforming moment." He comes alive not in contemplation, but in "the deed." One might say, in fact, that the most important, latent, function of ideology is to tap emotion. DANIEL BELL, *The End of Ideology*, 1960.

The way you hold beliefs is more important than what you hold. If somebody's been a rigid Communist, he becomes a rigid anti-Communist—the rigidity being the constant. DANIEL BELL, quoted in *Christian Science Monitor*, March 12, 1990.

Intellectuals have a dangerous facility to imagine themselves occupying the seats of power in the wake of, so to speak, the revolution of their choice. With revolutionaries as with generals, one ought to beware of those who manage to philosophize about their lust for battle. . . . PETER L. BERGER, *Pyramids of Sacrifice: Political Ethics and Social Change*, 1974.

Intellectuals have always had the propensity to endow their libidinal emotions with philosophical significance, in sex as in politics, and in both areas one often suspects that the need for philosophy arises from an unfortunate combination of strong ambitions and weak capabilities. PETER L. BERGER, *Pyramids of Sacrifice: Political Ethics and Social Change*, 1974.

Revolutionary warfare (contrary to the ideology of revolutionary intellectuals) is very largely not a matter of "winning the hearts and minds of the people," but rather a competition as to which side can make more people afraid of it. PETER L. BERGER, *Pyramids of Sacrifice: Political Ethics and Social Change,* 1974.

One belief, more than any other, is responsible for the slaughter of individuals on altars of the great historical ideas—justice or progress or happiness of future generations . . . or emancipation of a nation or race or class. . . . this is the belief that somewhere . . . there is a final solution. SIR ISAIAH BERLIN, *Two Concepts of Liberty,* 1958.

An ideology is a belief system which explains the nature of the world and man's place in it. It explains the nature of man and the derivative relationships of humans to one another. GORDON C. BJORK, *Ideology and the American Experience* (Roth and Whittemore), 1986.

A system is nothing more than the subordination of all aspects of the universe to any one such aspect. JORGE LUIS BORGES, *Labyrinths,* 1962.

The new ideas of one age become the ideologies of the next, by which time they will in all probability be out of date and inapplicable. GERALD BRENAN.

Intellectuals are people who believe that ideas are of more importance than values . . . their own ideas and other people's values. GERALD BRENAN.

An ideologue—one who thinks ideologically—can't lose. He can't lose because his answer, his interpretation and his attitude have been determined in advance of the particular experience or observation. They are derived from the ideology, and are not subject to the facts. JAMES BURNHAM (1905–1987), *Suicide of the West,* 1964.

Once beliefs have been adopted by an individual or community, many forces operate to give them continued sway, even though they may be erroneous, and even though occurrences are frequent which might be expected to throw doubt upon them. . . . A belief once adopted is not a merely contemplative affair, it is an established habit, providing ready guidance for action on the objects with which the belief is concerned. EDWIN ARTHUR BURTT, *Right Thinking,* 1946.

Tedious polemic writers are more severe to their readers than those they contend with. SAMUEL BUTLER (1612–1680), *Prose Observations,* 1660–80.

Political ideology helps people avoid ambiguity in their lives and provides them with a sense of certainty and security. If people see powerful and unpredictable forces around them, ideological faith becomes a sanctuary. It permits them to believe in something outside and beyond themselves, in ideas and prospects derived from a higher power, whether religious, historical, or scientific. REO M. CHRISTIANSON et al., *Ideologies and Modern Politics,* 1975.

Ideology thereby makes the future more predictable. The potency of this human need for predictability, and its fulfillment by ideology, is indicated by the human tendency to think in black-and-white stereotypes and simplified either-or dichotomies, and to overlook apparent contradictions and incongruities in their own ideologies. REO M. CHRISTIANSON et al., *Ideologies and Modern Politics,* 1975.

The attractiveness of the Marxist ideology is apparent. To the dissatisfied, the malcontent, the powerless, the suffering, it offers hope. It offers a pinpointed explanation for what is wrong with modern society. It assigns blame. It provides a plan for action. It assures the victory of justice and international brotherhood even if nothing is done. REO M. CHRISTIANSON et al., *Ideologies and Modern Politics,* 1975.

By "ideology," is meant here any intellectual structure consisting of a set of beliefs about man's nature and the world in which he lives; a claim that the two sets are interdependent; and a demand that those beliefs should be professed . . . by anyone who is to be considered a full member of a certain social group. PATRICK CORBETT, *Ideology,* 1965.

Where ideology differs from even the most heretical forms of religion is that it is entirely centered on this world and claims to depend entirely on reason, as opposed to faith or revelation. MAURICE CRANSTON, *The American Spectator,* June 1985.

Ideology simplifies things at the same time it constructs its elaborate theoretical edifices; if it is philosophy, it is philosophy for the masses at the same time as it is philosophy for the rootless, rebellious intellectual class in whom our culture's "self-loathing" is most pronounced. MAURICE CRANSTON, *The American Spectator,* June 1985.

Beliefs serve the interests of the community. Like force, belief induces the individual to conform to the demands of the group. Unlike force, belief gets the individual to conform and boast about it. Even more interesting, belief gets the individual to conform to the interests of the collective and not even know it. . . . In relatively simple societies, belief systems are powerful agents of social control insofar as they are not challenged. They possess the qualities of an ideal use of force as an agent of social control. RAY P. CUZZORT, *Using Social Thought,* 1989.

Just now the favorite ideological psychological candidate for control of human activity is love of power. JOHN DEWEY (1859–1952), *Freedom and Culture,* 1939.

[Ideology] is a system of related beliefs about how the political world does and should operate. . . . One who holds an ideology has, in effect, a series of expectations or a map in his mind, orienting him and telling him how things work. Thus, he knows where to fit facts that he perceives and how to understand their significance. KENNETH M. DOLBEARE and PATRICIA DOLBEARE, *American Ideologies,* 1971.

[Patriotism is] the more or less conscious conviction of a person that his own welfare and that of the significant groups to which he belongs are dependent upon the preservation or expansion (or both) of the power and culture of his society. LEONARD W. DOOB, *Patriotism and Nationalism: Their Psychological Foundations,* 1964.

[Nationalism is] the set of more or less uniform demands (1) which people in a society share, (2) which arise from their patriotism, (3) for which justifications exist and can be readily expressed, (4) which incline them to make personal sacrifices in behalf of their government's aims, and (5) which may or may not lead to appropriate action. LEONARD W. DOOB, *Patriotism and Nationalism: Their Psychological Foundations,* 1964.

Man has such a predilection for systems and abstract deductions that he is ready to distort truth intentionally, he is ready to deny the evidence of his senses only to justify his logic. FYODOR DOSTOEVSKY (1821–1881), *Notes from the Underground,* 1864.

I suspect that in our loathing of totalitarianism, there is infused a good deal of admiration for its efficiency. T. S. ELIOT (1888–1965), 1939.

A truly committed movement participant experiences an intensity of involvement over ideological differences that the ordinary person feels only for events which threaten his immediate well-being, his family, or home. LUTHER P. GERLACH, in *Social Movements of the Sixties and Seventies* (Jo Freeman, ed.), 1983.

To the ideologist, reality has at last bared her secrets and the world is waiting for conquest by those who have the necessary knowledge that man himself is the ultimate creator of reality. Knowledge and power are joined in ideology in such a way that the only knowledge deserving of the name is that which is instrumental to attaining power and dominion over the environment and, ultimately, over man himself in his innermost being. Reality to ideological thought is something that needs to be "made up" rather than "made out." DANTE GERMINO, *The Revival of Political Theory,* 1967.

All ideologies are relative; the only absolute is the torment men inflict on each other. YEVGENIA GINSBERG.

It is a maxim of government to deal with men not as they ought to be but as they are. JOHANN WOLFGANG von GOETHE (1749–1832), quoted in *Conversations with Goethe* (Johann Peter Eckermann), 1833.

People who intensely believe in any extreme political ideology, whether left or right, are also likely to believe that some small groups conspire to achieve their evil ends by manipulating the social structure. WILLIAM J. GOODE, *The Celebration of Heroes,* 1978.

[Ideology is] those sets of beliefs which have or are meant to have wide implications for the conduct of political life and even, in some cases, for its complete refashioning. The principal instances are very familiar—socialism, liberalism, conservatism, nationalism, Marxism and fascism. GORDON GRAHAM, *Politics in Its Place,* 1986.

Modern ideologies and the simplicities of ideological thinking have developed to meet the needs of societies based on the conception of popular sovereignty and the general will. Their function is to make the people one in thought and action, to make them singular rather than plural. Their function is to displace the mind that thinks for itself, to afford the comfort of certainty where there is no certainty, to eliminate questioning. LOUIS J. HALLE, *The Ideological Imagination,* 1972.

If all men, accepting the principle of commitment, should surrender their minds to one or another of the rival ideologies that contend for dominance, mankind's most precious qualities would be lost, its most hopeful possibilities would be foreclosed, and perhaps earth would become a stage on which mindless hordes tore each other to pieces in the name of unquestionable truth. LOUIS J. HALLE, *The Ideological Imagination,* 1972.

It is not easy to define what gives a body of doctrine power over the minds of men in the mass. Especially for those who are unlearned and have intellectual pretensions, a vague immensity of conception, a high level of abstraction, and obscurity of language seems to be essential. LOUIS J. HALLE, *The Ideological Imagination,* 1972.

The intellectual is *engagé*—he is pledged, committed, enlisted. . . . [He feels imperatively] that ideas and abstractions are of signal importance in human life. RICHARD HOFSTADTER (1916–1970), *Anti-Intellectualism in American Life,* 1963.

The passionate partisanship of double standards also conflicts with conventional wisdom about intellectuals which attributes to them higher levels of rationality, objectivity, and detachment, and thus a lesser likelihood of being carried away by political passions and bias. It is always in the service of political commitments and to salvage political beliefs that double standards arise. . . . Correspondingly, moral indignation or outrage is stilled or inflamed depending not on what is done but who has done it. PAUL HOLLANDER, *Society,* July–August 1983.

[Ideology is] . . . a system of ideas concerned with the distribution of political and social values and acquiesced in by a significant social group. SAMUEL P. HUNTINGTON, *American Political Science Review,* vol. 51, June 1957.

An ideology is a complex of ideas or notions which represents itself to the thinker as an absolute truth for the interpretation of the world and his situation within it; it leads the thinker to accomplish an act of self-deception for the purpose of justification, obfuscation, evasion in some sense or other to his advantage. KARL JASPERS (1883–1969), *The Origin and Goal of History,* 1968.

In relation to their systems, most systematizers are like a man who builds an enormous castle and lives in a shack close by; they do not live in their own enormous systematic buildings. SØREN KIERKEGAARD (1813–1855), Journal, 1864.

Totalitarian ideologues share a general tendency to underestimate the difficulties of achieving social and cultural character change. The reason doubtless lies in their original assumption that the observed imperfections of man are the result of bad institutions. JEANE J. KIRKPATRICK, *Dictatorships and Double Standards,* 1982.

Almost every discussion with myth-addicts, whether public or private, is doomed to failure. The debate is from the beginning removed from the level of objectivity; arguments are not considered on their merit, but by whether they fit the system, and if not, how they can be made to fit. ARTHUR KOESTLER (1904–1983), *The Yogi and the Commissar,* 1945.

Changing ideas is a strain not to be lightly incurred, particularly when these ideas are intimately related to one's self-esteem . . . men have elaborated an explanation for their situation in life. . . . Their rationales are endowed with moral qualities. ROBERT E. LANE, *Political Ideology,* 1962.

Ideologies have consequences. The ideologies of a society shape its social and political institutions; when ideologies and institutions are more than normally out of phase, one may expect trouble. When men act without beliefs to justify and give meaning to their acts, they are coerced, confused, or moving like automatons through social routines, and, like automatons, are easily led to do something else. ROBERT E. LANE, *Political Ideology,* 1962.

An ideology, once accepted, perpetuates itself with remarkable vitality. The individuals born into the state direct some of their love toward the symbols which sustain the system. . . . Some destructive tendencies are directed against rivals, traitors, heresies, and counterdemands. HAROLD D. LASSWELL, *Politics: Who Gets What, When, How?,* 1936.

It is a fair criticism of many philosophies, and not only determinism, that they are hoist with their own petard. The Marxist who says that all ideologies have no independent validity and merely reflect the class interests of those who hold them can be told in that case his Marxist views merely express the economic interests of his class, and have no more claim to be adjudged true or valid than any other views. J. R. LUCAS, *The Freedom and the Will,* 1970.

[Ideology is] that peculiar disease of intellectuals, that infatuation with ideas at the expense of experience, that compels experience to conform to bookish expectations. ARCHIBALD MACLEISH (1892–1982).

Social movements can be seen as vehicles for personal crusades; those which do not build a base or structure that extends beyond the fiefdom of the leader may not last long. But . . . the resolution of a succession crisis may permit a movement to become a bureaucracy and thus perpetuate itself in the image of the founder. The founding leader may thus leave an indelible impression on a movement, and through it on society. WILLIAM McPHERSON, *Ideology and Change,* 1973.

The danger with the scholar's conceptual theory is that it suffers a constant tendency to abstraction, to remoteness from real life. . . . [T]he inherent logic of internal consistency is liable to become more important than correspondence with facts. JOHN MADGE, *The Tools of Social Science,* 1965.

Belief systems are . . . based on ideas that are held to be self-evidently true. And as they are self-evident there is obviously no need to prove that they are true. "To those who do not believe no explanation is possible." ANDREW MALCOLM, *The Tyranny of the Group,* 1975.

The distrust and suspicion which men everywhere evidence toward their adversaries, at all stages of historical development, may be regarded as the immediate precursor to the notion of ideology. KARL MANNHEIM (1893–1947), *Ideology and Utopia,* 1936.

Liberalism is virtually unique amongst ideologies in that it is addressed to all men regardless of race, class, religion, nationality or language. It is addressed to every man in the world as an individual and nothing else. D. J. MANNING, *Liberalism,* 1976.

[The] center of ideological understanding . . . consists in the view that the evils of life are not . . . part of an immemorial human condition which is beyond human power to change, or a set of problems to each of which a specific solution may be hazarded, as politicians often suggest, but that they are part of a single system of dehumanization which determines everything that happens, and which cannot be changed except by a complete transformation. KENNETH MINOGUE, *Alien Powers: The Pure Theory of Ideology,* 1985.

Ideology is systematically destructive of political ideas and values because it represents the imperfections of the human condition as the necessary deficiencies of an oppressive system, judging everything in terms of a concealed absolute constructed from the human essense itself. KENNETH MINOGUE, *Alien Powers: The Pure Theory of Ideology,* 1985.

Ideologies always stem from a real grievance, an intolerable situation, a threat. . . . Then someone elaborates a theory in the center of which is found that correction of the situation, a redress of the grievance. However, the theory concentrates so exclusively on the originating cause that it becomes one-sided, obliquely relevant to the entirety of man's situation. THOMAS MOLNAR, *Utopia: The Perennial Heresy,* 1967.

I distrust all systematizers, and avoid them. The will to a system shows a lack of honesty. FRIEDRICH NIETZSCHE (1844–1900), *Twilight of the Gods,* 1889.

Religious ideologies and their fanaticisms are dangerous enough, but when these or other ideologies become frenzied elements of the political area, the only area of absolute power over human lives . . . they become potentially dangerous in their impact on a free society. ROBERT NISBET, *Prejudices: A Philosophical Dictionary,* 1982.

No dogma or superstition in any religion yet uncovered by anthropologists is more tyrannical, and more intellectually absurd, than that of the historically inevitable or necessary. ROBERT NISBET, *Twilight of Authority,* 1981.

There is a natural crisis-mindedness, I think, among intellectuals generally; a fondness for the great changes and great decisions which the crisis of war makes possible. ROBERT NISBET, *Twilight of Authority,* 1981.

A political ideology purports to be an abstract principle, or set of related abstract principles, which has been independently premeditated. It supplies in advance of the activities of attending to the arrangements of a society a formulated end to be pursued, and in so doing it provides a means of distinguishing between those desires which ought to be encouraged and those which ought to be suppressed. MICHAEL OAKSHOTT, *Rationalism and Politics,* 1962.

For beliefs to be ideological . . . they must be shared by a group of people, the must concern matters important to the group, and must be in some way functional in relation to it: they must serve to hold it together or to justify activities and attitudes characteristic of its members. JOHN PLANENATZ, *Ideology,* 1970.

Ideology inhibits independent thinking and all the work that thinking entails; it offers support for like-minded folk who have also put their minds out to pasture. PETER S. PRESCOTT, *Newsweek,* October 10, 1988.

The word "ideologie," as introduced by Destutt de Tracy in 1796, refers to a program of reductive semantic analysis which aims to study the formation of ideas, their expression and combination in language and logic, and their application in economic, moral, and legal areas. DOUGLAS B. RASMUSSEN, in *Ideology and the American Experience* (Roth and Whittemore), 1986.

By "ideology" I mean here a system of ideas, values, and beliefs, both normative and allegedly factual, which purport to explain complex social phenomena and which also aid to justify and direct public policy and action. ANDREW J. RECK, in *Ideology and the American Experience* (Roth and Whittemore), 1986.

The fact that political ideologies are tangible realities is not a proof of their vitally necessary character. The bubonic plague was an extraordinarily powerful social reality, but no one would have regarded it as vitally necessary. WILHELM REICH (1897–1957), *The Mass Psychology of Fascism,* 1933.

Ideology refers to a more or less institutionalized set of beliefs—"the views someone picks up." Belief-disbelief systems contain those too but, in addition, they contain highly personalized pre-ideological beliefs. MILTON ROKEACH, *The Open and Closed Mind,* 1960.

The belief system is conceived to represent all the beliefs, sets, expectancies, or hypotheses, conscious and unconscious, that a person at a given time accepts as true of the world he lives in. MILTON ROKEACH, *The Open and Closed Mind,* 1960.

In ideological movements, time perspectives appear to be typically future-oriented. The past hardly exists, and the present is unimportant in its own right. The present is a vestibule to the future rather than something to be enjoyed and appreciated in its own right; it is a means to a future end rather than an end in itself. It is the future that counts and the suffering and injustice existing in the present is sometimes condoned, even glorified, for the sake of securing some future heaven, Utopia, promised land, Platonic or classless society. MILTON ROKEACH, *The Open and Closed Mind*, 1960.

Every philosopher knows that his own system rests on no surer foundations than the rest, but he maintains it because it is his own. There is not one of them who, if he chanced to discover the difference between truth and falsehood, would not prefer his own lie to the truth which another had discovered. JEAN-JACQUES ROUSSEAU (1712–1778), *Émile*, 1762.

We are now again in an epoch of wars of religion, but a religion is now called an "ideology." BERTRAND RUSSELL (1872–1970), *Unpopular Essays*, 1950.

Where a profound change in philosophy, ideology, or ethics occurs, the hidden but encompassing struggle is particularly significant. Thus conversion cannot be regarded as a sudden or dramatic event. LEON SALZMAN, *Psychiatry*, 1953.

An ideology is a value or belief system that is accepted as fact by some group. It is composed of sets of attitudes toward the various institutions and processes of society. It provides the believer with a picture of the world both as it is and as it should be, and in so doing, it organizes the tremendous complexity of the world into something fairly simple and understandable. LYMAN T. SARGENT, *Contemporary World Ideologies*, 1969.

An ideology or a belief system can be clearly distinguished from an individual's belief in something. An ideology must be a more or less interrelated collection of beliefs that provide the believer with a fairly thorough picture of the entire world. LYMAN T. SARGENT, *Contemporary World Ideologies*, 1969.

Activity proneness in the service of an ideology . . . leads the individual into an irreversible series of commitments from which is forged an identity to which the individual inevitably becomes strongly attached psychologically. EDGAR W. SCHEIN, *Coercive Persuasion*, 1961.

Liberalism regards all absolutes with profound skepticism, including both moral imperatives and final solutions. . . . Insistence upon any particular solution is the mark of an ideologue. . . . ARTHUR M. SCHLESINGER, JR., *The Crisis of Confidence*, 1969.

Historicism always implicitly carries within itself an immanent and secularized form of the doctrine of judgement. It sees value in historical events and institutions—and indeed in people—only in their quality of "leading up to" the real focus of the historicist's interest: whatever it is he says history is progressing toward. HERBERT SCHLOSSBERG, *Idols for Destruction*, 1990.

Neoconservatives tend to take things personally. Personal attacks are one of their specialities. . . . They tend to be very ideological, in the old Trotskyite tradition. The language is that of denunciation and manifestoes. It's not based on reason and compromise and civility. The world is divided between Us and Them. WILLIAM SCHNEIDER, *Washington Post*, February 2, 1987.

Every occurrence which will later acquire significance is constituted by a complex of tiny occurrences . . . which are drawn in a concentric irresistible motion toward an invisible center . . . no tiny occurrence is accidental, incidental, fortuitous—each part, however minute, has its purpose—and thus its justification—in the whole. And the whole in the parts. LEONARDO SCIASCIA, *The Moro Affair*.

We believe that our conclusions represent "eternal truths" because we are not certain that they in fact do. We believe because we are uncomfortable with doubts, for doubting—reinforced by the presence of other men and women who just as firmly believe in their competing ideologies—reminds us of our own uncertainties and the limited nature of our understanding. BUTLER D. SHAFFER, *Calculated Chaos*, 1985.

Political ideology is a form of thought that presents a pattern of complex political ideas simply and in a manner that inspires action to achieve certain goals. MAX SKIDMORE, *Ideologies: Politics in Action*, 1989.

The reason that ideology has been represented so often as a type of religiosity is, of course, a response to the terrifying fervor expressed by the member of modern mass-movements. It is the emotional element of Nazism, communism, and other revolutionary movements all over the world that is so reminiscent of many of the old popular heresies. JUDITH SKLAR, in *Utopias and Utopian Thought* (F. Manuel), 1966.

The man of system . . . is often so enamored with the supposed beauty of his ideal plan of government, that he cannot suffer the smallest deviation from any part of it. ADAM SMITH (1723–1790), *The Theory of Moral Sentiments*, 1759.

Around this theme of "proof" we have piled our confusions which have intensi-fied anxiety until some of us are unable to relate to anything. Instead, we try to find a system to fuse ourselves with, or spin our ideologies and chain ourselves to them. LILLIAN SMITH (1897–1966), *Killers of the Dream*, 1949.

What is striking about communist thinking—and about other "hard" ideologies that monopolize the social vision of their adherents—is that its argument proceeds in many respects under a momentum quite its own, producing political analysis and directives by virtue of the logic of its own categories of reasoning. TONY SMITH, *Thinking Like a Communist*, 1987.

A hard political ideology is "comprehensive" in that it offers a self-sufficient worldview able to explain in terms of an integrated set of axioms why virtually any significant social or historical event occurs as it does. "Fundamentalist" religions frequently offer equivalent perspectives, which may be why communism is so often referred to as a secular religion. TONY SMITH, *Thinking Like a Communist*, 1987.

The intellectual Communists seemed extremely interested in theory, very little in evidence which might conflict with theory. . . . The same disregard for scrupulousness in anything but theory applied to behavior. The ends justified the means. STEPHEN SPENDER, *The God That Failed*, 1949.

A resistance ideology, potentially an extremist position in its own right, often exists in opposition to social reform. Resistence groups evidence the same paranoid mode of thinking as do reforming extremists, although intellectual convictions are opposite. DAVID W. SWANSON et al., *The Paranoid*, 1970.

Ideologue: A person who uses ideas as incantations. **True believer:** A person who accepts incantations as ideas. Skeptic: A person who assumes that ideas are incantations until proven otherwise. THOMAS SZASZ, *The Untamed Tongue*, 1990.

An ideology corresponds to a basic set of attitudes: it is related to the unconscious and to family structure. A doctrine, on the other hand, is intellectually articulated but exists purely on a verbal level: it is a conscious phenomenon. EMMANUAL TODD, *The Explanation of Ideology*, 1985.

Ideology is not the product of thought; it is the habit or the ritual of showing respect for certain formulas which, for various reasons have to do with emotional safety, we have very strong ties of whose meaning and consequences we have no clear understanding. LIONEL TRILLING (1905–1975), *The Liberal Imagination*, 1950.

Every person we meet in the course of our daily life . . . is groping with sentences toward a sense of his life and his position in it; and he has what almost always goes with an impulse to ideology, a good deal of animus and anger. LIONEL TRILLING (1905–1975), *The Liberal Imagination*, 1950.

For the dream of a perfect society communism [Marxism-Leninism] substitutes the cult of the perfect Party. In it the fighter for socialism will find what he cannot realize on earth until the distant day of communism: perfect equality and infallible authority, brotherhood and discipline. ADAM ULAM, in *Utopias and Utopian Thought* (F. Manuel), 1966.

The actual content of the given ideology is of no consequence in regard to the reality created by acceptance of that ideology. PAUL WATZLAWICK, *The Invented Reality*, 1984.

Because the cosmic order is incomprehensible to the average man, an ideology is all the more convincing the more it relies upon an unusual, superhuman, or at least brilliant originator. PAUL WATZLAWICK, *The Invented Reality*, 1984.

The idea of possessing the ultimate truth first leads to a messianic attitude that clutches the belief that the truth qua truth will prevail in and of itself. At this point the Champion of an ideology may still believe in the teachability or in the possibility of convincing the heretic. But because the world soon proves to be obdurate, unwilling, or unable to open up to the truth, the next inevitable step results in what Hermann Lubbe calls the self-authorization to use violence. PAUL WATZLAWICK, *The Invented Reality*, 1984.

It follows from the assumption of a universally valid ideology, just as night follows day, that other positions are heresy. PAUL WATZLAWICK, *The Invented Reality,* 1984.

Ideology carries satisfactions, even if it is not totally credible. Symbols carry much weight; people like to have answers to the big questions, whether the answers help them materially or not. . . . Whatever the psychological power of ideology, its specific content and ideas are much less significant than they are frequently made to seem. . . . An ideological movement soon finds that persuasion alone does not suffice, and it must offer firmer reasons for obedience. ROBERT WESSON, *Politics: Individual and State,* 1988.

Ideology . . . gives significance to the lives of individuals who might otherwise be overwhelmed by a sense of purposelessness and insignificance. Usually some kind of black-and-white picture is an inherent part of the ideology, and gives meaning to the struggle between the good guys and the bad guys. . . . RALPH K. WHITE, *Nobody Wanted War,* 1968.

Individual Liberties and Personal Freedom

By liberty I mean the assurance that every man shall be protected in doing what he believes his duty against the influence of authority and majorities, custom and opinion. LORD ACTON (1834–1902), *The History of Freedom in Antiquity.*

Be not intimidated . . . nor suffer yourselves to be wheedled out of your liberties by any pretenses of politeness, delicacy, or decency. These, as they are often used, are but three different names for hypocrisy, chicanery and cowardice. JOHN ADAMS (1732–1826), 1765.

Driven from every corner of the earth, Freedom of Thought and The Right of Private Judgment in matters of conscience direct their course to this happy country as their last asylum. SAMUEL ADAMS (1722–1803), Speech, 1776.

Mankind is at its best when it is most free. This will be clear if we grasp the principle of liberty. We must recall that the basic principle is freedom of choice, which saying many have on their lips but few in their mind. DANTE ALIGHIERI (1265–1321), *On Monarchy,* 1309.

For what is liberty but the unhampered translation of will into act. DANTE ALIGHIERI (1265–1321), Letters.

A free and open society is an ongoing conflict, interrupted periodically by compromises. SAUL ALINSKY (1909–1972), *Rules for Radicals,* 1971.

Liberty means that a man is recognized as free and treated as free by those who surround him. MIKHAIL A. BAKUNIN (1814–1876), *God and the State,* 1871.

Intellectual slavery, of whatever nature it may be, will always have as a natural result both political and social slavery. MIKHAIL A. BAKUNIN (1814–1876), *Federalism, Socialism and Anti-Theologism,* 1868.

The notion that the church, the press, and the universities should serve the state is essentially a Communist notion. In a free society these institutions must be wholly free—which is to say that their function is to serve as checks upon the state. ALAN BARTH, *The Loyalty of Free Men,* 1951.

[Natural rights are] moral claims to those spheres of action which are necessary for the welfare of the individual and the development of his personality. M. SEARLE BATES (1897–1978), *Religious Liberty: An Inquiry,* 1945.

One of the best ways to get yourself a reputation as a dangerous citizen these days is to go about repeating the very phrases which our founding fathers used in the great struggle for independence. CHARLES A. BEARD (1874–1948), 1935.

False is the idea of utility that sacrifices a thousand real advantages for one imaginary or trifling inconvenience; that would take fire from men because it burns, and water because one may drown in it; that has no remedy for evils, except destruction. The laws that forbid the carrying of arms are laws of such a nature. They disarm only those who [are] neither inclined nor determined to commit crimes. CESARE BECCARIA (1738–1794), *On Crimes and Punishments*, 1764.

Liberty is the soul's right to breathe. HENRY WARD BEECHER (1813–1887), *Life Thoughts*, 1858.

Civilization exists precisely so that there may be no masses but rather men alert enough never to constitute masses. GEORGES BERNANOS (1888–1948), *Last Essays of George Bernanos*, 1955.

Freedom of the mind requires not only, or not even specially, the absence of legal constraints but the presence of alternative thoughts. The most successful tyranny is not the one that uses force to assure uniformity but the one that removes the awareness of other possibilities. ALAN BLOOM (1930–1992), *The Closing of the American Mind*, 1987.

The free man is he who does not fear to go to the end of his thought. LEON BLUM (1872–1950).

The right to be alone—the most comprehensive of rights, and the right most valued by civilized men. LOUIS B. BRANDEIS (1856–1941), U.S. Supreme Court Justice, *Olmstead* v. *United States*, 1928.

Those who won our independence believed that the final end of the State was to make men free to develop their faculties. . . . They valued liberty both as an end and as a means. They believed liberty to be the secret of happiness and courage to be the secret of liberty. LOUIS D. BRANDEIS (1856–1941), U.S. Supreme Court Justice, *Whitney* v. *California*, 1927.

None who have always been free can understand the terrible fascinating power of the hope of freedom to those who are not free. PEARL S. BUCK (1892–1973), *What America Means to Me*, 1943.

Personal liberty is the paramount essential to human dignity and human happiness. EDWARD GEORGE BULWER-LYTTON (1803–1873).

Without bigots, eccentrics, cranks and heretics the world would not progress. FRANK GELETT BURGESS (1866–1951).

The true danger is when liberty is nibbled away, for expedients, and by parts. EDMUND BURKE (1729–1797), Letter to the Sheriffs of Bristol, April 3, 1777.

Among a people generally corrupt, liberty cannot long exist. EDMUND BURKE (1729–1797), Letter to the Sheriffs of Bristol, 3 April 1777.

The people never give up their liberties but under some delusion. EDMUND BURKE (1729–1797), Speech, 1784.

He that complies against his will is of his opinion still. SAMUEL BUTLER (1612–1680), *Hudibras,* 1664.

When we regard a man as morally responsible for an act, we regard him as a legitimate object of moral praise or blame in respect of it. But if seems plain that a man cannot be a legitimate object of moral praise or blame for an act unless in willing the act he is in some important sense a 'free' agent. Evidently free will in some sense, therefore, is a precondition of moral responsibility. C. ARTHUR CAMPBELL, *In Defence of Free Will,* 1967.

Men seldom, or rather never for a length of time and deliberately, rebel against anything that does not deserve rebelling against. THOMAS CARLYLE (1795–1881).

No iron chain, or outward force of any kind, could ever compel the soul of man to believe or disbelieve. THOMAS CARLYLE (1795–1881), *The French Revolution,* 1837.

We must get rid of fear; we cannot act at all till then. A man's acts are slavish, not true but specious; his very thoughts are false, he thinks too as a slave and coward, till he have got fear under his feet. THOMAS CARLYLE (1795–1881), *The French Revolution,* 1837.

The Republic may not give wealth or happiness; she has not promised these. It is the freedom to pursue these, not their realization, which the Declaration of Independence claims. ANDREW CARNEGIE (1835–1919), *Triumphant Democracy,* 1886.

The revolt against individualism naturally calls artists severely to account, because the artist is of all men the most individual: those who were not have been long forgotten. WILLA CATHER (1873–1947), *On Writing.*

I call the mind free which jealously guards its intellectual rights and powers, which calls no man master, which does not content itself with a passive or hereditary faith, [and] receives new truth as an angel from Heaven. WILLIAM ELLERY CHANNING (1780–1842), *Spiritual Freedom,* 1848.

Freedom suppressed and again regained bites with keener fangs than freedom never endangered. MARCUS TULLIUS CICERO (106–43 B.C.).

Machines from the Maxim gun to the computer, are for the most part means by which a minority can keep free men in subjection. KENNETH CLARK (1903–1983), *Civilisation,* 1970.

A right is not what someone gives you; it's what no one can take from you. RAMSEY CLARK, U.S. Attorney General, *New York Times,* October 2, 1977.

Small groups or communities may be far more oppressive to the individual than larger ones. Men are in many ways freer in large cities than in small villages. MORRIS R. COHEN (1880–1947), *Reason and Nature,* 1931.

A free society cherishes nonconformity. It knows that from the non-conformist, from the eccentric, have come many of the great ideas. . . . HENRY STEELE COMMAGER, *Freedom, Loyalty and Dissent,* 1954.

The American people . . . have a stake in nonconformity, for they know that the American genius is nonconformist. HENRY STEELE COMMAGER, *Harper's Magazine,* September 1947.

Freedom is not a luxury that we can indulge in when at last we have security and prosperity and enlightenment; it is, rather, antecedent to all of these, for without it we can have neither security nor prosperity nor enlightenment. HENRY STEELE COMMAGER, *Freedom, Loyalty and Dissent,* 1954.

Liberty is not collective, it is personal. All liberty is individual liberty. CALVIN COOLIDGE (1872–1933), U.S. President, Speech, 1924.

Individuality is the aim of political liberty. By leaving to the citizen as much freedom of action and of being as comports with order and the rights of others, the institutions render him truly a free man. He is left to pursue his means of happiness in his own manner. JAMES FENIMORE COOPER (1789–1851), *The American Democrat,* 1838.

There is a moment when individualism becomes a uniform in spite of itself. MALCOLM COWLEY.

It is always the task of the intellectual to "think otherwise." This is not just a perverse idiosyncrasy. It is an absolutely essential feature of a society. HARVEY COX, *The Secular City,* 1966.

It will be found an unjust and unwise jealousy to deprive a man of his natural liberty upon a supposition that he may abuse it. OLIVER CROMWELL (1599–1658).

You can only protect your liberties in this world by protecting the other man's freedom. You can only be free if I am free. CLARENCE S. DARROW (1857–1938), Address, Communist Trial, 1920.

This nation was conceived in liberty and dedicated to the principle—among others—that honest men may honestly disagree; that if they all say what they think, a majority of the people will be able to distinguish truth from error; that in the competition of the marketplace of ideas, the sounder ideas will win. ELMER DAVIS (1890–1958), *But We Were Born Free,* 1954.

Democracy means freeing intelligence for independent effectiveness—the emancipation of mind as an individual organ to do its own work. We naturally associate democracy, to be sure, with freedom of action, but freedom of action without freed capacity of thought behind it is only chaos. JOHN DEWEY (1859–1952), *The Elementary School Teacher,* December 1903.

The privacy and dignity of our citizens [are] being whittled away by sometimes imperceptible steps. Taken individually, each step may be of little consequence. But when viewed as a whole, there begins to emerge a society quite unlike any we have seen—a society in which government may intrude into the secret regions of a [person's] life. WILLIAM O. DOUGLAS (1898–1980), U.S. Supreme Court Justice, Dissenting opinion, *Osborne* v. *United States,* 385 U.S. 323.

The right to be let alone is indeed the beginning of all freedoms. WILLIAM O. DOUGLAS (1898–1980), U.S. Supreme Court Justice, *Public Utilities Commission* v. *Pollack,* 1952.

We are rapidly entering the age of no privacy, where everyone is open to surveillance at all times; where there are no secrets from government. WILLIAM O. DOUGLAS (1898–1980), U.S. Supreme Court Justice, *Osborn* v. *U.S.,* 1966.

Among the liberties of citizens that are guaranteed are . . . the right to believe what one chooses, the right to differ from his neighbor, the right to pick and choose the political philosophy that he likes best, the right to associate with whomever he chooses, the right to join groups he prefers. . . . WILLIAM O. DOUGLAS (1898–1980), U.S. Supreme Court Justice, 1958.

Ideas are indeed the most dangerous weapons in the world. Our ideas of freedom are the most powerful political weapons man has ever forged. WILLIAM O. DOUGLAS (1898–1980), *An Almanac of Liberty.*

The great and invigorating influences in American life have been the unorthodox: the people who challenge an existing institution or way of life, or say and do things that make people think. WILLIAM O. DOUGLAS (1898–1980), Interview, 1958.

I didn't know I was a slave until I found out I couldn't do what I wanted. FREDERICK DOUGLASS (1817–1895), *Narrative of the Life of Frederick Douglass,* 1845.

Of all the tyrannies on human kind, / the worst is that which persecutes the mind. JOHN DRYDEN (1631–1700), *The Hind and the Panther,* 1687.

The real guarantee of freedom is an equilibrium of social forces in conflict, not the triumph of any one force. MAX EASTMAN (1883–1969), *Reflections on the Failure of Socialism,* 1955.

But we know that freedom cannot be served by the devices of the tyrant. As it is an ancient truth that freedom cannot be legislated into existence, so it is no less obvious that freedom cannot be censored into existence. And any who act as if freedom's defenses are to be found in suppression and suspicion and fear confess a doctrine that is alien to America. DWIGHT D. EISENHOWER (1890–1969), U.S. President, Letter, June 24, 1953.

Society everywhere is in conspiracy against the manhood of every one of its members. The virtue in most demand is conformity. Self-reliance is its aversion. It loves not realities and creators, but names and customs. RALPH WALDO EMERSON (1803–1882).

Man exists for his own sake and not to add a laborer to the State. RALPH WALDO EMERSON (1803–1882), Journal, 1839.

No man is wholly free. He is a slave to wealth, or to fortune, or the laws, or the people restrain him from acting according to his will alone. EURIPIDES (480–405 B.C.), *Hecuba*, 426 B.C.

We must be free not because we claim freedom, but because we practice it. WILLIAM FAULKNER (1897–1962), *Harper's Magazine*, June 1956.

We must not overlook the role that extremists play. They are the gadflies that keep society from being too complacent. ABRAHAM FLEXNER (1866–1959), *Universities*, 1930.

Two cheers for democracy; one because it admits variety and two because it permits criticism. E. M. FORSTER (1879–1970), *Two Cheers for Democracy*, 1951.

The mark of a truly civilized man is confidence in the strength and security derived from the inquiring mind. FELIX FRANKFURTER (1882–1965), U.S. Supreme Court Justice, *Dennis* v. *United States*, 1950.

It was a wise man who said that there is no greater inequality than the equal treatment of unequals. FELIX FRANKFURTER (1882–1965), U.S. Supreme Court Justice, *Dennis* v. *United States*, 1950.

In those wretched countries where a man cannot call his tongue his own, he can scarce call anything his own. Whoever would overthrow the liberty of a nation must begin by subduing the freeness of speech. BENJAMIN FRANKLIN (1706–1790), *Dogwood Papers*.

Those who would give up essential liberty to purchase a little temporary safety, deserve neither liberty nor safety. BENJAMIN FRANKLIN (1706–1790), November 11, 1755.

Without freedom of thought, there can be no such thing as wisdom; and no such thing as public liberty, without freedom of speech. BENJAMIN FRANKLIN (1706–1790).

A society that puts equality . . . ahead of freedom will end up with neither equality nor freedom. MILTON FRIEDMAN and ROSE FRIEDMAN, *Free to Choose*, 1979.

The member of a primitive clan might express his identity in the formula "I am we"; he cannot yet conceive of himself as an "individual," existing apart from his group. ERICH FROMM (1900–1980).

To deny the freedom of the will is to make morality impossible. J. A. FROUDE (1818–1894), *Calvinism*.

A natural right to liberty, irrespective of the ability to defend it, exists in nations as much as and no more than it exists in individuals. J. A. FROUDE (1818–1894), *The English in Ireland in the Eighteenth Century*, 1872.

Most human beings are capable of achieving the measure of autonomy and mature individuality required by our conceptions of individual dignity and worth. But certain kinds of separation of the self from all that is beyond the self are inherently destructive and intolerable to human beings. JOHN W. GARDNER, *Self-Renewal,* 1964.

No person shall rule over me with my consent. I will rule over no man. WILLIAM LLOYD GARRISON (1805–1879).

Every man who rises above the common level has received two educations: the first from his teachers; the second, more personal and important, from himself. EDWARD GIBBON (1737–1794), *Memoirs,* 1795.

Unless men are taught to rely upon themselves they can never be truly worthy of freedom. WILLIAM E. GLADSTONE (1809–1898), Prime Minister of England, Speech, April 26, 1870.

The individual is the true reality of life. A cosmos in himself, he does not exist for the State, nor for that abstraction called "society," or the "nation," which is only a collection of individuals. EMMA GOLDMAN (1869–1940), *The Place of the Individual in Society.*

Laissez faire, laissez passer (Liberty of action, liberty of movement). JEAN CLAUDE VINCENT de GOURNAY (1712–1759), 1758.

The doctrine of blind obedience and unqualified submission to any human power, whether civil or ecclesiastical, is the doctrine of despotism, and ought to have no place among Republicans and Christians. ANGELICA GRIMKE (1805–1879), *Anti-Slavery Examiner,* September 1836.

If what is best in mankind, and what its progress depends on, manifests itself primarily in the individual and only secondarily in the mass, then our objectives should be to maintain such freedom as allows the individual to think and speak for himself. LOUIS J. HALLE, *The Ideological Imagination,* 1972.

The revolt against freedom, which can be traced back so far, is associated with a revolt against reason that [gives] sentiment primacy, to evaluate actions and experiences according to the subjective emotions with which they are associated. LOUIS J. HALLE, *The Ideological Imagination,* 1972.

The social molds civilization fits us into have no more relation to our actual shapes than the conventional shapes of the constellations have to real star patterns. THOMAS HARDY (1840–1928), *Jude the Obscure,* 1895.

Socialism was embraced by the greater part of the intelligentsia as the apparent heir to the liberal tradition: therefore it is not suprising that to them the idea of socialism's leading to the opposite of liberty should appear inconceivable. FRIEDRICH A. HAYEK (1899–1992), *The Road to Serfdom,* 1944.

I hate to be near the sea, and to hear it raging and roaring like a wild beast in its pen. It puts me in mind of the everlasting efforts of the human mind, struggling to be free and ending just where it began. WILLIAM HAZLITT (1778–1830), *Characteristics*, 1823.

We hold that the greatest right in the world is the right to be wrong, that in the exercise thereof people have an inviolable right to express their unbridled thoughts on all topics and personalities, being liable only for the use of that right. WILLIAM RANDOLPH HEARST (1863–1951), *New York Journal.*

Freedom is the fundamental character of the will, as weight is of matter. . . . That which is free is the will. Will without freedom is an empty word. GEORG WILHELM FRIEDRICH HEGEL (1770–1831), 1821.

The history of the world is none other than the progress of the consciousness of freedom. GEORG WILHELM FRIEDRICH HEGEL (1770–1831), Introduction to *The Philosophy of History*, 1832.

Radicals are only to be feared when you try to suppress them. You must demonstrate that you will use the best of what they offer. FRANK HERBERT, *Dune*, 1965.

Laws to suppress tend to strengthen what they would prohibit. This is the fine point on which all the legal professions of history have based their job security. FRANK HERBERT, *Dune*, 1965.

Seek freedom and become captive to your desires. Seek discipline and find your liberty. FRANK HERBERT, *Dune*, 1965.

The liberty of the individual is the greatest thing of all, it is on this and this alone that the true will of the people can develop. ALEXANDER IVANOVICH HERZEN (1812–1870), *From the Other Shore*, 1849.

The sooner we all learn to make a decision between disapproval and censorship, the better off society will be. . . . Censorship cannot get at the real evil, and it is an evil in itself. GRANVILLE HICKS.

The National Socialist party will prevent in the future, by force if necessary, all meetings and lectures which are likely to exercise a depressing influence on the German state. ADOLF HITLER (1889–1945), Speech, January 4, 1921.

A free man is he that, in those things which by his strength and wit he is able to do, is not hindered to do what he has a will to. THOMAS HOBBES (1588–1679), *Leviathan*, 1651.

Excess of liberty contradicts itself. In short there is no such thing: there is only liberty for one and restraint for another. LEONARD T. HOBHOUSE (1864–1929), *Social Evolution and Political Theory*, 1911.

The tendency of all strong governments has always been to suppress liberty, partly in order to ease the processes of rule, partly from sheer disbelief in innovation. JOHN A. HOBSON (1858–1940), *Free Thought in the Social Sciences*, 1926.

There can be no freedom without freedom to fail. ERIC HOFFER (1902–1983), *The Ordeal of Change*, 1964.

A university's essential character is that of being a center of free inquiry and criticism—a thing not to be sacrificed for anything else. RICHARD HOFSTADTER (1916–1970), 1968 Commencement Address, Columbia University.

To prevent inquiry is among the worst of evils. THOMAS HOLCROFT (1745–1816), *The Adventures of Hugh Trevor*, 1794.

There never was an idea stated that woke men out of their stupid indifference but its originator was spoken of as a crank. OLIVER WENDELL HOLMES, SR. (1809–1884), *Over the Teacups*, 1891.

Liberty is often a heavy burden on a man. It involves the necessity for perpetual choice which is the kind of labor men have always dreaded. OLIVER WENDELL HOLMES, SR. (1809–1884), *Elsie Venner*, 1861.

If there is any principle of the Constitution that more imperatively calls for attachment than any other it is the principle of free thought—not free thought for those who agree with us but freedom for the thought that we hate. OLIVER WENDELL HOLMES, JR. (1841–1935), U.S. Supreme Court Justice, *U.S.* v. *Schwimmer*, 1928.

Honest difference of views and honest debate are not disunity. They are the vital process of policy among free men. HERBERT CLARK HOOVER (1874–1964), U.S. President, Speech, 1950.

Freedom conceives that the mind and spirit of man can be free only if he is free to pattern his own life, to develop his own talents, free to earn, to spend, to save, to acquire property as the security of his old age and his family. HERBERT CLARK HOOVER (1874–1964), U.S. President, *Addresses upon the American Road.*

Who, then, is free? The wise who can command his passions, who fears not want, nor death, nor chains, firmly resisting his appetites and despising the honors of the world, who relies wholly on himself, whose angular points of character have all been rounded off and polished. HORACE (65 B.C.–8 B.C.), *Satires*, 25 B.C.

An idea that is not dangerous is unworthy of being called an idea at all. ELBERT G. HUBBARD (1856–1915).

When we lose the right to be different, we lose the privilege to be free. CHARLES EVANS HUGHES (1862–1948), U.S. Supreme Court Justice, Speech, June 17, 1925.

Our institutions were not devised to bring about uniformity of opinion; if they had been we might well abandon hope. It is important to remember, as has well been said, "the essential characteristic of true liberty is that under its shelter many different types of life and character and opinion and belief can develop unmolested and unobstructed." CHARLES EVANS HUGHES (1862–1948), U.S. Supreme Court Justice, *Forbes* magazine, November 1, 1957.

I believe the State exists for the development of individual lives, not individuals for the development of the state. JULIAN HUXLEY (1887–1975).

The most dangerous foe to truth and freedom in our midst is that compact majority, yes, the damned compact liberal majority. HENRIK IBSEN (1826–1906).

The strongest man is the one who stands most alone. HENRIK IBSEN (1826–1906), *An Enemy of the People,* 1882.

The enemies of freedom do not argue; they shout and they shoot. WILLIAM RALPH INGE (1860–1954), *The End of an Age.*

Intellectual liberty is the air of the soul, the sunshine of the mind, and without it, the world is a prison, the universe is a dungeon. ROBERT G. INGERSOLL (1833–1899), "Some Reasons Why."

Mental slavery is mental death, and every man who has given up his intellectual freedom is the living coffin of his dead soul. ROBERT G. INGERSOLL (1833–1899).

By physical liberty I mean the right to do anything which does not interfere with the happiness of another. By intellectual liberty I mean the right to think and the right to think wrong. ROBERT G. INGERSOLL (1833–1899).

The man who does not do his own thinking is a slave, and is a traitor to himself and his fellow-men. ROBERT G. INGERSOLL (1833–1899).

Heresy is what the minority believe; it is the name given by the powerful to the doctrines of the weak. ROBERT G. INGERSOLL (1833–1899), *Heretics and Heresies.*

There is no such thing as an achieved liberty: like electricity, there can be no substantial storage and it must be generated as it is enjoyed, or the lights go out. ROBERT H. JACKSON (1892–1954), U.S. Supreme Court Justice, *American Bar Association Journal,* 1953.

I tolerate with utmost latitude the right of others to differ with me in opinion without imputing to them criminality. I know too well all the weaknesses and uncertainty of human reason to wonder at its different results. THOMAS JEFFERSON (1743–1826), U.S. President, Letter To Mrs. Adams, 1804.

All, too, will bear in mind this sacred principle, that though the will of the majority is in all cases to prevail, that will, to be rightful, must be reasonable; that the minority possess their equal rights, which equal laws must protect, and to violate which would be oppression. THOMAS JEFFERSON (1743–1826), U.S. President, First Inaugural Address, March 4, 1801.

We hold these truths to be self-evident: that all men are created equal; that they are endowed by their Creator with certain unalienable rights; that among these are life, liberty, and the pursuit of happiness. THOMAS JEFFERSON (1743–1826), Declaration of Independence, 1776.

I would rather be exposed to the inconveniencies attending too much liberty than those attending too small a degree of it. THOMAS JEFFERSON (1743–1826), Letter, December 23, 1791.

It behooves every man who values liberty of conscience for himself, to resist invasions of it in the case of others; or their case may, by change of circumstances, become his own. THOMAS JEFFERSON (1743–1826), Letter, April 21, 1803.

We are reluctant to admit that we owe our liberties to men of a type that today we hate and fear—unruly men, disturbers of the peace, men who resent and denounce what Whitman called "the insolence of elected persons"—in a word, free men. . . . Freedom is always purchased at a great price, and even those who are willing to pay it have to admit that the price is great. GERALD W. JOHNSON (1890–1980), *American Freedom and the Press,* 1958.

They make a point about universal liberty, without considering that all that is to be valued, or indeed can be enjoyed by individuals, is private liberty. SAMUEL JOHNSON (1709–1784), in Boswell's *Life of Johnson,* 1791.

All theory is against the freedom of the will; all experience for it. SAMUEL JOHNSON (1709–1784), in Boswell's *Life of Johnson,* 1791.

Resistance to the organized mass can be effected only by the man who is as well organized in his individuality as the mass itself. CARL GUSTAV JUNG (1875–1961).

A shoe that fits one person pinches another; there is no recipe for living that suits all cases. CARL GUSTAV JUNG (1875–1961), *Modern Man in Search of a Soul,* 1933.

Freedom is independence of the compulsory will of another, and in so far as it tends to exist with the freedom of all according to a universal law, it is the one sole original inborn right belonging to every man in virtue of his humanity. IMMANUEL KANT (1724–1804).

Freedom is the faculty which enlarges the usefulness of all other faculties. IMMANUEL KANT (1724–1804), Lecture, 1775.

As long as man remains an inquiring animal, there can never be a complete unanimity in our fundamental beliefs. The more diverse our paths, the greater is likely to be the divergence of beliefs. SIR ARTHUR KEITH (1866–1927).

Security is mostly a superstition. It does not exist in nature, nor do the children of men as a whole experience it. Avoiding danger is no safer in the long run than outright exposure. Life is either a daring adventure, or nothing. HELEN KELLER (1880–1968), *The Open Door,* 1957.

The wave of the future is not the conquest of the world by a single dogmatic creed but the liberation of the diverse energies of free nations and free men. JOHN FITZGERALD KENNEDY (1917–1963), U.S. President, Speech, University of California, March 23, 1963.

In a free society art is not a weapon. . . . Artists are not engineers of the soul. JOHN FITZGERALD KENNEDY (1917–1963), U.S. President, 1963.

Conformity is the jailer of freedom and the enemy of growth. JOHN F. KENNEDY (1917–1963), U.S. President, U.N. General Assembly, September 25, 1961.

At the heart of western freedom and democracy is the belief that the individual man . . . is the touchstone of value, and all society, groups, the state, exist for his benefit. Therefore the enlargement of liberty for individual human beings must be the supreme goal and the abiding practice of any western society. ROBERT F. KENNEDY (1925–1968), Speech, University of Capetown, June 6, 1966.

True individualists tend to be quite unobservant; it is the snob, the . . . sophisticate, the frightened conformist, who keeps a fascinated or worried eye on what is in the wind. LOUIS KRONENBERGER (1904–1980), *Company Manners*, 1954.

Are we not all slaves, occasionally? To custom? To a situation? To an idea? Who among us is truly free? LOUIS L'AMOUR (1908–1988), *The Walking Drum*, 1984.

The love of justice is, in most men, nothing more than the fear of suffering justice. FRANÇOIS, DUC de LA ROCHEFOUCAULD (1613–1680), *Maxims.*

The only real security for social well-being is the free exercise of men's minds. HAROLD J. LASKI (1893–1950), *Authority in the Modern State*, 1919.

Every State is known by the rights it maintains. HAROLD J. LASKI (1893–1950), *A Grammar of Politics*, 1925.

Men are freest when they are most unconscious of freedom. The shout is a rattling of chains and always was. D. H. LAWRENCE (1885–1930).

Men fight for liberty and win it with hard knocks. Their children, brought up easy, let it slip away again, poor fools. And their grand-children are once more slaves. D. H. LAWRENCE (1885–1938), 1915.

No truly sophisticated proponent of repression would be stupid enough to shatter the facade of democratic institutions. MURRAY B. LEVIN, *Political Hysteria in America*, 1971.

This is a world of compensation; and he who would be no slave must consent to have no slave. Those who deny freedom to others, deserve it not for themselves. ABRAHAM LINCOLN (1809–1865), U.S. President, Speech, 1856.

Private property was the original source of freedom. It still is its main bulwark. WALTER LIPPMANN (1889–1974), *An Inquiry into the Principles of a Good Society*, 1937.

In a free society the state does not administer the affairs of men. It administers justice among men who conduct their own affairs. WALTER LIPPMANN (1889–1974), *An Inquiry into the Principles of the Good Society*, 1937.

No man is entitled to the blessings of freedom unless he be vigilant in its preservation. DOUGLAS MACARTHUR (1880–1964), *MacArthur: A Soldier Speaks.* 1965.

What is freedom? Freedom is the right to choose; the right to create for yourself the alternatives of choice. Without the responsibility and exercise of choice a man is not a man but a member, an instrument, a thing. ARCHIBALD MACLEISH (1892–1982).

The dissenter is every human being at those times of his life when he resigns momentarily from the herd and thinks for himself. ARCHIBALD MACLEISH (1892–1982), December 4, 1937.

Freedom is not a fixed and possessed thing. It is a quality of life. And like action itself, it is something experienced only by individuals. NEIL A. McDONALD, *Politics: A Study of Control Behavior,* 1965.

I believe there are more instances of the abridgement of the freedom of the people by gradual and silent encroachments of those in power than by violent and sudden ursurpations. JAMES MADISON (1751–1836), U.S. President, Speech, June 16, 1788.

He is free who knows how to keep in his own hands the power to decide, at each step, the course of his life, and who lives in a society which does not block the exercise of that power. SALVADOR de MADARIAGA (1886–1978), *New York Times,* January 29, 1957.

The classic liberal understanding of freedom is this: every individual should care for his own interests and mind his own business. No one should deem himself his brother's keeper unless his brother unequivocally asks him to. Every individual is a world unto himself, is a being in himself and is presupposed to be the best judge of his own affairs; everyone should respect the wishes, beliefs, and way of life of others. . . . MIESZYSLAW MANELI, *Freedom and Tolerance,* 1984.

To change masters is not to be free. JOSÉ MARTI y PÉREZ (1853–1895).

Morality cannot exist one minute without freedom. . . . Only a free man can possibly be moral. Unless a good deed is voluntary, it has no moral significance. EVERETT DEAN MARTIN, *Liberty,* 1930.

If a nation values anything more than freedom, it will lose its freedom; and the irony of it is that if it is comfort or money that it values more, it will lose that, too. W. SOMERSET MAUGHAM (1874–1965), *Strictly Personal,* 1941.

Whatever the immediate gains and losses, the dangers to our safety arising from political suppression are always greater than the dangers to that safety resulting from political freedom. Suppression is always foolish. Freedom is always wise. ALEXANDER MEIKLEJOHN (1872–1964), 1955.

Human progress is furthered, not by conformity, but by aberration. H. L. MENCKEN (1880–1956), *Prejudices: Third Series,* 1922.

The whole drift of our law is toward the absolute prohibition of all ideas that diverge in the slightist form from the accepted platitudes, and behind that drift of law there is a far more potent force of growing custom, and under that custom there is a natural philosophy which erects conformity into the noblest of virtues and the free functioning of personality into a capital crime against society. H. L. MENCKEN (1880–1956), quoted in *New York Times Magazine,* August 9, 1964.

Eccentricity has always abounded when and where strength of character has abounded; and the amount of eccentricity in a society has generally been proportional to the amount of genius, mental vigor, and moral courage which it contained. JOHN STUART MILL (1806–1873), *On Liberty,* 1859.

There is never any fair and thorough discussion of heretical opinions. . . . The greatest harm done is to those who are not heretics, and whose whole mental development is cramped and their reason cowed, by the fear of heresy. JOHN STUART MILL (1806–1873), *On Liberty,* 1859.

Mankind are greater gainers by suffering each other to live as seems good to themselves, than by compelling each to live as seems good to the rest. JOHN STUART MILL (1806–1873), *On Liberty,* 1859.

The only freedom which deserves the name, is that of pursuing our own good in our own way, so long as we do not attempt to deprive others of theirs, or impede their efforts to obtain it. JOHN STUART MILL (1806–1873), *On Liberty,* 1859.

The only purpose for which power can be rightfully exercised over any member of a civilised community, against his will, is to prevent harm to others. His own good, either physical or moral, is not a sufficient warrant. JOHN STUART MILL (1806–1873), *On Liberty,* 1859.

Whatever crushes individuality is despotism, by whatever name it may be called. JOHN STUART MILL (1806), *On Liberty,* 1859.

No man is great enough or wise enough for any of us to surrender our destiny to. The only way in which anyone can lead us is to restore to the belief in our own guidance. HENRY MILLER (1891–1980), *The Wisdom of the Heart,* 1941.

Let us by wise and constitutional measures promote intelligence among the people as the best means of preserving our liberties. JAMES MONROE (1758–1831), U.S. President, First Inaugural Address, March 4, 1817.

Once conform, once do what others do because they do it, and a kind of lethargy steals over all the finer senses of the soul. MICHEL de MONTAIGNE (1532–1592), *Essays,* 1588.

A man must keep a little back shop where he can be himself without reserve. In solitude alone can he know true freedom. MICHEL de MONTAIGNE (1532–1592), *Essays,* 1588.

No one can be free unless he is independent. . . . In reality, he who is served is limited in his independence. . . . MARIA MONTESSORI (1870–1952).

If none of us ever read a book that was "dangerous," had a friend who was "different" or joined an organization that advocated "change," we would all be just the kind of people Joe McCarthy wants. Whose fault is that? Not really [McCarthy's]. He didn't create this situation of fear. He merely exploited it, and rather successfully. EDWARD R. MURROW (1908–1965), "See It Now," CBS TV, March 7, 1954.

Liberty is not an end, it is a means. As a means, it needs to be controlled and dominated. BENITO MUSSOLINI (1883–1945), Speech, 1922.

Against individualism, the fascist conception is for the State; and it is for the individual in so far as he coincides with the State, which is the conscience and universal will of man in his historical experience. BENITO MUSSOLINI (1883–1945), "The Doctrine of Fascism," Encyclopedia Italiana, 1932.

Fascism conceives of the State as an absolute, in comparison with which all individuals or groups are relative, only to be conceived of in their relation to the state. BENITO MUSSOLINI (1883–1945), New York Times, January 11, 1935.

A people which is able to say everything becomes able to do everything. NAPOLEON BONAPARTE (1761–1821), Maxims, 1815.

To be independent is the business of a few only; it is the privilege of the strong. FRIEDRICH NIETZSCHE (1844–1900), Beyond Good and Evil, 1886.

Then what is freedom? It is the will to be responsible to ourselves. FRIEDRICH NIETZSCHE (1844–1900), Twilight of the Idols, 1888.

There are . . . certain freedoms that are like circuses. Their very existence, so long as they are individual and enjoyed chiefly individually as by spectators, diverts men's mind from the loss of other, more fundamental, social and economic and political rights. ROBERT NISBET, Twilight of Authority, 1981.

In military or in war society anything resembling true freedom of thought, true individual initiative in the intellectual and cultural and economic areas, is made impossible—not only cut off when they threaten to appear but worse, extinguished more or less at the root. ROBERT NISBET, Twilight of Authority, 1981.

Yet we can maintain a free society only if we recognize that in a free society no one can win all the time. No one can have his way all the time, and no one is right all the time. RICHARD M. NIXON, U.S. President, Speech, September 16, 1970.

Even as it stands, the home guard can only exist in a country where men consider themselves free. The totalitarian states can do great things. There's one thing they cannot do: they cannot give a factory worker a rifle and tell him to take it home and keep it in his bedroom. That rifle hanging on the wall . . . is the symbol of democracy. It is our job to see that it stays there. GEORGE ORWELL (1903–1950), quoted in *Orwell: A Life* (Bernard Crick).

The American constitutions were to liberty, what a grammar is to language: they define its parts of speech and practically construct them into syntax. THOMAS PAINE (1737–1809), *The Rights of Man,* 1791.

An avidity to punish is always dangerous to liberty. It leads men to stretch, to misinterpret, and to misapply even the best of laws. He that would make his own liberty secure must guard even his enemy from oppression: for if he violates his duty he establishes a precedent that will reach to himself. THOMAS PAINE (1737–1809), *Dissertation on First Principles of Government,* July 7, 1795.

No free people can lose their liberties while they are jealous of liberty. But the liberties of the freest people are in danger when they set up symbols of liberty as fetishes, worshipping the symbol instead of the principle it represents. WENDELL PHILLIPS (1811–1884), quoted in *Liberty and the Great Libertarians* (Charles Spradling).

Necessity is the plea of every infringement of human freedom. It is the argument of tyrants; it is the creed of slaves. WILLIAM PITT (1759–1806), Speech, November 18, 1783.

The freedom of the ego here and now, and its independence of the causal chain, is a truth that comes from the immediate dictate of the human consciousness. MAX PLANCK (1858–1947), *Where Is Science Going?,* 1932.

The first destroyer of the liberties of a people is he who first gave them bounties and largesses. PLUTARCH (46–120 A.D.).

Those persons who live in obedience to reason are worthy to be accounted free. PLUTARCH (46–120 A.D.).

We must plan for freedom, and not only for security, if for no other reason than only freedom can make security more secure. SIR KARL POPPER, *The Open Society and Its Enemies,* 1966.

In the past generation we have come to see, with increasing clarity, that the individualism of the American frontier was an individualism of personal self-reliance and of hardihood and stamina rather than an individualism of intellectual independence and personal self-expression. DAVID M. POTTER, in *Innocence and Power* (Gordon Mills, ed.), 1965.

The guarantee of equal protection cannot mean one thing when applied to one individual and something else when applied to a person of another color. If both are not accorded the same protection, then it is not equal. LEWIS F. POWELL, U.S. Supreme Court Justice, *Regents of the University of California* v. *Bakke,* 1978.

Adjustment as an educational goal is a pricked balloon. To adjust to the twentieth century is to come to terms with madness. What is needed is the adjustment of our environment to ourselves, or rather what we would like ourselves to be. MAX RAFFERTY, *Suffer Little Children,* 1962.

The modern mystics of muscle who offer you the fraudulent alternative of "human rights" versus "property rights," as if one could exist without the other, are making a last, grotesque attempt to revive the doctrine of soul versus body. Only a ghost can exist without material property: only a slave can work with no right to the product of his effort. AYN RAND (1905–1982), *Atlas Shrugged,* 1957.

What a state of society is this in which freethinker is a term of abuse, and in which doubt is regarded as sin. W. WINWOOD READE, *The Martyrdom of Man,* 1972.

If you give me six lines written by the most honest man, I will find something in them to hang him. CARDINAL RICHELIEU (1585–1642).

Individuality is to be preserved and respected everywhere, as the root of everything good. JEAN PAUL RICHTER (1763–1825), *Titan,* 1803.

Men are created different; the lose their social freedom and their individual autonomy in seeking to become like each other. DAVID REISMAN, *The Lonely Crowd,* 1950.

It is not that you set the individual apart from society but that you recognize in any society that the individual must have rights that are guarded. ELEANOR ROOSEVELT (1884–1962), *New York Times,* February 4, 1947.

It is a good thing to demand liberty for ourselves and for those who agree with us, but it is a better thing and a rarer thing to give liberty to others who do not agree with us. FRANKLIN D. ROOSEVELT (1882–1945), U.S. President, Radio Address, November 22, 1933.

The only tyrannies from which men, women and children are suffering in real life are the tyrannies of minorities. THEODORE ROOSEVELT (1858–1919), U.S. President, 1912.

Liberty is not to be found in any form of government; she is in the heart of the free man; he bears her with him everywhere. JEAN-JACQUES ROUSSEAU (1712–1741).

There is no subjugation so perfect as that which keeps the appearance of freedom, for in that way one captures volition itself. JEAN-JACQUES ROUSSEAU (1712–1741), *Émile,* 1762.

The problem is to find a form of association which will defend and protect with the whole common force the person and goods of each associate, and in which each, while uniting himself with all, may still obey himself alone, and remain as free as before. JEAN-JACQUES ROUSSEAU (1712–1778), *The Social Contract,* 1762.

Controversy is only dreaded by the advocates of error. BENJAMIN RUSH (1745–1813).

One evening, when I was yet in my nurse's arms, I wanted to touch the tea urn, which was boiling merrily. . . . My nurse would have taken me away from the urn, but my mother said "Let him touch it." So I touched it—and that was my first lesson in the meaning of liberty. JOHN RUSKIN (1819–1900), *The Story of Arachne,* 1870.

True, it is evil that a single man should crush the herd, but see not there the worse form of slavery, which is when the herd crushes out the man. ANTOINE de SAINT-EXUPÉRY (1900–1944), *Citadelle,* 1948.

I know of but one freedom and that is the freedom of the mind. ANTOINE de SAINT-EXUPÉRY (1900–1944), *The Wisdom of the Sands,* 1950.

Freedom can't be kept for nothing. If you set a high value on liberty, you must set a low value on everything else. LUCIUS ANNAEUS SENECA (4 B.C.– 65 A.D.), *Letters to Lucilius,* 65 A.D.

What is freedom? It means not being a slave to any circumstance, to any restraint, to any chance. . . . LUCIUS ANNAEUS SENECA (4 B.C.–65 A.D.), *Letters to Lucilius,* 65 A.D.

Our lack of constant awareness has also permitted us to accept definitions of freedom that are not necessarily consistent with the actuality of being free. Because we have learned to confuse the word with the reality the word seeks to describe, our vocabulary has become riddled with distorted and contradictory meanings smuggled into the language. BUTLER D. SHAFFER, *Calculated Chaos,* 1985.

Every great historic change has been based on nonconformity, has been bought either with the blood or with the reputation of nonconformists. BEN SHAHN (1898–1969), *Atlantic Monthly,* September 1957.

Liberty means responsibility. That is why most men dread it. GEORGE BERNARD SHAW (1856–1950), *Maxims for Revolutionists.*

The right to know is like the right to live. It is fundamental and unconditional in its assumption that knowledge, like life, is a desirable thing. GEORGE BERNARD SHAW (1856–1950), *The Doctor's Dilemma,* 1906.

People are always blaming their circumstances for what they are. I don't believe in circumstances. The people who get on in this world are the people who get up and look for the circumstances they want, and if they can't find them, make them. GEORGE BERNARD SHAW (1856–1950), *Mrs. Warren's Profession.*

Liberty is the possibility of doubting, the possibility of making a mistake, the possibility of searching and experimenting, the possibility of saying "No" to any authority—literary, artistic, philosophic, religious, social and even political. IGNAZIO SILONE (1900–1978), *The God That Failed,* 1950.

There is no "slippery slope" toward loss of liberty, only a long staircase where each step down must first be tolerated by the American people and their leaders. ALAN K. SIMPSON, U.S. Senator, *New York Times,* September 26, 1982.

The thing we have to fear in this country is the influence of the organized minorities, because somehow or other the great majority does not seem to organize. ALFRED E. SMITH (1873–1944), Speech, Harvard University, 1933.

The liberty the citizen enjoys is to be measured not by the governmental machinery he lives under, whether representative or other, but by the paucity of restraints it imposes upon him. HERBERT SPENCER (1820–1903), *The Man versus the State*, 1884.

Every man has freedom to do all that he wills, providing he infringes not on the equal freedom of any other man. HERBERT SPENCER (1820–1903), *Social Statics*, 1851.

A man's liberties are none the less aggressed upon because those who coerce him do so in the belief that he will be benefitted. HERBERT SPENCER (1820–1903), *Social Statics*, 1850.

The first great struggle for liberty was in the realm of thought. The libertarians reasoned that freedom of thought would be good for mankind; it would promote knowledge, and increased knowledge would advance civilization. But the authoritarians protested that freedom of thought would be dangerous, that people would think wrong, that a few were divinely appointed to think for the people. CHARLES T. SPRADLING, *Liberty and the Great Libertarians*.

Just as the right to speak and the right to refrain from speaking are complementary components of a broader concept of individual freedom, so also the individual's freedom to choose his own creed is the counterpart of his right to refrain from accepting the creed established by the majority. JOHN PAUL STEVENS, U.S. Supreme Court Justice, *Wallace* v. *Jaffree*, 1985

My definition of a free society is a society where it safe to be unpopular. ADLAI E. STEVENSON (1900–1965), Speech, 1952.

If we value the pursuit of knowledge, we must be free to follow wherever that search may lead us. ADLAI E. STEVENSON (1900–1965), Speech, 1952.

The dichotomy between personal liberties and property rights is a false one. Property does not have rights. People have rights. . . . In fact, a fundamental interdependence exists between the personal right to liberty and the personal right in property. POTTER STEWART (1915–1985), U.S. Supreme Court Justice, *Lynch* v. *Household Finance Corp.*, 1972.

Distinctions between citizens solely because of their ancestry are by their very nature odious to a free people whose institutions are founded upon the doctrine of equality. HARLAN F. STONE (1872–1946), U.S. Supreme Court Justice, *Hirabayashi* v. *United States*, 1943.

History teaches us that there have been but few infringements of personal liberty by the state which have not been justified . . . in the name of righteousness and the public good, and few which have not been directed, as they are now, at politically helpless minorities. HARLAN F. STONE (1872–1946), U.S. Supreme Court Justice, *Minersville School District* v. *Gobitis*, 1940.

If I want to be free from any other man's dictation, I must understand that I can have no other man under my control. WILLIAM GRAHAM SUMNER (1840–1910), *The Forgotten Man and Other Essays*, 1919.

Civil liberty is the status of the man who is guaranteed by law and civil institutions the exclusive employment of all his own powers for his own welfare. WILLIAM GRAHAM SUMNER (1840–1910), *The Forgotten Man and Other Essays*, 1919.

Men love liberty because it protects them from control and humiliation by others, thus affording them the possibility of dignity; they loathe liberty because it throws them back on their own abilities and resources, thus confronting them with the possibility of insignificance. THOMAS SZASZ, *The Untamed Tongue*, 1990.

If you shut your door to all errors truth will be shut out. RABINDRANATH TAGORE (1861–1941), *Stray Birds*, 1916.

It is probable that democracy owes more to nonconformity than to any other single movement. R. H. TAWNEY (1880–1962), *Religion and the Rise of Capitalism*, 1926.

Under a government which imprisons any unjustly, the true place for a just man is also a prison. HENRY DAVID THOREAU (1817–1862), *Civil Disobedience*, 1849.

There will never be a free and enlightened State until the State comes to recognize the individual as a higher and independent power, from which all its own power and authority are derived, and treats them accordingly. HENRY DAVID THOREAU (1817–1862), *Civil Disobedience*, 1849.

I know of no country in which there is so little independence of mind and real freedom of discussion as in America. ALEXIS de TOCQUEVILLE (1805–1859), *Democracy in America*, 1835.

Discipline is the destruction of reason and of liberty in man, and cannot have any other purpose than merely the preparation for the commission of such malefactions as not one man will commit in his normal condition. LEO TOLSTOY (1828–1910), *The Slavery of Our Times*.

We human beings do have some genuine freedom of choice and therefore some effective control over our destinies. I am not a determinist. But I also believe that the decisive choice is seldom the latest choice in the series. More often than not, it will turn out to be some choice made relatively far back in the past. ARNOLD J. TOYNBEE (1889–1975), *New York Times*, March 5, 1961.

To force a man to pay for the violation of his own liberty is indeed an addition of insult to injury. This is exactly what the state is doing. BENJAMIN TUCKER (1854–1939), *Instead of a Book*, 1893.

Irreverence is the champion of liberty and its only sure defense. MARK TWAIN (1835–1910), Notebook.

No man should be a serf, nor do homage or any manner of service to any lord, but should give fourpence rent for an acre of land, and that no one should work for any man but as his own will, and on terms of a regular covenant. WAT TYLER (?–1381), *Anonimalle Chronicle.*

Liberty is the hardest test that one can inflict on a people. To know how to be free is not given equally to all men and all nations. PAUL VALÉRY (1871–1945), *Reflections on the World Today,* 1931.

The world acquires value only through its extremists and endures only through its moderates; extremists make the world great, moderates keep it stable. PAUL VALÉRY (1871–1945).

All the citizens of a state cannot be equally powerful, but they may be equally free. VOLTAIRE (1694–1778), *Philosophical Dictionary,* 1764.

Every man is the creature of the age in which he lives; very few are able to raise themselves above the ideas of the times. VOLTAIRE (1694–1778), *Candide,* 1759.

Liberty is not and cannot be anything but the power of doing what we will. VOLTAIRE (1694–1778), *Philosophical Dictionary,* 1764.

I tell you true, liberty is the best of all things; never live beneath the noose of a servile halter. WILLIAM WALLACE (1270–1305), Address to the Scots, c. 1300.

A free people ought to be armed, but disciplined. GEORGE WASHINGTON (1732–1799), U.S. President, Message to Congress, 1790.

Liberty consists in the ability to choose. SIMONE WEIL (1910–1943), *The Need for Roots.*

Heresies are experiments in man's unsatisfied search for truth. H. G. WELLS (1866–1946).

We are only so free that others may be free as well as we. BENJAMIN WHICHCOTE (1609–1683), *Moral and Religious Aphorisms,* 1753.

Liberty is never out of bounds or off limits; it spreads wherever it can capture the imagination of men. E. B. WHITE (1899–1985), *The Points of My Compass,* 1960.

Liberty is the only thing you cannot have unless you are willing to give it to others. WILLIAM ALLEN WHITE (1868–1944).

Democracy . . . is a society in which the unbeliever feels undisturbed and at home. If there were only half a dozen unbelievers in America, their well-being would be a test of our democracy. ALFRED NORTH WHITEHEAD (1861–1947), quoted in *The New Yorker,* February 18, 1956.

The eager and often inconsiderate appeals of reformers and revolutionists are indispensable to counterbalance the inertia and fossilism marking so large a part of human institutions. WALT WHITMAN (1819–1892), *Democratic Vistas,* 1871.

Art is individualism, and individualism is a disturbing and disintegrating force. Therein lies its immense value. For what it seeks is to disturb is monotony of type, slavery of custom, tyranny of habit, and the reduction of man to the level of a machine. OSCAR WILDE (1854–1900), *The Soul of a Man under Socialism,* 1891.

Whenever we take away the liberties of those whom we hate we are opening the way to loss of liberty for those we love. WENDELL L. WILKIE (1892–1944).

Liberty does not consist in mere declarations of the rights of man. It consists in the translation of those declarations into definite action. WOODROW WILSON (1856–1924), U.S. President, Speech, 1914.

I have always in my own thought summed up individual liberty, and business liberty, and every other kind of liberty, in the phrase that is common in the sporting world, "A free field and no favor." WOODROW WILSON (1856–1924), U.S. President, Speech, 1915.

Liberty has never come from the government. Liberty has always come from the subjects of it. The history of liberty is a history of resistance. The history of liberty is a history of the limitations of government power, not the increase of it. WOODROW WILSON (1856–1924), U.S. President, Speech, 1912.

Man free, man working for himself, with choice of time, and place, and object. WILLIAM WORDSWORTH (1770–1850), *The Prelude,* 1805.

If liberty has any meaning it means freedom to improve. PHILIP G. WYLIE (1902–1971), *A Generation of Vipers,* 1942.

Logic

To reason analogically is to reason that because two or more things or types of things are alike in some one or more respects (we may call this the antecedent resemblence), they will therefore be found alike in some other respect(s)—and consequent resemblance. ROBERT W. ALLEN and LORNE GREENE, *The Propaganda Game,* 1966.

The maxim of science is simply that of common sense—simple cases first; begin with seeing how the main force acts when there is as little as possible to impede it, and when you thoroughly comprehend that, add to it in succession the separate effects of each of the encumbering and interfering agencies. WALTER BAGEHOT (1826–1877), *Economic Studies.*

Ad baculum argument (appeal to force): Strictly speaking, an ad baculum argument is any argument that fallaciously employs a threat as though it were a logical reason for believing a conclusion. In a looser sense, when someone stops offering arguments and resorts to force, he may be said to be resorting to the ad baculum "argument." STEPHEN F. BARKER, *The Elements of Logic,* 1965.

Ad misericordiam argument (appeal to pity): Any argument whose premises, rather than containing evidence having a direct bearing on the conclusion, instead give reasons why acceptance of the conclusion would prevent someone's misery. STEPHEN F. BARKER, *The Elements of Logic,* 1965.

Ad verecundiam argument (appeal to authority): Any arguments whose premises, rather than containing evidence having a direct bearing on the conclusion, instead give evidence that some supposed authority advocates the conclusion. Such arguments are often, but not always, fallacious. STEPHEN F. BARKER, *The Elements of Logic,* 1965.

Argument from Analogy: An unsound form of inductive argument, in which two things of different sorts are asserted to have a number of characteristics in common, one of the two things is then asserted to have a further characteristic, and it is concluded that the other thing has the same characteristic. MONROE C. BEARDSLEY, *Thinking Straight,* 1966.

The fallacy of special pleading occurs when someone, because of subjective limitations produced by his own personal concerns or by deliberate intent, presents only one side of a case, the one favorable to him. JOHN B. BENNETT, *Rational Thinking,* 1980.

The fallacy of accident consists in moving from a generally accepted rule or principle to a special case—a case that lacks the features of cases to which the rule generally applies, or a case which is quite different from the general run of cases. JOHN B. BENNETT, *Rational Thinking,* 1980.

Rationalizing is the procedure whereby one justifies a position on the basis of a reason that he offers instead of a frank appraisal of his real reason or reasons. In rationalizing, one must first of all ignore principles of logic which he might otherwise recognize. But the results of adopting clear facts and relating them logically yields conclusions he does not relish. So he supplants them with propositions more palatable to him. JOHN B. BENNETT, *Rational Thinking,* 1980.

If an idea presents itself to us, we must not reject it simply because it does not agree with the logical deductions of a reigning theory. CLAUDE BERNARD (1813–1878), *An Introduction to the Study of Experimental Medicine,* 1865.

A fact is in itself nothing. It is valuable only for the idea attached to it, or for the proof which it furnishes. CLAUDE BERNARD (1813–1878), *An Introduction to the Study of Experimental Medicine,* 1865.

Hypothesis is a tool which can cause trouble if not used properly. We must be ready to abandon our hypothesis as soon as it is shown to be inconsistent with the facts. WILLIAM I. B. BEVERIDGE (1879–1963), *The Art of Scientific Investigation,* 1950.

While playing the part of the detective the investigator follows clues, but having captured his alleged fact, he turns judge and examines the case by means of logically arranged evidence. Both functions are equally essential but they are different. WILLIAM I. B. BEVERIDGE (1879–1963), *The Art of Scientific Investigation,* 1950.

Careful and correct use of language is a powerful aid to straight thinking, for putting into words precisely what we mean necessitates getting our own minds quite clear on what we mean. WILLIAM I. B. BEVERIDGE (1879–1963), *The Art of Scientific Investigation,* 1950.

Induction is a kind of reasoning by which we examine a number of particulars or specific instances and on the basis of them arrive at a generalized conclusion. . . . The probability grows stronger and the induction becomes sounder when a substantial number of instances are examined, when the instances examined are typical, and when the exceptions, if any, are infrequent and explainable. A conclusion based on too few instances is called a hasty generalization. It is the most common fallacy in inductive reasoning. NEWMAN P. BIRK and GENEVIEVE B. BIRK, in *Forms of Rhetoric* (T. Kakonis and J. C. Wilcox, eds.), 1969.

Deduction is reasoning from stated propositions or premises to a conclusion. If the conclusion follows logically from the premises and if the premises are true, deduction arrives at proof or certainty. NEWMAN P. BIRK and GENEVIEVE B. BIRK, in *Forms of Rhetoric* (T. Kakonis and J. C. Wilcox, eds.), 1969.

Logic is like the sword—those who appeal to it shall perish by it. SAMUEL BUTLER (1835–1902), Notebooks.

Analogy is reasoning based on the assumption that if two things are alike in several important known respects, they will probably be alike in other respects not known or investigated. . . . Deductive reasoning is inference from a general statement to specific instances; generalization is inference from specific instances to a general statement; analogy is inference from one specific instance to another specific instance. G. R. CAPP and T. R. CAPP, *Principles of Argumentation and Debate*, 1965.

The evidence for generalizations, of no matter what type, takes the form of an argument from observed instances. Such an argument is never more than probable, that is, never certain. ALBUREY CASTELL, *A College Logic*, 1935.

There is the fallacy of logic—of assuming that because something is logical it is true, because something is illogical it is false, and because something appears evil its opposite is good. It is necessary to evaluate carefully the premises of an ideology and to relate its propositions to reality. REO M. CHRISTENSON et al., *Ideologies and Modern Politics*, 1975.

. . . [T]here is the fallacy of values defined as facts. Ideologies frequently dress their values in the garb of facts, leading people to falsely believe that they are correcting their knowledge of the facts, not changing their values. REO M. CHRISTENSON et al., *Ideologies and Modern Politics*, 1975

. . . [T]here is the fallacy of scientific and moral certitude. Absolute certainty of political wisdom or morality is unattainable. We are doomed to decide and act on the basis of inadequate evidence and a fallible intellect . . . . Political certainty is to be found only in deceptive simplicities or resounding generalities. . . . REO M. CHRISTENSON et al., *Ideologies and Modern Politics*, 1975.

The prejudice against careful analytic procedure is part of the human impatience with technique which arises from the fact that men are interested in results and would like to attain them without the painful toil which is the essence of our moral finitude. MORRIS R. COHEN (1880–1947).

The argument that we should believe certain things because they are helpful to what we have assumed to be practical interests, is a willful confusion between what may be pleasant for the time being and what is determined by the weight of rational evidence. MORRIS R. COHEN (1880–1947), *Journal of Philosophy and Scientific Method*, 1925.

Facts are not truths; they are not conclusions; they are not even premises, but in the nature and parts of premises. The truth depends on, and is only arrived at, by a legitimate deduction from all the facts which are truly material. SAMUEL TAYLOR COLERIDGE (1772–1834), *Table-Talk*, 1831.

Peace rules the day, where reason rules the mind. WILLIAM COLLINS (1721–1759), *Persian Eclogues*, 1742.

Reasoning is a special kind of thinking in which inference takes place, in which conclusions are drawn from premises. . . . The logician is concerned only with the correctness of the completed process. The question is always: does the conclusion reached follow from the premises used or assumed? IRVING M. COPI, *Introduction to Logic,* 1978.

The fallacy of *argumentum ad ignorantiam* is illustrated by the argument that there must be ghosts because no one has ever been able to prove that there aren't any. [It] is committed whenever it is argued that a proposition is true simply on the basis that it has not been proved false, or that it is false because it has not been proved true. IRVING M. COPI, *Introduction to Logic,* 1978.

The difference between the reason of man and the instinct of the beast is this, that the beast does but know, but the man knows that he knows. JOHN DONNE (1572–1631), *Sermons.*

It is a capital mistake to theorize before one has data. Insensibly, one begins to twist facts to suit theories instead of theories to suit facts. SIR ARTHUR CONAN DOYLE (1859–1930), *The Adventures of Sherlock Holmes,* 1891.

[The] factual aspect of a proposition refers to a part of reality, hence it can be tested by reference to the facts. In this way we can check its truth. The moral aspect of a proposition, however, expresses only the emotional response of an individual to a state of real or presumed facts. . . . DAVID EASTON, *The Political System,* 1953.

[In science] the grand aim . . . is to cover the greatest number of empirical facts by logical deduction from the smallest number of hypotheses or axioms. ALBERT EINSTEIN (1879–1955).

Argument by analogy [is] an argument by the consideration of similar cases. The trouble is that they may be taken to be more similar than they really are. . . . Analogies can never be validly used to establish conclusions although they may sometimes point to them. E. M. EMMET, *Handbook of Logic,* 1967.

The fallacy of division lies in assuming that what holds true for all members of a class taken together is necessarily true for each alone. W. WARD FEARNSIDE and WILLIAM B. HOLTHER, *Fallacy: The Counterfeit of Argument,* 1959.

There are . . . terms, however, the use of which usually implies the existence of entities in the situation unverifiable in principle. The usual occasion of the use of such terms as "destiny" and "fate" provides no clue for reduction and strongly suggests hypostatization of entitles. Such use is commonly called Word Magic. W. WARD FEARNSIDE and WILLIAM B. HOLTHER, *Fallacy: The Counterfeit of Argument,* 1959.

The inconsistency of acting on two opposite principles . . . rarely troubles the common man; indeed he is seldom even aware of it. His affair is to act, not to analyze the motives of his action. If mankind had always been logical and wise, history would not be a long chronicle of folly and crime. SIR JAMES GEORGE FRASER (1854–1941), *The Golden Bough.*

It is indeed not the least of the logician's tasks to indicate the pitfalls laid by language in the way of the thinker. GOTTLOB FREGE (1848–1925).

Factual evidence can never "prove" a hypothesis; it can only fail to disprove it, which is what we generally mean when we say, somewhat inexactly, that the hypothesis is "confirmed" by experience. MILTON FRIEDMAN, *Essays in Positive Economics*, 1953.

The only relevant test of the validity of a hypothesis is comparison of its predictions with experience. MILTON FRIEDMAN, *Essays in Positive Economics*, 1953.

Men are apt to mistake the strength of their feeling for the strength of their argument. The heated mind resents the chill touch and relentless scrutiny of logic. WILLIAM GLADSTONE (1809–1898).

Where many factors are at work, the fallacy of 'post hoc ergo propter hoc' has a fateful plausibility to the simple mental economy of the uncritical multitude as well as to impatient men of action. A Hoover will be held accountable for a depression whose seeds were planted long before his advent. SIDNEY HOOK (1902–1989), *The Hero in History*, 1955.

If we be, therefore, engaged by arguments to put trust in past experience, and to make it the standard of our future judgement, these arguments must be probable only. DAVID HUME (1711–1776).

Science is simply common sense at its best—that is, rigidly accurate in observation and merciless to fallacy in logic. . . . It is wrong for a man to say that he is certain of the objective proof of any proposition unless he can produce evidence which logically justifies that certainty. THOMAS HENRY HUXLEY (1825–1895).

Logic is not satisfied with assertion. It cares nothing for the opinions of the great—nothing for the prejudices of the many, and least of all for the superstitions of the dead. ROBERT G. INGERSOLL (1833–1899), *Prose-Poems and Selections*, 1884.

The basic difficulty with the absolutist or objective view of truth is that different theories may employ different epistemological (or metatheoretical) assumptions. Since the validity of these assumptions cannot be tested empirically, the frameworks themselves are not comparable or commensurable. THOMAS S. KUHN, *The Structure of Scientific Revolution*, 1970.

Logic is the art of making truth prevail. JEAN de LA BRUYÈRE (1645–1696), *Les Caractères*, 1688.

Anyone who conducts an argument by appealing to authority is not using his intelligence; he is just using his memory. LEONARDO DA VINCI (1452–1519).

There are two kinds of truths: those of reasoning and those of fact. The truths of reasoning are necessary and their opposite is impossible; the truths of fact are contingent and their opposite is possible. GOTTFRIED W. LEIBNIZ (1646–1716), *The Monadology*, 1714.

The facts to be explained should follow demonstratively from the hypothesis. But this alone is not enough. The implications of the hypothesis must accord not only with the facts in which we happen to be interested, but with all the facts on which it bears. Most hypotheses will imply many things which have not been observed. It is by determining the accordance of the implications with the facts, in every case, that the hypothesis is tested. CECIL ALEC MACE, 1933.

No one, if pressed, can ultimately be sure that his argument is valid unless he can reduce it to a syllogism; and conversely, an argument so reduced will satisfy the most confirmed skeptic. Reduction to syllogism is the one method of ultimately satisfying oneself of the validity of inference. CHARLES RICHARD MORRIS, 1933.

Rational thought is interpretation according to a scheme which we cannot escape. FRIEDRICH NIETZSCHE (1844–1900), 1887.

Logic is useful for proof but almost never for making discoveries. A man receives certain impressions; under their influence he states—without being able to say either how or why, and if he attempts to do so he deceives himself— a proposition, which can be verified experimentally. VILFRED PARETO (1848–1923), *Manual of Political Economy*, 1906.

Reason commands us far more imperiously than a master; in disobeying the latter we are made unhappy, in disobeying the former, fools. BLAISE PASCAL (1623–1662), *Pensées*, 1670.

. . . [T]he woof and warp of all thought and all research is symbols, and the life of thought and science is the life inherent in symbols; so it is wrong to say that a good language is important to good thought, merely; for it is the essence of it. CHARLES SANDERS PEIRCE (1839–1914).

. . . [T]o call an argument illogical, or a proposition false, is a special kind of moral judgment. CHARLES SANDERS PEIRCE (1839–1914), *Collected Papers*.

Logic is one thing, the human animal another. You can quite easily propose a logical solution to something and at the same time hope in your heart of hearts that it won't work out. LUIGI PIRANDELLO (1867–1936), *The Pleasure of Honesty*, 1917.

Logic, which alone can give certainty, is the instrument of demonstration; intuition is the instrument of invention. JULES-HENRI POINCARÉ (1854–1912), *The Value of Science*.

A system [is] empirical or scientific only if it is capable of being tested by experience. These considerations suggest that not the verifiability but the falsifiability of a system is to be taken as a criterion of demarcation. . . . It must be possible for an empirical or scientific system to be refuted by experience. SIR KARL POPPER, *The Logic of Scientific Discovery*, 1935.

The history of science, like the history of all human ideas, is a history of irresponsible dreams, of obstinacy, and of error. But science is one of the very few human activities—perhaps the only one—in which errors are systematically criticized and fairly often, in time, corrected. This is why we can say that, in science, we often learn from our mistakes, and why we can speak clearly and sensibly about making progress there. SIR KARL POPPER, *Conjectures and Refutations.*

Logic is the science of proof. What the logical man insists on is simply this: that if you claim that you have proved a point—about anything at all—then your proof should be scrutinized in terms of the adequacy of your evidence. Logic shows us how to make this scrutiny. . . . Logic helps us to confound . . . irrational attitudes by showing us that there is much more room for doubt than is dreamed of by dogmatic prophets and proclaimers. Thus logic encourages a bit of skepticism. LIONEL RUBY, *The Art of Making Sense,* 1968.

We want our theoretical views to yield statements about the empirical world that are in some respects falsifiable. . . . To be empirically falsifiable, a theory should yield statements for which, in principle, contrary evidence might be adduced. Falsifiable theories afford the possibility of organizing research so as to seek potentially undermining evidence. They enable us to envisage evidence compatible with one theory yet tending to cast doubt on another. JAMES B. RULE, *Theories of Civil Violence,* 1988.

Because language is misleading, as well as because it is diffuse and inexact when applied to logic (for which it was never intended), logical symbolism is absolutely necessary to any exact or thorough treatment of our subject. BERTRAND RUSSELL (1872–1970).

Reason deserves to be called a prophet; for in showing us the consequence and effect of our actions in the present, does it not tell us what the future will be? ARTHUR SCHOPENHAUER (1788–1860), *Parerga and Paralipomena,* 1851.

In these anxious times many of us are less astonished that reason is ever suspended than that it should even prevail, even during the briefest of intervals. MORTON IRVING SEIDEN, *The Paradox of Hate,* 1967.

Rhetoric without logic is like a tree with leaves, blossoms but no root; yet more are taken with rhetoric than logic, because they are caught with fine expressions when they understand not reason. JOHN SELDEN (1584–1654), *Table-Talk,* 1689.

Empirical thinking leads to a basically objective view of the world, belief leads to a view of the world in which the distinction between objective and subjective is blurred. . . . Thus cause is apt to be mistaken for effect, the wish confused with its fulfillment, the symbol with the thing. GEORGE SERBAN, *The Tyranny of Magical Thinking,* 1982.

The argument by analogy is not necessarily dishonest or crooked, although it is a dangerous one always requiring careful examination. To an extraordinary extent, intelligent people become convinced of highly improbable things because they have heard them supported by analogies whose unsoundness would be apparent to an imbecile. R. H. THOULESS, 1932.

In formal logic, a contradiction is the signal of a defeat: but in the evolution of real knowledge it marks the first step in progress towards a victory. This is the one great reason for the utmost toleration of variety of opinion. ALFRED NORTH WHITEHEAD (1861–1947), *Science in the Modern World*, 1925.

Mass Movements and Revolutions

Two forces which are the worst enemies of civil freedom are the absolute monarchy and the revolution. LORD ACTON (1834–1902), *The Home and Foreign Review*, July 1862.

The secret agent is a journalist who assumes prominence in the opposition press for his strident calls to violence; he is the speaker who addresses proletarian meetings and urges them to put an end to capitalism. . . . [Revolutionaries'] suspicion of each other contributes far more to their helplessness than to their safety. L. ANDRIEUX, *Recollections of a Prefect of Police*, Paris, vol. 1, 1885.

The most radical revolutionary will become a conservative the day after the revolution. HANNAH ARENDT (1906–1975), *The New Yorker*, September 12, 1970.

Revolutionaries do not make revolutions. The revolutionaries are those who know when power is lying in the street and they can pick it up. Armed uprising by itself has never yet led to revolution. HANNAH ARENDT (1906–1975).

Revolutions in democracies are mainly the work of demagogues. Partly by persecuting men of property and partly by arousing the master against them, they induce them to unite, for a common fear brings even enemies together. ARISTOTLE (384–322 B.C.), *Politics*.

Inferiors revolt in order that they may be equal and equals that they may be superior. Such is the state of mind which creates revolutions. ARISTOTLE (384–322 B.C.), *Politics*.

Thinkers prepare the revolution; bandits carry it out. MARIONO AZUELA (1873–1952), *The Flies*, 1918.

The revolutionist is a doomed man. He has no personal interests, no affairs, sentiments, attachments, property, not even a name of his own. Everything in him is absorbed by one exclusive interest, one thought, one passion—the revolution. MIKHAIL A. BAKUNIN (1814–1876), *Catechism of the Revolution*.

Our first work must be the annihilation of everything as it now exists. The old world must be destroyed and replaced by a new one. When you have freed your mind from the fear of God, and that childish respect for the fiction of right, then all the remaining chains that bind you—property, marriage, morality, and justice—will snap asunder like threads. MIKHAIL A. BAKUNIN (1814–1876), *God and the State*, 1882.

The revolutionist has no personal right to anything. Everything he has or earns belongs to the cause. Everything, even his affections. ALEXANDER BERKMAN (1870–1936), *Prison Memoirs of an Anarchist,* 1912.

They are not reformers who simply abhor evil. Such men become in the end abhorrent themselves. HENRY WARD BEECHER (1813–1887), *Life Thoughts,* 1858.

Revolution, n. In politics, an abrupt change in the form of misgovernment. AMBROSE BIERCE (1842–1914), *The Devil's Dictionary,* 1906.

Insurrection, n. An unsuccessful revolution. Disaffection's failure to substitute misrule for bad government. AMBROSE BIERCE (1842–1914), *The Devil's Dictionary,* 1906.

[Revolutions] begin as anarchistic movements against bureaucratic state organization, which they inevitably destroy; they continue by setting in place another, in most cases stronger, bureaucratic organization, which suppresses all free mass movements. FRANZ BORKENAU (1900–1957), *Sociological Review,* vol. 29 (1937).

It may be laid down as an axiom that a man who does not live the life of the mob will not think its thoughts either. LEWIS BROWNE (1897–1949).

A reform is a correction of abuses; a revolution is a transfer of power. EDWARD GEORGE BULWER-LYTTON (1803–1873), Speech, House of Commons, 1866.

Make the revolution a parent of settlement, and not a nursery of future revolutions. EDMUND BURKE (1729–1797), *Reflections on the Revolution in France,* 1790.

We must enter and take possession of the consciences of the children, of the consciences of the young, because they do belong and should belong in the revolution. PLUTARCO CALLES (1877–1945), Speech at Guadalajara, July 19, 1934.

Every revolutionary ends by becoming either an oppressor or a heretic. ALBERT CAMUS (1913–1960), *The Rebel,* 1951.

All modern revolutions have ended in a reinforcement of the power of the state. ALBERT CAMUS (1913–1960), *The Rebel,* 1951.

You can never have a revolution in order to establish a democracy. You must have a democracy in order to have a revolution. GILBERT KEITH CHESTERTON (1874–1936), *Tremendous Trifles,* 1909.

It is an easy and a vulgar thing to please the mob, and no very arduous task to astonish them; but essentially to benefit and to improve them is a work fraught with difficulty, and teeming with danger. CHARLES CALEB COLTON (1780–1832), *Lacon,* 1820.

An agitation to attain a political or economic end must rest upon an implied willingness and ability to use force. Without that it is mere wind and attitudinizing. JAMES CONNOLLY (1870–1916), *Forward,* March 14, 1914.

The revolutionary spirit is mightily convenient in this: that it frees one from all scruples as regards ideas. JOSEPH CONRAD (1857–1924), *A Personal Record,* 1912.

The way of even the most justifiable revolutions is prepared by personal impulses disguised into creeds. JOSEPH CONRAD (1857–1924), *The Secret Agent,* 1907.

A violent revolution falls into the hands of narrow-minded fanatics and tyrannical hypocrites at first. Afterward comes the turn of all the pretentious intellectual failures of the time. The scrupulous and the just, the noble . . . may begin a movement—but it passes away from them. . . . They are its first victims. JOSEPH CONRAD (1857–1924), *Under Western Eyes,* 1911.

It was the best of times, it was the worst of times; it was the age of wisdom, it was the age of foolishness; it was the epoch of belief, it was the epoch of incredulity; it was the season of Light, it was the season of Darkness; it was the spring of hope, it was the winter of despair; we had everything before us, we had nothing before us; we were all going directly to Heaven, we were all going the other way. CHARLES DICKENS (1812–1870), *A Tale of Two Cities,* 1868.

Nothing is clearer in history than the adoption by successful rebels of the methods they were accustomed to condemn in the forces they deposed. WILL DURANT (1885–1981) and ARIEL DURANT (1898–1981), *The Lessons of History,* 1968.

The world is always childish, and with each new gewgaw of a revolution or new constitution that it finds, thinks it shall never cry any more. RALPH WALDO EMERSON (1803–1882), Journals, 1847.

A mob is a society of bodies voluntarily bereaving themselves of reason, and traversing its work. The mob is man voluntarily descending to the nature of the beast. RALPH WALDO EMERSON (1803–1882), *Compensation,* 1841.

Let us remember that revolutions do not always establish freedom. Our own free institutions were not the offspring of own revolution. They existed before. MILLARD FILLMORE (1800–1874), U.S. President, Message to Congress, December 5, 1852.

The mob, which everywhere is the majority, will always let itself be led by scoundrels. FREDERICK THE GREAT (1712–1786), Letter, 1782.

[W]hen individuals come together in a group all their individual inhibitions fall away and all the cruel, brutal and destructive instincts, which lie dormant in individuals as relics of a primitive epoch, are stirred up to find free expression. SIGMUND FREUD (1856–1939), *Group Psychology and the Analysis of the Ego,* 1921.

The successful revolutionary is a statesmen; the unsuccessful one a criminal. ERICH FROMM (1910–1980), *Escape from Freedom,* 1941.

A nonviolent revolution is not a program of seizure of power. It is a program of transformation of relationships, ending in a peaceful transfer of power. MOHANDAS K. GANDHI (1869–1948), *Non-Violence in Peace and War,* 1948.

Multiplicity of leadership and lack of centralized control ensures the survival of the movement even if leaders are jailed or otherwise removed. In fact, such action stimulates emergence of new leadership because of heightened commitment in the face of opposition. Autonomy and self-sufficiency of local cells make effective suppression of the movement extremely difficult. LUTHER P. GERLACH, in *Social Movements of the Sixties and Seventies* (Jo Freeman, ed.), 1983.

Though a revolution may call itself "national," it always marks the victory of a single party. ANDRÉ GIDE (1869–1951), Journals, 1941.

The mob that would die for a belief seldom hesitates to inflict death upon any opposing heretical groups. ELLEN GLASGOW (1874–1945), *I Believe.*

Revolutions are the product of passion, not of sober, tranquil reason. There must be obstinate resistance to improvement on the one side, to engender a furious determination of realizing a system at a stroke on the other. WILLIAM GODWIN (1756–1836), *An Enquiry concerning Political Justice,* 1793.

Revolution is engendered by an indignation with tyranny, yet is itself pregnant with tyranny. . . . An attempt to scrutinize men's thoughts and punish their opinions is of all kinds of despotism the most odious: yet this is peculiarly characteristic of a period of revolution. . . . There is no period more at war with the existence of liberty. WILLIAM GODWIN (1756–1836), *An Enquiry concerning Political Justice,* 1793.

No revolution ever succeeds as a factor of liberation unless the Means used to further it be identified in spirit and tendency with the Purpose to be achieved. EMMA GOLDMAN (1869–1940), *My Further Disillusion,* 1925.

There are only two great currents in the history of mankind: the baseness which makes conservatives and the envy which makes revolutionaries. EDMOND de GONCOURT (1822–1896) and JULES de GONCOURT (1830–1870), Journal, July 12, 1867.

The spirit of revolution, the spirit of insurrection, is a spirit radically opposed to liberty. FRANÇOIS PIERRE GUIZOT (1787–1874), Premier of France, Speech, December 29, 1830.

The men who make revolutions are always despised by those who profit from them. FRANÇOIS PIERRE GUIZOT (1787–1874), Premier of France, *Corneille and His Times,* 1855.

Revolutions begin with infatuation and end with incredulity. In their origin proud assurance is dominant; the ruling opinion disclaims doubt, and will not endure contradiction. At their completion, skepticism takes the place of disdain, and there is no longer any care for individual convictions, or any belief in truth. FRANÇOIS PIERRE GUIZOT (1787–1874), Premier of France, 1851.

[For] many intelligent and well-informed terrorists . . . the unshakable belief that they work, fight, and die for purposes transcending their own narrow interests gives them the fanatic self-righteousness which makes their often self-destructive acts so destructive, dangerous, and contagious. FREDERICK HACKER, *Terrorism,* vol. 4, 1980.

In this grandiose identification with a sacred cause and its representatives, the terrorist, by giving up his individual will, individual responsibility, and individual interest, experiences the "high" of "liberation" from his individual problems, guilts and anxiety. FREDERICK HACKER, *Terrorism,* vol. 4, 1980.

So long as we read about revolution in books, they all look very nice—like those landscapes which, as artistic engravings on white vellum, look so pure and friendly. Dung heaps engraved on copper do not smell, and the eye can easily wade through an engraved morass. HEINRICH HEINE (1797–1856).

Martyrs are needed to create incidents. Incidents are needed to create revolutions. Revolutions are needed to create progress. CHESTER BOMAR HIMES (1909–1984), "Mary," *Crisis* magazine, 1944.

We used to think that revolutions are the cause of change. Actually it is the other way around: change prepares the ground for revolution. ERIC HOFFER (1902–1983), *The Temper of Our Time,* 1967.

The history of mankind is one long record of giving revolution another trial, and limping back at last to sanity, safety, and work. EDGAR WATSON HOWE (1853–1937), Preaching from an Audience, 1926.

The effect of boredom on a large scale in history is underestimated. It is a main cause of revolutions. WILLIAM RALPH INGE (1860–1954), *End of an Age.*

If there is one safe generalization in human affairs, it is that revolutions always destroy themselves. How often have fanatics proclaimed "the year one!" DEAN WILLIAM INGE (1860–1954), *Outspoken Essays: First Series,* 1919.

Secession, like any other revolutionary act, may be morally justified by the extremity of oppression; but to call it a constitutional right is confounding the meaning of the term. ANDREW JACKSON (1767–1845), U.S. President, 1832.

The spirit of resistance to government is so valuable on certain occasions, that I wish it to be always kept alive. It will often be exercised when wrong but better so than not to be exercised at all. I like a little rebellion now and then. It is like a storm in the atmosphere. THOMAS JEFFERSON (1743–1846), U.S. President, Letter to Abigail Adams, February 22, 1787.

Every revolution evaporates and leaves behind only the slime of a new bureaucracy. FRANZ KAFKA (1883–1924).

Now it is a fact that humor and revolutionary fervor are never congenial bedfellows. The lack of a sense of humor is doubtless one of the most salient characteristics of the revolutionary. Wit and humor appeared as counterrevolutionary vices. . . . [I]t reveals a state of mind that the revolutionaries . . . would not have denied, for they took life very seriously and attached a quasi-religious significance to words. JEFFREY KAPLOW, *New Perspective on the French Revolution,* 1965.

A revolution requires of its leaders a record of unbroken infallibility. If they do not possess it they are expected to invent it. MURRAY KEMPTON, *Part of Our Time,* 1955.

Revolutionary theory is not a collection of petrified dogmas and formulas, but a militant guide to action in transforming the world. NIKITA KHRUSHCHEV (1894–1971), Report to Central Committee of the Communist Party, 1956.

Revolutions conducted in the name of liberty more often than not refine new tools of authority. HENRY KISSINGER, *White House Years,* 1979.

The rebel turns his indignation now against this injustice, now against another; the revolutionary is a consistent hater who has invested all the power of hatred in one object. The rebel has a touch of the Quixotic; the revolutionary is a bureaucrat of Utopia. The rebel is an enthusiast; the revolutionary, a fanatic. ARTHUR KOESTLER (1904–1983), *Arrow in the Blue,* 1952.

All true faith is uncompromising, radical, purist; hence the true traditionalist is always a revolutionary zealot in conflict with the pharisaic society. ARTHUR KOESTLER (1904–1983), *The God That Failed,* 1949.

Men of courage, not satisfied with words, but ever searching for means to transform them into action—men of integrity for whom the act is one with the idea, for whom prison, exile, and death are preferable to a life contrary to their principles,—intrepid souls who know that it is necessary to dare in order to succeed. PRINCE PETER KROPOTKIN (1842–1921), *Kropotkin's Revolutionary Pamphlets* (R. Baldwin, ed.), 1970.

The reformer, in the eyes of the militant, is the despicable betrayer of the true cause. . . . The revolutionary, in the eyes of the moderate, is the crazed subverter of a fragile social order. He comes to destroy. He adores the fire and longs for the ashes. . . . His demands can never be met. M. J. LASKY, *Utopia and Revolution,* 1976.

Mental contagion is the most powerful factor in the propagation of a revolutionary movement. In certain men, the revolutionary spirit is a mental condition independent of the object on which it is exercised. No concession could appease them. GUSTAVE LE BON (1841–1931), *Aphorisms of Present Times,* 1913.

The revolutionary dictatorship is power won and maintained by the violence of the proletariat against the bourgeoisie, power that is unrestricted by any laws. V. I. LENIN (1870–1924), *The Proletarian Revolution and the Renegade Kautsky,* 1924.

Every mob, in its ignorance and blindness and bewilderment, is a League of Frightened Men that seeks reassurance in collective action. MAX LERNER, *The Unfinished Country*, 1959.

There is no grievance that is a fit object of redress by mob law. ABRAHAM LINCOLN (1809–1865), U.S. President, Speech, January 27, 1838.

Revolution or dictatorship can sometimes abolish bad things, but they can never create good and lasting ones. Impatience is fatal in politics. THOMAS MASARYK (1850–1937), *The Foundations of Marxist Theory*, 1899.

Women hate revolutions and revolutionists. They like men who are docile, and well-regarded at the bank, and never late at meals. H. L. MENCKEN (1880–1956), *Prejudices*, 1924.

The public, with its yearning to be instructed, edified, and pulled by the nose, demands certainties. H. L. MENCKEN (1880–1956), *Prejudices*, 1924.

Moderation is fatal to factions, just as it is the vital principle of established power. To ask malcontents to be moderate is like asking them to destroy the foundations of their existence. PRINCE CLEMENS von METTERNICH (1773–1859), Letter, 1834.

Every generation revolts against its fathers and makes friends with its grandfathers. LEWIS MUMFORD (1895–1990), *The Brown Decades*, 1931.

All revolutions are the work of a minority. MAX NORDAU (1849–1923), 1897.

Revolution is not the uprising against preexisting order, but the setting up of a new order contradictory to the old one. JOSÉ ORTEGA y GASSET (1883–1955), *Revolt of the Masses*, 1930.

Most revolutionaries are potential Tories, because they imagine that everything can be put to rights by altering the shape of society. GEORGE ORWELL (1903–1950), *Nineteen Eighty-Four*, 1949.

Power is not a means, it is an end. One does not establish a dictatorship in order to safeguard a revolution. One makes the revolution in order to establish the dictatorship. The object of persecution is persecution. The object of torture is torture. The object of power is power. GEORGE ORWELL (1903–1950), *Nineteen Eighty-Four*, 1949.

The art of revolutionizing and overturning states is to undermine established customs, by going back to their origin, in order to mark their want of justice. BLAISE PASCAL (1623–1662), *Pensées*, 1670.

Revolutions are not made; they come. A revolution is as natural a growth as an oak. It comes out of the past. Its foundations are laid far back. WENDELL PHILLIPS (1811–1884), Speech, January 8, 1852.

Perseverance is more prevailing than violence; and many things which cannot be overcome when they are taken together, yield themselves up when taken little by little. PLUTARCH (ca. 46–ca. 120 A.D.), *The Parallel Lives* (Sertorius).

The nose of the mob is its imagination. By this, at any time, it can be quietly led. EDGAR ALLAN POE (1809–1849), *Marginalia,* 1844–49.

The mob is easily led and may be moved by the smallest force, so that its agitations have a wonderful resemblance to those of the sea. POLYBIUS (ca. 200–118 B.C.), *Histories,* 125 B.C.

Every successful revolt is termed a revolution, and every unsuccessful one a rebellion. JOSEPH PRIESTLY (1733–1804), Letter to Edmund Burke, 1791.

The slogan, "The end justifies the means," a great favorite of revolutionists and opportunists, is an affirmation of activist ethics. It sounds like a realistic, down-to-earth principle and is often cited to counter ethical arguments based on "abstract" moral considerations or on sentiment. What are a few hundred drops at the guillotine weighed against the ends. ANATOL RAPOPORT, *Operational Philosophy,* 1953.

All assemblages of men are different from the men themselves. Neither intelligence nor culture can prevent a mob from acting as a mob. The wise man and the knave lose their identity and merge themselves into a new being. THOMAS BRACKET REED (1839–1902), Speech at Bowdoin College, July 25, 1902.

The foundation of popular government in time of revolution is at once virtue and terror; virtue, without which terror is fatal; terror, without which virtue is powerless. ROBESPIERRE (1758–1794), Speech, 1794.

You can talk a mob into anything. JOHN RUSKIN (1819–1900), *Sesame and Lilies,* 1865.

Revolution is a transfer of property from class to class. LEON SAMSON, *The New Humanism,* 1930.

Revolutions are ambiguous things. Their success is generally proportionate to their power of adaption and to the reabsorption with them of what they rebelled against. GEORGE SANTAYANA (1863–1952), *The Life of Reason,* 1906

The revolutionary wants to change the world; he transcends it and moves toward the future, towards an order of values which he himself invents. The rebel is careful to preserve the abuses from which he suffers so that he can go on rebelling against them. JEAN-PAUL SARTRE (1905–1980), *Baudelaire,* 1947.

When the people contend for their liberty, they seldom get anything for their victory but new masters. GEORGE SAVILE (1633–1695), *Political Thoughts and Reflections.*

It is the proof of a bad cause when it is applauded by the mob. LUCIUS ANNAEUS SENECA (4 B.C.–65 A.D.), *Epistles.*

Revolutionary movements attract those who are not good enough for established institutions as well as those who are too good for them. GEORGE BERNARD SHAW (1856–1950), *The Revolutionist's Handbook,* 1903.

Revolutions have never lightened the burden of tyranny; they have only shifted it to another shoulder. GEORGE BERNARD SHAW (1856–1950), *The Revolutionist's Handbook,* 1903.

Violence, once employed by the revolutionist, has a tendency to so enamor him of its use that he becomes unaware of other possibilities. MULFORD Q. SIBLEY (1912–1991).

The effect of number is to impart to all members of a crowd a sense of their sudden, extraordinary and uncontrollable power, such that no one can judge or punish their actions; and this assurance leads them to commit acts which they [individually] condemn, feeling them unjust. SCIPIO SIGHELE, *The Criminal Masses: Essay on Collective Psychology,* 1892.

Experience has always shown us hitherto that revolutionaries plead "reasons of state" as soon as they get into power, that they employ police methods and look upon justice as a weapon which they may use unfairly against their enemies. GEORGES SOREL (1847–1922), *Reflections on Violence,* 1906.

In the language of politics, the term "revolution" stands for a certain kind of historical change: an old order dissolves and a new one emerges; old rulers are replaced by new; men feel that the tempo of events is quickening and that, willingly or unwillingly, they are breaking with the past; and the transition is enlivened by more or less spectatular bursts of violence. ROBERT STRAUSZ-HUPE, *Protracted Conflict,* 1958.

It is axiomatic that the revolutionary side must strive, by graduated and sometimes imperceptible pressures, to weaken the status quo forces, strengthen its own forces, and bring about a piecemeal, yet ultimately decisive, shift in the distribution of power. ROBERT STRAUSZ-HUPE, *Protracted Conflict,* 1958.

Every revolution by force only puts more violent means of enslavement into the hands of the persons of power. LEO TOLSTOY (1828–1910), 1893.

Every successful revolution puts on in time the robes of the tyrant it has deposed. BARBARA TUCHMAN (1912–1989).

The word "revolution" is a word for which you kill, for which you die, for which you send the laboring masses to their death, but which does not possess any content. SIMONE WEIL (1909–1943), *Reflections concerning the Causes of Liberty and Social Oppression,* 1934.

The saddest illusion of the revolutionary is that revolution itself will transform the nature of human beings. SHIRLEY WILLIAMS, Labour MP, 1977.

Mysticism, Metaphysics, and Religion

Fanaticism in religion is the alliance of the passions she condemns with the dogmas she professes. LORD ACTON (1834–1902).

A man is quickly convinced of the truth of religion, who finds it not against his interests that it should be true. JOSEPH ADDISON (1672–1719), *The Spectator,* August 23, 1712.

The insatiableness of our desires asserts our personal imperishableness. A. BRONSON ALCOTT (1799–1888), *Tablets,* 1868.

The philosopher aspires to explain away all mysteries, to dissolve them into light. Mystery, on the other hand, is demanded and pursued by the religious instinct; mystery constitutes the essence of worship. HENRI FRÉDÉRIC AMIEL (1821–1881), *Journal intime,* 1849–1872.

Man never knows what he wants; he aspires to penetrate mysteries and as soon as he has, wants to reestablish them. Ignorance irritates him and knowledge cloys. HENRI FRÉDÉRIC AMIEL (1821–1881), *Journal intime,* 1882–1884.

We are always making God our accomplice so that we may legalize our own inequities. Every successful massacre is consecrated by a *Te Deum,* and the clergy have never been wanting in benedictions for any victorious enormity. HENRI FRÉDÉRIC AMIEL (1821–1881), *Journal intime,* 1866.

There can be no doubt that the idea of a happy immortality, serving as a harbor of refuge from the tempests of this mortal existence . . . carries with it inexpressible consolation to those who are wearied, burdened, and tormented by pain and suffering. To feel one's self individually cared for and protected by God gives a special dignity and beauty to life. HENRI FRÉDÉRIC AMIEL (1821–1881), *Journal intime,* 1873.

Faith is a certitude without proofs . . . a sentiment, for it is a hope; it is an instinct, for it precedes all outward instruction. HENRI FRÉDÉRIC AMIEL (1821–1881), *Journal intime,* 1882–1884.

It is almost impossible to exaggerate the proneness of the human mind to take miracles as evidence, and to seek for miracles as evidence. MATTHEW ARNOLD (1822–1888), *Literature and Dogma,* 1873.

The Christian opium makes the people passive, the Communist opium invites them to revolt. RAYMOND ARON (1905–1983), *The Great Debate,* 1965.

Faith is to believe what you do not yet see; the reward of this faith is to see what you believe. SAINT AUGUSTINE (340–430), *Sermons.*

The fact that people have religious experiences is interesting from the psychological point of view, but it does not in any way imply that there is such a thing as religious knowledge. . . . Unless he can formulate his "knowledge" in propositions that are empirically verifiable, we may be sure that he is deceiving himself. A. J. AYER, *Language, Truth and Logic,* 1936.

[Metaphysics is] an elaborate, diabolical invention for mystifying what was clear, and confounding what was intelligible. WILLIAM E. AYTOUN (1813–1865).

Atheism leaves a man to sense, to philosophy, to natural piety, to laws, to reputation, all which may be guides to an outward moral virtue, though religion were not; but superstition dismounts all these, and erects an absolute monarchy in the minds of men . . . the master of superstition is the people; and arguments are fitted to practice, in a reversed order. SIR FRANCIS BACON (1561–1626), "Of Superstition."

In every age Natural Philosophy had a troublesome adversary and hard to deal with; namely, superstition, and the blind and immoderate zeal of religion. SIR FRANCIS BACON (1561–1626), *Novum Organum,* 1620.

The general root of superstition is that men observe when things hit, and not when they miss, and commit to memory the one, and pass over the other. SIR FRANCIS BACON (1561–1626).

The greatest vicissitude of things among men is the vicissitude of sects and religions. SIR FRANCIS BACON (1561–1626), *Essays,* 1597.

All religions, with their gods, demigods, prophets, messiahs and saints, are the product of the fancy and credulity of men who have not yet reached the full development and complete possession of their intellectual powers. MIKHAIL A. BAKUNIN (1814–1876), *God and the State,* 1871.

People go to church for the same reasons they go to a tavern: to stupefy themselves, to forget their misery, to imagine themselves, for a few minutes anyway, free and happy. MIKHAIL A. BAKUNIN (1814–1876), *Circular Letter to My Friends in Italy.*

It is not within the power of the President, nor of Congress, nor of any judicial tribunal of the United States, to take or even hear testimony or in any mode to inquire into or decide upon the religious belief of any official. THOMAS F. BAYARD (1828–1898), U.S. Secretary of State, Letter, 1885.

In the matters of religion, it is very hard to deceive a man, and very hard to undeceive him. PIERRE BAYLE (1647–1705), *Dictionary,* 1697.

The idea of death, the fear of it, haunts the human animal like nothing else; it is a mainspring of human activity—activity designed largely to avoid the fatality of death, to overcome it by denying . . . it. ERNEST BECKER, *The Denial of Death*, 1973.

No power of government ought to be employed in the endeavor to establish any system or article of belief on the subject of religion. JEREMY BENTHAM (1748–1832), *Constitutional Code*, 1830.

Faith is the substance of things hoped for, the evidence of things not seen. BIBLE, Hebrews 11:1.

Faith, n. Belief without evidence in what is told by one who speaks without knowledge, of things without parallel. AMBROSE BIERCE (1842–1914), *The Devil's Dictionary*, 1906.

Heathen, n. A benighted creature who has the folly to worship something he can see and feel. AMBROSE BIERCE (1842–1914), *The Devil's Dictionary*, 1906.

Religion, n. A daughter of Hope and Fear, explaining to Ignorance the nature of the Unknowable. AMBROSE BIERCE (1842–1914), *The Devil's Dictionary*, 1906.

The pig is taught by sermons and epistles, / To think the god of swine has snout and bristles. AMBROSE BIERCE (1842–1914), *The Devil's Dictionary*, 1906.

The First Amendment has erected a wall between church and state. That wall must be kept high and impregnable. We could not approve the slightest breach. . . . State power is no more to be used so as to handicap religions than it is to favor them. HUGO L. BLACK (1886–1971), U.S. Supreme Court Justice, *Everson* v. *Board of Education*, 1947.

Prisons are built with stones of law, brothels with bricks of religion. WILLIAM BLAKE (1757–1827), *Proverbs of Hell*.

The humanist is reconciled to reality and makes his home there, and has a horror of the black-and-white fantasy of heaven and hell. H. J. BLACKHAM, in *The Humanist Frame* (Julian Huxley, ed.), 1961.

Religions are not revealed: they are evolved. If a religion were revealed by God, that religion would be perfect in whole and in part, and would be as perfect at the first moment of its revelation as after ten thousand years of practice. There has never been a religion that fulfills those conditions. ROBERT BLATCHFORD (1851–1943), *God and My Neighbor*, 1903.

To die for a religion is easier than to live it absolutely. JORGE LUIS BORGES (1899–1986), *Labyrinths*.

No object is mysterious. The mystery is in your eye. ELIZABETH BOWEN (1899–1973), *The House in Paris*, 1935.

The atheist does not say, "There is no God," but he says, "I know not what you mean by God; the word God is to me a sound conveying no clear or distinct affirmation." CHARLES BRADLAUGH (1833–1891), *A Plea for Atheism*, 1864.

Metaphysics is the finding of bad reasons for what we believe on instinct; but to find these reasons is no less an instinct. F. H. BRADLEY (1846–1924), *Appearance and Reality*, 1894.

In religion fear and approval to some extent must always combine. . . . In religion approval implies devotion, and devotion seems hardly possible, unless there is some fear, if only the fear of estrangement. F. H. BRADLEY (1846–1924), *Appearance and Reality*, 1894.

The sole result of the mystic projection of "another" reality is that it incapacitates man psychologically for this one. NATHANIEL BRANDEN, *Psychology of Self-Esteem*, 1969.

Faith is the commitment of one's consciousness to beliefs for which one has no sensory evidence or proof. When a man rejects reason as his standard of judgement, only one alternative standard remains: his feelings. A mystic is a man who treats his feelings as tools of cognition. A mystic equates feelings with knowledge. NATHANIEL BRANDEN, *The Psychology of Self-Esteem*, 1969.

The door of the Free Exercise Clause [of the First Amendment] stands tightly closed against any governmental regulation of religious beliefs as such. Government may neither compel affirmation of a repugnant belief, nor penalize or discriminate against individuals or groups because they hold religious views abhorrent to the authorities. WILLIAM J. BRENNAN, JR., U.S. Supreme Court Justice, *Sherbert* v. *Verner*, 1963.

Superstition is the religion of feeble minds. EDMUND BURKE (1729–1797), *Reflections on the Revolution in France*, 1790.

Nothing is so fatal to religion as indifference, which is, at least, half infidelity. EDMUND BURKE (1729–1797), 1795.

One religion is as true as another. ROBERT BURTON (1577–1640), *The Anatomy of Melancholy*, 1621.

A credulous mind . . . finds most delight in believing strange things, and the stranger they are the easier they pass with him; but never regards those that are plain and feasible, for every man can believe such. SAMUEL BUTLER (1612–1680), *Characters*, 1667–79.

Is there any religion whose followers can be pointed to as distinctly more amiable and trustworthy than those of any other? If so, this should be enough. SAMUEL BUTLER (1835–1902), Notebooks.

It must be remembered that we have heard only one side of the case. God has written all the books. SAMUEL BUTLER (1835–1902), Notebooks.

The grand thing about the human mind is that it can turn its own tables and see meaninglessness as ultimate meaning. JOHN CAGE (1912–1992), *Silence,* 1961.

The certainty of a God giving meaning to life far surpasses in attractiveness the ability to behave badly with impunity. ALBERT CAMUS (1913–1960), *The Myth of Sisyphus,* 1942.

There can be no Creator, simply because his grief at the fate of his creation would be inconceivable and unendurable. ELIAS CANETTI, *The Human Province,* 1878.

I will call metaphysical all those propositions which claim to represent knowledge about something which is over or beyond all experience. . . . Metaphysicians cannot avoid making their propositions non-verifiable, because if they make them verifiable, the decision about the truth or falsehood of their doctrines would depend upon experience and therefore belong to the region of empirical science. R. CARNAP (1891–1970), *Philosophy and Logical Syntax,* 1935.

Religion claims to be in possession of an absolute truth; but its history is a history of errors and heresies. It gives us the promise and prospect of a transcendent world—far beyond the limits of our human experience—and it remains human, all too human. ERNST CASSIRER (1874–1945), *An Essay on Man,* 1944.

The real substratum of myth is not a substratum of thought but of feeling. Myth and primitive religion are by no means entirely incoherent, they are not bereft of sense or reason. But their coherence depends much more upon unity of feeling than upon logical rules. This unity is one of the strongest and most profound impulses of primitive thought. ERNEST CASSIRER (1874–1945), *An Essay on Man,* 1944.

Mythical thought is, by its origin and by its principle, traditional thought. . . . For the primitive mind there is no more sacred thing than the sacredness of age. It is age that gives to all things, to physical objects and to human institutions, their value, their dignity, their moral and religious worth. ERNEST CASSIRER (1874–1945), *An Essay on Man,* 1944.

The well-meaning person who, by merely studying the logical side of things, has decided that "faith is nonsense" does not know how truly he speaks; later it may come back to him that nonsense is faith. GILBERT KEITH CHESTERTON (1874–1936), *In Defense of Nonsense.*

It is very good for a man to talk about what he does not understand; as long as he understands that he does not understand it. GILBERT KEITH CHESTERTON (1874–1936), *A Handful of Authors.*

Without the hope of immortality no one would ever face death for his country. MARCUS TULLIUS CICERO (106–43 B.C.).

Religion is not removed by removing superstition. MARCUS TULLIUS CICERO (106–43 B.C.), *De divinatione,* 78 B.C.

Each mystic brings back confirmation of his own creed. . . . The mystic brings his theological beliefs to the mystical experience; he does not derive them from it. GEORGE A. COE, *The Hibbert Journal,* vol. VI, 1907–1908.

The predominant emphasis on the motive of fear for the enforcement of absolute commands has made religious morality develop the most intense cruelty that the human heart has known. MORRIS R. COHEN (1880–1947), in *Religion Today* (A. L. Swift, ed.), 1933.

To most people religion is just a matter of loyalty to the accepted ways hallowed by our ancestors. MORRIS R. COHEN (1880–1947), in *Religion Today* (A. L. Swift, ed.), 1933.

To doubt has more faith, even to disbelieve, than blank negation of all such thoughts and feelings which is the lot of the herd of church-and-meeting trotters. SAMUEL TAYLOR COLERIDGE (1772–1834).

Whenever philosophy has taken into its plan religion, it has ended in skepticism; and wheneve religion excludes philosophy, or the spirit of free inquiry, it leads to wilful blindness and superstition. SAMUEL TAYLOR COLERIDGE (1772–1834), *Letters, Conversations and Recollections of Samuel Taylor Coleridge* (Allsop), 1836.

Precisely in proportion to our own intellectual weakness will be our credulity as to those mysterious powers assumed by others. CHARLES CALEB COLTON (1780–1832), *Lacon,* 1825.

Religion has treated knowledge sometimes as an enemy, sometimes as a hostage; often as a captive and more often as a child. . . . CHARLES CALEB COLTON (1780–1832), *Lacon,* 1825.

We have no reliable guarantee that the afterlife will be any less exasperating than this one, have we? NOEL COWARD (1899–1973), *Blithe Spirit,* 1941.

It was a man who first made men believe in gods. CRITIAS (ca. 480–403 B.C.), Fragment, 425 B.C.

The one big difficulty is not why there is a Hell but why God chooses a world in which there should have to be one. MARTIN C. D'ARCY (1888–1976), *The Problem of Evil,* 1928.

I do not pretend to know where many ignorant men are sure—that is all that agnosticism means. CLARENCE S. DARROW (1857–1938), 1925.

The assumed instinctive belief in God has been used by many persons as an argument for His existence. But this is a rash argument, as we should thus be compelled to believe in the existence of many cruel and malignant spirits, only a little more powerful than man; for the belief in them is far more general than in a beneficent Diety. CHARLES DARWIN (1809–1882), *The Descent of Man,* 1871.

A myth is a fixed way of looking at the world which cannot be destroyed because, looked at through the myth, all evidence supports the myth. EDWARD DE BONO, *Beyond Yes and No.*

Nothing sways the stupid more than arguments they can't understand. CARDINAL de RETZ (1614–1679), *Memoires,* 1762–79.

The moment religion organizes into a specific creed it becomes a political force. From Moses down to Brigham Young, every creed-founder has been a State-builder. DANIEL de LEON (1852–1914), *The Vatican in Politics,* 1891.

Intellectually, religious emotions are not creative but conservative. They attach themselves readily to the current view of the world and consecrate it. JOHN DEWEY (1859–1952), *The Influence of Darwin on Philosophy,* 1909.

Some people have an unconquerable love of riddles. They may have the chance of listening to plain sense, or to such wisdom as explains life; but no, they must go and work their brains over a riddle, just because they do not understand what it means. ISAK DINESEN (1885–1962), *Seven Gothic Tales,* 1934.

Man is a being born to believe. And if no church comes forward with its title-deeds of truth to guide him, he will find altars and idols in his own heart and his own imagination. BENJAMIN DISRAELI (1804–1881).

So long as man remains free he strives for nothing so incessantly and so painfully as to find something to worship. . . . [W]hat is essential is that all may be together in it. The craving for community or worship is the chief misery of . . . all humanity. For the sake of common worship they've slain each other with the sword. FYODOR DOSTOEVSKY (1821–1881), *The Brothers Karamazov,* 1879.

Religion is a bandage that man has invented to protect a soul made bloody by circumstance. THEODORE DREISER (1871–1945).

Religion has its origin and its support in dissatisfaction with life, resulting from reflection on the failure of life to satisfy the primary desires of man. KNIGHT DUNLAP (1875–1949), *Social Psychology,* 1925.

Religions are born and may die, but superstition is immortal. Only the fortunate can take life without mythology. WILL DURANT (1885–1981) and ARIEL DURANT (1898–1981), *The Age of Reason Begins,* 1961.

Does history support a belief in God? If by God we mean not the creative vitality of nature but a supreme being intelligent and benevolent, the answer must be a reluctant negative. Like other departments of biology, history remains at bottom a natural selection of the fittest individuals and groups in a struggle where goodness receives no favors, misfortunes abound, and the final test is the ability to survive. . . . [T]he total evidence suggests either a blind or an impartial fatality. . . . WILL DURANT (1885–1981) and ARIEL DURANT (1898–1981), *The Lessons of History,* 1968.

One strength of the Communist system. . . . is that it has some of the characteristics of a religion and inspires the emotions of a religion. ALBERT EINSTEIN (1879–1955), *Out of My Later Life,* 1950.

The idea of a Being who interferes with the sequence of events in the world is absolutely impossible. ALBERT EINSTEIN (1879–1955), *Has Science Discovered God?* (E. H. Cotton), 1931.

Your dunce who can't do his sums always has a taste for the infinite. GEORGE ELIOT (1819–1880), *Felix Holt, The Radical,* 1860.

The whole religious complexion of the modern world is due to the absense from Jerusalem of a lunatic asylum. HAVELOCK ELLIS (1859–1939), *Impressions and Comments,* 1914.

Heaven always bears some proportion to earth. The god of the cannibal will be a cannibal, of the crusades a crusader, and of the merchants a merchant. RALPH WALDO EMERSON (1803–1882), *The Conduct of Life,* 1860.

The most tedious of all discourses are on the subject of the Supreme Being. RALPH WALDO EMERSON (1803–1882), Journals, 1836.

Do we, holding that the gods exist, deceive ourselves with unsubstantiated dreams, and lies, while random careless chance and change alone rule the world? EURIPIDES (484–406 B.C.).

Whenever morality is based on theology, whenever right is made dependent on divine authority, the most immoral, unjust, infamous things can be justified and established. LUDWIG FEUERBACH (1804–1872), *The Essence of Christianity,* 1841.

Intuition attracts those who wish to be spiritual without any bother, because it promises a heaven where the intuitions of others can be ignored. E. M. FORSTER (1879–1970), *Abinger Harvest,* 1936.

Faith, to my mind, is a stiffening process, a sort of mental starch, which ought to be applied as sparingly as possible. . . . I do not believe in it for its own sake at all. E. M. FORSTER (1879–1970), *Two Cheers for Democracy,* 1951.

That the mythology of the shaman does not correspond to objective reality does not matter. The patient believes in it and belongs to a society that believes in it. The protecting spirits, the evil spirits, the supernatural monsters and magical monsters are elements of a coherent system. JEROME D. FRANK, *Persuasion and Healing,* 1961.

[Humanism] rejects supernaturalism and moral absolutism and argues that the best possibilities of human beings can be achieved only by a combination of informed intelligence and candid recognition that man must bear the responsibility for whatever standards he adopts. CHARLES FRANKEL (1917–1979), *New York Times Book Review,* January 14, 1962.

Homeopathic magic is founded on the association of ideas by similarity: contagious magic is founded on the association of ideas by contiguity. Homeopathic magic commits the mistake of assuming that things which resemble each other are the same: contagious magic commits the mistake of assuming things which have once been in contact with each other are always in contact. SIR JAMES GEORGE FRAZER (1854–1941), *The Golden Bough*, 1922.

The fatal flaw of magic lies not in its general assumption of a sequence of events determined by law, but in its total misconception of the nature of the particular laws which govern that sequence. SIR JAMES GEORGE FRAZER (1854–1941), *The Golden Bough*, 1922.

Religion is the idol of the mob; it adores everything it does not understand. . . . We know the crimes that fanaticism in religion has caused; let us be careful not to introduce fanaticism in philosophy. FREDERICK THE GREAT (1712–1768), Letter to Voltaire, 1737.

All religions must be tolerated, and the sole concern of the authorities should be to see that one does not molest another, for here every man must be saved in his own way. FREDERICK THE GREAT (1712–1768), Cabinet Order, 1740.

Superstition is the weakness of the human mind; it is inherent in that mind; it has always been, and always will be. FREDERICK THE GREAT (1712–1768), Letter to Voltaire, 1766.

A religion, even if it calls itself a religion of love, must be hard and unloving to those who do not belong to it. SIGMUND FREUD (1856–1939), *Group Psychology and the Analysis of the Ego*, 1921.

Religion is an illusion and it derives its strength from the fact that it falls in with our instinctual desires. SIGMUND FREUD (1856–1939), *New Introductory Lectures on Psychoanalysis*, 1933.

Religion is an attempt to get control over the sensory world, in which we are placed, by means of the wish-world which we have developed inside us as a result of biological and psychological necessities. SIGMUND FREUD (1856–1939), *Moses and Monotheism*, 1939.

If faith cannot be reconciled with rational thinking, it has to be eliminated as an anachronistic remnant of earlier stages of culture and replaced by science dealing with facts and theories which are intelligible and can be validated. ERICH FROMM (1900–1980), *Man for Himself*, 1947.

I understand by religion any system of thought and action shared by a group which gives the individual a frame of orientation and an object of devotion. ERICH FROMM (1900–1980), *Psychoanalysis and Religion*, 1950.

The most heinous and the most cruel crimes of which history has record have been committed under the cover of religion or equally noble motives. MOHANDAS K. GANDHI (1869–1948), *Young India*, July 7, 1927.

So urgent on the vulgar is the necessity of believing, that the fall of any system of mythology will probably be succeeded by the introduction of some other mode of superstition. EDWARD GIBBON (1737–1794), *Decline and Fall of the Roman Empire,* 1776–88.

The various modes of worship which prevailed in the Roman world were all considered by the people as equally true; by the philosopher as equally false, and by the magistrate as equally useful. EDWARD GIBBON (1737–1794), *Decline and Fall of the Roman Empire,* 1776–88.

There's no religion so irrational but can boast its martyrs. JOSEPH GLANVILLE (1636–1680), *The Vanity of Dogmatizing,* 1661.

We are so constituted that we believe the most incredible things: and, once they are engraved upon the memory, woe to him who would endeavor to erase them. JOHANN WOLFGANG von GOETHE (1749–1832), *Sorrows of Young Werther,* 1771.

Superstition is rooted in a much deeper and more sensitive layer of the psyche than skepticism. JOHANN WOLFGANG von GOETHE (1749–1832).

The people like neither the true nor the simple: they like novels and charlatans. EDMOND de GONCOURT (1822–1896) and JULES de GONCOURT (1830–1870), *Journal,* 1861.

There is something odd about the weakness which irreligious men feel for religion. Almost invariably it becomes their favorite topic. PHILIP GUEDELLA (1889–1944), *A Gallery,* 1924.

The garb of religion is the best cloak for power. WILLIAM HAZLITT (1778–1830).

Metaphysicians, like all other men who cannot give convincing reasons for their statements, are usually not very polite in controversy. One's success against them may be measured approximately by the increasing want of politeness in their replies. HERMANN von HELMHOLTZ (1821–1894), *On Thought in Medicine,* 1877.

One of the marks of a true mystic is the tenacious and heroic energy with which he pursues a definite moral idea. J. H. HEUBA, *Revue Philosophique,* July 1902.

Mystical experience appears to be no less a product of the nervous system than is the reflex action to a pinprick or the appreciation of a Beethoven symphony. HUDSON HOAGLAND, in *Science Ponders Religion* (Harlow Shapley), 1960.

Fear of things invisible, is the natural seed of that which every one in himself calleth religion. THOMAS HOBBES (1588–1679), *Leviathan,* 1651.

The atheist is a man who destroys the chimeras which afflict the human race, and so leads men back to nature, to experience and to reason. BARON d'HOLBACH (1723–1789), *The System of Nature,* 1770.

All religions are ancient monuments to superstition, ignorance, ferocity; and modern religions are only ancient follies rejuvenated. BARON d'HOLBACH (1723–1789), 1772.

Nature tells man to consult reason, and to take it for his guide: religion teaches him that his reason is corrupted, that it is only a treacherous guide. . . . Nature tells man to enlighten himself, to search after truth, to instruct himself in his duties: religion enjoins him to examine nothing, to remain in ignorance, to fear truth. BARON d'HOLBACH (1723–1789), *The System of Nature,* 1770.

Had it not been for religion, that most harmful of evils, the progress of mind would have been unbounded. . . . Religion has been the scourge of mankind, and it has been made worse by having something of morality, that is, of truth mixed with it. THOMAS HOLCROFT (1745–1809), in *The Life of Thomas Holcroft* (E. Colby), 1925.

Men are idolators, and want something to look at and kiss, or throw themselves down before; they always did, they always will; and if you don't make it of wood, you must make it of words. OLIVER WENDELL HOLMES, SR. (1809–1894), *The Poet at the Breakfast Table,* 1872.

We are all tattooed in our cradles with the beliefs of our tribe; the record may seem superficial, but it is indelible. You cannot educate a man wholly out of the superstitious fears which were implanted in his imagination, no matter how utterly his reason may reject them. OLIVER WENDELL HOLMES, SR. (1809–1894).

[Secularism is] a form of opinion which concerns itself only with questions, the issues of which can be tested by the experience of this life. G. J. HOLYOAKE (1817–1906), *The Origin and Nature of Secularism,* 1896.

As a set of cognitive beliefs, religion is a speculative hypothesis of an extremely low order of probability. SIDNEY HOOK (1902–1989), *The Partisan Review,* March 1950.

If your faith is opposed to experience, human learning and investigation, it is not worth the breath used in giving it expression. EDGAR WATSON HOWE (1853–1937), *Ventures in Common Sense,* 1919.

Religion is but a desperate attempt to find an escape from the truly dreadful situation in which we find ourselves. Here we are in this wholly fantastic universe with scarcely a clue as to whether our existence has any real significance. No wonder then that many people feel the need for some belief that gives them a sense of security, and no wonder that they become very angry with people like me who say that this is illusory. FRED HOYLE, *The Nature of the Universe,* 1950.

Metaphysics is an attempt to define a thing and by so doing escape the bother of understanding. ELBERT HUBBARD (1856–1915), *The Roycroft Dictionary and Book of Epigrams,* 1923.

Theology is an attempt to explain a subject by men who do not understand it. The intent is not to tell the truth but to satisfy the questioner. ELBERT HUBBARD (1856–1915), *The Philistine*.

No man should dogmatize except on the subject of theology. Here he can take his stand, and by throwing the burden of proof on the opposition, he is invincible. We have to die to find out whether he is right. ELBERT HUBBARD (1856–1915), *The Note Book*.

Theology is an attempt to explain a subject by men who do not understand it. The intent is not to tell the truth but to satisfy the questioner. ELBERT HUBBARD (1856–1915), *The Philistine*.

Faith is the effort to believe what your common sense tells you is not true. ELBERT HUBBARD (1856–1915).

A mystic is a person who is puzzled before the obvious, but who understands the nonexistent. ELBERT HUBBARD (1856–1915).

There is not to be found, in all history, any miracle attested by a sufficient number of men, of such unquestioned goodness, education, and learning as to secure us against all delusion in themselves; of such undoubted integrity as to place them beyond all suspicion of any design to deceive others; of such credit and reputation in the eyes of mankind as to have a great deal to lose in case of their being detected in any falsehood; and at the same time attesting facts, performed in such a public manner, and in so celebrated a part of the world, as to render the detection unavoidable. DAVID HUME (1711–1776), *An Enquiry concerning Human Understanding*, 1748.

Morals excite passions, and produce or prevent actions. Reason of itself is utterly impotent in this particular. The roles of morality, therefore, are not conclusions of our reasons. DAVID HUME (1711–1776), *A Treatise of Human Nature*.

The believer is happy; the doubter is wise. HUNGARIAN PROVERB.

You never see animals going through the absurd and often horrible fooleries of magic and religion. . . . Only man behaves with such gratuitous folly. ALDOUS HUXLEY (1894–1963).

[Religion is] a consciously accepted system of make-believe. ALDOUS HUXLEY (1894–1963), *Texts and Pretexts*, 1932.

[Humanism] will have nothing to do with Absolutes, including absolute truth, absolute morality, absolute perfection and absolute authority. JULIAN HUXLEY (1887–1975), *The Humanist Frame*, 1961.

It is wrong for a man to say that he is certain of the objective truth of any proposition unless he can produce evidence which logically justifies that certainty. This is what agnosticism asserts. THOMAS HENRY HUXLEY (1825–1895), *Essays upon Controversial Questions*, 1889.

The foundation of morality is to . . . give up pretending to believe that for which there is no evidence, and repeating unintelligible propositions about things beyond the possibilities of knowledge. THOMAS HENRY HUXLEY (1825–1895), *Essays upon Controversial Questions, 1889.*

[Agnosticism is] not a creed, but a method, the essence of which lies in the rigorous application of a single principle . . . that every man should be able to give a reason for the faith that is in him. THOMAS HENRY HUXLEY (1825–1895).

Agnosticism simply means that a man shall not say he knows or believes that for which he has no grounds for professing to believe. THOMAS HENRY HUXLEY (1825–1895), in *What Great Men Think of Religion* (Ira Cardiff, ed.).

It is the customary fate of new truths to begin as heresies and to end as superstitions. THOMAS HENRY HUXLEY (1825–1895), *The Coming of Age of* The Origin of Species.

I neither deny nor affirm the immortality of man. I see no reason for believing in it, but, on the other hand, I have no means of disproving it. THOMAS HENRY HUXLEY (1825–1895), Letter, 1860.

To become a popular religion, it is only necessary for a superstition to enslave a philosophy. WILLIAM RALPH INGE (1860–1954), *Outspoken Essays,* 1919.

No man with any sense of humor ever founded a religion. ROBERT G. INGERSOLL (1833–1899), *Prose-Poems and Selections,* 1884.

. . . [I]n nature there are neither rewards nor punishments—there are consequences. ROBERT G. INGERSOLL (1833–1899).

It seems almost impossible for religious people to really grasp the ideas of intellectual freedom. They seem to think that a man is responsible for his honest thoughts; that unbelief is a crime, that investigation is sinful; that credulity is a virtue, and that reason is a dangerous guide. ROBERT G. INGERSOLL (1833–1899), "Atheist Truth versus Religion's Ghosts."

It has always seemed absurd to suppose that a god would choose for his companions, during all eternity, the dear souls whose highest and only ambition is to obey. ROBERT G. INGERSOLL (1833–1899), "Individuality."

Our hope of immortality does not come from any religions, but nearly all religions come from that hope. ROBERT G. INGERSOLL (1833–1899), *Chicago Times,* November 14, 1879.

In the name of religion, one tortures, persecutes, builds pyres. In the guise of ideologies, one massacres, tortures and kills. In the name of equality and brotherhood there is suppression and torture. There is nothing in common between the means and the end . . . ideologies and religion . . . are the alibis of the means. EUGENE IONESCO, *Esquire* magazine, 1974.

Man is a venerating animal. He venerates as easily as he purges himself. When they take away from him the gods of his fathers, he looks for others abroad. MAX JACOB (1876–1944), 1922.

Religion . . . shall mean for us, the feelings, acts, and experiences of individual men in their solitude, so far as they apprehend themselves to stand in relation to whatever they may consider divine. WILLIAM JAMES (1842–1910), *The Varieties of Religious Experience*, 1902.

It is only in the lonely emergencies of life that our creed is tested: then routine maxims fail, and we fall back on our Gods. WILLIAM JAMES (1842–1910), *The Will to Believe*, 1896.

A man's religious faith . . . means for me essentially his faith in the existence of an unseen order of some kind in which the riddles of the natural order may be found. WILLIAM JAMES (1842–1910).

Faith means belief in something concerning which doubt is still theoretically possible. WILLIAM JAMES (1842–1910), *Princeton Review*, July 1882.

Religious experience, in other words, spontaneously and inevitably engenders myths, superstitions, dogmas, creeds, and metaphysical theologies, and criticisms of one set of these by the adherents of another. WILLIAM JAMES (1842–1910), *The Varieties of Religious Experience*, 1902.

Religion may be defined as the natural belief in a Power or Powers beyond our control, and upon whom we feel ourselves dependent. MORRIS JASTROW (1861–1921), *The Study of Religion*, 1911.

On the dogmas of religion, as distinguished from moral principles, all mankind, from the beginning of the world to this day, have been quarreling, fighting, burning and torturing one another, for abstractions unintelligible to themselves and to all others, and absolutely beyond the comprehension of the human mind. THOMAS JEFFERSON (1743–1826), U.S. President, 1816.

I am for freedom of religion, and against all maneuvers to bring about a legal ascendency of one sect over another. THOMAS JEFFERSON (1743–1826), U.S. President, Letter, 1799.

I never will, by any word or act, bow to the shrine of intolerance, or admit a right of inquiry into the religious opinions of others. THOMAS JEFFERSON (1743–1826), U.S. President, Letter, 1803.

To compel a man to furnish contributions of money for the propagation of opinions which he disbelieves, is sinful and tyrannical. THOMAS JEFFERSON (1743–1826), Acts for Establishing Religious Freedom in Virginia, 1786.

Nothing is so firmly believed as that which is least known. FRANCIS JEFFREY (1773–1850).

Be not to hasty to trust or admire the teachers of morality; they discourse like angels but they live like men. SAMUEL JOHNSON (1709–1784), *Rasselas*, 1759.

No man will be found in whose mind airy notions do not sometime tyrannize, and force him to hope or fear beyond the limits of sober probability. SAMUEL JOHNSON (1709–1784), *Rasselas,* 1759.

There is no doctrine will do good when nature is wanting. BEN JONSON (1573–1637), *Timber,* 1640.

What excellent fools religion makes of men. BEN JONSON (1573–1637), *Sejanus,* 1603.

That one man of ten thousand or ten million men find a dogma acceptable does not argue for its soundness. DAVID STARR JORDAN (1851–1931), in *What Great Men Think of Religion* (Ira Cardiff, ed.).

Superstition is the only religion of which base souls are capable. JOSEPH JOUBERT (1754–1824), *Pensées,* 1842.

There is holy mistaken zeal in politics as well as in religion. By persuading others, we convince ourselves. JUNIUS (1769–1771).

All mystics set out to say . . . that the incomprehensible is uncomprehensible, and that we knew before. FRANZ KAFKA (1883–1924).

All beliefs on which you bet your life are fundamentally religious beliefs, and atheism can be as much a religion as theism. H. M. KALLEN (1882–1974), *Religion and Freedom,* 1958.

The human heart refuses to believe in a universe without a purpose. IMMANUEL KANT (1724–1804).

Faith means intense, usually confident, belief that is not based on evidence sufficient to command assent from every reasonable person. WALTER KAUFMANN, *Faith of a Heretic,* 1961.

The course of human history is determined, not by what happens in the skies, but by what takes place in the hearts of men. SIR ARTHUR KEITH (1866–1927).

The anatomy of any myth is the anatomy of the men who believed in it and suffered by it. MURRAY KEMPTON, *Part of Our Time,* 1955.

We have used the Bible as if it was a constable's handbook—an opium-dose for keeping beasts of burden patient while they are being overloaded. CHARLES KINGSLEY (1819–1875).

The unbelievers shall have garments of fire fitted unto them; boiling water shall be poured on their heads; their bowels shall be dissolved thereby, and also their skins, and they shall be beaten with maces of iron. KORAN.

To the religious [Rev. Jim] Jones offered religion; to the ideological, he offered politics; to the ignorant and gullible, he offered miracles. CHARLES A. KRAUSE, *Guyana Massacre,* 1978.

The skeptic has no illusions about life, nor a vain belief in the promise of immortality. Since this life here and now is all we can know, our most reasonable option is to live it fully. In not being deluded about the human condition we recognize that we are responsible in large part for what will happen to us. PAUL KURTZ, *The Transcendental Temptation*, 1986.

The basic methodological principle of science is that we should seek natural causal explanations for phenomena. The occult or transcendental temptation is anti-scientific. Where there is uncertainty, the most sensible response is agnosticism or the withholding of judgment. But this is often very difficult. Magical, occult, religious thinking persists in many areas of life, particularly when we are beset by quandaries. It is on the borderlands of knowledge and in areas concerning human meaning and purpose that the transcendental leap is especially tempting. The dissatisfaction with ambiguity and the quest for order often tempts us to invoke unknown occult or magical causes. PAUL KURTZ, *The Transcendental Temptation*, 1986.

To what excesses will men not go to for the sake of a religion in which they believe so little and which they practice so imperfectly. JEAN de LA BRUYÈRE (1645–1696), *Les Caractères*, 1688.

Humanism believes, contrary to all theories of universal predestination, determinism or fatalism, that human beings possess true freedom of creative action and are, within reasonable limits, the masters of their own destiny. CORLISS LAMONT, *The Independent Mind*, 1951.

Even the weakest disputant is made so conceited by what he calls religion, as to think himself wiser than the wisest who thinks differently from him. WALTER SAVAGE LANDOR (1775–1864), *Imaginary Conversations*, 1824–1853.

Every sect is a moral check on its neighbor. Competition is as wholesome in religion as in commerce. WALTER SAVAGE LANDOR (1775–1864).

A belief is an act of faith not requiring proof and which, besides, almost always is not verifiable by any. If faith imposed itself only by rational argument, very few beliefs would have been formed during the course of the centuries. GUSTAVE LE BON (1841–1931), *Opinions and Beliefs*, 1911.

Mystical logic can dominate affective logic to the point of nullifying the instinct for self-preservation. GUSTAVE LE BON (1841–1931), *Aphorisms of Present Times*, 1913.

The equal toleration of all religions . . . is the same thing as atheism. POPE LEO XIII (1810–1903), *Immortal? Dei*, 1885.

Many a man who is now willing to be shot down for the sake of his belief in a miracle would have doubted, if he had been present, the miracle itself. GEORGE CHRISTOPH LICHTENBERG (1742–1799), *Reflections*, 1799.

All the different religions are only so many religious dialects. GEORGE CHRISTOPH LICHTENBERG (1742–1799), *Reflections*, 1799.

Most men of education are more superstitious than they admit—nay, than they think. GEORGE CHRISTOPH LICHTENBERG (1742–1799), *Reflections,* 1799.

The same marvelous faculty that drives us along the road to morality often acts as a sadistic slave driver, a self-accusing fury, and a tireless jobber in guilt. JOSHUA LIEBMAN (1907–1948), *Peace of Mind,* 1946.

Theoretically, religion wishes to make men serene and inwardly peaceful by reaching a loving and forgiving God. But in practice, there is too much undissolved wrath and punishment in most religions. JOSHUA LIEBMAN (1907–1948), *Peace of Mind,* 1946.

There is no arguing with the pretenders to a divine knowledge and to a divine mission. They are possessed with the sin of pride, they have yielded to the perennial temptation. WALTER LIPPMANN (1889–1974), *The Public Philosophy,* 1955

The magic relationship exists not only between and thing and its analogous imitation—equally mystical is the connection between a thing and its name. Even philosophers like Plato and Aristotle believed that the name of a thing is contained in it like an invisible kernel and that the name determines its very nature. Only during the last two thousand years have the Middle European peoples developed the idea that words are mere symbols for the objects they designate and that the things exist independently from the names by which we describe them. JULIUS E. LIPS (1895–1950), *The Origin of Things,* 1956.

In our minds, the relationship between cause and effect is the result of our logical thinking, based especially on our experiences in the natural sciences. In the minds of primitive men, cause and effect are not restricted to the small domain of the physical world, but they are associated with the powers and phenomena beyond the visible world. To the primitive, this all-pervading power is completely natural, because to his way of thinking, the supernatural is concrete reality. JULIUS E. LIPS (1895–1950), *The Origin of Things,* 1956.

Faith is the assent to any proposi ion not . . . made out by the deductions of reason, but upon the credit of the proposer, as coming from God, in some extraordinary way of communication. JOHN LOCKE (1632–1704), *An Essay concerning Human Understanding,* 1690.

The ignorant man always adores what he cannot understand. CESARE LOMBROSO (1853–1909), *The Man of Genius.*

Round about what is, lies a whole mysterious world of might be, a psychological romance of possibilities of things that do not happen. HENRY WADSWORTH LONGFELLOW (1807–1882).

We forbid our Protestant subjects to meet . . . for the exercise of their [religion] in any public place or any private home, under any pretext whatever. LOUIS XIV (1638–1715), Edict, 1685.

[Religion is] a sense of something transcending the expected or natural, a sense of the Extraordinary, Mysterious, or Supernatural. ROBERT H. LOWIE (1883–1957), *Primitive Religion*, 1924.

We should always be disposed to believe that that which appears to us to be white is really black, if the hierarchy of the Church so desires. IGNATIUS LOYOLA (1491–1556), *Spiritual Exercises*, 1541.

The modern theory that you should always treat the religious convictions of other people with profound respect finds no support in the Gospels. Mutual tolerance of religious views is the product not of faith, but of doubt. ARNOLD LUNN (1888–1974).

Reason is the greatest enemy that faith has: it never comes to the aid of spiritual things, but—more frequently than not—struggles against the divine word, treating with contempt all that emanates from God. MARTIN LUTHER (1483–1546).

It is therefore the duty of princes and heads of republics to uphold the foundations of the religion of their countries, for then it is easy to keep their people religious, and consequently well conducted and united. NICCOLO MACHIAVELLI (1469–1527), *Discourses on the First Ten Books of Livy*, 1517.

Our religion has glorified those of meek and contemplative character rather than those of action. Further, it places the highest good in humility, lowliness, and the contempt for worldly things. . . . This manner of life, then, seems to have rendered the world weak, and to have given it over as a prey to wicked men. NICCOLO MACHIAVELLI (1469–1527), *Discourses on the First Ten Books of Livy*, 1517.

By myths we mean the value-impregnated beliefs and notions that men hold, that they live by or live for. . . . We imply nothing concerning the grounds of belief, so far as belief claims to interpret reality. ROBERT M. MACIVER (1882–1957), *The Web of Government*, 1947.

Religion is an emotion resting on a conviction of a harmony between ourselves and the universe at large. JOHN McTAGGART ELLIS (1866–1925), *Some Dogmas of Religion*, 1906.

Religious bondage shackles and debilitates the mind, and unfits it for every noble enterprise. JAMES MADISON (1751–1836), U.S. President, Letter to William Bradford, Jr., January 24, 1774.

Absolute atheism starts in an act of faith in reverse gear and is a full-blown religious commitment. JACQUES MARITAIN (1882–1973).

I count religion but a childish toy, and hold there is no sin but ignorance. CHRISTOPHER MARLOWE (1564–1593), *The Jew of Malta*, 1589.

What the religous interest strives to do is to preserve intact an infantile image of the ideal father, perfect and "pure" and sinless. E. D. MARTIN, *The Mystery of Religion*, 1924.

. . . [A]lmost without exception cultic belief systems all manifest a type of institutional dogmatism and pronounced intolerance for any position but their own. . . . [T]his line of reasoning [is] resistant to change and penetration since the cults thrive on conformity, ambiguity and extremeness of belief. WALTER R. MARTIN, *The Kingdom of the Cults,* 1965.

It has been said that metaphysics is the finding of bad reasons for what we believe on instinct. W. SOMERSET MAUGHAM (1874–1965), *The Summing Up,* 1938.

Metaphysics is almost always an attempt to prove the incredible by an appeal to the unintelligible. H. L. MENCKEN (1880–1956), *Minority Report,* 1956.

The curse of man, and cause of nearly all of his woes, is his stupendous capacity for believing the incredible. H. L. MENCKEN (1880–1956), *A Mencken Chrestomathy,* 1949.

The most costly of all follies is to believe passionately in the palpably not true. H. L. MENCKEN (1880–1956), *A Mencken Chrestomathy,* 1949.

God is the immemorial refuge of the incompetent, the helpless, the miserable. They find not only sanctuary in his arms, but also a kind of superiority, soothing to their macerated egos; He will set them above their betters. H. L. MENCKEN (1880–1956), *Minority Report,* 1956.

[Metaphysicians are] men with no taste for exact facts, but only a desire to transcend and forget them as quickly as possible. H. L. MENCKEN (1880–1956).

Faith may be defined briefly as an illogical belief in the occurrence of the improbable. H. L. MENCKEN (1880–1956), *Prejudices.*

Let us next consider the subject of metaphysics. Alas, what an immensity of nonsense awaits us! J. B. MENCKEN, *De Charlanteria eruditorum,* 1715.

Metaphysics pleases me because it is never ending. PROSPER MERIMÉE (1803–1870), *Letters to an Unknown,* 1854.

A being who can create a race of men devoid of real freedom and inevitably foredoomed to be sinners, and then punish them for being what he has made them, may be omnipotent and various other things, but he is not what the English language has always intended by the adjective holy. JOHN STUART MILL (1806–1873), *Examination of Sir William Hamilton's Philosophy,* 1865.

The tendency has always been strong to believe that whatever receives a name must be an entity or being, having an independent existence of its own; and if no real entity answering to the name could be found, men did not for that reason suppose that none existed, but imagined that it was something peculiarly abstruse and mysterious, too high to be an object of sense. JOHN STUART MILL (1806–1873).

The world would be astonished if it knew how great a proportion of its brightest ornaments, of those most distinguished even in popular estimation for wisdom and virtue, are complete skeptics in religion. JOHN STUART MILL (1806–1873), in *What Great Men Think of Religion* (Ira Cardiff, ed.).

The notion that truths external to the human mind may be known by intuition or consciousness, independently of observation or experience, is, I am persuaded, in these times, the great intellectual support of false doctrines and bad institutions. By the aid of this theory, every inveterate belief and every intense feeling, of which the origin is not remembered, is enabled to dispense with the obligation of justifying itself by reason, and is erected into its own all-sufficient voucher and justification. JOHN STUART MILL (1806–1873), *Autobiography.*

Safe upon the solid rock the ugly houses stand: / Come and see my shining palace built upon the sand! EDNA ST. VINCENT MILLAY (1892–1950), "A Few Figs from Thistles," 1921.

Life has to be given a meaning because of the obvious fact that it has no meaning. HENRY MILLER (1891–1980), *The Wisdom of the Heart,* 1941.

The greatest burden in the world is superstition, not only of the ceremonies in the Church, but of imaginary and scarecrow sins at home. JOHN MILTON (1608–1674).

Man is certainly stark mad. He cannot make a flea, and yet he will be making gods by the dozen. MICHEL de MONTAIGNE (1533–1592). *Essays,* 1588.

The most gross and childish ravings are most found in those authors who treat of the most elevated subjects. MICHEL de MONTAIGNE (1533–1592), *Essays,* 1588.

Miracles appear to be so, according to our ignorance of nature, and not according to the essence of nature. MICHEL de MONTAIGNE (1533–1592), *Essays,* 1580.

If triangles had a God, he would have three sides. CHARLES-LOUIS de SECONDAT, BARON de MONTESQUIEU (1689–1755), *Lettres persanes,* 1721.

Christian mysticism, whether of the quasi or the mixed type, is connected with a craving for intensity of experience at the cost of clarity and sanity. PAUL ELMER MORE (1864–1937), *The Catholic Faith,* 1931.

Where it is a duty to worship the sun, it is pretty sure to be a crime to examine the laws of heat. JOHN MORLEY (1832–1923), *Voltaire,* 1872.

Religion is excellent stuff for keeping the common people quiet. NAPOLEON BONAPARTE (1769–1821).

I would believe in a religion if it existed ever since the beginning of time, but when I consider Socrates, Plato, Mohamet, I no longer believe. All religions have been made by men. NAPOLEON BONAPARTE (1769–1821), To Gaspard Gourmond at St. Helena, January 28, 1817.

Man's uneasiness is such, that the vagueness and the mystery which religion presents are absolutely necessary to him. NAPOLEON BONAPARTE (1769–1821), *Maxims,* 1804–1815.

It too often happens that the religiously disposed are in the same degree intellectually deficient. JOHN HENRY NEWMAN (1801–1890), *The Idea of a University,* 1852.

There is no social evil, no form of injustice, whether of the feudal or capitalist order, which has not been sanctified in some way or another by religious sentiment and thereby rendered more impervious to change. REINHOLD NIEBUHR (1892–1971), *Christian Realism and Political Problems,* 1953.

A scientific humanism frequently offends the dignity of man, which it ostensibly extols, by regarding human beings as subject to manipulation and as mere instruments of some "socially approved" ends. REINHOLD NIEBUHR (1892–1971), *Christian Realism and Political Problems,* 1953.

The religious interpretation of the world is essentially an insistence that the ideal is real and that the real can be understood only in the light of the ideal. REINHOLD NIEBUHR (1892–1971).

Religion is so frequently a source of confusion in political life, and so frequently dangerous to democracy, precisely because it introduces absolutism into the realm of relative values. REINHOLD NIEBUHR (1892–1971), quoted in *Brown Alumni Monthly,* May 1989.

The desire for a strong faith is not the proof of a strong faith, rather the opposite. If one has it one may permit oneself the beautiful luxury of scepticism: one is secure enough, firm enough, fixed enough for it. FRIEDRICH NIETZSCHE (1844–1900), *Twilight of the Idols,* 1888.

Wherever on earth the religious neurosis has appeared we find it tied to three dangerous dietary demands: solitude, fasting, and sexual abstinence. FRIEDRICH NIETZSCHE (1844–1900), *Beyond Good and Evil,* 1886.

The Christian concept of a god—the god as the patron of the sick, the god as a spinner of cobwebs, the god as a spirit—is one of the most corrupt concepts that has ever been set up in the world: it probably touches the low-water mark in the ebbing evolution of the god-type. FRIEDRICH NIETZSCHE (1844–1900), *The Antichrist.*

Religious ideologies and their fanaticisms are dangerous enough, but when these or other ideologies become frenzied elements of the political area, the only area of absolute power over human lives . . . they become potentially dangerous in their impact on a free society. ROBERT NISBET, *Prejudices: A Philosophical Dictionary,* 1982.

The lie of a pipe dream is what gives life to the whole misbegotten mad lot of us, drunk or sober. EUGENE O'NEILL (1888–1953), *The Iceman Cometh,* 1946.

. . . [T]he sort of atheist who does not so much disbelieve in God as personally dislikes him. GEORGE ORWELL (1903–1950), *Down and Out in Paris and London,* 1933.

The desire for immortality seems never to have had a very strong hold upon mankind, and the belief is less widely held than is usually stated. SIR WILLIAM OSLER (1849–1919), *Science and Immortality,* 1904.

[Religious mystery is] the standard device for getting around a logical contradiction by elevating it to the status of a truth beyond logic. MAX C. OTTO, *Religious Liberals Reply,* 1947.

Morality is the means for the satisfaction of human wants. In other words, morality must justify itself at the bar of life, not life at the bar of morality. MAX C. OTTO, *Things and Ideals,* 1924.

Society, democratic from end to end, can brook no such radical class distinction as that between a supreme being favored with eternal and absolute perfection and the man of beings doomed to the lower ways of imperfect struggle. HARRY A. OVERSTREET, *Hibbert Journal,* vol. XI, 1913.

It is expedient that gods should exist: since it is expedient, let us believe they do. OVID (43 B.C.–17 A.D.), *Ars amatoria,* 2 B.C.

Whenever we read the obscene stories, the voluptuous debaucheries, the cruel and torturous executions, the unrelenting vindictiveness, with which more than half the Bible is filled, it would be more consistent that we called it the word of a demon than the word of God. It is a history of wickedness that has served to corrupt and brutalize mankind. THOMAS PAINE (1737–1809), *The Age of Reason,* 1795.

Inborn religious faculty is the basis and cause of all religion. . . . If man have not a religious element in his nature, miraculous or other "Revelations" can no more render him religious than fragments of sermons and leaves of the Bible can make a lamb religious when mixed and eaten with its daily food. THEODORE PARKER (1810–1860), *Views of Religion,* 1855.

When life is colorful and varied, religion can be austere and unimportant. Where life is appallingly monotonous, religion must be emotional, dramatic and intense. C. NORTHCOTE PARKINSON, *East and West,* 1963.

Men never do evil so completely and cheerfully as when they do it from a religious conviction. BLAISE PASCAL (1623–1662), *Pensées,* 1670.

God must have loved the people in power, for he made them so much like their own image of him. KENNETH PATCHEN (1911–1972), *Some Little Sayings and Observations,* 1956.

When an age is found occupied in proving its creed, this is but a token that the age has ceased to have a proper belief in it. MARK PATTISON (1813–1884), *Tendencies of Religious Thought in England,* 1860.

Religion consists of believing that everything that happens is extraordinarily important. It can never disappear from the world, precisely for this reason. CESARE PAVESE (1908–1950), *The Business of Living: Diaries,* 1935–1950.

You are never dedicated to something you have complete confidence in. When people are fanatically dedicated to political or religious faiths, or any other kind of dogma or goals, it's always because these dogmas or goals are in doubt. ROBERT M. PERSIG, *Zen and the Art of Motorcycle Maintenance,* 1974.

It was fear that first brought gods into the world. PETRONIUS (d. 65 A.D.), *Satyricon,* ca. 50 A.D.

But when the divine part began to fade away, they then behaved unseemly and grew visibly debased, full of avarice and righteous power. PLATO (427–347 B.C.).

It is ridiculous to suppose that the great head of things, whatever it may be, pays any regard to human affairs. PLINY THE ELDER (ca. 23–79 A.D.), *Natural History.*

Since the masses of the people are inconstant, full of unruly desires, passionate, and reckless of consequence, they must be filled with fears to keep them in order. The ancients did well, therefore, to invent gods, and the belief in punishment after death. POLYBIUS (c. 200–118 B.C.), *Histories,* 125 B.C.

Our civilization . . . has not yet fully recovered from the shock of its birth— the transition from the tribal or "closed society," with its submission to magical forces, to the "open society" which sets free the critical powers of man. SIR KARL POPPER, *The Open Society and Its Enemies,* 1966.

Cults can insure members' obedience by establishing a spiral of escalating commitment; the cult member, at first, agrees to simple requests that become increasingly more demanding. ANTHONY PRATKANIS and ELLIOT ARONSON, *Age of Propaganda,* 1991.

Although we talk so much about coincidence we do not really believe in it. In our heart of hearts we think better of the universe, we are secretly convinced that it is not such a slipshod, haphazard affair, that everything in it has meaning. J. B. PRIESTLY (1894–1984).

Everything great in the world is done by neurotics; they alone founded our religions and created our masterpieces. MARCEL PROUST (1871–1922), *The Perpetual Pessimist.*

No miracle has ever taken place under conditions which science can accept. Experience shows, without exception, that miracles occur only in times and in countries in which miracles are believed in, and in the presence of persons who are disposed to believe them. ERNEST RENAN (1823–1890), *The Life of Jesus,* 1863.

Mysticism is, in essence, little more than a certain intensity and depth of feeling in regard to what is believed about the universe. BERTRAND RUSSELL (1872–1970), *Mysticism and Logic,* 1917.

Religions, which condemn the pleasures of sense, drive men to seek the pleasures of power. Throughout history power has been the vice of the ascetic. BERTRAND RUSSELL (1872–1970), 1938.

By religion I mean a set of beliefs held as dogmas, dominating the conduct of life, going beyond or contrary to evidence, and inculcated by methods which are emotional, or authoritarian, "not intellectual." BERTRAND RUSSELL (1872–1970), *Practice and Theory of Bolshevism,* 1920.

In every writer on philosophy there is a concealed metaphysic, usually unconscious; even if his subject is metaphysics, he is almost certain to have an uncritically believed system which underlies his specific arguments. BERTRAND RUSSELL (1872–1970), in *The Philosophy of John Dewey* (P. A. Schilpp, ed.).

Faith in the supernatural is a desperate wager made by man at the lowest ebb of his fortunes. GEORGE SANTAYANA (1863–1952), *Reason in Science,* 1906.

Proofs are the last thing looked for by a truly religious mind which feels the imaginative fitness of its faith. GEORGE SANTAYANA (1863–1952), *Interpretations of Poetry and Religion,* 1900.

Even the heretics and atheists, if they had profundity, turn out after a while to be forerunners of some new orthodoxy. What they rebel against is a religion alien to their nature; they are atheists only by accident, and relatively to the conventions which inwardly offend them. . . . GEORGE SANTAYANA (1863–1952), *Reason in Religion,* 1905.

The brute necessity of believing something so long as life exists does not justify any belief in particular. GEORGE SANTAYANA (1863–1952), *Skepticism and Animal Faith,* 1923.

[Metaphysics is] an attempt to learn matters of fact by means of logical or moral or rhetorical constructions. GEORGE SANTAYANA (1863–1952), *Skepticism and Animal Faith,* 1923.

Men become superstitious, not because they have too much imagination, but because they are not aware that they have any. GEORGE SANTAYANA (1863–1952), *Little Essays,* 1920.

Skepticism is a discipline fit to purify the mind of prejudice and render it all the more apt, when the time comes, to believe and act wisely. GEORGE SANTAYANA (1863–1952).

Religion is the natural reaction of the imagination when confronted by the difficulties in a truculent world. GEORGE SANTAYANA (1863–1952), *Atlantic Monthly,* 1953.

Miracles are propitious accidents, the natural causes of which are too complicated to be readily understood. GEORGE SANTAYANA (1863–1952), *Introduction to the Ethics of Spinoza,* 1910.

The most malicious kind of hatred is that which is built upon a theological foundation. GEORGE SARTON (1884–1955), *History of Science.*

There are still a few old-fashioned rationalists, freethinkers, or professional atheists, who mourn the failures of humanitarianism as a universal religion, and who are therefore willing to call themselves religious humanists. HERBERT WALLACE SCHNEIDER, *Religion in the Twentieth Century,* 1952.

All religions promise a reward . . . for excellences of the will or heart, but none for excellences of the head or understanding. ARTHUR SCHOPENHAUER (1788–1860), *The World as Will and Idea,* 1819.

The chief objection I have to pantheism is that it says nothing. To call the world God is not to explain it; it is only to enrich our language with a superfluous synonym for the word world. ARTHUR SCHOPENHAUER (1788–1860), *A Few Words on Pantheism,* 1851.

Astrology furnishes a splendid proof of the contemptible subjectivity of men. It refers the course of celestial bodies to the miserable ego; it establishes a connection between the comets in heaven and squabbles and rascalities on earth. ARTHUR SCHOPENHAUER (1788–1860), *Parerga and Paralipomena,* 1851.

Every religion or cause grows out of a desire either to make one's own life more effortless, or to control and manipulate other people in order to enforce behavior in conformity with the expectations of the true believers. BUTLER D. SHAFFER, *Calculated Chaos,* 1985.

The fact that a believer is happier than a skeptic is no more to the point than that a drunken man is happier than a sober one. GEORGE BERNARD SHAW (1856–1950).

Heaven, as conventionally described, is a place so inane, so dull, so useless, so miserable, that nobody has ever ventured to describe a whole day in heaven, though plenty of people have described a day at the seaside. GEORGE BERNARD SHAW (1856–1950), *Misalliance,* 1910.

[Christianity] was a religion perfectly tailored to appeal to the lower classes; it preached that those who do well have done wrong and that those who have done nothing constructive are the most worthy of all. ROBERT SHEAFFER, *Resentment against Achievement,* 1988.

Our reason can never admit the testimony of men who not only declare that they were eyewitnesses of miracles, but that the Deity was irrational; for He commanded that He should be believed, He proposed the highest rewards for faith, eternal punishment for disbelief. PERCY BYSSHE SHELLEY (1792–1822), *Queen Mab,* 1813.

[Religion is] the reaction of mankind to something apprehended but not comprehended. JAMES SHOTWELL (1874–1965), *The Religious Revolution of Today,* 1924.

[Agnostics are] people who, like myself, confess themselves to be hopelessly ignorant concerning a variety of matters, about which metaphysicians and theologians, both orthodox and heterodox, dogmatize with the utmost confidence. HERBERT SPENCER (1820–1903), 1863.

A miracle signifies nothing more than an event . . . the cause of which cannot be explained by another familiar instance, or . . . which the narrator is unable to explain. BARUCH SPINOZA (1632–1677).

I found nothing grand in the history of the Jews nor in the morals inculcated in the Pentateuch. I know of no other books that so fully teach the subjection and degradation of women. ELIZABETH CADY STANTON (1815–1902), *Eighty Years and More*, 1898.

The religious superstitions of women perpetuate their bondage more than all other adverse influences. ELIZABETH CADY STANTON (1815–1902).

All religions are founded on the fear of the many and the cleverness of the few. STENDHAL (1783–1842).

Early man and his later brothers doubted that eath was natural and attributed it to the action of supernatural, and often malevolent, agencies. The search for a cause has led man to suspect the sun, moon, stars, animals, ghosts, ancestors and family members. Intense fear produced generalizations attributing to these entities not only the cause of disease but other misfortunes. Thus in his demonology primitive man attributed to nonhuman and even inanimate nature his own human motivations and methods—an early but vivid illustration of projective reasoning. DAVID W. SWANSON et al., *The Paranoid*, 1970.

Paranoid thinking, specifically the project of human inefficacy or wrongdoing onto a noncorporeal entity, is evident in both ancient and current religious thinking. Evil spirits, gods of the underworld and Satan have been held responsible for natural catastrophes, misfortune, war, crime and unacceptable thoughts. DAVID W. SWANSON et al., *The Paranoid*, 1970.

Mysticism joins and unites; reason divides and separates. People crave belonging more than understanding. Hence, the prominent role of mysticism, and the limited role of reason, in human affairs. THOMAS SZASZ, *The Untamed Tongue*, 1990.

The more strongly a belief is held, the harder it is to see evidence of its disproof. JOHN TAYLOR, *Science and the Supernatural*, 1980.

Philosophy seeks knowledge for the sake of understanding, while religion seeks knowledge for the sake of worship. WILLIAM TEMPLE (1881–1944), *Nature, Man and God*, 1934.

There lives more faith in honest doubt, believe me, than in half the creeds. ALFRED, LORD TENNYSON (1809–1892), *In Memoriam*, 1850.

All religious notions are uniformly founded on authority; all the religions of the world forbid examination, and are not disposed that men should reason upon them. PAUL HENRI THIRY (1723–1789).

Defensible agnosticism is that of the person who admits that he does not know, and is consequently open to learning. DAVID E. TRUEBLOOD, *Philosophy of Religion,* 1957.

Whatever a man prays for, he prays for a miracle. Every prayer reduces itself to this: "Great God, grant that twice two be not four." IVAN S. TURGENEV (1818–1883).

God's contempt for human minds is evidenced by miracles. He judges them unworthy of being drawn to Him by other means than those of stupefaction and the crudest modes of sensibility. PAUL VALÉRY (1871–1945), *Tel quel,* 1941-43.

Imagination is more robust in proportion as reasoning power is weak. GIOVANNI BATTISTA VICO (1668–1744), *Principles of a New Science Concerning the Common Nature of Nations,* 1720–25.

[Fanaticism is] the effect of a false conscience, which makes religion subservient to the caprices of the imagination, and the excesses of the passions. VOLTAIRE (1694–1778).

When one speaks to another man who doesn't understand him, and when the man who's speaking no longer understands, it's metaphysics. VOLTAIRE (1694–1778), *Candide,* 1759.

Theological religion is the source of all imaginable follies and disturbances; it is the parent of fanaticism and civil discord; it is the enemy of mankind. VOLTAIRE (1694–1778), *Philosophical Dictionary,* 1764.

Faith consists of believing when it is beyond the power of reason to believe. It is not enough that a thing be possible for it to be believed. VOLTAIRE (1694–1778), *Questions sur l'encyclopédie.*

If god did not exist, it would be necessary to invent him. VOLTAIRE (1694–1778).

Say what you will about the sweet miracle of unquestioning faith. I consider a capacity for it terrifying and absolutely vile. KURT VONNEGUT, JR.

Today there is but one religious dogma in debate: What do you mean by "God"? . . . This is the fundamental religious dogma, and all other dogmas are subsidiary to it. ALFRED NORTH WHITEHEAD (1861–1947), *Religion in the Making,* 1926.

Even in religious fervor there is a touch of animal heat. WALT WHITMAN (1819–1892), *Democratic Vistas,* 1870.

So many gods, so many creeds, / So many paths that wind and wind, / While just the art of being kind, / Is all the sad world needs. ELLA WHEELER WILCOX (1850–1919), *The World's Need.*

The value of an idea has nothing whatsoever to do with the sincerity of the man who expresses it. OSCAR WILDE (1854–1900).

Truth in matters of religion, is simply the opinion that has survived. OSCAR WILDE (1854–1900), *The Critic as Artist,* 1891.

Religions die when they are proved to be true. Science is the record of dead religions. OSCAR WILDE (1854–1900), 1894.

[A believer is] one in whom persuasion and belief had ripened into faith and faith became a passionate intuition. WILLIAM WORDSWORTH (1770–1850).

The Ethiopians say that their gods are snub-nosed and black, the Thracians that theirs have light blue eyes and red hair. XENOPHANES (ca. 560–ca. 478 B.C.), Fragment 15.

Political Psychology

To be a human being means to possess a feeling of inferiority which constantly presses towards its own conquest. . . . The greater the feeling of inferiority that has been experienced, the more powerful is the urge to conquest and the more violent the emotional agitation. ALFRED ADLER (1870–1967), in *The Individual Psychology of Alfred Adler* (Ansbacher), 1933.

The trouble with modern theories of behaviorism is not that they are wrong but that they could become true, that they actually are the best possible conceptualization of certain obvious trends in modern society. It is quite conceivable that the modern age—which began with such an unprecedented and promising outburst of human activity—may end in the deadliest, most sterile passivity history has ever known. HANNAH ARENDT (1906–1975), *The Human Condition*, 1959.

Pleasure and nobility between them supply the motives for all actions whatsoever. ARISTOTLE (384–322 B.C.), *The Nicomachean Ethics*, 340 B.C.

The power of authority is never more subtle and effective than when it produces a psychological "atmosphere" or "climate" favorable to the life of certain modes of belief, unfavorable, and even fatal, to the life of others. ARTHUR BALFOUR (1848–1930), *The Foundations of Belief*, 1895.

The herd instinct makes the average man afraid to stand alone; he is always afraid to stand alone for an idea, no matter how good, simply as a matter of prejudice. Our herd, like every herd, when stampeded is liable to trample under its feet anybody who does not run with it. VICTOR BERGER (1860–1929).

All forms of tampering with human beings, getting at them, shaping them against their will to your own pattern, all thought control and conditioning is therefore a denial of that in man which makes them men and their values ultimate. SIR ISAIAH BERLIN, *Two Concepts of Liberty*, 1958.

What the fanatical theocrat lacks in artistic imagination, he makes up in paranoia. There can be no pluralism, no diversity, no individuality in his kingdom. Such things are, to him, manifestations of evil. . . . On every hand, so he imagines, are heretics, saboteurs, wreckers, hatching their sinister conspiracies. From such paranoia comes the purge, the assassination. LLOYD BILLINGSLEY, *Religion's Rebel Son: Fanaticism in Our Time*, 1986.

One of the cardinal causes of war, in the opinion of the present writer, is the fact that national leadership frequently falls to men of abnormal makeup. There are ill-balanced men of history who have been directed by a star of destiny, an inner voice, or a guiding light. Other men, free from hallucinations, have been motivated by hatred or suspicion having a paranoid quality. C. S. BLUEMEL, *War, Politics and Insanity,* 1948.

Persons in groups may experience both loss of self-awareness and evaluation apprehension, a process called deindividuation. . . . Group situations that produce anonymity and draw attention away from each person seem most likely to foster the deindividuation process. MARTIN BOLT, "Group Dynamics," in Baker, *Encyclopedia of Psychology* (David G. Benner, ed.), 1985.

We often do not know ourselves the grounds / On which we act, though plain to others. BERTOLT BRECHT (1898–1956), *Roundheads and Peakheads,* 1933.

Certain subjects are clearly emotionally loaded. Discussing them generates peculiar resistances that are hardly amenable to rational argument. . . . [T]hese resistances are the result of a longstanding conditioning, going back to earliest childhood. . . . The net result is a powerful reinforcement and perpetuation of the dominant ideology and . . . individuals ready at a later stage to accept the authority of the school teacher, priest, employer and politician. MAURICE BRINTON, *The Irrational in Politics.*

The radical tends to cut himself off from the rest of the community and depends more on his political associates for love and friendship. The radical organization is likely to lose members who fail to find satisfying primary relations within the group or find them elsewhere. LEONARD BROOM and PHILIP SELZNICK, *Sociology,* 1957.

Since a political mass movement has to compete with other demands for loyalty, it is initially against both religion and the family, as the two social bodies which attract the most deep-rooted emotions. JAMES A. C. BROWN (1911–1964), *Techniques of Persuasion,* 1963.

Communism and fascism or nazism, although poles apart in their intellectual content are similar in this, that both have emotional appeal to the type of personality that takes pleasure in being submerged in a mass movement and submitting to superior authority. JAMES A. C. BROWN (1911–1964), *Techniques of Persuasion,* 1963.

Revolutionary leaders belong to the category of the rejected, the minority group, the social misfits, the mentally unbalanced, the power-seeking . . . the jealous lower middle class, the discontented ex-serviceman, and the self-centered who have lost faith in themselves. For these, the mass movement has attractions, not by reason of its doctrine alone, but because it can cure their frustrations by freeing them from their ineffectual selves and submerging them in a closely knit and confident corporate whole. JAMES A. C. BROWN (1911–1964), *Techniques of Persuasion,* 1963.

Nowhere are prejudices more mistaken for truth, passion for reason, and invective for documentation than in politics. That is a realm, peopled only by villains or heroes, in which everything is black or white and gray is a forbidden color. JOHN MASON BROWN (1900–1969), *Through These Men,* 1956.

How little solidity and substance there is in the political or social beliefs of nineteen persons out of twenty. These beliefs, when examined, mostly resolve themselves into two or three prejudices and aversions, two or three prepossessions for a particular party or section of a party, two or three phrases or catch-words suggesting or embodying arguments which the man who repeats them has not analyzed. JAMES BRYCE (1849–1926), *The American Commonwealth.*

Fascism, therefore, must be fought with Freudian as well as Marxist weapons. And, like fascism, communism will have to call on sadistic and masochistic love. Masochistic tendencies must be excited in the fascist masses, and sadistic tendencies among the Communists. . . . But we must never forget that the dominant revolutionary complex is to be sadistic. This means that hatred of the father should always be stronger than love of the brother. NICOLAS CALAS, *Partisan Review,* January–February 1940.

On behalf of emotional conviction a man will sacrifice position, wealth, honor, honesty, ethics, and life. The most honorable of men considers it his honorable duty to lie, cheat, steal, and murder for his emotional convictions. It is essential, if we are to understand the real problems of the world in which we actually live, that we recognize and acknowledge that emotional conviction outweighs any and all other considerations. JOHN W. CAMPBELL, *Analog,* December 1960.

All passions exaggerate; it is only because they exaggerate that they are passions. NICOLAS SEBASTIEN CHAMFORT (1741–1794), 1805.

In the history of social behavior there certainly are some patterns which in their main outlines recur again and again, revealing as they do so similarities which become ever more recognizable. And this is nowhere more evident than in the case of highly emotional mass movements. . . . The old symbols and the old slogans have indeed disappeared, to be replaced by new ones; but the structure of the basic phantasies seems to have changed scarcely at all. NORMAN COHN, *The Pursuit of the Millennium,* 1957.

Politics is turning a complex problem of the head into a simple moral question of the heart. FRANK MOORE COLBY (1865–1925).

A man's most open actions have a secret side to them. JOSEPH CONRAD (1857–1924), *Under Western Eyes,* 1911.

In groups that appeal only to a peripheral part of the members' personality . . . conflicts are apt to be less sharp and violent than in groups wherein ties . . . [involve] the total personality of the members. LEWIS A. COSER, *The Functions of Social Conflict,* 1956.

The quest for authority results from a wide range of factors . . . the dissolution of conventional moral codes; the erosion of traditional authority. . . . As a result, large numbers of people have begun to suffer a kind of choice fatigue. They hunger for an authority that will simplfy, straighten out, assure. HARVEY COX, *Psychology Today,* July 1977.

When the mind is dissatisfied, whether upon grounds just or unjust, it ever views objects through an exaggerated medium. CHARLOTTE DACRE, *Zofloya,* 1806.

If a set of beliefs prescribes a corresponding code of conduct, if the believer has internalized this code, and if he now perceives himself as living up to it, he is also likely to experience a gain in his own feelings of righteousness. . . . KARL W. DEUTSCH, in *Sanity and Survival: Psychological Aspects of War and Peace* (Jerome Frank), 1967.

The mind cannot support moral chaos for long. Men are under as strong a compulsion to invent an ethical setting for their behavior as spiders are to weave webs. JOHN DOS PASSOS (1896–1970).

A failure to feel any guilt or shame about his misdeeds is considered the mark of a psychopath, if the lack of guilt or shame pervades all or most aspects of his life. PAUL EKMAN, *Telling Lies,* 1985.

For when established identities become outworn or unfinished ones threaten to remain incomplete, special crises compel men to wage holy wars, by the cruelest means, against those who seem to question or threaten their unsafe ideological bases. ERIK H. ERIKSON, *Childhood and Society,* 1950.

The process of American identity formation seems to support an individual's ego identity as long as he can preserve a certain element of deliberate tentativeness of autonomous choice. The individual must be able to convince himself that the next step is up to him. ERIK M. ERIKSON, *Childhood and Society,* 1950.

There is no necessary connection between the desire to lead and the ability to lead. . . . Leadership is more likely to be assumed by the aggressive than by the able, and those who scramble to the top are more often motivated by their own inner torments. BERGEN EVANS (1904–1978), *The Spoor of Spooks and Other Nonsense,* 1954.

The fact that every sort of reform movement teems with neuropaths is to be explained by the transference of interest from censored egoistic (erotic or violent) tendencies of the unconscious to fields where they can work themselves out without any self-reproach. SANDOR FERENCZI (1873–1933), *Introjection and Transference,* 1909.

[Cognitive dissonance] theory centers around the idea that if a person knows various things that are not psychologically consistent with one another, he will, in a variety of ways, try to make them more consistent. Two items of information that psychologically do not fit together are said to be in a dissonant relation to each other. The items of information may be about behavior, feelings, opinions . . . and so on. . . . Such items can, of course, be changed. A person chan change his opinion, he can change his behavior, thereby changing the information he has about it; he can even distort his perception and his information about the world around him. LEON FESTINGER, in *Readings about the Social Animal* (Aronson), 1973.

We may say that hysteria is a caricature of an artistic creation, a compulsion neurosis a caricature of a religion, and a paranoiac delusion a caricature of a philosophic system. SIGMUND FREUD (1856–1939), *Totem and Taboo,* 1918.

The great majority of people have a strong need for authority which they can admire, to which they can submit, and which dominates and sometimes even ill-treats them. . . . SIGMUND FREUD (1856–1939), *Moses and Monotheism,* 1939.

A group is extraordinarily credulous and open to influence, it has no critical faculty, and the improbable does not exist for it. It thinks in images, which call one another up by association . . . and whose agreement with reality is never checked by any reasonable agency. The feelings of a group are always very simple and very exaggerated, so that a group knows neither doubt nor certainty. SIGMUND FREUD (1856–1939), *Group Psychology and the Analysis of the Ego.*

Not only do people accept violence if it is perpetrated by legitimate authority, they also regard violence against certain kinds of people as inherently legitimate, no matter who commits it. EDGAR Z. FRIEDENBERG, 1966.

The lure of secrecy consists for the possessor of a secret partly in the possibility of betraying it. It gives the possessor of a secret a certain sense of exclusivity whereby he is set apart from ordinary mortals. CARL J. FRIEDRICH, *The Pathology of Politics,* 1972.

Man is so educable an animal that it is difficult to distinguish between that part of his character which has been acquired through education and circum-stance, and that which was in the original grain of his constitution. FRANCIS GALTON (1822–1911), *Inquiry into Human Faculty,* 1883.

Delusional imagery frequently evolves around critical political relationships: victimizer/victim; master/slave; controller/controlled. In terms of their effect, these internal structures exercise as much power over the self as any external tyranny. JAMES M. GLASS, *Delusion,* 1985.

For the fanatic, delusional readings of reality, hallucinations, divinations, reve-lations—all coalesce as claims to power and draw on a community or group's own uncertainty and fear. The fantasy of power depends on domination; it may even become the vehicle for a collective identity, with the delusional world being shared publicly as national policy or revenge. JAMES M. GLASS, *Delusion,* 1985.

The mind can protect itself against anxiety by diminished awareness. This mechanism creates a blind spot: a zone of blocked attention and self-deception. Such blind spots occur at each major level of behavior from the psychological to the social. DANIEL GOLEMAN, *Vital Lies, Simple Truths: The Psychology of Self-Deception,* 1985.

The primary source of the human capacity for violence appears to be the frustration-aggression mechanism. . . . If frustrations are sufficiently prolonged or sharply felt, aggression is quite likely, if not certain, to occur. TED ROBERT GURR, *Why Men Rebel,* 1970.

There is genuine idealism and there is the Pharisaism that imitates it; there is the psychological need to be dedicated to a cause, which is what makes the profession more than a profession, a vocation; there is the appeal of comradeship in the cause, the intoxication of marching in step with others, open hand or clenched fist upraised; there is the satisfaction of having an enemy in the form of a monstrous abstraction to whose image one can attach all the evils of our common life. Finally, there is the appeal of being free to indulge as a virtue the destructive impulse we all know. LOUIS J. HALLE, *The Ideological Imagination,* 1972.

The free individual feels himself, moreover, too small to cope with the immensity of the world in which he finds himself. Alone, he is no more than a mite in a maelstrom. Because his individual identity seems so insufficient, he feels the need to adopt, by association, another identity that represents the greatness and power that he lacks. LOUIS J. HALLE, *The Ideological Imagination,* 1972.

Men and all the political, social, economic, religious, intellectual, aesthetic and psychological systems by which he has so far organized his life, are persistently being rendered incoherent. . . . This breaking of connections, and there the destruction of the capacity to deal with the most basic issues of social life, is the persistent challenge of the modern age. MANFRED HALPERN, 1969.

Irritation at the imperfection of the surrounding world—at other people, parents, etc.—is actually irritation resulting from the realization of the non-reality of megalomaniacal ideas of perfection. This . . . is linked to the narcissistic structures of certain intellectuals, pushing them to aggressiveness which can become deadly. ANDRE HAYNAL et al., *Fanaticism,* 1983.

When our individual interests and prospects do not seem worth living for, we are in desperate need for something apart from us to live for. All forms of dedication, devotion, loyalty and self-surrender are in essence a desperate clinging to something which might give worth and meaning to our lives. ERIC HOFFER (1902–1983), *The True Believer,* 1951.

The implacable stand is directed more against the doubt within than the assailant without. ERIC HOFFER (1902–1983), *The Passionate State of Mind,* 1954.

There is a vital difference between the paranoid spokesman in politics and the clinical paranoiac: although both tend to be overheated, oversuspicious, overaggressive, grandiose, and apocalyptic in expression, the clinical paranoid sees the hostile and conspiratorial world in which he feels himself to be living as directed specifically against him; whereas the spokesman of the paranoid style finds it directed against a nation, a culture, a way of life whose fate affects not himself alone but millions of others. RICHARD HOFSTADTER (1916–1970), *The Paranoid Style in American Politics,* 1965

There is something deeply satisfying about drawing the world's attention to evil and injustice; by doing so, the critic has automatically placed himself into the ranks of the virtuous, whose heart is in the right place. PAUL HOLLANDER, *Society,* July–August 1983.

In fantasies where the person is the victim of someone else's cruelty, there is a sense of moral superiority and power that comes, perhaps, in dying nobly and well. ALTHEA HORNER, *The Wish for Power and the Fear of Having It,* 1989.

Everyone has observed how much more dogs are animated when they hunt in a pack, than when they pursue their game apart. We might, perhaps, be at a loss to explain this phenomenon, if we had not experience of a similar in ourselves. DAVID HUME (1711–1776), *A Treatise of Human Nature,* 1739.

We never remark of any passion or principle in others, of which, in some degree or another, we may not find a parallel in ourselves. DAVID HUME (1711–1776), *A Treatise of Human Nature,* 1739.

Defined in psychological terms, a fanatic is a man who consciously overcompensates a secret doubt. ALDOUS HUXLEY (1894–1963).

The trouble with most people is, they bow to what is called authority; they have a certain reverence for the old because it is old. They think a man is better for being dead, especially if he has been dead a long time. ROBERT G. INGERSOLL (1833–1899), "Individuality."

Each individual in the group feels himself to be under an injunction to avoid making penetrating criticisms that might bring on a clash with fellow members and destroy the unity of the group. . . . The various devices to enhance self-esteem require an illusion of unanimity about all important judgments. Without it, the sense of group unity would be lost. IRVING JANIS, *Victims of Groupthink,* 1972.

The more amiable the esprit de corps among the members of a policy-making in-group, the greater is the danger that independent critical thinking will be replaced by groupthink. IRVING JANIS, *Victims of Groupthink,* 1972.

The various devices to enhance self-esteem require an illusion of unanimity about all important judgments. Without it, the sense of group unity would be lost, gnawing doubts would start to grow. . . . IRVING JANIS, *Victims of Groupthink,* 1972.

Are we seeking the truth about man that sets all men free? Or are the truths we discover only making some men more free and powerful, while others become more vulnerable to manipulation? SIDNEY JOURARD, 1964.

Whenever an inferiority complex exists, there is a good reason for it. There is always something inferior there, although not just where we persuade ourselves that it is. CARL GUSTAV JUNG (1875–1961), 1943.

But, just as the introvert causes trouble by the violence of his passions, the extrovert irritates by his half-conscious thoughts and feelings, incoherently and abruptly applied in the form of tactless and unsparing judgements of his fellow men. CARL JUNG (1875–1961), *Psychological Types,* 1921.

There is a holy, mistaken zeal in politics, as well as religion. By persuading others we convince ourselves. JUNIUS (1589–1677), *Letters.*

Paranoia creates a self-fulfilling prophecy, a vicious circle in which suspicion breeds suspicion, threat breeds counterthreat. Passive-aggressive victims bring on themselves the aggression they obsessively fear. . . . Paranoids [begin] with imagined enemies and end up with real ones as the cycle of reaction turns into a complex historical conflict. . . . [E]nemies become hypnotized by each other and become locked in a prison of mirrors. SAM KEEN, *Faces of the Enemy,* 1986.

Paranoia reduces anxiety and guilt by transferring to the other all the characteristics one does not want to recognize in oneself. It is maintained by selective perception and recall. We only see and acknowledge those negative aspects of the enemy that support the stereotype we have already created. SAM KEEN, *Faces of the Enemy,* 1986.

As a metaphysic of threat, paranoia eliminates in advance any evidence that might contradict its basic assumption about the malevolent intent of the enemy. Hence, it makes it impossible to discriminate between realistic and purely imaginative dangers. SAM KEEN, *Faces of the Enemy,* 1986.

Members of the new class are defined not by what they own, but by what they do. They constitute what Harold Lasswell termed a "skill" class, trained in the manipulation of ideas, words, and meanings. . . . [T]he new class can be recognized not by its socioeconomic characteristics but by its relationship to culture: to the meanings that constitute a culture and the symbols by which those meanings are expressed. JEANE J. KIRKPATRICK, *Dictatorships and Double Standards,* 1982.

The crusader role has an unusual capacity for giving the feeling of "rightness." . . . The crusade's power of conferring rightness resembles that of a cult in giving a deep moral, rather than technical, sense of rightness, and in making life more exciting. ORRIN E. KLAPP, *Collective Search for Identity,* 1969.

The inner defenses are unconscious. They consist of a kind of magic aura which the mind builds around its cherished belief. Arguments which penetrate into the magic aura are not dealt with rationally but by a specific type of pseudo-reasoning. Absurdities and contradictions . . . are made acceptable by specious rationalizations. ARTHUR KOESTLER (1904–1983), *The Yogi and the Commissar,* 1945.

People divorced from community, occupation and association are first and foremost among supporters of extremism. WILLIAM KORNHAUSER, *The Politics of Mass Society,* 1959.

Once people can be induced to experience a situation in a similar way, they can be expected to behave in similar ways. Induce people all to want the same thing, hate the same thing, feel the same threat, then their behavior is already captive—you have acquired your consumers or your cannon fodder. R. D. LAING, *The Politics of Experience,* 1967.

Authoritarianism contains a strictly interpersonal component: the tendency to divide the world into "we" and "they," "in-groups" and "out-groups." This is a product of a more basic tendency to conceive of the world in somewhat hostile terms, in which case the most important question to ask of a person is, "Is he for me or is he against me?" ROBERT E. LANE, *Political Ideology,* 1962.

This corrosive need to be liked seems often to reflect a special kind of uncertainty about the self, an uncertainty about one's rightness or correctness in style, manner, and thought. It reflects, that is, a need for self-validation. ROBERT E. LANE, *Political Thinking and Consciousness,* 1969.

[There is] a tendency for someone in the grip of relatively strong aggressive feelings that he cannot accept to develop a philosophy of opposition to aggression. It is the ideology of reaction formation; it is the syndrome of the belligerent pacifist. ROBERT E. LANE, *Political Thinking and Consciousness,* 1969.

As an agency of social discipline, the school . . . both reflects and contributes to the shift from authoritarian sanctions to psychological manipulation and surveillance—the redefinition of political authority in therapeutic terms—and to the rise of a professional and managerial elite that governs society not by upholding authoritative moral sanctions but by defining normal behavior and by invoking allegedly nonpunitive, psychiatric sanctions against deviance. CHRISTOPHER LASCH, *Democracy,* January 1981.

Political prejudices, preferences, and creeds are often formulated in highly rational form, but they are grown in highly irrational ways. When they are seen against the developmental history of the person, they take on meanings which are quite different from the phrases in which they are put. HAROLD D. LASSWELL (1902–1978), *Psychopathology and Politics,* 1930.

The political type is characterized by an intense craving for deference. HAROLD D. LASSWELL (1902–1978), *Power and Personality,* 1948.

The essential mark of the agitator is the high value he places on the emotional response of the public. Whether he attacks or defends social institutions is a secondary matter. HAROLD D. LASSWELL (1902–1978), *Psychopathology and Politics,* 1930.

Dogma is a defensive reaction against doubt in the mind of the theorist, but doubt of which he is unaware. HAROLD D. LASSWELL (1902–1978), *Psychopathology and Politics,* 1930.

Every man has a mob self and an individual self, in varying proportions. D. H. LAWRENCE (1885–1930), 1929.

Whoever be the individuals that compose it, however like or unlike be their mode of life, their occupations, their character, or their intelligence, the fact that they have been transformed into a crowd puts them into possession of a sort of collective mind which makes them think, feel, and act in a manner quite different from that in which each individual of them would think, feel and act were he in a state of isolation. GUSTAVE LE BON (1841–1931), *The Crowd,* 1896.

The individual forming part of a crowd acquires solely from numerical considerations a sentiment of invincible power allowing him to yield to instincts which, had he been alone, he would perforce have kept under restraint. He will be the less disposed to check himself from the consideration that, a crowd being anonymous and in consequence irresponsible, the sentiment of responsibility which always controls individuals disappears entirely. GUSTAVE LE BON (1841–1931), *The Crowd,* 1896.

Crowds are cognizant only of simple and extreme sentiments; the opinions, ideas and beliefs suggested to them are accepted or rejected as a whole, and considered as absolute truths or as no less absolute errors. GUSTAVE LE BON (1841–1931), *The Crowd,* 1896.

All organizations recapitulate the basic family structure. . . . Our earliest experiences with our parents are repeated in our subsequent relationships with authority. Early family life determines our assumptions of how power is distributed, and as we grow up we form groups on the same model. HARRY LEVINSON, *Psychology Today,* December 1977.

Often we think we believe a thing, and yet do not believe it. Nothing is more impenetrable than the motivation of our actions. GEORGE C. LICHTENBERG (1742–1799), *Reflections,* 1799.

The most basic feature of the thought reform environment, the psychological current upon which all else depends, is the control of human communication. Through this milieu control the totalist environment seeks to establish domain over not only the individual's communication with the outside . . . but also, in its penetration of his inner life, over what he may speak of in his communication with himself. ROBERT J. LIFTON, *Thought Reform and the Psychology of Totalism,* 1961.

The language of the totalist environment is characterized by the thought-terminating cliché. The most far-reaching and complex of human problems are compressed into brief, highly reductive, definitive-sounded phrases, easily memorized and easily expressed. ROBERT J. LIFTON, *Thought Reform and the Psychology of Totalism,* 1961.

It is characteristic of all movements and crusades that the psychopathic element rises to the top. ROBERT LINDNER (1914–1956), *Must You Conform,* 1956.

More than any other system that has offered itself in recent years as a vessel for human hopes and aspirations, Marxism in the guise of communism fulfills the deep compulsion we humans have to defend ourselves against a terrifying outside environment and the raging instinctual forces within us; a compulsion to defend ourselves by believing, and by organizing such beliefs into those patterns that go by the name of religion. ROBERT LINDNER (1914–1956), *Must You Conform,* 1956.

Once you touch the biographies of human beings, the notion that political beliefs are logically determined collapses like a pricked balloon. WALTER LIPPMANN (1889–1974), *A Preface to Politics,* 1914.

By myths we mean the value-impregnated beliefs and notions that men hold, that they live by and for. Every society is held together by a myth-system, a complex of dominating thought-forms that determines and sustains all activities. All social relations, the very texture of human society, are myth-born and myth-sustained. ROBERT M. MACIVER (1882–1970), *The Web of Government,* 1947.

To be an individual in a complex and bewildering world is very difficult. Sensing their smallness and relative helplessness, many people are strongly inclined to submerge themselves in what they perceive to be the vastly more powerful identity of the group. . . . Alone they are weak; together, they are a force that commands respect. ANDREW MALCOLM, *The Tyranny of the Group,* 1975.

Every intellectual attitude is latently political. THOMAS MANN (1875–1956).

[They] try frantically to order and stabilize the world so that no unmanageable, unexpected or unfamiliar dangers will ever appear. They hedge themselves about with all sorts of ceremonials, rules and formulas so that no new contingencies may appear. They are much like the brain injured cases . . . who manage to mantain their equilibrium by avoiding anything unfamiliar and strange and by ordering their restricted world in such a neat, disciplined, orderly fashion that everything in the world can be counted upon. ABRAHAM MASLOW, *Psychological Review,* 1943.

Deeds of violence in our society are performed largely by those trying to establish their self-esteem, to defend their self-image, and to demonstrate that they, too, are significant. Violence arises not out of superfluity of power but out of powerlessness. ROLLO MAY, *Power and Innocence,* 1972.

The bulk of the totalitarian-minded in the democratic societies are men and women who are attracted to this destructive way of life for inner emotional reasons unknown to themselves. JOOST A. MERLOO, *The Rape of the Mind,* 1956.

The more an individual feels himself to be part of the group, the more easily can he become the victim of mass suggestion. This is why primitive communications, which have a high degree of social integration and identification, are so sensitive to suggestion. JOOST A. MERLOO, *The Rape of the Mind,* 1956.

In my own experience, I have been amazed to see how unrealistic are the bases for political opinion in general. Only rarely have I found a person who has chosen any particular political party—democratic or totalitarian—through study and comparison of principles. JOOST A. MERLOO, *The Rape of the Mind,* 1956.

Little difference exists in their mind between what they have seen and what they have thought. Momentary impressions and hazy memories become fact. Chains of unconnected facts are fitted together. An inexorable course from imagination to supposition to suspicion takes place, and soon a system of invalid and unshakeable belief has been created. THEODORE MILTON, *Disorders of Personality,* 1982.

One will not go far wrong if one attributes extreme actions to vanity, average ones to habit, and petty ones to fear. FRIEDRICH NIETZSCHE (1844–1900), *Human All Too Human,* 1878.

What gives the new despotism its peculiar effectiveness is indeed its liaison with humanitarianism, but beyond this fact its capacity for entering into the smallest details of human life. ROBERT NISBET, *Twilight of Authority,* 1981.

Ritual is the dramatization of thought and faith. It converts ordinary, utilitarian behavior into sequential acts which are given a meaning that is far above anything deducible from the mere existence of the behavior. ROBERT NISBET, *Prejudices: A Philosophical Dictionary,* 1982.

Political language—and with variations this is true of all political parties, from Conservatives to Anarchists—is designed to make lies sound truthful and murder respectable, and to give the appearance of solidarity to pure wind. GEORGE ORWELL (1903–1950), *Shooting an Elephant,* 1950.

Stereotypes develop because they are useful. They reduce the tremendous complexity of the world around us into a few simple guidelines which we can use in our everyday thought and decisions. STUART OSKAMP, *Attitudes and Opinions,* 1977.

The person who vehemently disbelieves is quite aware of the possibility of believing. Even those ideas that a man never learns to take seriously are nonetheless within the scope of his potential belief. . . . No rejected belief is ever completely discredited. What has once been believed lingers on as a faint possibility. SNELL and GAIL J. PUTNEY, *The Adjusted American,* 1964.

The fanatic who refused to admit the existence of a feared facet of himself may eventually be confronted with undeniable evidence that he harbors the very attitudes or desires he has sought to eradicate in others. SNELL and GAIL J. PUTNEY, *The Adjusted American,* 1964.

In the ranks of any political party there are few whose allegiance is predicated on a rational decision. People offer numerous and plausible explanations for their political convictions, but these "good reasons" were discovered long after their convictions were established. SNELL and GAIL J. PUTNEY, *The Adjusted American,* 1964.

Extremes of belief are generally recognizable, not in terms of the content or nature of the idea itself, but in terms of its dominance. If the subject is wrapped up in his belief . . . if he holds an idea with pronounced intensity and his considerations of it clearly spring from heightened emotion, the observer will have doubts as to whether his evaluation is based on rational analysis. GRAHAM REED, *The Psychology of Anomalous Experience,* 1988.

People with overvalued ideas are prominent in political movements and religious cults, as well as in crank organizations and extreme minority groups. . . . In all these areas of activity, it is not so much the content of the belief that is significant but its preoccupying power, and the degree to which the believer finds it necessary to force his ideas on others. GRAHAM REED, *The Psychology of Anomalous Experience,* 1988.

This infantile value system knows only absolute perfection and complete destruction; it belongs to the early time in life when only black and white existed, good and bad, pleasure and pain, but nothing in between. There are no shadings, no degrees, there are only extremes. Reality is judged exclusively from the standpoint of the pleasure principle; to evaluate it objectively is still impossible. ANN REICH, *Psychoanalytic Contributions,* 1973.

The otherdirected person . . . starts group life in fear of the taunt, "So you think you're big," and . . . occasionally struggles against his gifts lest these bring him into conflict with others. DAVID RIESMAN, *Faces in the Crowd,* 1952.

We are incredibly heedless in the formation of ou beliefs, but find ourselves filled with an illicit passion for them when anyone proposes to rob us of their companionship. It is obviously not the ideas themselves that are dear to us, but our self-esteem, which is threatened. JAMES HARVEY ROBINSON (1863–1936), *The Mind in the Making,* 1921.

The human mind operates on different levels and in different ways. Parts of it, indeed probably the principal parts of it, are still primitive, archaic and irrational. . . . A part of the mind conceives of wishes and thoughts as being omnipotent. Although this part is obscure to us we can recognize some of its modern remains. Modern man, just as his primitive ancestors, still burns his enemies in effigy. O. JOHN ROGGE, *Why Men Confess,* 1959.

Fantasies of world destruction are also a characteristic of various forms of schizophrenia. It is as if feelings of self-hatred are so great that they cannot be absorbed by projections to single persons but require fantasies involving complete destruction of the world. THEODORE ISAAC RUBIN, *Compassion and Self-Hate,* 1975.

The megalomaniac differs from the narcissist by the fact that he wishes to be powerful rather than charming, and seeks to be feared rather than loved. To this type belong many lunatics and most of the great men of the world. BERTRAND RUSSELL (1872–1970), *The Conquest of Happiness.*

Before we can understand the nature of cruelty, we must begin to see that it does serve a psychological function for those who resort to it; it is a mechanism of defense used by the ego to ward off the threat of annihilation. The ego, when threatened with destruction, for reasons that are almost impossible to explain, can reaffirm its existence by making others suffer. ELI SAGAN, *At the Dawn of Tyranny,* 1986.

The ego, when faced with attack by someone in the world, attempts to defend itself against annhilation by identifying with the attacker. Instead of being an entity about to be destroyed, it becomes the destroyer. ELI SAGAN, *At the Dawn of Tyranny,* 1986.

The typical citizen drops down to a lower level of mental performance as soon as he enters the political field. He argues and analyzes in a way he would readily recognize as infantile within the sphere of his real interests. He becomes a primitive again. JOSEPH A. SCHUMPETER (1883–1950), *Capitalism, Socialism and Democracy,* 1950.

Capitalism inevitably and by virtue of the very logic of its civilization creates, educates and subsidizes a vested interest in social unrest. JOSEPH A. SCHUMPETER (1883–1950).

Every religion or cause grows out of a desire either to make one's own life more effortless, or to control and manipulate other people in order to enforce behavior in conformity with the expectations of the true believers. BUTLER D. SHAFFER, *Calculated Chaos,* 1985.

The State . . . has had a vested interest in promoting attitudes that would tend to make us skeptical of our own abilities, fearful of the motives of others, and emotionally dependent upon external authorities for purpose and direction in our lives. BUTLER D. SHAFFER, *Calculated Chaos,* 1985.

[For the paranoid] a subjective world can be constructed in which facts, accurately enough perceived in themselves, are endowed with a special interpretive significance in place of their actual significance. . . . Thus, the subject matter of his interest has to do with hidden motives, underlying purposes, special meanings, and the like. He does not necessarily disagree with the normal person about the existence of any given fact; he disagrees only about its significance. DAVID SHAPIRO, *Neurotic Styles,* 1965.

"Projection" . . . means the attribution to external figures of motivations, drives, or other tensions that are repudiated and intolerable in oneself. This mental operation or mechanism is . . . central to our understanding of paranoid pathology. DAVID SHAPIRO, *Neurotic Styles,* 1965.

Externalization occurs when an individual, often responding unconsciously, senses an analogy between a perceived environmental event and some unresolved inner problem. He adopts an attitude toward the event in question which is a transformed version of his way of dealing with his inner difficulty. M. BREWSTER SMITH et al., *Opinions and Personality,* 1956.

Policies are judged by their consequences but crusades are judged by how good they make the crusaders feel. THOMAS SOWELL, *Compassion versus Guilt,* 1987.

When the crowd hurls itself in blind fury upon its victims. . . . this collective murder does not seem so frightful to them because they share a feeling of unity and purposefulness. EUGÈNE SUE (1804–1857), *The Wandering Jew,* 1845.

The life of a society can be powerfully influenced by a paranoid person or group. The impact may be felt in any phase of community life. Paranoid accusations are directed by single individuals toward an entire community and by entire communities toward one individual. DAVID W. SWANSON et al., *The Paranoid,* 1970.

A paranoid approach is recognizable in the actions of certain political groups, most obviously those of the extreme left and the extreme right. These extremist political groups emphasize the inefficiency, corruptness and malice of those in power. Often their accusations have a certain accuracy, in that those in power are doing everything possible to sustain control and to deny known faults; also, the power faction is quite unwilling to recognize the extremist group's demand for a hearing. DAVID W. SWANSON et al., *The Paranoid,* 1970.

The aggressiveness of a person with a paranoid style may be masked, but no less powerful, when it is expressed in intellectual or ideological terms. In such a subtle and controlled form it usually has a greater impact on others. . . . As individuals, extremist reformers utilize psychological mechanisms which resemble those observed in the paranoid individual. DAVID W. SWANSON et al., *The Paranoid,* 1970.

A quick glance around the world reveals that nuclear family systems everywhere are incapable of producing totalitarian ideologies or political forms which seek and achieve the total absorption of civil society by the state. EMMANUAL TODD, *The Explanation of Ideology,* 1985.

All socialist ideologies correspond to complex family structures. Only the light, nuclear systems—absolute or egalitarian—and the anomic ones if they are not too dense in practice, escape the temptation of socialism. EMMANUAL TODD, *The Explanation of Ideology,* 1985.

Ideology is not the product of thought; it is the habit or the ritual of showing respect for certain formulas which, for various reasons, have to do with emotional safety. We have very strong ties of whose meaning and consequences we have no clear understanding. LIONEL TRILLING (1905–1975), *The Liberal Imagination,* 1950.

In religion and politics people's beliefs and convictions are in almost every case gotten at second hand, and without examination, from authorities who have not themselves examined the questions at issue but have taken them at second hand from other nonexaminers. MARK TWAIN (1835–1910). *Autobiography.*

If we look closely, we will discover that because of externalizations and projections the enemy is not unlike the self. The enemy resembles his opponent, and although physically and psychologically "out there," the enemy is nevertheless linked to his opponent, having become a reservoir for the threatened group's externalizations and projections. VAMIK D. VOLKAN, *The Need to Have Enemies and Allies,* 1988.

What is madness? To have erroneous perceptions and reason correctly from them. VOLTAIRE (1694–1778), *Philosophical Dictionary,* 1764.

Most of the political opinions of men are the result, not of reason tested by experience but of unconscious or half-conscious inference fixed by habit. GRAHAM WALLIS (1858–1932), *Human Nature in Politics,* 1908.

It is inherent in the concept of paranoia that it rests upon a fundamental assumption that is held to be absolutely true. . . . Strict logical deductions are then made from this fundamental premise and create a reality in which any failures and inconsistencies of the system are attributed to the deductions, but never to the original premise itself. PAUL WATZLAWICK, *The Invented Reality,* 1984.

A self-fulfilling prophecy is an assumption or prediction that, purely as a result of having been made, causes the expected or predicted event to occur and thus confirms its own accuracy. PAUL WATZLAWICK, *The Invented Reality,* 1984.

Propaganda and Persuasion

Abuse of words has been the great instrument of sophistry and chicanery, of party, faction, and division of society. JOHN ADAMS (1735–1826), U.S. President, 1819.

This shuffling trick of misstating the question, and setting up a man of straw to make a pompous demonstration of knocking him down. . . . JOHN QUINCY ADAMS (1767–1848), Diary, February 12, 1841.

Ridicule is man's most potent weapon. SAUL ALINSKY, *Rules for Radicals,* 1971.

The *ad hominem* attack often takes the form of discounting a proposition by attributing prejudice or bias to its supporters. But what motivates us to believe as we do, say what we say, is one thing. The truth or falsity, validity or invalidity, of what we say is another. It is possible to be prejudiced but right. ROBERT W. ALLEN and LORNE GREENE, *The Propaganda Game,* 1966.

Propaganda is a soft weapon: hold it in your hands too long, and it will move about like a snake, and strike the other way. JEAN ANOUILH, *The Lark,* 1955.

The trouble with lying and deceiving is that their efficiency depends entirely upon a clear notion of the truth that the liar and the deceiver want to hide. HANNAH ARENDT (1906–1975), *Crisis of the Republic,* 1972.

The fundamental reason for the superiority of totalitarian propaganda over the propaganda of other parties and movements is that its content, for the members of the movement at any rate, is no longer an objective issue about which people may have opinions, but has become as real and untouchable an element in their lives as the rules of arithmetic. HANNAH ARENDT (1906–1975), *The Origins of Totalitarianism,* 1968.

How do you persuade another person? Our culture distinguishes two ways. The first is the Platonic way, the use of reason. . . . The other form of persuasion (direct use of the passions) seeks to eliminate the mind and the critical faculties. It provokes feeling rather than thought. It is employed when the persuader suspects that the logical steps in the argument will not survive critical examination. F. G. BAILEY, *The Tactical Uses of Passions,* 1983.

A metaphor is a direct comparison of two things that equates one thing with a special feature of the other. The use of metaphor often makes it possible to substitute politically useful meanings for potentially damaging realities. W. LANCE BENNETT, *Public Opinion in American Politics,* 1980.

Given sufficient control over information and enough public distance from the reality of events, even the most unlikely situations can be endowed with powerful emotional trappings. W. LANCE BENNETT, *Public Opinion in American Politics,* 1980.

People tend to see and hear communications that are favorable or congenial to their dispositions; they are more likely to see and hear congenial communications than neutral or hostile ones. And the more interested they are in the subject, the more likely is such selective attention. BERNARD BERELSON and GARY A. STEINER, *Human Behavior: An Inventory of Scientific Findings,* 1964.

I am aware that the word "propaganda" carries to many minds an unpleasant connotation. Yet, whether, in any instance, propaganda is good or bad depends upon the merit of the cause urged, and the correctness of the information published. EDWARD L. BERNAYS, *Propaganda,* 1928.

Judgment of the art work in the National Socialist State can be made only on the basis of the National Socialist viewpoint of culture. Only the Party and the State are in a position to determine artistic values. ALFRED INGEMAR BERNDT (Reich Minister for Popular Enlightenment and Propaganda), *Völkischer Beobachter,* April 3, 1936.

In manipulating the public, he [the propagandist] attempts to discover the emotional opinions which they already accept. He then fastens or conditions the emotions he desires to one of these already established beliefs. WILLIAM W. BIDDLE, *Manipulating the Public,* 1931.

It [propaganda] relies upon the drive of certain preponderant emotions to result in the desired behavior. Theoretically, any emotion can be "drained off" into any activity by skillful manipulation. WILLIAM W. BIDDLE, *Propaganda and Education,* 1932.

While seeking to legitimatize their revolution by sanctifying a place, a process, or even a picture, Frenchmen still sought to define their beliefs in words. There was a trend toward radical simplification, however, as they increasingly tended to substitute labels for arguments. JAMES H. BILLINGTON, *Fire in the Minds of Men,* 1980.

In dealing with the Communists, remember that in their mind what is secret is serious, and what is public is merely propaganda. CHARLES E. BOHLEN (1904–1974), *New York Times,* January 2, 1966.

The purpose of education—both East and West—is the mass production of robots . . . who have so internalized social constraints that they submit to them automatically. MAURICE BRINTON, *The Irrational in Politics.*

Propaganda by censorship takes two forms: the selective control of information to favor a particular viewpoint, and the deliberate doctoring of information in order to create an impression different from that originally intended. JAMES A. C. BROWN, *Techniques of Persuasion,* 1963.

The potency of Hitler's propaganda, however, has been grossly exaggerated. Democracy had failed, and the only real choice open to the Germans was between Communism and the Nazis. JAMES A. C. BROWN, *Techniques of Persuasion,* 1963.

One can only speak of propaganda when alternative views exist, and it is therefore not propaganda to teach a belief which is universal at a particular time or place. JAMES A. C. BROWN, *Techniques of Persuasion,* 1963.

The real struggle is not between East and West, or capitalism and communism, but between education and propaganda. MARTIN BUBER (1878–1965).

To the degree that propaganda is freed from legal and moral restrictions, it will not be content with interpreting events but will attempt to bring about such events as are necessary to its purposes. HANS BUCHHEIM, *Totalitarian Rule,* 1968.

Totalitarian propaganda owes an essential part of its effectiveness to political romanticism—romanticism concerning the Reich, romanticism of elites, romanticism of revolution, romanticism of nihilism. . . . The romantic imagination likes to use even the horrors of totalitarian rule as a suitable back ground to present most impressively man's "depravity." HANS BUCHHEIM, *Totalitarian Rule,* 1968.

People on the whole are very simple-minded, in whatever country one finds them. They are so simple as to take literally, more often than not, the things their leaders tell them. PEARL S. BUCK (1892–1973), *What America Means to Me,* 1943.

Constant repetition of the item to be inculcated unsupported by any reasons will have an immense effect on the suggestible, herd-minded human. An opinion, an idea, or a code acquired in this manner can be so firmly fixed that one who questions its essential rightness will be regarded as foolish, wicked, or insane. Suggestion, then, is the key to inculcating discipline, esprit, and morale. JOHN H. BURNS, *Infantry Journal,* December 1928.

Propaganda itself, pretending to be truth, does not rest solely on people's love of truth. It is more subtle. It is aimed partly at their love of wish-fulfillment— to make them feel safe, proud, and strong. JOYCE CARY (1888–1957), *Power in Men,* 1939.

"When I use a word," Humpty Dumpty said in a rather scornful tone, "it means just what I choose it to mean—neither more nor less." "The question is," said Alice, "whether you can make words mean so many different things." "The question is," said Humpty Dumpty, "which is to be master—that's all." LEWIS CARROLL (1832–1898), *Through the Looking Glass,* 1872.

"I can't believe that," said Alice. "Can't you?" the Queen said in a pitying tone. "Try again; draw a long breath, and shut your eyes." LEWIS CARROLL (1832–1889), *Through the Looking Glass,* 1872.

Semantics teaches us to watch our prejudices, and to take our exercise in other ways than jumping to conclusions. Semantics is the propagandist's worse friend. STUART CHASE (1888–1985), *Guide to Straight Thinking,* 1956.

Most people have ears, but few have judgment; tickle those ears, and, depend upon it, you will catch their judgment. LORD CHESTERFIELD (1694–1773), Letter to his son, December 9, 1749.

To please people is the greatest step toward persuading them. LORD CHESTERFIELD (1694–1773), Letter to his son, November 1, 1739.

Indoctrination is to democracy what coercion is to dictatorship—naturally, since the stick that beats the people is labeled "the people's stick." NOAM CHOMSKY, *Toward a New Cold War,* 1982.

Any expert in indoctrination will confirm, no doubt, that it is far more effective to constrain all possible thought within a framework of tacit assumption than to try to impose a particular explicit belief with a bludgeon. NOAM CHOMSKY, *Toward a New Cold War,* 1982.

In every society there will emerge a caste of propagandists who labor to disguise the obvious, to conceal the actual workings of power, and to spin a web of mythical goals and purposes utterly benign, that allegedly guide national policy. A typical thesis of the propaganda system is that the nation is guided by certain ideals and principles. NOAM CHOMSKY, *Foreign Policy and the Intelligensia.*

The most fundamental requirement in constructing a persuasive message is to select arguments that are consistent with the beliefs and values of the audience. RUTH ANNE CLARK, *Persuasive Messages,* 1984.

The ideologue does not perform miracles. Very fittingly he confines himself to the deceptive charm of the realized abstraction. GEORGES CLEMENCEAU (1841–1929), Premier of France, *In the Evening of My Thought,* 1929.

For the Communist, freedom, democracy, equality and, above all, peace can come only when communism is firmly established throughout the world. Whatever forces oppose communism, they are by their very nature reactionary, undemocratic, fascist, anti-popular and repressive. When we study the communist viewpoint, we must consider it in terms of these double values. JOHN C. CLEWS, *Communist Propaganda Techniques,* 1964.

Falsehood is never so successful as when she baits her hook with the truth, and no opinions so fastly mislead us as those that are not wholly wrong, as no watch so effectually deceive as those that are sometimes right. CHARLES CALEB COLTON (1780–1832), *Lacon.*

Slogans are both exciting and comforting, but they are also powerful opiates for the conscience. JAMES BRYANT CONANT (1893–1978), Baccalaureate Address, Harvard University, June 17, 1934.

Some of mankind's most terrible misdeeds have been committed under the spell of certain magic words or phrases. JAMES BRYANT CONANT (1893–1978), Baccalaureate Address, Harvard University, June 17, 1934.

Unless one understands the power of words, he will never understand men. CONFUCIUS (551–479 B.C.), *Analects.*

He who wants to persuade should put his trust not in the right argument, but in the right word. The power of sound has always been greater than the power of sense. JOSEPH CONRAD (1857–1924), *A Personal Record,* 1912.

Whatever it is that makes ridicule work among human beings, a small amount of it seems to go a long, long way. Ridicule is powerful as a control agent. RAY P. CUZZORT, *Using Social Thought,* 1989.

[Propaganda is] . . . a systematic attempt by an interested individual (or individuals) to control the attitudes of groups of individuals through the use of suggestion, and, to control their actions. LEONARD W. DOOB, *Public Opinion and Propaganda,* 1966.

Among intentional propagandists the Idea is worshipped above all else. . . . For intentional propagandists are convinced that it is Ideas which make the world go round and which therefore are peculiarly a symptom of their own genius. LEONARD W. DOOB, *Public Opinion and Propaganda,* 1966.

"It is later than you think"—almost every propagandist tries to employ this slogan in a direct or indirect form during his propaganda campaign. The impression he wishes to create is that time is running out; he who hesitates is lost; the moment for action is now. LEONARD W. DOOB, *Public Opinion and Propaganda,* 1966.

All rumor is psychologically effective because the person who spreads the propaganda has a certain prestige as a result of the social situation; the listener naively assumes that the speaker has no ulterior motive and, therefore, can be trusted. LEONARD W. DOOB, *Propaganda: Its Psychology and Technique,* 1935.

The essence of education . . . seems to be its objectivity in light of the scientific truths prevalent at the time, whereas propaganda, intentionally or unintentionally, is an attempt to control the attitudes of people. LEONARD W. DOOB, *Propaganda: Its Psychology and Technique,* 1935.

Modern methods of communication and propaganda give modern dictators a hold over nations which bears no comparison with ancient tyrants. . . . Today authority has powerful arms at its disposal which make any resistance on the part of citizens more difficult. MAURICE DUVERGER, *The Ideas of Politics,* 1964.

There are two major forms of lying: concealment, leaving out true information; and falsification, or presenting false information as if it were true. Other ways to lie include: misdirecting, acknowledging an emotion but misidentifying what caused it; telling the truth falsely, or admitting the truth but with such exaggeration or humor that the target remains uninformed or misled; half-concealment, or admitting only part of what is true, so as to deflect the target's interest in what remains concealed; and the incorrect inference dodge, or telling the truth but in a way that implies the opposite of what is said. PAUL EKMAN, *Telling Lies,* 1985.

When there is a choice about how to lie, liars usually prefer concealing to falsifying. There are many advantages. For one thing, concealing is easier than falsifying. Nothing has to be made up. There is no chance of getting caught without having the whole story worked out in advance. PAUL EKMAN, *Telling Lies,* 1985.

To be effective, propaganda must constantly short-circuit all thought and decision. It must operate on the individual at the level of the unconscious. He must not know that he is being shaped by outside forces. JACQUES ELLUL, *Propaganda: The Formation of Men's Attitudes,* 1965.

For action makes propaganda's effect irreversible. He who acts in obedience to propaganda can never go back. He is now obligated to believe in that propaganda because of his past action. . . . He is what one calls committed. JACQUES ELLUL, *Propaganda: The Formation of Men's Attitudes,* 1965.

Propaganda must be continuous and lasting—continuous in that it must not leave any gaps . . . lasting in that it must function over a very long period of time . . . for propaganda is not the touch of the magic wand. It is based on slow, constant impregnation. It creates convictions and compliance through imperceptible influences that are effective only by continuous repetition. JACQUES ELLUL, *Propaganda: The Formation of Men's Attitudes,* 1965.

Condense some daily experience into a glowing symbol, and an audience is electrified. RALPH WALDO EMERSON (1803–1882), *Eloquence,* 1877.

Propaganda is persuading people to make up their minds while withholding some of the facts from them. HAROLD EVANS.

Governments have ever been careful to hold a high hand over the education of the people. They know, better than anyone else, that their power is based almost entirely on the school. Hence, they monopolize it more and more. FRANCISCO FERRER (1859–1909), *The Modern School.*

The enemy aggressor is always pursuing a course of larceny, murder, rapine, and barbarism. We are always moving forward with high mission, a destiny imposed by the Deity to regenerate our victims while incidentally capturing their markets, to civilize savage and senile and paranoid peoples while blundering accidentally into their oil wells and metal mines. JOHN T. FLYNN (1883–1964), *As We Go Marching,* 1944.

Education's chief concern is its search for truth; propaganda's chief concern is its determination to incite action or active belief. True education always seeks its goal by discarding all that it discovers to be false, biased and misleading, while propaganda often seeks its goal by either hiding and ignoring the false and the misleading or deliberately distorting and using them to advantage in its efforts to support with emotional fervor biased attitudes and opinions. NICK AARON FORD, *Language in Uniform*, 1967.

I like truth. I think mankind needs it; but people have a greater need of lies— lies that flatter, console, and open endless possibilities. Without lies, humanity would die of boredom and futility. ANATOLE FRANCE (1844–1924), *La Vie en fleur*, 1923.

When you would persuade, speak of interest, not of reason. BENJAMIN FRANKLIN (1706–1790), 1732.

A group is subject to the truly magical power of words. SIGMUND FREUD.

Propaganda of the act, if multiplied beyond a certain limit, also creates an atmosphere of total emergency, not merely crisis, which readies the public for an autocratic takeover by the military or by some totalitarian movement, be it Communist or Fascist. CARL J. FRIEDRICH, *The Pathology of Politics*, 1972.

Even doubtful accusations leave a stain behind them. THOMAS FULLER (1654– 1734), *Gnomologia*, 1732.

We are apt to be deluded into false security by political catch-words, devised to flatter rather than instruct. JAMES A. GARFIELD (1831–1881), U.S. President, Speech, Hudson College, July 2, 1873.

Propaganda involves identifying one's cause with values which are unquestioned. TIMOTHY GARTON-ASH, *The Uses of Authority*, 1989.

Newspapers nowadays use facts merely as the raw material for propaganda. By suppression, or alteration, or overemphasis, or by the trick of false perspective, or by scare headlines and editorial comment, the "facts" are made to convey exactly the particular idea which the newspaper desires to suggest to its readers. PHILIP GIBBS (1877–1962), in *Public Enemy the Press* (A. E. Mander), 1944.

Sudden and irrestible conviction is chiefly the offspring of living speech. WILLIAM GODWIN (1756–1836), *Thoughts on Man*, 1831.

This is the secret of propaganda: to totally saturate the person, whom the propaganda wants to lay hold of, with the ideas of the propaganda, without him even noticing that he is being saturated. Propaganda has of course a purpose, but this purpose must be disguised with such shrewdness and virtuosity that he who is supposed to be filled with this purpose never even knows what is happening. JOSEPH GOEBBELS (1897–1962), quoted in *Words Make People* (Wolf Schneider), 1976.

When an idea is wanting, a word can always be found to take its place. JOHANN WOLFGANG von GOETHE (1749–1832).

The frame around a picture is a visual directive focusing our gaze toward what it surrounds and away from everything else. It defines what is in the picture and what is out. The framer's art is to build margins that blend with a picture so we notice what is framed rather than the frame itself. DANIEL GOLEMAN, *Vital Lies, Simple Truths: The Psychology of Self-Deception,* 1985.

Many political advertisements are unfair appeals to bias and emotion, distortions of logic intended to subvert the reasoned evaluation that ideally lies at the heart of the democratic process. DANIEL GOLEMAN, *New York Times,* October 27, 1992.

There is no political group in the world which understands the value of words as thoroughly as do the Communists. NATALIE GRANT, *Research Institute on the Sino-Soviet Bloc,* 1961.

Propaganda, as inverted patriotism, draws nourishment from the sins of the enemy. If there are no sins, invent them! The aim is to make the enemy appear so great a monster that he forfeits the rights of a human being. He cannot bring a libel action, so there is no need to stick at trifles. SIR IAN HAMILTON (1853–1947), *The Soul and Body of an Army,* 1921.

The power of reiterated suggestion and consecrated platitude . . . has brought our entire civilization to imminent peril. It is possible by these means to shape [one's] tastes, feelings, hopes . . . and convert him into a fanatic zealot, ready to torture and destroy and suffer mutilation and death for an obscene faith, baseless in fact, and morally monstrous. LEARNED HAND (1872–1961), U.S. Supreme Court Justice, 1951.

Successful propagandists have succeeded because the doctrine they bring into form is that which their listeners have for some time felt without being able to shape. THOMAS HARDY (1840–1928), *The Return of the Native,* 1878.

In all major socializing forces you will find an underlying movement to gain and maintain power through the use of words. From witch doctor to priest to bureaucrat it is all the same. A governed populace must be conditioned to accept power-words as actual things, to confuse the symbolized system with the tangible universe. FRANK HERBERT, *Dune,* 1965.

Motivating people, forcing them to your will, gives you a cynical attitude toward humanity. It degrades everything it touches. FRANK HERBERT, *Dune,* 1965.

The concept of propaganda has been redefined by national socialism. It has been closely linked to the totalitarian organization of society and may more aptly becalled "psychological management" than propaganda. It does not want to persuade or convince. It introduces the element of fear, and aims at the elimination of rationality. H. HERMA, *Social Research,* vol. 10, no. 2, 1943.

Only constant repetition will finally succeed in imprinting an idea on the memory of the crowd. ADOLF HITLER (1889–1945), *Mein Kampf,* 1925–27.

Through clever and constant propaganda, people can be made to see paradise as hell and vice versa, to consider the most wretched sort of life as heaven itself. ADOLF HITLER (1889–1945), *Mein Kampf,* 1925–27.

Propaganda must not serve the truth, especially not insofar as it might bring out something favorable for the opponent. ADOLPH HITLER (1889–1945), *Mein Kampf,* 1925–27.

The receptive ability of the great masses is only very limited, their understanding is small; on the other hand, their forgetfulness is great. This being so, all effective propaganda should be limited to a very few points which, in turn, should be used as slogans until even the very last man is able to imagine what is meant by such words. ADOLPH HITLER (1889–1945), *Mein Kampf,* 1925–27.

Eloquent speakers are inclined to ambition; for eloquence seemeth wisdom, both to themselves and others. THOMAS HOBBES (1588–1679), *Leviathan,* 1651.

Outlets for propaganda are necessary in any society, and they are particularly necessary in a democracy. Our freedom of the press is really only a freedom to be propagandized, but it deserves to be defended on that ground. One of the great dangers of our time is the threat against freedom of speech and freedom of the press, two liberties that are unknown today through a large part of our world. WILLIAM HUMMELL and KEITH HUNTRESS, *The Analysis of Propaganda,* 1949.

The propagandist's purpose is to make one set of people forget that the other set of people are human. ALDOUS HUXLEY (1894–1963), *The Olive Tree,* 1937.

Propaganda gives force and direction to the successive movements of popular feeling and desire; but it does not do much to create those movements. The propagandist is a man who canalizes an alreading existing stream. ALDOUS HUXLEY (1894–1963), *Harper's Magazine,* December 1936.

In regard to propaganda the early advocates of universal literacy and a free press envisaged only two possibilities: that propaganda might be good or it might be false. They did not foresee what in fact has happened above all in our Western capitalistic democracies—the development of a vast communications industry, concerned in the main neither with the true nor the false but the . . . more or less totally irrelevant. In a word, they failed to take into account man's almost infinite appetite for distractions. ALDOUS HUXLEY (1894–1963), *Brave New World Revisited,* 1958.

The greatest triumphs of propaganda have been accomplished, not by doing something, but by refraining from doing. Great is truth, but still greater from a practical point of view, is silence about truth. ALDOUS HUXLEY (1894–1963), *Brave New World,* 1932.

Situations sometimes arise in practical propaganda in which the logical mode (*ad rem*) does not produce the necessary effect, despite the convincingness of the arguments and correctness of the propagandist's positions. The psychological mode (*ad hominem*) proves to be more effective, for the propagandist takes into account the usual course of reasoning and conclusions to which the listener resorts proceeding from his interests and convictions. Psychological arguments make the propagandist's words more convincing, comprehensible, and clear. INSTITUTE OF SOCIAL SCIENCES (USSR), *Social Psychology and Propaganda*, 1985.

The first casualty when war comes is truth. HIRAM WARREN JOHNSON (1866–1945), U.S. Senator, 1917.

Among the calamities of war may be justly numbered the diminution of the love of truth by the falsehoods which interest dictates and credulity encourages. SAMUEL JOHNSON (1709–1784), *The Idler,* 1758.

Propaganda is a form of communication that is different from persuasion because it attempts to achieve a response that furthers the desired intent of the propagandist. Persuasion is interactive and attempts to satisfy the needs of both persuader and persuadee. GARTH JOWETT and VICTORIA O'DONNELL, *Propaganda and Persuasion,* 1986.

The persuasiveness of a low-credibility communicator can be enhanced when he argues against his own best interest, or when he is identified after, rather than before, presentation of his appeal. MARVIN KARLINS and HERBERT I. ABELSON, *Persuasion: How Opinions and Attitudes Are Changed,* 1970.

A communicator's effectiveness is increased if he initially expresses some views that are also held by his audience. MARVIN KARLINS and HERBERT I. ABELSON, *Persuasion: How Opinions and Attitudes Are Changed,* 1970.

A propagandist is a person who uses the mass media in an attempt to persuade people to his point of view. MARVIN KARLINS and HERBERT I. ABELSON, *Persuasion: How Opinions and Attitudes Are Changed,* 1970.

In all propaganda, the face of the enemy is designed to provide a focus for our hatred. He is the other. The outsider. The alien. He is not human. If we can only kill him, we will be rid of all within and without ourselves that is evil. SAM KEEN, *Faces of the Enemy,* 1986.

The purpose of propaganda is to paralyze thought, to prevent discrimination, and condition individuals to act as a mass. SAM KEEN, *Faces of the Enemy,* 1986.

The individual is likely to perceive what he expects to perceive. If he thinks of himself as ambitious, then he will be more sensitive to the evaluations of others that might reinforce this perception. JOHN W. KINCH, *Social Psychology,* 1973.

Use such phrases as "it is said," "there are those who believe," "the opinion is held in well-informed quarters," "some experts have come to the conclusion." Why keep on saying "I think," and "I believe," when you can put over the same idea much more persuasively by quoting someone else? EDWARD

KLAUBER, in *The Golden Webb* (Eric Barnouw, ed.), 1968.

The most important things must be said simply, for they are spoiled by bombast; whereas trivial things must be described grandly, for they are supported only by aptness of expression, tone and manner. JEAN de LA BRUYÈRE (1645–1696), *Les Caractères,* 1688.

Anything pleasant easily persuades, and while it gives pleasure it fixes itself in the heart. LACTANTIUS (ca. 240–320 A.D.), *Divine Institutions,* ca. 310 A.D.

Eloquence lies as much in the tone of the voice, in the eyes, and in the speaker's manner, as in his choice of words. FRANÇOIS, DUC de LA ROCHEFOUCAULD (1613–1680), *Maxims,* 1665.

The passions are the only advocates which always persuade. The simplest man with passion will be more persuasive than the most eloquent without. FRANÇOIS, DUC de LA ROCHEFOUCAULD (1613–1680), *Maxims,* 1665.

The object of revolution, like war, is to attain coercive predominance over the enemy as a means of working one's will with him. Revolutionary propaganda selects symbols which are calculated to detach the affections of the masses from the existing symbols of authority and to attach their affections to challenging symbols and to direct hostilities toward existing symbols of authority. HAROLD D. LASSWELL (1902–1978), *World Politics and Personal Insecurity,* 1965.

The modern propagandist, like the modern psychologist, recognizes that men are often poor judges of their own interests, flitting from one alternative to the next without solid reason or clinging timorously to the fragments of some mossy rock of ages. HAROLD D. LASSWELL (1902–1978), "Propaganda," *Encyclopedia of the Social Sciences,* 1934.

Reason and argument are incapable of combatting certain words and formulas. They are uttered with solemnity in the presence of crowds, and as soon as they have been pronounced an expression of respect is visible on every countenance, and all heads are bowed. GUSTAVE LE BON (1841–1931), *The Crowd,* 1895.

The power of words is bound up with the images they evoke, and is quite independent of their real significance. Words whose sense is the most ill-defined are sometimes those that possess the most influence. Such, for example, are the terms democratic, socialism, equality, liberty, etc., whose meaning is so vague that thick volumes do not suffice to fix it precisely. GUSTAVE LE BON (1841–1931), *The Crowd,* 1895.

Name calling—giving an idea a bad label—is used to make us reject and condemn the idea without examining the evidence. . . . Glittering generality—associating something with a "virtue word"—is used to make us accept and approve the thing without examining the evidence. Testimonial consists in having some respected or hated person say that a given idea or program or product or person is good or bad. . . . Card Stacking involves the selection or use of facts or falsehoods, illustrations or distractions, and logical or illogical statements in order to give the best or the worst possible case for an idea, program, person, or product. ALFRED McCLUNG LEE and ELIZABETH BRIANT LEE, *The Fine Art of Propaganda,* 1939.

The surest way of discrediting a new political idea, and of damaging it, is to reduce it to absurdity while ostensibly defending it. For every truth is "exorbitant," if it is exaggerated, if it is carried beyond the limits in which it can be actually applied, can be reduced to absurdity, and is even found to become an absurdity under the conditions. V. I. LENIN (1870–1924), *Left-Wing Communism, An Infantile Disorder,* 1920.

No amount of manifest absurdity could deter those who wanted to believe from believing. BERNARD LEVIN, *The Pendulum Years,* 1976.

[Propaganda is when the] complex is made into the simple, the hypothetical into the dogmatic, and the relative into the absolute. WALTER LIPPMANN (1889–1974).

We must remember that in time of war what is said on the enemy's side of the front is always propaganda and what is said on our side of the front is truth and righteousness, the cause of humanity and a crusade for peace. WALTER LIPPMANN (1889–1974), 1966.

Propaganda is promotion which is veiled in one way or another as to (1) its origin or sources, (2) the interests involved, (3) the methods employed, (4) the content spread, and (5) the results accruing to the victims—any one, any two, any three, any four, or all five. FREDERICK E. LUMLEY (1880–1954), *The Propaganda Machine,* 1933.

The propagandist . . . is powerfully motivated to let into the channels of communication . . . only that which, in his judgment, will evoke the desired responses; he keeps back, suppresses, or extinguishes all the rest. FREDERICK E. LUMLEY (1880–1954), *The Propaganda Machine,* 1933.

The object of oratory is not truth but persuasion. THOMAS BABINGTON MACAULAY (1800–1859), *The Athenian Orators,* 1824.

Persuasion as a means of control always involves the introduction of a consideration not naturally relevant to the situation but deliberately made relevant. The persuader must deliberately create and alleviate discomforts in order to control behavior. NEIL A. McDONALD, *Politics: A Study of Control Behavior,* 1965.

One is convinced . . . when he arrives at a course of action by direct and independent examination of the consequences of alternative courses of action. Persuasion suggests acting on faith, belief, feelings, hunch, unconsciousness and uncertainty. The psychological bases of persuasion are likes and dislikes, attractions and repulsions, comforts and discomforts. . . . NEIL A. McDONALD, *Politics: A Study of Control Behavior,* 1965.

Though fraud in other activities be detestable, in the management of war it is laudable and glorious, and he who overcomes an enemy by fraud is as much to be praised as he who does so by force. NICCOLO MACHIAVELLI (1469–1527), *Discourses on the First Ten Books of Livy,* 1517.

One of the great secrets of the day is to know how to take possession of popular prejudices and passions, in such a way as to introduce a confusion of principles which makes impossible all understanding between those who speak the same language and have the same interests. NICCOLO MACHIAVELLI (1469–1527).

Give me the writing of a nation's advertising and propaganda, and I care not who governs its politics. HUGH MACLENNAN, *MacLean's,* November 5, 1960.

Education aims at independence of judgment. Propaganda offers ready-made opinions for the unthinking herd. Education and propaganda are directly opposed both in aim and method. . . . The educator tries to tell people HOW to think; the propagandist WHAT to think. The educator strives to develop individual responsibility; the propagandist, mass effects. The educator fails unless he achieves an open mind; the propagandist unless he achieves a closed mind. EVERETT DEAN MARTIN (1880–1941), *Forum,* vol. 81, 1929.

It is hard to believe that a man is telling the truth when you know that you would lie if you were in his place. H. L. MENCKEN (1880–1956).

There is an old story of blind men trying to describe an elephant. One felt the elephant's leg and declared that the creature was like a tree, another felt the enormous side and said the elephant was like a wall, while a third, feeling the tail, was positive the animal was like a rope. Each man had a notion of reality that was limited by the number and kind of attributes he had perceived. WAYNE C. MINNICK, *The Art of Persuasion,* 1957.

That eloquence prejudices the subject it would advance which wholly attracts us to itself. MICHEL de MONTAIGNE (1533–1592), *Essays,* 1580.

Every method is used to prove to men that in given political, economic and social situations they are bound to be happy, and those who are unhappy are made either criminals or monsters. ALBERTO MORAVIA, *Man As an End,* 1964.

Slogans are apt to petrify man's thinking . . . every slogan, every word almost, that is used by the socialist, the communist, the capitalist. People hardly think nowadays. They throw words at each other. JAWAHARLAL NEHRU (1889–1964).

Nothing is more common than for men to think that because they are familiar with words, they understand the ideas they stand for. CARDINAL JOHN NEWMAN (1801–1890).

Propaganda is any effort to change opinions or attitudes. . . . The propagandist is anyone who communicates his ideas with the intent of influencing others. MARBURY B. OGLE, *Public Opinion and Political Dynamics,* 1950.

Oratory is just like prostitution: you must have little tricks. One of my favorite tricks is to start a sentence and leave it unfinished. Everyone racks his brains and wonders what I was going to say. . . . VITTORIO EMANUELE ORLANDO, *Time,* December 8, 1952.

Words are weapons, and it is dangerous in speculation, as in politics, to borrow them from your enemies. JOSÉ ORTEGA y GASSET (1883–1955), *Obiter Scripta,* 1936.

A person growing up with Newspeak as his sole language would no more know that equal had once had the secondary meaning of "politically equal," or that free had once meant "intellectually free." GEORGE ORWELL (1903–1950), *Nineteen Eighty-Four,* 1949.

The whole aim of Newspeak is to narrow the range of thought. In the end we shall make thoughtcrime literally impossible, because there will be no words in which to express it. Every concept that can ever be needed will be expressed by exactly one word, with its meaning rigidly defined and all its subsidiary meanings rubbed out and forgotten. GEORGE ORWELL (1903–1950), *Nineteen Eighty-Four,* 1949.

It was perceived that in thus abbreviating a name one narrowed and subtly altered its meaning, by cutting out most of the associations that would otherwise cling to it. GEORGE ORWELL (1903–1950), *Nineteen Eighty-Four,* 1949.

In elections where people's enduring commitments are relevant, political propaganda generally serves merely to reinforce their preexisting attitudes. But in elections where enduring commitments are not called into play, attitudes and votes are more labile, and political persuasion may have major effects. STUART OSKAMP, *Attitudes and Opinions,* 1977.

A doctrine capable of being stated only in obscure and involved terms is open to reasonable suspicion of being either crude or erroneous. SIR FREDERICK POLLOCK (1845–1937), 1946.

Falsehood is a recognized and extremely useful weapon in warfare, and every country uses it quite deliberately to deceive its own people, to attract neutrals, and to mislead the enemy. ARTHUR PONSONBY (1871–1946), *Falsehood in Wartime,* 1928.

To the Communists, words are tools to achieve effects, not means to communicate in the search for truth. STEFAN T. POSSONY.

Each end of the political spectrum has, I suppose, its own favorite style of propaganda. The Right tends to prefer gross, straightforward sentimentality. The Left, a sort of surface intellectualizing. But it is very important, it seems to me, to note that the response required of us, in each instance, is a passionate, uncritical acceptance of a point of view. NEIL POSTMAN, *Et Cetera,* Summer 1979.

[Propaganda] is a manipulation designed to lead you to a simplistic conclusion rather than a carefully considered one. It is an abuse of persuasion techniques because it tries to short-circuit critical scrutiny, thoughtful evaluations and counterarguments. ANTHONY PRATKANIS, *New York Times,* October 27, 1992.

The power of guilt to convince and to persuade stems, as with most emotional appeals, from its power to direct our thoughts and to channel our energies. When we feel guilty we typically pay little attention to the cogency of an argument, to the merits of a suggested course of action. Instead, our thoughts and actions are directed to removing the feeling of guilt—to somehow making things right or doing the right thing. We fall into the rationalization trap. ANTHONY PRATKANIS and ELLIOT ARONSON, *The Age of Propaganda,* 1991.

If you have a weak candidate and a weak platform, wrap yourself up in the American flag and talk about the constitution. MATTHEW QUAY (1833–1904).

The abuse of language occurs when its metaphorical nature is hidden, if the representation is identified with the thing represented. Therefore the linguistically hygienic use of metaphor depends on the full recognition of its limitations, that is, on critical consciousness of the generalizations, analogies, and abstractions involved. ANATOLE RAPOPORT, *Operational Philosophy,* 1953.

There are some things about which the public always wants to be deceived. CARDINAL de RETZ (1614–1679), *Mémoires.*

Through an emotional speech, a charismatic leader is able to "infect" followers, to stir them to action. It is the charismatic speaker's skill in emotional expressivity that people most often associate with charisma. . . . Sensitivity to nonverbal and emotional messages is a second critical component of charisma. . . . RONALD E. RIGGIO, *The Charisma Quotient,* 1987.

The essence of lying is in its deception, not in words; a lie may be told by silence, by equivocation, by the accent on a syllable, by a glance of the eyes attaching a peculiar significance to a sentence. . . . JOHN RUSKIN (1819–1900), *Modern Painters,* 1872.

Why is propaganda so much more successful when it stirs up hatred than when it tries to stir up friendly feeling? BERTRAND RUSSELL (1872–1970), *The Conquest of Happiness,* 1936.

To acquire immunity to eloquence is of the utmost importance to the citizens of a democracy. BERTRAND RUSSELL (1872–1970), *Power,* 1938.

To prevent resentment, governments attribute misfortunes to natural causes; to create resentment, oppositions attribute them to human causes. BERTRAND RUSSELL (1872–1970), *Unpopular Essays,* 1928.

The content and forms of American communications—the myths and the means of transmitting them—are devoted to manipulation. When successfully employed, as they invariably are, the result is individual passivity, a state of inertia that precludes action. HERBERT SCHILLER, *The Mind Managers,* 1973.

There is no absurdity so palpable but that it may be firmly planted in the human head if only you begin to inculcate it before the age of five, by constantly repeating it with an air of great solemnity. ARTHUR SCHOPENHAUER (1788–1860).

The reduction of political discourse to sound bites is one of the worst things that's happened in American political life. JOHN SILBER, *USA Today,* October 1, 1990.

Every event, once it has occurred, can be made to appear inevitable by a competent historian. LEE SIMONSONA (1888–1967).

The words men fight and die for are the coins of politics, where by much usage they are soiled and by much manipulation debased. This has evidently been the fate of the word "democracy." It has come to mean whatever anyone wants it to mean. BERNARD SMITH, *The Democratic Spirit,* 1941.

Print is the sharpest and the strongest weapon of our party. JOSEPH STALIN (1879–1953), Speech, April 19, 1923.

There is no lie that many men will not believe; there is no man who does not believe many lies; and there is no man who believes only lies. JOHN STERLING (1806–1844), *Essays and Tales,* 1848.

Eloquence, smooth and cutting, is like a razor whetted with oil. JONATHAN SWIFT (1667–1745), *Thoughts on Various Subjects,* 1706.

Whenever there is an organized movement to persuade people to believe or do something, whenever an effort is made to "propagate" a creed or set of opinions or convictions or to make people act as we want them to act, the means employed are called propaganda. EDWARD A. TENNEY, *A Primer for Readers,* 1942.

We love eloquence for its own sake, and not for any truth which it may utter, or any heroism it may inspire. HENRY DAVID THOREAU (1817–1862), *Cape Cod,* 1865.

Words began to change their ordinary meaning, and to take on that which was not given to them. Reckless audacity came to be considered the courage of a loyal ally; prudent hesitation, specious cowardice; moderation was held to be a cloak for unmanliness; ability to see all sides of a question, inaptness to act on any. THUCYDIDES (460–400 B.C.), *History of the Peloponnesian War.*

History is the propaganda of the victors. ERNEST TOLLER (1893–1939).

Perhaps the most outstanding device in film propaganda is the use of contrasts. Not only do strong contrasts contain a greater emotional intensity than the more subtle nuances, but they also guide the audience's sympathies with more certainty. DAVID WELCH, *Propaganda and the German Cinema: 1933-1945,* 1983.

Propaganda has its best chance of success when it clearly designates a target as the source of all misery and suffering. . . . One of the most striking means by which the cinema has influenced social attitudes—changing or reinforcing opinions—has been through the use of stereotypes . . . conventional figures that have come to be regarded as representative of particular classes, races, and so on. DAVID WELCH, *Propaganda and the German Cinema: 1933–1945,* 1983.

A good catchword can obscure analysis for fifty years. WENDELL L. WILKIE (1892–1944), Debate, 1938.

Such force hath the tongue, and such is the power of eloquence and reason, that most men are forced even to yield in that which most standeth against their will. THOMAS WILSON (1525–1581), *The Arte of Rhetorique,* 1553.

[Propaganda is] . . . the more or less deliberately planned and systematic use of symbols, chiefly through suggestion and related psychological techniques, with a view to altering and controlling opinions, ideas, and values, and ultimately to changing overt actions along predetermined lines. Propaganda may be open and its purpose avowed, or it may conceal its intentions. KIMBALL YOUNG, *Handbook of Social Psychology.*

Public Opinion and Mass Media

The abuses of the press are notorious. License of the press is no proof of liberty. When a people are corrupted, the press may be made an engine to complete their ruin. JOHN ADAMS (1735–1826), *Boston Gazette,* February 6, 1775.

There is nothing that more betrays an ungenerous spirit than the giving of secret stabs to a man's reputation. Lampoons and satires, that are written with wit and spirit, are like poisoned darts, which not only inflict a wound, but make it incurable. JOSEPH ADDISON (1672–1719), *The Spectator,* 1711–1712.

The American people should be made aware of the trend toward monopolization of the great public information vehicles and the concentration of more and more power over public opinion in fewer and fewer hands. SPIRO AGNEW, U.S. Vice-President, November 13, 1969.

The vested interests—if we explain the situation by their influence—can only get the public to act as they wish by manipulating public opinion, by playing either upon the public's indifference, confusions, prejudices, pugnacities or fears. SIR NORMAN ANGELL (1874–1967), *The Great Illusion,* 1933.

The evil that men do lives on in the front pages of greedy newspapers, but the good is oft interred apathetically inside. BROOKS ATKINSON, *Once around the Sun,* 1951.

Opinion is the main thing which does good or harm in the world. It is our false opinions of things which ruin us. MARCUS AURELIUS (121–180 A.D.), *Meditations.*

You may talk of the tyranny of Nero and Tiberius, but the real tyranny is the tyranny of your next-door neighbor. What espionage of despotism comes to your door so effectively as the eye of the man who lives at your door? Public opinion is a permeating influence. It requires us to think other men's thoughts. . . . WALTER BAGEHOT (1826–1877), *The English Constitution,* 1867.

Character assassination is at once easier and surer than physical assault; and it involves far less risk for the assassin. It leaves him free to commit the same deed over and over again, and may, indeed, win him the honors of a hero even in the country of his victim. ALAN BARTH, *The Loyalty of Free Men,* 1951.

Vilify! Vilify! Some of it will always stick. PIERRE BEAUMARCHAIS (1732–1799).

There is nothing that makes more cowards and feeble men than public opinion. HENRY WARD BEECHER (1813–1887), *Proverbs from Plymouth Pulpit*, 1887.

Critics are like eunuchs in a harem: they know how it's done, they've seen it done every day, but they're unable to do it themselves. BRENDAN BEHAN (1923–1964).

Journalists say a thing that they know isn't true, in the hope that if they keep on saying it long enough it will be true. ARNOLD BENNET (1867–1931), *The Title.*

If people find emotional and social significance in the distant world of news politics, the media and the government are in possession of a powerful mechanism of political and social control. The temptation always exists for political actors to propose magical solutions and fantastic political scenarios through the use of myths, stereotypes, scapegoats and other symbolic devices. W. LANCE BENNETT, *News: The Politics of Illusion*, 1983.

Perhaps the most obvious political effect of controlled news is the advantage it gives powerful people in getting their issues on the political agenda and defining those issues in ways likely to influence their resolution. W. LANCE BENNETT, *News: The Politics of Illusion*, 1983.

Many powerful social beliefs are based less on the capacity to prove or disprove the belief than on the side benefits that follow from the belief. W. LANCE BENNETT, *News: The Politics of Illusion*, 1983.

Image has become everything. EDWARD L. BERNAYS, *Life* magazine, Fall 1990.

The deeper problems connected with advertising come less from the unscrupulousness of our "deceivers" than from our pleasure in being deceived, less from the desire to seduce than from the desire to be seduced. DANIEL J. BOORSTIN, *The Image*, 1962.

Our national politics has become a competition for images or between images, rather than between ideals. DANIEL BOORSTIN, *The Image*, 1962.

Objectivity is impossible to a normal human being. Fairness, however is attainable, and this is what we are striving for—not objectivity but fairness. DAVID BRINKLEY, *Newsweek*, January 6, 1969.

It is proof of a base and low mind for one to wish to think with the masses or majority, merely because the majority is the majority. Truth does not change because it is, or is not, believed by a majority of the people. GIORDANO BRUNO (1548–1600).

Towering over Presidents and State Governors, over Congress and state legislatures, over conventions and the vast machinery of party, public opinion stands out, in the United States, and the great source of Power, the master of servants who tremble before it. JAMES BRYCE (1838–1922), *The American Commonwealth*, 1880.

When the people have no tyrant, their own public opinion becomes one. EDWARD GEORGE BULWER-LYTTON (1803–1873).

The most important service rendered by the press and the magazines is that of educating people to approach printed matter with distrust. SAMUEL BUTLER (1835–1902).

The public buys its opinions as it buys its meat, or takes its milk, on the principle that it is cheaper to do this than to buy a cow. So it is, but the milk is more likely to be watered. SAMUEL BUTLER (1835–1902), Notebooks, 1912.

The world is naturally averse, / To all the truth it sees or hears; / But swallows nonsense, and a lie, / With greediness and gluttony. SAMUEL BUTLER (1612–1680), *Hudibras*, 1664.

Burke said that there were three estates in Parliament; but in the reporters' gallery yonder, there sat a fourth estate, more important by far than all. THOMAS CARLYLE (1795–1881), *On Heroes, Hero-Worship, and the Heroic in History*, 1841.

There are two kinds of restrictions on human liberty—the restraint of law and that of custom. No written law has ever been more binding than unwritten custom supported by popular opinion. CARRIE CHAPMAN CATT (1859–1947), Speech, February 8, 1900.

The world is governed much more by opinion than by laws. It is not the judgment of courts but the moral judgement of individuals and masses of men, which is the chief wall of defense around property and life. WILLIAM ELLERY CHANNING (1780–1842), Letter, 1839.

Flatterers look like friends, as wolves like dogs. GEORGE CHAPMAN (1559–1634), *The Conspiracy of Byron*, 1608.

When the public mood is not mere indifference, it is a rapidly alternating sense of likes and dislikes, or what Matthew Arnold called hot fits and cold fits; all of them arising from certain hasty impressions about our own advantage or disadvantage; and none of them founded on anything but newspaper stories. GILBERT KEITH CHESTERTON (1874–1936), *The End of the Armistice*, 1936.

Guesses about the fashions of the future are generally quite wide of the mark, because they are founded on a very obvious fallacy. They always imply that public taste will continue to progress in its present direction. GILBERT KEITH CHESTERTON (1874–1936), *Robert Louis Stevenson*, 1927.

The monopoly of communications also facilitates the political "education" of the mass, reaching with equal vigor toward the youngest generational levels. It is a striking and significant fact that totalitarian leaders have uniformly expressed a high priority interest in the political potential of youth. REO M. CHRISTENSON et al., *Ideologies and Modern Politics,* 1975.

Nothing is so swift as calumny; nothing is more easily uttered; nothing more readily received; nothing more widely dispersed. MARCUS TULLIUS CICERO (106–43 B.C.)

Our major mistakes have not been the result of democracy, but of the erosion of democracy made possible by the mass media's manipulation of public opinion. ROBERT CIRINO, *Don't Blame the People,* 1971.

As long as the media owners were able to make the question of objectivity respectable enough for argument, they were able to keep the public from asking the right question. The right question is whether all viewpoints have an equal opportunity to use bias, not the already answered question of whether or not bias is being used by this or that news media. ROBERT CIRINO, *Don't Blame the People,* 1971.

The humbug and hypocrisy of the press begin only when the newspapers pretend to be "impartial" or "servants of the public." And this becomes dangerous as well as laughable when the public is fool enough to believe it. CLAUD COCKBURN, *In Time of Trouble,* 1956.

[The mass media] may not be successful much of the time in telling people what to think, but it is stunningly successful in telling its readers what to think about. . . . The world will look different to different people, depending . . . on the map that is drawn for them by writers, editors, and publishers of the papers they read. BERNARD COHEN, quoted in *Communication Yearbook II* (Rogers and Dearing), 1988.

A people are free in proportion as they form their own opinions. SAMUEL TAYLOR COLERIDGE (1772–1834), *The Watchman,* 1796.

The modern press itself is a new phenomenon. Its typical unit is the great agency of mass communication. These agencies can facilitate thought and discussion. They can stifle it. . . . They can play up or down the news and its significance, foster and feed emotions, create complacent fictions and blind spots, misuse the great words and uphold empty slogans. Their scope and power are increasing every day as new instruments become available to them. These instruments can spread lies faster and farther than our forefathers dreamed when they enshrined freedom of the press in the First Amendment to the Constitution. COMMISSION on FREEDOM of the PRESS, *A Free and Responsible Press,* 1947.

Protection against government is now not enough to guarantee that a man who has something to say shall have a chance to say it. The owners and managers of the press determine which person, which facts, which version of the facts, and which ideas shall reach the public. COMMISSION on FREEDOM of the PRESS, *A Free and Responsible Press,* 1947.

It is the besetting vice of democracies to substitute public opinion for law. This is the usual form in which the masses of men exhibit their tyranny. JAMES FENIMORE COOPER (1789–1851), *The American Democrat,* 1838.

In a democracy, as a matter of course, every effort is made to seize upon and create public opinion, which is, substantially, securing power. JAMES FENIMORE COOPER (1789–1851), *The American Democrat,* 1838.

Democracies are necessarily controlled by public opinion, and failing of the means of obtaining power more honestly, the fraudulent and ambitious find a motive to mislead, and even to corrupt the common sentiment, to attain their ends. JAMES FENIMORE COOPER (1789–1851), *The American Democrat,* 1838.

The constant appeals to public opinion in a democracy, though excellent as a corrective of public vices, induce private hypocrisy, causing men to conceal their own convictions when opposed to those of the mass, the latter being seldom wholly right, or wholly wrong. JAMES FENIMORE COOPER (1789–1851), *The American Democrat,* 1838.

I had grown tired of standing in the lean and lonely front line facing the greatest enemy that ever confronted man—public opinion. CLARENCE DARROW (1857–1938), *The Story of My Life,* 1932.

Exploitation of the "unconscious" has rapidly opened up the field of political psychology, including factors that enter into public opinion, leadership, policy decisions, motives, ideologies, and organizational behavior. No subject of political science, and no applications of political science, are untouched by the new knowledge that has flowed from the realization that political man can be only understood and acted upon through his hidden and concealed drives, feelings, and predispositions. ALFRED de GRAZIA, *Politics and Government,* 1962.

What the lawmaker has to ascertain is not the true belief but the common belief. PATRICK DEVLIN, *The Enforcement of Morals,* 1965.

Genuine ignorance is . . . profitable because it is likely to be accompanied by humility, curiosity, and open-mindedness; whereas ability to repeat catch-phrases, cant terms, familiar propositions, gives the conceit of learning and coats the mind with varnish waterproof to new ideas. JOHN DEWEY (1859–1952).

What we call public opinion is generally public sentiment. BENJAMIN DISRAELI (1804–1881), Speech, August 3, 1880.

The constitution of man is such that for a long time after he has discovered the incorrectness of the ideas prevailing around him he shrinks from openly emancipating himself from their domination; and, constrained by the force of circumstances, he publicly applauds what his private judgment condemns. J. W. DRAPER (1811–1882), *History of the Intellectual Development of Europe,* 1863.

If by the people you understand the multitude, the hoi polloi, 'tis no matter what they think; they are sometimes in the right, sometimes in the wrong;

their judgment is a mere lottery. JOHN DRYDEN (1631–1700), *Essay on Dramatic Poetry.*

Nor is the people's judgment always true: The most may err as grossly as the few. JOHN DRYDEN (1631–1700), *Absalom and Achitophel,* 1682.

The critical element in political maneuver for advantage is the creation of meaning: the construction of beliefs about the significance of events, of problems, of crises, of policy changes, and of leaders. The strategic need is to immobilize opposition and mobilize support. While coercion and intimidation help to check resistance in all political systems, the key tactic must always be the evocation of meanings that legitimize favored courses of action. MURRAY EDELMAN, *PS,* Winter 1985.

It is not "reality" in any testable or observable sense that matters in shaping political consciousness and behavior, but rather the beliefs that language helps evoke about the causes of discontents and satisfactions, about policies that will bring about a future closer to the heart's desire, and about other unobservables. MURRAY EDELMAN, *PS,* Winter 1985.

The [American] Press, which is mostly controlled by vested interests, has an excessive influence on public opinion. ALBERT EINSTEIN (1879–1955), *Ideas and Opinions of Albert Einstein.*

You must pay for conformity. All goes well as long as you run with conformists. But you, who are an honest man in other particulars, know that there is alive somewhere a man whose honesty reaches to this point also, that he shall not kneel to false gods, and, on the day when you meet him, you sink into the class of counterfeits. RALPH WALDO EMERSON (1803–1882), *English Traits,* 1856.

Leave this hypocritical prating about the masses. Masses are rude, lame, unmade, pernicious in their demands and influence, and need not to be flattered but to be schooled. I wish not to concede anything to them, but to tame, drill, divide, and break them up, and draw individuals out of them. RALPH WALDO EMERSON (1803–1882).

The problem of journalism in America proceeds from a simple but inescapable bind: journalists are rarely, if ever, in a position to establish the truth about an issue for themselves, and they are therefore almost entirely dependent on self-interested "sources" for the version of reality that they report. EDWARD JAY EPSTEIN, *Between Fact and Fiction,* 1975.

When journalists are presented with secret information about issues of great import, they become, in a very real sense, agents for the surreptitious source. EDWARD JAY EPSTEIN, *Between Fact and Fiction,* 1975.

Our opinions exert a powerful tyranny over us, especially when we are simultaneously uncertain whence they derive yet nonetheless determined to live lives congruent with them. JOSEPH EPSTEIN, *Political Passages* (John H. Bunzel, ed.), 1988.

It is a good part of sagacity to have known the foolish desires of the crowd and their unreasonable notions. DESIDERIUS ERASMUS (1466–1536), *Colloquies,* 1516.

Governments have ever been known to hold a high hand over the education of the people. They know, better than anyone else, that their power is based almost entirely on the school. Hence, they monopolize it more and more. FRANCISCO FERRER (1857–1909), *The Modern School.*

The education of today is nothing more than drill. . . . [C]hildren must be accustomed to obey, to believe, to think according to the social dogmas which govern us. FRANCISCO FERRER (1857–1909), *The Modern School.*

No mighty king, no ambitious emperor, no pope, or prophet ever dreamt of such an awesome pulpit, so potent a magic wand [television]. FRED W. FRIENDLY, Foreword, *Presidential Television,* 1973.

The fabric of popular culture that relates the elements of existence to one another and shapes the common consciousness of what is, what is important, what is right and what is related to what else is now largely a manufactured product. GEORGE GERBNER, *Scientific American,* September 1972.

Little people like to talk about what the great are doing. GERMAN PROVERB.

Taken together, the changes produced by polling contribute to the transformation of public opinion from an unpredictable, extreme, and often dangerous force into a more docile expression of public sentiment. Opinion stated through polls imposes less pressure and makes fewer demands on government than would more spontaneous or natural assertions of popular sentiment. BENJAMIN GINSBERG, *The Captive Mind,* 1986.

Using polling, media, and public relations techniques, modern states have learned a good deal about the manipulation and management of mass opinion. Indeed, in the modern era the censor has been supplanted—or at least joined—by the public relations officer as the government functionary most responsible for dealing with public opinion. BENJAMIN GINSBERG, *The Captive Mind,* 1986.

There is scarce any truth, but its adversaries have made it an ugly vizard, by which it's exposed to the hate and disesteem of superficial examiners. For an oppropbrious title, with vulgar believers, is as good as an argument. JOSEPH GLANVILLE (1636–1680), *Scepsis Scientifica,* 1655.

Congruity of opinions, whether true or false, to our natural constitution is one great incentive to their belief and reception. JOSEPH GLANVILLE, *The Vanity of Dogmatizing,* 1661.

No maxim can be more pernicious than that which would teach us to consult the temper of the times, and to tell only so much as we imagine our contemporaries will be able to bear. WILLIAM GODWIN (1756–1830), *An Enquiry concerning Political Justice,* 1793.

It is seldom that we are persuaded to adopt opinions, or persuaded to abandon them, by the mere force of arguments. The change is produced silently, and unperceived except in its ultimate results by him who suffers it. Our creed is, ninety nine times in a hundred, the pure growth of our temper and social feelings. The human intellect is a sort of barometer, directed by the variations that surround it. WILLIAM GODWIN (1756–1830), *Thoughts Occasioned by the Perusal of Dr. Parr's Spiritual Sermon*, 1801.

Not every item of news should be published: rather must those who control news policies endeavor to make every item of news serve a certain purpose. PAUL JOSEPH GOEBBELS (1897–1945), Diary, March 14, 1943.

It is the absolute right of the state to supervise the formation of public opinion. PAUL JOSEPH GOEBBELS (1897–1945), Address, October 1933.

Prestige is a system of social control that shapes much of social life. All people share the universal need to gain the respect and esteem of others . . . and all individuals and groups give and withhold prestige and approval as a way of rewarding or punishing others. WILLIAM J. GOODE, *The Celebration of Heroes*, 1978.

It is no exaggeration to say that the press of Europe and America busies itself assiduously and almost exclusively with the task of lowering the cultural level of its readers, a level which is already sufficiently low. MAXIM GORKY (1868–1936), *To American Intellectuals*, 1932.

He who speaks of the people, speaks of a madman; for the people is a monster full of confusion and mistakes; and the opinions of the people are as far removed from the truth as, according to Ptolemy, the Indies are from Spain. FRANCESCO GUICCIARDINI (1483–1540), *Storie d'Italia*, 1564.

The ethics of salesmanship have infected every area of life. Politics has become a branch of public relations. Persuasion has been substituted for debate and the search for the right image has replaced the search for the right policy. STUART HALL and PADDY WHANNEL, *The Popular Arts*.

No character, however upright, is a match for constantly reiterated attacks, however false. ALEXANDER HAMILTON (1755–1804).

The hand that rules the press, the radio, the screen and the far-spread magazine, rules the country. LEARNED HAND (1872–1961), U.S. Supreme Court Justice, 1942.

The people cannot see, but they can feel. JAMES HARRINGTON (1611–1677), *The Commonwealth of Oceana*, 1658.

Public opinion is the most potent monarch this world knows. BENJAMIN HARRISON (1833–1901), Speech, 1888.

Life is the art of being well-deceived and in order that the deception may succeed it must be habitual and uninterrupted. WILLIAM HAZLITT (1778–1830), *The Round Table*, 1817.

Calumny requires no proof. The throwing of malicious imputations against any character leaves a stain which no after-refutation can wipe out. To create an unfavorable impression, it is not necessary that certain things be true, but only that they have been said. WILLIAM HAZLITT (1778–1830), *Selected Essays*.

Nothing is more unjust or capricious than public opinion. WILLIAM HAZLITT (1778–1830), *Characteristics,* 1823.

When a thing ceases to be a subject of controversy, it ceases to be a subject of interest. WILLIAM HAZLITT (1778–1830), *Collected Works.*

Trying to determine what is going on in the world by reading the newspaper is like trying to tell the time by watching the second hand of a clock. BEN HECHT (1894–1964).

Historians exercise great power and some of them know it. They recreate the past, changing it to fit their own interpretations. Thus, they change the future as well. FRANK HERBERT, *Dune,* 1965.

In relation to the political decontamination of our public life, the government will embark upon a systematic campaign to restore the nation's moral and material health. The whole educational system, theater, film, literature, the press, and broadcasting—all these will be used as a means to this end. ADOLPH HITLER (1889–1945), *Völkischer Beobachter,* March 23, 1933.

They that approve a private opinion, call it opinion; but they that dislike it, heresy; and yet heresy signifies no more than private opinion. THOMAS HOBBES (1588–1679), *Leviathan,* 1651.

Those who in vague rhetoric dwell on education as the substitute for force and revolution often mean a doped, standarized, and servile education. JOHN A. HOBSON (1858–1940), *Free Thought in the Social Sciences,* 1926.

The thought control of dictatorships is imposed by force, but discussion, criticism and debate can be stifled by fear as well as by force. Persecution [by] public opinion can be as powerful as purges and pogroms. Frightened men are, at best, irresponsible in their actions and, at worst, dangerous. Of all the forms of tyranny over the mind of man, none is more terrible than fear—to be afraid of being one's self among one's neighbors. PAUL G. HOFFMAN (1891–1974), Address, Freedom House Award, 1951.

With effervescing opinions, as with champagne, the quickest way to let them get flat is to let them get exposed to air. OLIVER WENDELL HOLMES, JR. (1841–1935), Letter, 1920.

One secret has been kept many centuries: the terrible worthlessness of the people collectively. EDGAR WATSON HOWE (1853–1937), *Country Town Sayings,* 1911.

That mysterious independent variable of political calculation, public opinion. THOMAS H. HUXLEY (1825–1895), *Universities, Actual and Ideal,* 1874.

And what can be said of the attitude assumed by the press of these leaders of the people who speak and write of freedom of thought, and at the same time make themselves the slaves of the supposed opinions of their subscribers? HENRIK IBSEN (1828–1906), Letter, 1882.

Public opinion is a vulgar, impertinent, anonymous tyrant who deliberately makes life unpleasant for anyone who is not content to be the average man. WILLIAM RALPH INGE (1860–1954), *Outspoken Essays,* 1919.

I would like to see all editors of papers and magazines agree to print the truth and nothing but the truth, to avoid all slander and misrepresentation, and to let the private affairs of men alone. ROBERT G. INGERSOLL (1833–1899).

The murderer only takes the life of the parent and leaves his character as a goodly heritage to his children, whilst the slanderer takes away his goodly reputation and leaves him a living monument to his children's disgrace. ANDREW JACKSON (1767–1845), U.S., President, Note, August 1837.

I really look with commiseration over the great body of my fellow citizens who, reading newspapers, live and die in the belief that they have known something of what has been passing in the world in their time. THOMAS JEFFERSON (1743–1826), U.S. President, Letter, 1807.

What is it men cannot be made to believe? THOMAS JEFFERSON (1743–1826), U.S. President, Letter, 1786.

The animosities of sovereigns are temporary and may be allayed; but those which seize the whole body of a people, and of a people, too, who dictate their own measures, produce calamities of long duration. THOMAS JEFFERSON (1743–1826), U.S. President, Letter, 1786.

Heroes are created by popular demand, sometimes out of the scantiest materials, or none at all. GERALD W. JOHNSON (1890–1980), *American Heroes and Hero-Worship,* 1943.

There is censorship in this country, all right, make no mistake about that, but also make no mistake about its source. . . . While the government will not censor, apparently the networks will. The irreparable damage to the public is all the same. NICHOLAS JOHNSON, Federal Communications Commissioner, *New York Times,* April 8, 1969.

If a man could say nothing against a character but what he can prove, history could not be written. SAMUEL JOHNSON (1709–1784), Boswell's *Life of Samuel Johnson,* 1791.

The liberty of the press is a blessing when we are inclined to write against others, and a calamity when we find ourselves overborn by the multitude of our assailants. SAMUEL JOHNSON (1709–1784).

That every man should regulate his actions by his own conscience, without any regard to the opinions of the rest of the world, is one of the first precepts of moral prudence. SAMUEL JOHNSON (1709–1784), *The Rambler,* 1750–52.

Calumny differs from most other injuries in this dreadful circumstance. He who commits it can never repair it. A false report may spread where a recantation never reaches. SAMUEL JOHNSON (1709–1784).

Just as an army cannot fight without arms, so the party cannot do ideological work successfuly without such a sharp and militant weapon as the press. We cannot put the press in unreliable hands. It must be in the hands of the most faithful, most trustworthy, most politically steadfast people devoted to our cause. NIKITA KHRUSHCHEV (1894–1971), *New York Times Magazine,* September 19, 1957.

The media, sometimes intentionally, but often unintentionally, have the function of providing models for behavior. In some instances, propaganda is used in a deliberate attempt to influence values and beliefs. In other instances, the content of the ads and entertainment functions to convey particular norms of society. JOHN W. KINCH, *Social Psychology,* 1973.

There is [an] area in which mass communication is extremely effective, and that is in the creation of opinion on new issues. By "new issues" I mean issues on which the individual has no opinion and on which his friends and fellow group members have no opinion. . . . The individual has no predisposition to defend, and so the communication falls, as it were, on defenseless soil. And once the opinion is created, then it is this new opinion which becomes easy to reinforce and hard to change. JOSEPH KLAPPER, *Modern Communications and Foreign Policy,* 1967.

To befool and mislead the people, to falsify public opinion, is to pervert and destroy a republican form of government. ROBERT M. LaFOLLETTE, SR. (1855–1925), *LaFollette's Magazine,* April 1918.

People may expect too much of journalism. Not only do they expect it to be entertaining, they expect it to be true. LEWIS LAPHAM.

The fame of men ought always to be estimated by the means used to acquire it. FRANÇOIS, DUC de LA ROCHEFOUCAULD (1613–1680), *Maxims,* 1665.

Publicity is to a contemporaneous culture what the great public monuments and churches and buildings of state are to more traditional societies, an instrument of solidarity; but because publicity is only generalized gossip of the in-group, the solidarity it creates is synthetic. CHRISTOPHER LASCH.

In our own day it would not be an unfair description of education to define it as the art which teaches men to be deceived by the printed word. HAROLD J. LASKI (1893–1950), *Liberty in the Modern State.*

It is a dangerous situation for . . . without accurate information it is difficult to be an effective citizen; and most people have neither the time nor the means to explore for truth in the news. HAROLD J. LASKI (1893–1950), *The American Democracy,* 1948.

The real power of the press comes from the effect of its continuous repetition of an attitude reflected in the facts which its readers have no chance to check, or by its ability to surround those facts by an environment of suggestion which, often half-consciously, seeps its way into the mind of the reader and forms his premises for him without his even being aware that they are really prejudices to which he has scarcely given a moment of thought. HAROLD J. LASKI (1893–1950), *The American Democracy,* 1948.

Daily new lies; lies by means of pure fact alone, lies by means of invented facts, lies by means of facts distorted into their opposites—such were the weapons with which we were fought! . . . [T]he newspapers in most cases even refused to print a correction. FERDINAND LASALLE (1825–1864).

The public, which is feebleminded like an idiot, will never be able to preserve its individual reactions from the tricks of the exploiter . . . because it can't distinguish between its own original feelings and feelings which are diddled into existence by the exploiter. D. H. LAWRENCE (1885–1930).

[Mass media may be] among the most respectable and efficient of social narcotics. They may be so fully effective as to keep the addict from recognizing his own malady. PAUL F. LAZARSFELD and THOMAS R. MERTON, in *The Communication of Ideas* (L. Bryson, ed.), 1948.

The audiences of mass media apparently subscribe to the circular belief: "If you really matter, you will be at the focus of mass attention, and if you are at the focus of mass attention, then surely you must really matter. PAUL F. LAZARSFELD and THOMAS R. MERTON, in *The Communication of Ideas* (L. Bryson, ed.), 1948.

Whatever has been a ruling power in the world, whether it be ideas or men, has in the main enforced its authority by means of the irresistible force expressed by the word "prestige." GUSTAVE LE BON (1841–1931), *The Crowd,* 1895.

I think our major problem, our real problem is that somehow we [the news media] have gotten it into our heads that we are truly the special people of this world, because we happened into journalism. . . . We became privileged people, above all laws, above all rules that the rest of society has to play by. JIM LEHRER, *The Dial,* April 1983.

Democracy, which began by liberating man politically, has developed a dangerous tendency to enslave him through the tyranny of majorities and the deadly power of their opinion. LUDWIG LEWISOHN (1882–1955), *The Modern Drama.*

Given network television's need for mass audiences, and the visual and experiental information it conveys, its emphasis is bound to be on the personal and dramatic rather than the abstract and discursive. S. ROBERT LICHTER et al., *The Media Elite,* 1986.

Freedom of the press is guaranteed only to those who own one. A. J. LIEBLING (1904–1963), *The Press.*

People everywhere confuse / What they read in newspapers with news. A. J. LIEBLING (1904–1963), *The New Yorker,* April 7, 1956.

Public opinion is everything. With public sentiment nothing can fail; without it, nothing can succeed. Consequently, he who molds public opinion goes deeper than he who enacts statutes or pronounces decisions. ABRAHAM LINCOLN (1809–1865), U.S. President.

Politicians tend to live "in character," and many a public figure has come to imitate the journalism which describes him. WALTER LIPPMANN (1889–1974), *A Preface to Politics,* 1914.

The subtlest and most pervasive of all influences are those which create and maintain the repertory of stereotypes. We are told about the world before we see it. We imagine most things before we experience them. And those preconceptions, unless education has made us acutely aware, govern deeply the whole process of perception. They mark out certain objects as familiar or strange, emphasizing the difference, so that the slightly familiar is seen as very familiar, and the somewhat strange as sharply alien. WALTER LIPPMANN (1889–1974), *Public Opinion,* 1922.

Fear always represents objects in their worst light. LIVY (59 B.C.–17 A.D.), *History of Rome.*

The pressure of public opinion is like the pressure of the atmosphere; you can't see it—but, all the same, it is sixteen pounds to the square inch. JAMES RUSSELL LOWELL (1819–1891).

The great majority of mankind are satisfied with appearances, as though they were realities, and are often more influenced by things that seem than by those that are. NICCOLO MACHIAVELLI (1469–1527), *The Prince,* 1513.

Men are never so good or so bad as their opinions. JAMES MACKINTOSH (1765–1832), *Progress of Ethical Philosophy,* 1830.

"The Medium is the Message" because it is the medium that shapes and controls the search and form of human associations and actions. MARSHALL McLUHAN (1911–1980), *Understanding Media,* 1964.

Television brought the brutality of the war into the comfort of the living room. Vietnam was lost in the living rooms of America, not on the battlefields of Vietnam. MARSHALL McLUHAN (1911–1980), *Montreal Gazette,* May 16, 1975.

It is almost impossible for public opinion to form any kind of verdict based on actual facts. Newspapers nowadays use facts merely as the raw material of propaganda. By suppression, or alteration, or overemphasis, or by the trick of false perspective, or by scare headlines and editorial comment, the "facts" are made to convey exactly the particular idea which the newspaper desires to suggest to its readers. A. E. MANDER, *Public Enemy The Press,* 1944.

Risk! Risk anything! Care no more for the opinion of others, for those voices. Do the hardest thing on earth for you. Act for yourself. Face the truth. KATHERINE MANSFIELD (1888–1923), Journals.

When I hear a man applauded by the mob I always feel a pang of pity for him. All he has to do to be hissed is to live long enough. H. L. MENCKEN (1880–1956), *Minority Report, 1956.*

Electronic media, especially television, have broken that age-old connection between location and experience, between where we are and our access and accessibility to other people, between place and appropriate behavior. The logic underlying social roles in a print-oriented society, therefore, has been radically subverted. JOSHUA MEYROWITZ, *Kettering Review,* Winter 1987.

At present individuals are lost in the crowd. In politics it is almost a triviality to say that public opinion now rules the world. JOHN STUART MILL (1806–1873), *On Liberty,* 1859.

There is a limit to the legitimate interference of collective opinion with individual independence; and to find that limit, and maintain it against encroachment, is as indispensable to a good condition of human affairs, as protection against political despotism. JOHN STUART MILL (1806–1873), *On Liberty,* 1859.

The engines of moral repression have been wielded more strenuously against divergence from the reigning opinion in self-regarding, than even in social matters; religion, the most powerful of the elements which have entered into the formation of moral feeling, having always been governed by the ambition of a hierarchy, seeking control over every department of human conduct, or by the spirit of Puritanism. JOHN STUART MILL (1806–1873), *On Liberty,* 1859.

Popular opinions, on subjects not palpable to sense, are often true, but seldom or never the whole truth. . . . Heretical opinions, on the other hand, are generally some of these suppressed and neglected truths, bursting the bonds which kept them down. JOHN STUART MILL (1806–1873), *On Liberty,* 1859.

And what the people but a herd confus'd, / A miscellaneous rabble, who extol things vulgar. JOHN MILTON (1608–1674), *Paradise Regained,* 1671.

The inability to draw a strong, sharp line between journalism and show business— which is ultimately to say, between fact and fiction—is one of the most critical problems in modern-day American journalism because of the crucial role television occupies in conveying news. DALE MINOR, *The Information War,* 1970.

The most effective way of attacking vice is to expose it to ridicule. We can stand rebukes, but not laughter; we don't mind seeming wicked, but we hate to look silly. MOLIÈRE (1622–1673), *Tartuffe,* 1664.

After all, it is setting a high value on our opinions to roast people alive on account of them. MICHEL de MONTAIGNE (1533–1592), *Essays,* 1588.

Opinion and force belong to different elements. To think that you are able by social disapproval or other coercive means to crush a man's opinion, is as one who fires off a blunderbus to put out a star. JOHN MORLEY (1838–1923), *On Compromise,* 1874.

The political consequences of the rising social status of journalism is that the press grows more and more influenced by attitudes genuinely hostile to American society and American government. DANIEL PATRICK MOYNIHAN, U.S. Senator, *Commentary,* March 1971.

Journalism is not a profession but a mission. Our newspaper is our party, our ideal, our soul, and our banner which will lead us to victory. BENITO MUSSOLINI (1883–1945), *Avanti!,* 1912.

Public opinion is a mysterious and invisible power which is impossible to resist. Nothing is more unsteady, more vague, or more powerful. . . . NAPOLEON BONAPARTE (1769–1821), *Maxims.*

I can calculate the motion of heavenly bodies but not the madness of people. ISAAC NEWTON (1642–1727).

The media are far more powerful than the President in creating public awareness and shaping public opinion, for the simple reason that the media always have the last word. RICHARD M. NIXON, U.S. President, *Memoirs,* 1978.

When I did well, I heard it never; / When I did ill; I heard it ever. OLD ENGLISH RHYME.

Doublethink means the power 1 holding contradictory beliefs in one's mind simultaneously, and accepting both of them. . . . To tell deliberate lies while genuinely believing them, to forget any facts that become inconvenient. GEORGE ORWELL (1903–1950), *Nineteen Eighty-Four,* 1949.

In a society where there is no law, and in theory no compulsion, the only arbiter of behavior is public opinion. But public opinion, because of the tremendous urge to conformity in gregarious animals, is less tolerant than any system of law. GEORGE ORWELL (1903–1950), 1949.

The centrality of a belief is its importance in the person's belief system, while a belief's intensity is how strongly it is held. Primitive beliefs are . . . formed either through direct contact with the object of belief or through accepting the statement of an unquestioned external authority. STUART OSKAMP, *Attitudes and Opinions,* 1977.

Derived beliefs . . . can be built up from basic underlying beliefs in a syllogistic type of structure. . . . Despite their syllogistic structure, beliefs are not usually completely logical or rational. They are built up of elements which "go together" comfortably in the person's value system. STUART OSKAMP, *Attitudes and Opinions,* 1977.

If all men knew what others say of them, there would not be four friends in the world. BLAISE PASCAL (1623–1662), *Pensées,* 1670.

Public opinion is a compound of folly, weakness, prejudice, wrong feeling, right feeling, obstinacy and newspaper paragraphs. ROBERT PEEL (1788–1850), Prime Minister of Great Britain, 1835.

Those who wish to control opinions and beliefs turn less to physical force than to mass persuasion in the form of news and views and entertainment. They use the advertising campaign and public-relations program instead of the threat of firing squad or concentration camp. THEODORE B. PETERSON, *The Mass Media and Modern Society,* 1965.

But even if modern democracies use psychological manipulation instead of totalitarianism's direct and violent forms of social control, the results are not necessarily less effective. Never before have such pervasive and ubiquitous means of communication existed; never before has public opinion been so completely at the mercy of whoever may control the instrument. THEODORE B. PETERSON, *The Mass Media and Modern Society,* 1965.

Truth is one forever absolute, but opinion is truth filtered through the moods, the blood, and the disposition of the spectator. WENDALL PHILLIPS (1811–1884), Lecture, October 4, 1859.

Let me make the newspapers and I care not what is preached in the pulpit or what is enacted in Congress. WENDALL PHILLIPS (1811–1884).

There is no tyranny so despotic as that of public opinion among a free people. DONN PIATT (1819–1891), *Memories of the Men Who Saved The Union,* 1887.

Every noble deed dies, if suppressed in silence. PINDAR (522–443 B.C.), Eulogy on Alexander, Son of Amyntas.

Between knowledge of what really exists and ignorance of what does not exist lies the domain of opinion. It is more obscure than knowledge, but clearer than ignorance. PLATO (428–347 B.C.).

A claim, whether true or untrue, must be made in language. More precisely, it must take the form of a proposition, for that is the universe of discourse from where such words as true and false come. If that universe is discarded, an advertisement is immune to the rigors of logical analysis or empirical tests. Such questions do not apply in the world of visual images. Through television the visual image, embedded in a variety of dramatic forms, has now emerged as our basic unit of political conversation. NEIL POSTMAN, *Kettering Review,* Winter 1987.

It seems to me self-evident that television and other modern media are altering the meaning of "being informed" by creating a species of information that might properly be called disinformation. I am using this word in almost the precise sense in which it is used by spies in the CIA or KGB. Disinformation does not mean false information. It means misleading information—misplaced, fragmented, irrelevant or superficial information—information that creates the illusion that one knows something but which, in fact, leads one away from knowing. NEIL POSTMAN, *Kettering Review,* Winter 1987.

Television in the United States has proved to be a highly effective medium for indirect and covert appeals to the irrational side of man's nature. DAVID M. POTTER, *Freedom and Its Limitations in American Life,* 1976.

Publicity is like power . . . it's a rare man who isn't corrupted by it. ANTHONY PRICE, *Colonel Butler's Wolf,* 1972.

Given a greatly expanded franchise, with its corollary of the need to base authority on the support of public opinion, political society invited the attention of the professional controller of public opinion. T. H. QUALTER, *Propaganda and Psychological Warfare,* 1962.

Autocratic regimes try to minimize the flow of communication in the population: they try to keep the channels silent. . . . Totalitarian regimes, on the other hand, utilize the communication channels to the utmost: they try to keep the channels clogged with their own brand of information, keeping all other brands out. . . . In short, an autocracy demands a silent submissive loyalty. The totalitarian regime demands a noisy, enthusiastic loyalty, with full participation of the population in politics. On this basis, totalitarian regimes often claim the status of democracies. ANATOLE RAPOPORT, *Operational Philosophy,* 1953.

[Forbidden is] anything which in any manner is misleading to the public, mixes selfish aims with community aims, tends to weaken the strength of the German Reich, outwardly or inwardly, the common will of the German people, the defense of Germany, its culture and economy . . . or offends the honor and dignity of Germany. REICH PRESS LAW, October 4, 1933.

The best way to compel weak-minded people to adopt our opinion is to terrify them from all others, by magnifying their danger. CARDINAL de RETZ (1614– 1679), *Political Maxims.*

There is little doubt that the public's knowledge of government depends not upon experience and observation, but rather on the news media, which set the agenda for public discussion. WILLIAM L. RIVERS, *Mass Media Issues,* 1977.

The most successful politician is he who says what the people are thinking most often and in the loudest voice. THEODORE ROOSEVELT (1858–1919), U.S. President.

The energies which lead men into newspapers are . . . the desire to startle and expose; the opportunity to project personal hostilities and feelings of injustice on public persons under the aegis of "journalistic duty"; inner drives for "action" plus inner anxieties about accepting the consequences of action. This last is particularly important. There is a sense of invulnerability attached to newspaper work. LEO ROSTEN, *The Washington Correpondents,* 1937.

Domination itself is servile when beholden to opinion; for you depend upon the prejudices of those you govern by means of their prejudices. JEAN-JACQUES ROUSSEAU (1712–1778), *Émile,* 1762.

One should respect public opinion in so far as is necessary to avoid starvation and to keep out of prison, but anything that goes beyond this is voluntary submission to an unnecessary tyranny. BERTRAND RUSSELL (1872–1970), *The Conquest of Happiness,* 1930.

In the average newspaper there is not a complete suppression of stories the sacred cows don't want printed. But rather what happens is that the stories get printed with stresses, colorations and emphasis that favor the sacred cows. CARL SANDBURG (1878–1967), Letter, 1941.

Isolation [is] probably the most terrifying of all human experiences. Primitive societies have always recognized this terror. Isolation or ostracism, means death to them and they use it to punish offenders. The custom—and the dread as well—survives in our prison mores where to be put "in solitary" is the severest punishment meted out to criminals. MILTON R. SAPERSTEIN, *Paradoxes of Everyday Life,* 1955.

To form a judgment intuitively is the privilege of the few; authority and example lead the rest of the world. They see with the eyes of others, they hear with the ears of others. Therefore it is easy to think as all the world now think; but to think as all the world would think thirty years hence, is not in the power of everyone. ARTHUR SCHOPENAUER (1788–1860), *Great Problems of Ethics,* 1841.

The theory of Agenda-Setting is based on two ideas—that the media are necessarily gatekeepers for reporting the news of the world . . . and, secondly, that people feel a continuing need for orientation to the complex world of politics. WILBUR SCHRAMM and WILLIAM E. PORTER, *Men, Women, Messages and Media,* 1982.

Wearied from doubt to doubt to flee, / We welcome fond credulity. SIR WALTER SCOTT (1771–1832), *Marmion,* 1808.

I believe that few people aside from myself have any idea of the tremendous almost invincible power and force of the daily press. . . . I am one of those who believe that at least in America the press rules the country; it rules its politics, its religion, its social practice. E. W. SCRIPPS (1854–1926), *Damned Old Crank,* 1951.

As long as the means of [mass] communication are not available for criticism of themselves, as long as we are prevented from thinking about the process by which we are hypnotized into not thinking, we remain at the mercy of our simplest appetites, our immediate and most childish sensations. GILBERT SELDES (1893–1970), *The Public Arts,* 1956.

Reputation, reputation, reputation O, I have lost my reputation! I have lost the immortal part of myself and what remains is bestial. WILLIAM SHAKE-SPEARE (1564–1616), *Othello,* 1604.

Reputation is an idle and most false imposition; oft got without merit, and lost without deserving. WILLIAM SHAKESPEARE (1564–1616), *Othello,* 1604.

Englishmen will never be slaves; they are free to do whatsoever the government and public opinion allow them to do. GEORGE BERNARD SHAW (1856–1950), *Man and Superman,* 1903.

The voice of the people is the voice of humbug. WILLIAM TECUMSEH SHERMAN (1820–1891), Letter, June 2, 1863.

Docudramas have removed the last remaining inhibitions against the assault on reality. At best they simplify reality, at worst pervert it. Television's make-believe makes belief in a way that words on the printed page cannot. It tends to loosen the viewers' grip on reality . . . relying on emotional manipulations. DANIEL SHORR, *Channels of Communication,* 1986.

The United States is *par excellence* a country where public opinion plays an important role, inspiring, orienting, and controlling the policy of the nation. Nothing can be achieved or endure without it. . . . It is characterized by the fact that it is both more spontaneous than anywhere else in the world and also more easily directed by efficient propaganda technique than in any other country. ANDRE SIEGFRIED (1875–1959), *America at Mid-Century,* 1955.

When you pick up your morning or evening newspaper and think you are reading the news of the world, what you are really reading is a propaganda which has been selected, revised, and doctored by some power which has an interest in you. UPTON SINCLAIR (1878–1968), *The Brass Check,* 1919.

A man may say what he likes on a public platform—he may publish whatever opinions he chooses—but he dare not wear a peculiar fashion of hat on the street. Eccentricity is an outlaw. ALEXANDER SMITH (1830–1867), *Dream-thorp,* 1863.

Hastiness and superficiality are the psychic diseases of the twentieth century, and more than anywhere else this disease is reflected in the press. ALEXANDER SOLZHENITSYN, Commencement Address, Harvard University, June 7, 1978.

Opinion is ultimately determined by the feelings, and not by the intellect. HERBERT SPENCER (1820–1903), *First Principles,* 1862.

If there is anything for which I have entire indifference, perhaps I might say contempt, it is the public opinion which is founded on popular clamor. THADDEUS STEVENS (1792–1868).

Those who corrupt the public mind are just as evil as those who steal from the public purse. ADLAI E. STEVENSON (1900–1965), 1952.

Man is a creature who lives not upon bread alone but primarily by catchwords. ROBERT LOUIS STEVENSON (1850–1894).

The respectable are not led so much by any desire of applause as by a positive need for countenance. The weaker and the tamer the man, the more will he require this support. ROBERT LOUIS STEVENSON (1850–1894), *Familiar Studies of Men and Books,* 1882.

Private opinion is weak, but public opinion is almost omnipotent. HARRIET BEECHER STOWE (1811–1896).

If you allow a political catchword to go on and grow, you will awaken some day to find it standing over you, arbiter of your destiny, against which you are powerless. WILLIAM GRAHAM SUMNER (1840–1910).

Education, or the presentation of information, is relatively ineffective in changing opinions or behavior. The perception and interpretation of "facts" is self-selective and the individual can "protect" himself against facts he does not wish to believe. EDWARD A. SUCHMAN et al., *Desegregation: Some Propositions and Research Suggestions,* 1958.

And since informed public opinion is the most potent of all restraints upon misgovernment, the suppression or abridgment of publicity afforded by a free press cannot be regarded otherwise than with grave concern. GEORGE SUTHER-LAND (1862–1942), U.S. Supreme Court Justice, *Grosjean* v. *American Press Co.,* 1936.

To journalists, like social scientists, the term "objectivity" stands as a bulwark between themselves and critics. Attacked for a controversial presentation of "facts," newspapermen invoke their objectivity almost as a Mediterranean peasant might wear a clove of garlic around his neck to ward off evil spirits. GAYE TUCHMAN, *American Journal of Sociology,* January 1972.

The most effective kind of field control of dissent, as of other behavior, is that imposed by the political environment itself, insofar as people are continually socialized to think and behave in terms of politically tolerable beliefs and values. AUSTIN J. TURK, *Political Criminality,* 1982.

Opinion has caused more trouble on this little earth than plagues or earthquakes. VOLTAIRE (1694–1778), Letter, 1759.

I know the people: they change in a day. The bestow prodigally their hatred and their love. VOLTAIRE (1694–1778), *La mort de César,* 1725.

The public is a ferocious beast: one must either chain it up or flee from it. VOLTAIRE (1694–1778), Letter, August 16, 1738.

To the extent that a relatively homogeneous symbolic environment is provided by the media, either through governmental direction or through common actions of private controllers, uniformity of political and social behavior is fostered. WALTER WEISS, *Mass Communications,* 1949.

Real rumors are very far from random. The distortion that accumulates as rumors are passed along tends to express the conscious and unconscious emotional needs of the persons involved—hostility, fear, wishful thinking, conformity with prevailing stereotypes. RALPH K. WHITE, *Nobody Wanted War,* 1970.

The power of conformity helps to explain the momentum and staying power of the black-and-white picture in any group, once it has become the view of a large majority of the articulate members of that group. Once that point is reached, conformity with "what everybody is saying" provides a kind of momentum. RALPH K. WHITE, *Nobody Wanted War,* 1970.

The power of the press in America is a primordial one. It sets the agenda of public discussion; and this sweeping political power is unrestrained by any law. It determines what people will talk and think about—an authority that in other nations is reserved for tyrants, priests, parties and mandarins. THEODORE WHITE, *The Making of the President,* 1972.

England . . . has invented and established public opinion, which is an attempt to organize the ignorance of the community, and to elevate it to the dignity of a physical force. OSCAR WILDE (1854–1900), *The Critic as Artist,* 1890.

Names are much more persistent than the functions upon which they were originally bestowed. WOODROW WILSON (1856–1924), *Congressional Government,* 1885.

When a subject is highly controversial . . . one cannot hope to tell the truth. One can only show how one came to hold whatever opinion one does hold. One can only give one's audience the chance of drawing their own conclusions as they observe the limitations, the prejudices, the ideosyncracies of the speaker. VIRGINIA WOOLF (1882–1941).

Not choice, but habit rules the unreflecting herd. WILLIAM WORDSWORTH (1770–1850).

I don't care what points I made in interviews, it practically never got printed the way I said it. I was learning under fire how the press, when it wants to, can twist and slant. . . . I developed a mental image of reporters as human ferrets—steadily sniffing, darting, probing for some way to trick me, somehow corner me in our interview exchanges. MALCOLM X (1925–1965), quoted in *Race and the News Media,* 1967.

Attitudes have generally been regarded as either mental readinesses or implicit predispositions which exert some general and consistent influence on a large class of evaluative responses. Attitudes are seen as enduring predispositions, but ones which are learned rather than innate. PHILIP ZIMBARDO and EBBE EBBESON, *Influencing Attitudes and Changing Behavior,* 1969.

Reason, Rationalism, and Freethought

Genius is the talent for seeing things straight. It is seeing things in a straight line without any bend or break or aberration of sight, seeing them as they are, without any warping of vision. MAUDE ADAMS (1872-1953).

Images are not arguments, they rarely even lead to proof, but the mind craves them. HENRY BROOKS ADAMS (1838-1918), *The Education of Henry Adams,* 1907.

Facts are stubborn things; and whatever may be our wishes, our inclinations, or the dictates of our passions, they cannot alter the state of facts and evidence. JOHN ADAMS (1735-1826), December 5, 1770.

Beware lest you lose the substance by grasping at the shadow. AESOP (620-560 B.C.), *Fables.*

I've always felt that a person's intelligence is directly reflected by the number of conflicting points of view he can entertain simultaneously on the same topic. LISA ALTHER.

A belief is not true because it is useful. HENRI FRÉDÉRIC AMIEL (1821-1881), *Amiel's Journal,* 1849-1872.

The judgment is weak that is built on rumor, or guided by appearances. JAMES ANNESLEY (1715-1760), *Memoirs of An Unfortunate Young Nobleman,* 1743.

In matters controversial, / My perception's rather fine. / I always see both points of view, / The one that's wrong and mine. ANONYMOUS.

Not everything that is more difficult is more meritorious. SAINT THOMAS AQUINAS (1225-1274).

Some men are just as sure of the truth of their opinions as others are of what they know. ARISTOTLE (384-322 B.C.), *Nicomachean Ethics.*

How many a dispute could have been deflated into a single paragraph if the disputants had dared to define their terms. ARISTOTLE (384-322 B.C.).

Some of the greatest controversies would cease in a moment, if one or other of the disputants took care to make out precisely, and in a few words, what he understands by the terms which are the subject of dispute. ANTOINE ARNAULD (1612-1694), *The Art of Thinking.*

Reality is always more conservative than ideology. RAYMOND ARON (1905–1983), *The Great Debate*, 1965.

When men are in doubt they always believe what is more agreeable. FLAVIUS ARRIANUS, *The Anabasis of Alexander the Great*, 2d c. A.D.

When the lay public rallies to an idea that is denounced by distinguished but elderly scientists and supports that idea with great fervor and emotion, the distinguished but elderly scientists are then, after all, right. ISAAC ASIMOV, *Fantasy and Science Fiction* magazine, 1977.

Life itself is neither good nor evil, but only a place for good and evil. MARCUS AURELIUS (121–180 A.D.), *Meditations*.

It is particularly incumbent on those who never change their opinion, to be secure of judging properly at first. JANE AUSTEN (1775–1817), *Pride and Prejudice*, 1813.

Read not to contradict and confute, nor to believe and take for granted . . . but to weigh and consider. SIR FRANCIS BACON (1561–1626).

There is nothing makes a man suspect much, more than to know a little. SIR FRANCIS BACON (1561–1626).

Knowledge and human power are synonymous, since the ignorance of the cause frustrates the effect. SIR FRANCIS BACON (1561–1626).

If a man begin with certainties, he shall end in doubts, but if he will be content to begin with doubts, he shall end in certainties. SIR FRANCIS BACON (1561–1626), *The Advancement of Learning*, 1605.

There are and can be only two ways of searching into and discovering truth. The one flies from the senses and particulars to the most general axioms, and from these principles, the truth of which it takes for settled and immovable, proceeds to judgment and to the discovery of middle axioms. This way is now in fashion. The other derives axioms from the senses and particulars, rising by a gradual and unbroken ascent, so that it arrives at the most general axioms last of all. This is the true way, but as yet untried. SIR FRANCIS BACON (1561–1626), *Novum Organum*, 1620.

There are things that cannot be made objectively true by consensus. This is exactly what "objective" means. . . . "[Su]bjective truths" of course have objective consequences . . . but they are not themselves made objectively true by consensus. F. G. BAILEY, *The Tactical Uses of Passion*, 1983.

Take as your motto this thought from Huxley: "God give me strength to face a fact though it slay me." BERNARD BARUCH (1870–1965), *A Philosophy for Our Time*, 1954.

It is pure illusion to think that an opinion which passes down from century to century, from generation to generation, may not be entirely false. PIERRE BAYLE (1647–1706), *Thoughts on the Comet*, 1682.

Whatever is almost true is quite false and among the most dangerous of errors. HENRY WARD BEECHER (1813–1887).

That truth which our age has forgotten more than any previous age ever did—the rare knowledge that proof is of various kinds. Proof is not of one sort only. It is multiple in character. The very word "'proof" takes on a different savor according to the matter toward which it is directed. HILAIRE BELLOC (1870–1950), 1933.

[Heresy is] the dislocation of complete and self-supporting scheme by the introduction of a novel denial of some essential part therein. HILAIRE BELLOC (1870–1950), *The Great Heresies,* 1938.

When faced with a choice between confronting an unpleasant reality and defending a set of comforting and socially accepted beliefs, most people choose the later course. W. LANCE BENNETT, *News: The Politics of Illusion,* 1983.

Consistency requires you to be as ignorant today as you were a year ago. BERNARD BERENSON (1865–1959), Notebook, 1892.

Philosophy doth open and enlarge the mind by the general views to which men are habituated in that study, and by the contemplation of more numerous and distant objects than fall within the sphere of mankind in the ordinary pursuits of life. GEORGE BERKELEY (1685–1763), *The Guardian,* June 1, 1713.

Men who have excessive faith in their theories are not only ill-prepared for making discoveries; they also make poor observations. CLAUDE BERNARD (1813–1878), *Introduction to the Study of Experimental Medicine,* 1865.

I had an immense advantage . . . inasmuch as I had no fixed ideas from long established practice to control and bias my mind, and did not suffer from the general belief that whatever is, is right. SIR HENRY BESSEMER (1813–1898).

Decide: To succumb to the preponderance of one set of influences over another set. AMBROSE BIERCE (1842–1914), *The Devil's Dictionary,* 1881–1911.

Impartial: Unable to perceive any promise of personal advantage from espousing either side of a controversy. AMBROSE BIERCE (1842–1914), *The Devil's Dictionary,* 1881–1911.

Absurd: A statement or belief manifestly inconsistent with one's own. AMBROSE BIERCE (1842–1914), *The Devil's Dictionary,* 1881–1911.

Wisdom don't consist in knowing more that is new, but in knowing less that is false. JOSH BILLINGS (1818–1885), *Everybody's Friend,* 1874.

A historian stands in a fiduciary position towards his readers, and if he withholds from them important facts likely to influence their judgment, he is guilty of fraud. AUGUSTINE BIRRELL (1850–1933), *Obiter Dicta,* 1884.

The man who never alters his opinions is like standing water, and breeds reptiles of the mind. WILLIAM BLAKE (1757–1827), *The Marriage of Heaven and Hell,* 1790.

There are two threats to reason: the opinion that one knows the truth about the most important things, and the opinion there is no truth about them. ALAN BLOOM (1930–1992), *Giants and Dwarfs: Essays 1960–1990,* 1990.

We suffer primarily not from our vices or our weaknesses, but from our illusions. We are haunted, not by reality, but by those images we have in place of reality. DANIEL J. BOORSTIN, *The Image,* 1962.

The mortalest enemy unto knowledge, and that which hath done the greatest execution unto truth, has been a peremptory adhesion unto authority, and especially of our belief upon the dictates of antiquities. SIR THOMAS BROWNE (1605–1682).

To most people nothing is more troublesome than the effort of thinking. JAMES BRYCE (1838–1922), *Studies in History and Jurisprudence,* 1901.

For those who do not think, it is best to rearrange their prejudices once in a while. LUTHER BURBANK (1849–1926).

Though discernment teaches us the folly of others, experience singly can teach us our own. FANNY BURNEY (1752–1840), *Cecilia,* 1782.

O wad some pow'r the giftie gie us, / To see ourselves as others see us! / It would frae many a blunder free us, / And foolish notion. ROBERT BURNS (1756–1796).

As compared with impulsive commitment to the first idea which dawns, that is, with intuitive action, reasoning is patient, exploratory of other possibilities, and deliberative. EDWIN ARTHUR BURTT, *Right Thinking,* 1946.

Creatures capable of reasoning often trust the intuitive method even in problems where some critical evaluation of suggestions would seem to be possible, and find satisfaction in doing so. We tend naturally to accept whatever directly satisfies us, and to avoid replacing it by something that is not so appealing . . . an emotionally attractive idea is directly satisfying just on that account. EDWIN ARTHUR BURTT, *Right Thinking,* 1946.

The credibility, or the certain truth of a matter of fact does not immediately prove anything concerning the wisdom or goodness of it. JOSEPH BUTLER (1692–1752), *The Analogy of Religion,* 1736.

Every bias, instinct, propension within is a natural part of our nature, but not the whole: add to these the superior faculty whose office it is to adjust, manage and preside over them, and take in this its natural superiority, and you complete the idea of human nature. JOSEPH BUTLER (1692–1752), *Sermons on Human Nature,* 1726.

People readily believe what they want to believe. JULIUS CAESAR (100–44 B.C.), *Gallic Wars,* 49 B.C.

The evil in the world almost always comes from ignorance. Good intentions may do as much harm as malevolence, if they lack understanding. ALBERT CAMUS (1913–1960), *The Plague,* 1947.

We are not certain, we are never certain. If we were we could reach some conclusions, and we could, at least, make others take us seriously. ALBERT CAMUS (1913–1960).

You cannot become a truly effective advocate unless you know all sides of your subject thoroughly, opposing arguments as well as your own. G. R. CAPP and T. R. CAPP, *Principles of Argumentation and Debate,* 1965.

Each theory becomes a Procrustean bed on which the empirical facts are stretched to fit a preconceived pattern. ERNST CASSIRER (1874–1945), *An Essay on Man,* 1944.

A man is not necessarily intelligent because he has plenty of ideas, any more than he is a good general because he has plenty of soldiers. SEBASTIEN CHAMFORT (1741–1794), 1805.

A little philosophy causes men to despise learning, but much philosophy makes them esteem it. NICOLAS CHAMFORT (1741–1794), *Maximes et Pensées,* 1785.

Error is the discipline through which we advance. WILLIAM ELLERY CHANNING (1780–1842), *The Present Age.*

Semantics teaches us to watch our prejudices, and to take our exercise in other ways than jumping to conclusions. Semantics is the propagandist's worst friend. STUART CHASE (1888–1956), *Guide to Straight Thinking,* 1956.

The most imaginative people are the most credulous, for to them everything is possible. ALEXANDER CHASE, *Perspectives,* 1966.

Observe any meetings of people, and you will always find their eargerness and impetuosity rise or fall in proportion to their numbers: when the numbers are very great, all sense and reason seem to subside, and one sudden frenzy to seize on all, even the coolest of them. LORD CHESTERFIELD (1694–1773), Letter to his son, September 13, 1748.

An imbecile habit has arisen in modern controversy of saying that such and such a creed can be held in one age but cannot be held in another. . . . What a man can believe depends upon his philosophy, not upon the clock of the century. . . . the point is not whether it was given in our time, but whether it was given in answer to our question. GILBERT KEITH CHESTERTON (1874–1936), *Orthodoxy.*

The first law is that the historian shall never dare to set down what is false; the second,that he shall never dare to conceal the truth; the third, that there shall be no suspicion in his work of either favoritism or prejudice. MARCUS TULLIUS CICERO (106-43 B.C.), *De oratore.*

Philosophy is the cultivation of the mental faculties; it roots out vices and prepares the mind to receive proper seed. MARCUS TULLIUS CICERO (106–43 B.C.), *Tusculanae disputationes*, 45 B.C.

When a distinguished but elderly scientists states that something is possible, he is almost certainly right. When he states that something is impossible, he is very probably wrong. ARTHUR C. CLARK, *Profile of the Future*, 1973.

The sociological historian uses his theory as the criterion for the selection of the relevant historical facts, and then on the basis of those selected facts he illustrates and confirms the theory by which they have been selected . . . success is built in. ALFRED COBBAN, *Sociological Interpretation of the French Revolution*, 1964.

By freethinking I mean the use of the understanding in endeavoring to find out the meaning of any proposition whatsoever, in considering the nature of the evidence for or against, and in judging of it according to the seeming force or weakness of the evidence. ANTHONY COLLINS (1676–1729), *A Discourse of Freethinking*, 1713.

Nothing so completely baffles one who is full of trick and duplicity himself, than straightforward and simple integrity in another. CHARLES CALEB COLTON (1780–1832), *Lacon*, 1825.

Though the proportion of those who think be extremely small, yet every individual flatters himself that he is one of the number. CHARLES CALEB COLTON (1780–1832), *Lacon*, 1825.

Falsehood can never be so successful as when she baits her hook with truth, and no opinions so falsely mislead us as those that are not wholly wrong, as no watches so effectually deceive the wearer as those that are sometimes right. CHARLES CALEB COLTON (1780–1832), *Lacon*, 1825.

All good intellects have repeated, since Bacon's time, that there can be no real knowledge but that which is based on observed facts. AUGUSTE COMTE (1798–1857), *The Positive Philosophy*, 1830–42.

When you know a thing, to hold that you know it; and when you do not know a thing, to allow that you do not know it; that is knowledge. CONFUCIUS, (551–478 B.C.), *Analects*.

Curiosity is freewheeling intelligence. . . . It endows the people who have it with a generosity in argument and a serenity in their own mode of life which spring from the cheerful willingness to let life take the forms it will. ALISTAIR COOKE, *Vogue*, January 1953.

There is no portion of human wisdom so select and faultless that it does not contain the seeds of its own refutation. JAMES FENIMORE COOPER (1789–1851), *The Monikins*, 1835.

Suspicion is a thing very few people can entertain without letting the hypothesis turn, in their minds, into fact. . . . DAVID CORT, *Social Astonishments*, 1963.

Wisdom consists of the anticipation of consequences. NORMAN COUSINS, *Saturday Review,* April 15, 1978.

It's amazing how many people are shocked by dishonesty, and how few by deception. NOEL COWARD (1899–1973).

Of all the threats to Phi Beta Kappa . . . probably none is more pervasive than that that of the so-called counterculture, with its elevation of instinct over intellect, mysticism over reason, consciousness over scholarship, sensitivity over discipline. PROFESSOR SIDNEY M. COULLING, *Wall Street Journal,* March 7, 1971.

It is always the task of the intellectual to "think otherwise." This is not just a perverse idiosyncrasy. It is an absolutely essential feature of a society. HARVEY COX, *The Secular City,* 1966.

As time goes on, new and remoter aspects of truth are discovered which can seldom be fitted into creeds that are changeless. CLARENCE DAY (1874–1935), *This Simian World,* 1926.

Give unqualified assent to no propositions but those the truth of which is so clear and distinct that they cannot be doubted. RENÉ DESCARTES (1596–1650).

Old ideas give way slowly; for they are more than abstract logical forms and categories. They are habits, predispositions, deeply ingrained attitudes of aversion and preference. JOHN DEWEY (1859–1952), *The Influence of Darwinism on Philosophy,* 1910.

I shall begin to believe that we care more for freedom than we do for imposing our own beliefs upon others in order to subject them to our will, when I see that the main purpose of our schools and other institutions is to develop powers of unremitting and discriminating observation and judgment. JOHN DEWEY (1859–1952), *Philosophy and Civilization,* 1931.

To be conscious that you are ignorant is a great step to knowledge. BENJAMIN DISRAELI (1804–1881), *Sybil,* 1895.

Man has such a predilection for systems and abstract deductions that he is ready to distort the truth intentionally, he is ready to deny the evidence of his senses only to justify his logic. FYODOR DOSTOEVSKY (1821–1881), *Notes from the Underground,* 1864.

The history of science is not a mere record of isolated discoveries; it is a narrative of the conflict of two contending powers, the expansive force of the human intellect on one side, and the compression arising from traditionary faith and human interest on the other. J. W. DRAPER, *History of the Conflict between Religion and Science,* 1874.

History is so indifferently rich that a case for almost any conclusion from it can be made by a selection of instances. Choosing evidence with a brighter bias, we might evolve some more comforting reflections. WILL DURANT (1885–1981) and ARIEL DURANT (1898–1981), *The Lessons of History,* 1968.

We must remind outselves again that history as usually written . . . is quite different from history as usually lived: the historian records the exceptional because it is interesting—because it is exceptional. WILL DURANT (1885–1981) and ARIEL DURANT (1898–1981), *The Lessons of History,* 1968.

A common fallacy: to imagine a measure will be easy because we have private motives for desiring it. GEORGE ELIOT (1819–1880), *Silas Marner,* 1861.

Wisdom lies more in affection and sincerity than people are apt to imagine. GEORGE ELIOT (1819–1880), *Middlemarch,* 1872.

The majority of mankind is lazy-minded, absorbed in vanities and. . . . incapable of much doubt or much faith. T. S. ELIOT (1888–1965), 1931.

It is when we take political and social metaphors literally that we must proceed with caution. Far more than we are aware, the way we use language determines what the social philosophy of our society will be. When we take figurative language literally, we are in danger of language behaving as if something were true which is manifestly not true, unless we proceed to make it so. WILLARD EMBLER, *Et Cetera,* Winter 1951.

People seem not to see that their opinion of the world is also a confession of character. RALPH WALDO EMERSON (1803–1882), *Conduct of Life,* 1880.

Our knowledge is the amassed thought and experience of innumerable minds. RALPH WALDO EMERSON (1809–1882), *Letters and Social Aims,* 1875.

The history of man is a series of conspiracies to win from nature some advantage without paying for it. RALPH WALDO EMERSON (1809–1882), *Demonology,* 1877.

Nothing astonishes men so much as common sense and plain dealing. RALPH WALDO EMERSON (1809–1882), *Art,* 1841.

To reason correctly from a false premise is the perfection of sophistry. DELOS C. EMMONS.

Wisdom is knowing when you can't be wise. PAUL ENGLE, *Poems in Praise,* 1959.

Here is the beginning of philosophy: a recognition of the conflicts between men, a search for their cause, a condemnation of mere opinion . . . and the discovery of a standard of judgment. EPICTETUS (ca. 55–135 A.D.), *Discourses.*

What is the first business of philosophy? To part with self-conceit. For it is impossible for anyone to begin to learn what he thinks he already knows. EPICTETUS (ca. 55–135 A.D.), *Discourses.*

Men are disturbed not by events which happen, but by the opinion they have of these events. EPICTETUS (ca. 55–135 A.D.), *Enchiridion.*

Authority sometimes proceeds from reason, but reason never from authority. For all authority that is not approved by true reason seems weak. But true reason, since it rests on its own strength, needs no reinforcement by any authority. JOHANNES SCOTUS ERIGENA (1266–1308), *De divisione naturae,* 1861.

A true philosopher is like an elephant: he never puts the second foot down until the first one is solidly in place. BERNARD de FONTENELLE (1657–1757) *History of Miracles,* 1687.

The mark of a truly civilized man is confidence in the strength and security derived from an inquiring mind. FELIX FRANKFURTER (1882–1965), U.S. Supreme Court Justice, *Dennis* v. *United States,* 1951.

The voice of the intellect is a soft one, but it does not rest until it has gained a hearing. Finally, after a countless succession of rebuffs, it succeeds. SIGMUND FREUD (1856–1939), *The Future of an Illusion,* 1927.

We are so made that we can derive intense enjoyment only from a contrast and very little from a state of things. SIGMUND FREUD (1856–1939), *Civilization and Its Discontents,* 1930.

Why abandon a belief merely because it ceases to be true? Cling to it long enough and . . . it will turn true again, for so it goes. Most of the change we think we see in life is due to truths being in and out of favor. ROBERT FROST (1874–1963)

Argument seldom convinces anyone contrary to his inclinations. THOMAS FULLER (1654–1734), *Gnomologia,* 1732.

Every man's private persuasion or belief, must be founded on evidence proposed to his own mind; and he cannot but believe, according as things appear to HIMSELF, not to others; to his own understanding, not to that of any other man. P. FURNEAUX, *Letters to the Honorable Mr. Justice Blackstone,* 1770.

Faced with the choice between changing one's mind and proving that there is no need to do so, almost everybody gets busy on the proof. JOHN KENNETH GALBRAITH.

If it's a despot you would dethrone, see first that his throne erected within you is destroyed. KAHLIL GIBRAN (1883–1931), *The Prophet,* 1923.

Say not, "I have found the truth," but rather, "I have found a truth." KAHLIL GIBRAN (1883–1931), *The Prophet,* 1923.

No progress of humanity is possible unless it shakes off the yoke of authority and tradition. ANDRÉ GIDE (1869–1951), Journal, March 17, 1931.

The most decisive actions of our life—I mean those that are most likely to decide the full course of our future are, more often than not, unconsidered. ANDRÉ GIDE (1869–1951).

Each of us really understands in others only those feelings he is capable of producing himself. ANDRÉ GIDE (1869–1951), Second Notebook, August 1921.

Nothing must be sustained, because it is ancient, because we have been accustomed to regard it as sacred, or because it has been unusual to bring its validity into question. WILLIAM GODWIN (1756–1836), *An Enquiry concerning Political Justice*, 1793.

We are never deceived. We deceive ourselves. JOHANN WOLFGANG von GOETHE (1749–1832).

We are so constituted that we believe the most incredible things: and once they are engraved upon the memory, woe to him who would endeavor to erase them. JOHANN WOLFGANG von GOETHE (1749–1832), *Sorrows of Young Werther*, 1771

Ages which are regressive and in process of dissolution are always subjective, whereas the trend in all progressive epochs is objective. JOHANN WOLFGANG von GOETHE (1749–1832).

Just being a Negro doesn't qualify you to understand the race situation any more than being sick makes you an expert on medicine. DICK GREGORY, *Nigger*, 1964.

There is no such thing as an evil in itself. Evil is not a thing, but a wrong function; it is the use of a good impulse at the wrong time, in the wrong place, towards a wrong end, that constitutes an evil function. J. A. HADFIELD, *Psychology and Morals*, 1923.

The conservative has but little to fear from the man whose reason is the servant of his passion, but let him beware of him in whom reason has become the greatest and most terrible of passions. J. B. S. HALDANE (1892–1964), *Daedalus or Science and the Future*.

A fool hath no dialogue with himself, the first thought carrieth him, without the reply of a second. GEORGE SAVILE, MARQUIS OF HALIFAX (1633–1695), *Moral Thoughts and Reflections*, 1788.

There is no fury like that against one who, we fear, may succeed in making us disloyal to beliefs we hold with passion, but have not really won. LEARNED HAND (1872–1961), U.S. Supreme Court Justice, Address, Harvard University, 1932.

Indeed, nothing is so likely to lead us astray as an abject reliance upon canons of any sort; so much the whole history of verbal interpretation teaches, if it teaches anything. LEARNED HAND (1872–1961), U.S. Supreme Court Justice, *Van Vranken* v. *Helvering*, 1940.

No man fully realizes what opinions he acts upon, or what his actions mean. THOMAS HARDY (1840–1928), *A Pair of Blue Eyes*, 1873.

You may be sure that when a man begins to call himself a realist he is preparing to do something that he is secretly ashamed of doing. SYDNEY J. HARRIS.

The last thing a scientist would do is cling to a map because he inherited it from his grandfather, or because it was used by George Washington or Abraham Lincoln. S. I. HAYAKAWA.

There is nothing more likely to drive a man mad than an obstinate constitutional preference of the true to the agreeable. WILLIAM HAZLITT (1778–1830).

He is a hypocrite who professes what he does not believe; not he who does not practice all that he wishes or approves. WILLIAM HAZLITT (1778–1830), *Sketches and Essays,* 1839.

Fraud may consist as well in the suppression of what is true as in the representation of what is false. JUSTICE HEATH, English Jurist, *Tapp* v. *Lee,* 1803.

For it is natural to man to indulge in the illusion of hope. We are apt to shut our eyes against a painful truth, and listen to the song of the siren, till she transforms us into beasts. PATRICK HENRY (1736–1799), Virginia Convention, March 23, 1775.

If you hate a person, you hate something in him that is part of yourself. What isn't part of ourselves doesn't disturb us. HERMANN HESSE (1877–1962).

Science is the knowledge of Consequences, and dependence of one fact upon another. . . . THOMAS HOBBES (1558–1679), *Leviathan,* 1651.

Self-righteousness is a loud din raised to drown the voice of guilt within us. ERIC HOFFER (1902–1983), *The True Believer,* 1951.

Those who remain in the dark about their own motives are as it were strangers to themselves. Hence perhaps their exceptional power of self-delusion—their ability to talk themselves into anything. ERIC HOFFER (1902–1983), *The Passionate State of Mind,* 1955.

There is in us a tendency to locate the shaping forces of our existence outside ourselves. Success and failure are unavoidably related in our minds with the state of things around us. ERIC HOFFER (1902–1983), *The True Believer,* 1956.

It is a talent of the weak to persuade themselves that they suffer for something when they suffer from something; that they are showing the way when they are running away; that they see the light when they feel the heat; that they are chosen when they are shunned. ERIC HOFFER (1902–1983), *The Passionate State of Mind,* 1955.

You never need think you can turn over any old falsehood without a terrible squirming and scattering of the horrid little population that dwells under it. OLIVER WENDELL HOLMES, SR. (1809–1894), *The Autocrat at the Breakfast Table,* 1858.

All generous minds have a horror of what are commonly called "facts." They are the brute beasts of the intellectual domain. OLIVER WENDELL HOLMES, SR. (1809–1894), *Autocrat at the Breakfast Table,* 1858.

Wisdom consists not so much in knowing what to do in the ultimate as in knowing what to do next. HERBERT CLARK HOOVER (1874–1964), U.S. President, *Reader's Digest,* July 1958.

Realism is nothing more and nothing less than the truthful treatment of material. WILLIAM DEAN HOWELLS (1837–1920), *Criticism and Fiction,* 1892.

Truth, in its struggles for recognition, passes through four distinct stages. First, we say it is damnable, dangerous, disorderly, and will surely disrupt society. Second, we declare it is heretical, infidelic and contrary to the Bible. Third, we say it is really a matter of no importance one way or the other. Fourth, we aver that we have always upheld and believed it. ELBERT HUBBARD (1856–1915), *The Roycroft Dictionary of Epigrams,* 1923.

There is no method of reasoning more common, and yet none more blamable, than, in philosophical disputes, to endeavor the refutation of any hypothesis, by a pretense of its dangerous consequence to religion and morality. DAVID HUME (1711–1776), *An Enquiry concerning Human Understanding,* 1758.

Belief consists not in the nature and order of our ideas, but in the manner of their conception, and in their feeling to the mind . . . something felt by the mind, which distinguishes the ideas of the judgment from the fictions of the imagination. DAVID HUME (1711–1776), *An Enquiry concerning Human Understanding,* 1758.

The first quality of an historian is to be true and impartial; the next to be interesting. DAVID HUME (1711–1776), Letter, 1754.

The consistent thinker, the consistently moral man, is either a walking mummy or else, if he has not succeeded in stifling all his vitality, a fanatical monomaniac. ALDOUS HUXLEY (1894–1963), *Do What You Will,* 1929.

My business is to teach my aspirations to conform themselves to fact, not to try and make facts harmonize with my aspirations. THOMAS HENRY HUXLEY (1825–1895).

Irrationally held truths may be more harmful than reasoned errors. THOMAS HENRY HUXLEY (1825–1895), *The Coming of Age of* The Origin of Species.

Logical consequences are the scarecrows of fools and the beacons of wise men. THOMAS HENRY HUXLEY (1825–1895), *Animal Automatism,* 1884.

Sit down before fact as a little child, be prepared to give up every preconceived notion, follow humbly wherever and to whatever abysses nature leads, or you shall learn nothing. THOMAS HENRY HUXLEY (1825–1895), Letter, September 23, 1860.

The great tragedy of science—the slaying of a beautiful hypothesis by an ugly fact. THOMAS HENRY HUXLEY (1825–1985), *Biogenesis and Abiogenesis,* 1870.

There are two kinds of fools: one says, "This is old, therefore it is good"; the other says, "This is new, therefore it is better." WILLIAM RALPH INGE (1860–1954).

The object of studying philosophy is to know one's own mind, not other people's. WILLIAM RALPH INGE (1860–1954), *Outspoken Essays,* 1922.

In nature there are neither rewards nor punishments—there are consequences. ROBERT G. INGERSOLL (1833–1899), *Some Reasons Why,* 1881.

Heresy is what the minority believe; it is the name given by the powerful to the doctrines of the weak. ROBERT G. INGERSOLL (1833–1899), "Heretics and Heresies."

Anger blows out the lamp of the mind. In the examination of a great and important question, everyone should be serene, slow-pulsed, and calm. ROBERT G. INGERSOLL (1833–1899).

Irrationalism, since it is not bound by any rules or consistency, may be combined with any kind of belief, including a belief in the brotherhood of man; but the irrationalist belief that emotions and passions rather than reason are the mainspring of human action tend to lead to an appeal to violence and brute force as the ultimate arbiter in any dispute. ROGER JAMES, *Return to Reason,* 1980.

Philosophical arguments are not directed against people, but against statements, or theories, or other arguments. All these have been proposed by people, they stand in their own right and are true or false regardless of the personality or character or reliability of their authors. ROGER JAMES, *Return to Reason,* 1980.

We never fully grasp the import of any true statement until we have a clear notion of what the opposite true statement would be. WILLIAM JAMES (1842–1910).

The facts of the world in their sensible diversity are always before us, but our theoretic need is that they should be conceived in a way that reduces their manifoldness to simplicity. Our pleasure at finding that a chaos of facts is the expression of a single underlying fact is like the relief of the musician at resolving a confused mass of sound into melodic or harmonic order. WILLIAM JAMES (1842–1910), *The Will to Believe,* 1896.

The art of being wise is the art of knowing what to overlook. WILLIAM JAMES (1842–1910), *Principles of Psychology,* 1890.

Reason and free inquiry are the only effectual agents against error. THOMAS JEFFERSON (1743–1826), *Notes on the State of Virginia,* 1782.

Nothing is so firmly believed as that which is least known. FRANCIS JEFFREY (1773–1850), *Contributions to the Edinburgh Review,* 1844.

In matters of philosophy and science authority has ever been the great opponent of truth. A despotic calm is usually the triumph of error. In the republic of the sciences sedition and even anarchy are beneficial in the long run. W. STANLEY JEVONS (1835–1882), *Theory of Political Economy,* 1871.

[Reason is] a free activity of the mind, reaching conclusions under no compulsion save that of evidence. C. E. M. JOAD (1891–1953), *Return to Philosophy,* 1936.

The "testing of hypothesis" is frequently merely a euphemism for obtaining plausible numbers to provide ceremonial adequacy for a theory chosen and defended on a priori grounds. HARRY G. JOHNSON (1923–1977), *American Economic Review,* 1971.

In order that all men may be taught to speak truth, it is necessary that all likewise should learn to hear it. SAMUEL JOHNSON (1709–1784), *The Rambler,* 1750–52.

In questions of law or of fact conscience is very often confounded with opinion. No man's conscience can tell him the rights of another man; they must be known by rational investigation or historical inquiry. SAMUEL JOHNSON (1709–1784), 1773.

All knowledge is of itself of some value. There is nothing so minute or inconsiderate that I would not rather know it than not. SAMUEL JOHNSON (1709–1784), 1775.

When speculation has done its worst, two and two still make four. SAMUEL JOHNSON (1709–1784), *The Idler,* 1758.

Integrity without knowledge is weak and useless, and knowledge without integrity is dangerous and dreadful. SAMUEL JOHNSON (1709–1784), *Rasselas,* 1759.

Those who never retract their opinions love themselves more than they love truth. JOSEPH JOUBERT (1754–1824), *Pensées,* 1842.

The aim of argument, or of discussion, should be not victory but progress. JOSEPH JOUBERT (1754–1824), *Pensées,* 1842.

The aphorism is a personal observation inflated into a universal truth, a private posing as a general. STEFAN KANFER, *Time,* July 11, 1983.

Faith means intense, usually confident, belief that is not based on evidence sufficient to command assent from every reasonable person. WALTER KAUFMANN (1921–1980), *Faith of a Heretic,* 1961.

An extensive knowledge is needful to thinking people—it takes away the heat and fever; and helps, by widening speculation, to ease the burden of the mystery. JOHN KEATS (1795–1821), Letter, 1818.

We should be as wary of psychologizing political events as we should be of politicizing psychological events. SAM KEEN, *Faces of the Enemy,* 1986.

The great enemy of truth is very often not the lie—deliberate, contrived and dishonest—but the myth—persistent, persuasive, and unrealistic. . . . We subject all facts to a prefabricated set of interpretations. We enjoy the comfort of opinions without the discomfort of thought. JOHN FITZGERALD KENNEDY (1917–1963), U.S. President, Address, Yale University, 1962.

The truth is sometimes a poor competitor in the market place of ideas—complicated, unsatisfying, full of dilemmas, always vulnerable to misinterpretation and abuse. GEORGE F. KENNEN, *American Diplomacy: 1900–1950*, 1951.

Many people today don't want honest answers insofar as honest means unpleasant or disturbing. They want a soft answer that turneth away anxiety. LOUIS KRONENBERGER, *The Cart and the Horse*, 1964.

If you can talk brilliantly about a problem, it can create the consoling illusion that it has been mastered. STANLEY KUBRICK.

There are some men who turn a deaf ear to reason and good advice, and willfully go wrong for fear of being controlled. JEAN de LA BRUYÈRE (1645–1696), *Les Caractères*, 1688.

There is nothing more horrible than the murder of a beautiful theory by a brutal gang of facts. FRANÇOIS, DUC de LA ROCHEFOUCAULD (1613–1680), *Maxims*, 1665.

Smallness of mind is the cause of stubbornness, and we do not credit readily what is beyond our view. FRANÇOIS, DUC de LA ROCHFOUCAULD (1613–1680), *Maxims*, 1665.

It is as easy to deceive oneself without perceiving it as it is difficult to deceive others without their perceiving it. FRANÇOIS, DUC de LA ROCHFOUCAULD (1613–1680), *Maxims*, 1665.

If in argument we can make a man angry with us, we have drawn him from the vantage ground and overcome him. WALTER SAVAGE LANDOR (1775–1864), *Imaginary Conversations*, 1824–53.

Principles do not mainly influence even the principled; we talk on principle, but we act on interest. WALTER SAVAGE LANDOR (1775–1864), *Imaginary Conversations*, 1824–54.

What sociologists and humanists call "rationality," or "reason," or what psychologists call cognitive development or cognitive complexity is a good in itself. It is not so much that knowledge is freedom, or that knowledge sets men free, but rather knowing, especially knowing how to know, is freedom and sets men free. ROBERT E. LANE, *Micropolitics*, vol. 1, no. 1, 1981.

A philosophy is characterized more by the formulation of its problems than by its solution of them. SUSANNE K. LANGER, *Philosophy in a New Key*, 1942.

The characteristics of the reasoning of crowds are the association of dissimilar things possessing a merely apparent connection . . . and the immediate generalization of particular cases. It is arguments of this kind that are always presented to crowds by those who know how to manipulate them. GUSTAVE LE BON (1841–1931), *The Crowd*, 1895.

Science has promised us truth—an understanding of such relationships as our minds can grasp; it has never promised us either peace or happiness. GUSTAVE LE BON (1841–1931), *The Crowd,* 1895.

The greater deception men suffer is from their own opinions. LEONARDO DA VINCI (1452–1519), Notebooks, ca. 1500.

Anyone who in discussion relies upon authority uses, not his understanding but rather his memory. LEONARDO DA VINCI (1452–1519), Notebooks, ca. 1500.

You do ill if you praise, but worse if you censure, what you do not rightly understand. LEONARDO DA VINCI (1452–1519), Notebooks, ca. 1500.

There is an enormous difference between the recognition of the role of the irrational and the glorification of it. It is our failure to make this distinction that has largely prevented us from making use of the new insights into the irrational. MAX LERNER, *Ideas Are Weapons,* 1939.

There is a great difference in still believing something and in believing it again. GEORG CHRISTOPH LICHTENBERG (1742–1799), *Aphorisms,* 1764–99.

To do just the opposite is also a form of imitation. GEORG CHRISTOPH LICHTENBERG (1742–1799), *Aphorisms,* 1764–99.

Here's an object more of dread, / Than aught the grave contains, / A human form with reason fled, / While wretched life remains. ABRAHAM LINCOLN (1809–1865), U.S. President, Letter to Andrew Johnson, 1846.

The dogmas of the quiet past, are inadequate to the stormy present. The occasion is piled high with difficulty, and we must rise with the occasion. As our case is new, so we must think anew and act anew. ABRAHAM LINCOLN (1809–1865), U.S. President, Message to Congress, December 1, 1862.

For the attempt to see things freshly and in detail, rather than as types and generalities, is exhausting, and among busy affairs practically out of the question. WALTER LIPPMANN (1889–1974), *Public Opinion,* 1922.

We should have a great many fewer disputes in the world if words were taken for what they are, the signs of our ideas only, and not for things themselves. JOHN LOCKE (1632–1704), *An Essay concerning Human Understanding,* 1690.

The imputation of inconsistency is one to which every sound politician and every honest thinker must sooner or later subject himself. The foolish and the dead alone never change their opinions. JAMES RUSSELL LOWELL (1819–1891), *My Study Windows,* 1871.

"Intellectuals," no doubt, are often tiresome enough, because they are often pseudo-intellectuals—ingenious fools too clever to be wise, though brilliant at inventing the most ingenious reasons for their fatuous beliefs. F. L. LUCAS (1884–1967), *The Search for Good Sense.*

The historian should be fearless and incorruptible; a man of independence, loving frankness and truth; one who, as the poet says, calls a fig a fig and a spade a spade. He should yield to neither hatred nor affection, but should be unsparing and unpitying. . . . He should never consider what this or that man will think, but should state the facts as they really occurred. LUCIAN (120–200 A.D.), *How History Should Be Written,* 170 A.D.

Large bodies are far more likely to err than individuals. The passions are inflamed by sympathy; and fear of punishment and the sense of shame are diminished by partition. THOMAS BABINGTON MACAULAY (1800–1859), *Edinburgh Review,* September 1828.

Ah, snug lie those that slumber, / Beneath Conviction's roof. / Their floors are study lumber, / Their windows weatherproof. / But I sleep cold forever, / And cold sleep all my kind, / For I was born to shiver, / In the draft from an open mind. PHYLLIS McGINLEY (1905–1978), *A Pocket Full of Wry,* 1940.

Nothing is simpler than to maintain that a certain type of thinking is feudal, bourgeois or proletarian, liberal, socialistic, or conservative, as long as there is no analytical method for demonstrating it and no criteria have been adduced which will provide a control over the demonstration. KARL MANNHEIM (1893–1947), *Ideology and Utopia,* 1936.

The sign of intelligent people is their ability to control emotions by the application of reason. MARYA MANNES, *More in Anger,* 1958.

The more conscious a philosopher is of the weak spots in his theory, the more certain he is to speak with an air of final authority. DON MARQUIS (1878–1937), *Archy and Mehitabel,* 1927.

If you make people think they're thinking, they'll love you. If you really make them think, they'll hate you. DON MARQUIS (1878–1937), *Archy and Mehitabel,* 1927.

The most reckless and treacherous of all theorists is he who professes to let facts speak for themselves, who keeps in the background the part he has played, perhaps unconsciously, in selecting and grouping them, and in suggesting the argument *post hoc ergo propter hoc.* ALFRED MARSHALL (1842–1924), *The Present Position of Economics,* 1885.

Man has always sacrificed truth in his vanity, comfort and advantage. He lives not by truth but by make-believe. W. SOMERSET MAUGHAM (1874–1965), *The Summing Up,* 1938.

The Vicar of Whitstable . . . had a great idea that one should stick to whatever one had begun. Like all weak men he laid an exaggerated stress on not changing one's mind. W. SOMERSET MAUGHAM (1874–1965), *Of Human Bondage,* 1915.

What plays the mischief with the truth is that men will insist upon the universal application of a temporary feeling or opinion. HERMAN MELVILLE (1819–1891).

Penetrating so many secrets, we cease to believe in the unknowable. But there it sits nevertheless, calmly licking its chops. H. L. MENCKEN (1880–1956), *Minority Report*.

The real advantage which truth has, consists in this, that when an opinion is true, it may be extinguished once, twice, or many times, but in the course of the ages there will generally be found persons to rediscover it. JOHN STUART MILL (1806–1873), *On Liberty*, 1859.

Indeed, the dictum that truth always triumphs over persecution, is one of those pleasant falsehoods which men repeat after one another till they pass into commonplaces, but which all experience refutes. History teems with instances of truth put down by persecution. If not suppressed for ever, it may be thrown back for centuries. . . . It is a piece of idle sentimentality that truth, merely as truth, has any inherent power denied to error, of prevailing against the dungeon and the stake. JOHN STUART MILL (1806–1873), *On Liberty*, 1859.

No one can be a great thinker who does not recognize that as a thinker it is his first duty to follow his intellect to whatever conclusions it may lead. JOHN STUART MILL (1806–1873).

The task of the real intellectual consists of analyzing illusions in order to discover their causes. ARTHUR MILLER.

Reason is but choosing. JOHN MILTON (1608–1674), *Areopagitica*, 1644.

There is no such thing as perfection in human knowledge. . . . The most elaborate theory that seems to satisfy completely our search for knowledge may one day be amended or supplanted by a new theory. Science does not give us absolute and final certainty. It only gives us assurance within the limits of our mental abilities and the prevailing state of scientific thought. LUDWIG von MISES (1881–1973), *Human Action*, 1963.

There is a momentous difference between coming to believe what we have been told and deciding, as Jefferson did, out of knowledge and thoughtful judgement, to "hold" something true. The former is a kind of slavery and easy to achieve; the latter is difficult, for it requires knowledge and governed intellect. RICHARD MITCHELL, *The Graves of Academe*, 1981.

What kind of truth is this which is true on one side of the mountain and false on the other? MICHEL de MONTAIGNE (1533–1592), *Essays*, 1580.

How many things that were articles of faith yesterday are fables today? MICHEL de MONTAIGNE (1533–1592), *Essays*, 1580.

The means prepare the end, and the end is what the means have made it. JOHN MORLEY (1838–1923), *Critical Miscellanies*, 1871–1908.

Our opinions are less important than the spirit and temper with which they posses us, and even good opinions are worth very little unless we hold them in a broad, intelligent, and spacious way. JOHN MORLEY (1838–1923), *Critical Miscellanies*, 1871–1908.

Where it is a duty to worship the sun it is pretty sure to be a crime to examine the laws of heat. JOHN MORLEY (1823–1923), *Critical Miscellanies,* 1871–1908.

Stupidity does not consist in being without ideas. Such stupidity would be the sweet, blissful stupidity of animals, mulluscs and the gods. Human stupidity consists in having lots of ideas, but stupid ones. HENRY de MONTHERLANT (1896–1972), Notebooks, 1930.

Indignation is the seducer of thought. No man can think clearly when his fists are clenched. GEORGE JEAN NATHAN (1882–1958), *The World In Falseface,* 1923.

There can be no absolute conclusions in economics, and no result can be asserted as positive, until all the causes which may affect it have been considered. SIMON NEWCOMB (1835–1909), *Principles of Political Economy,* 1886.

A liberal education is the education which gives a man a clear, conscious view of his own opinions and judgments, a truth in developing them, an eloquence in expressing them, and a force in urging them. It teaches him to see things as they are, to go right to the point, to disentangle a skein of thought, to detect what is sophistical, and to discard what is irrelevant. JOHN HENRY NEWMAN (1801–1890), quoted in *Saturday Review,* November 21, 1953.

We are inclined to judge ourselves by our ideals; others by their acts. HAROLD NICOLSON (1886–1968).

Beware of notions like genius and inspiration; they are a sort of magic wand and should be used sparingly by anybody who wants to see things clearly. JOSÉ ORTEGA y GASSET (1883–1955), *Notes on the Novel,* 1925.

A long habit of not thinking a thing wrong gives it a superficial appearance of being right, and raises at first a formidable outcry in defense of custom. THOMAS PAINE (1737–1809), *Common Sense,* 1776.

The greater intellect one has, the more originality one finds in men. Ordinary persons find no differences between men. BLAISE PASCAL (1623–1662), *Pensées,* 1670.

It is your own assent to yourself, and the constant voice of your own reason, and not that of others, that should make you believe. BLAISE PASCAL (1623–1662), *Pensées,* 1670.

It is much better to know something about everything than to know everything about one thing. BLAISE PASCAL (1623–1662), *Pensées,* 1670.

When we wish to correct with advantage, and to show another that he errs, we must notice from what side he views the matter, for on that side it is usually true. BLAISE PASCAL (1623–1662), *Pensées,* 1670.

People are generally better persuaded by reasons which they themselves have discovered than by those which come into the mind of others. BLAISE PASCAL (1623–1662), *Pensées,* 1670.

Our whole dignity consists in thought. Let us indeavor, then, to think well: this is the principle of ethics. BLAISE PASCAL (1623–1662), *Pensées,* 1670.

All progress of mind consists for the most part in differentiation, in the resolution of an obscure and complex subject into its component aspects. WALTER PATER (1839–1894), *Style,* 1888.

Truth often suffers more by the heat of its defenders than from the arguments of its opponents. WILLIAM PENN (1644–1718), *Some Fruits of Solitude,* 1693.

Knowledge is the treasure, but judgment the treasurer of a wise man. He that has more knowledge than judgment is made for another man's use more than his own. WILLIAM PENN (1644–1718), *Some Fruits of Solitude,* 1693.

Arguments that make their point by means of similarities are imposters, and, unless you are on your guard against them, will quite readily deceive you. PLATO (428–348 B.C.).

A man should never be ashamed to own he has been in the wrong, which is but saying that he is wiser today than he was yesterday. ALEXANDER POPE (1688–1744), *Thoughts on Various Subjects,* 1706.

There are certain times when most people are in a disposition of being informed, and 'tis incredible what a vast good a little truth might do, spoken in such seasons. ALEXANDER POPE (1688–1744), Letter, 1705.

Of nearly every theory it may be said that it agrees with many facts: this is one of the reasons why a theory can be said to be corroborated only if we are unable to find refuting facts, rather than if we are able to find supporting facts. SIR KARL POPPER, *The Poverty of Historicism,* 1963.

Irrational emphasis upon emotion and passion leads ultimately to what I can only describe as crime. One reason for this opinion is that this attitude, which is at best one of resignation towards the irrational of human beings, at worst one of scorn for human reason, must lead to an appeal to violence and brutal force as the ultimate arbiter in any dispute. SIR KARL POPPER, *The Open Society and Its Enemies,* 1966

Irrationalism expresses itself in various ways. One of them is . . . the attitude of looking at once for the unconscious motives and determinants in the social habitat of the thinker, instead of first examining the validity of the argument itself. SIR KARL POPPER, *The Open Society and Its Enemies,* 1966.

In men it is necessary that the rational principle, or the intellectual discernment of right and wrong, should be aided by instinctive determinations. The dictates of mere reason, being slow and deliberate, would otherwise be much too weak. RICHARD PRICE (1723–1791), *The Principal Question in Morals,* 1758.

A powerful idea communicates some of its power to the man who contradicts it. MARCEL PROUST (1871–1922), *Remembrance of Things Past,* 1911.

The chief danger to our philosophy, apart from laziness and wooliness, is scholasticism . . . which is treating that which is vague as if it were more precise.

FRANK P. RAMSEY (1903–1951), *Foundations of Mathematics and Other Logical Essays,* 1931.

We arrive at causes by noting coincidences; yet, now and then, coincidences are deceitful. CHARLES READE (1814–1884), *The Cloister and the Hearth,* 1861.

Metaphor . . . is the synthesis of several units of observation into one commanding image; it is the expression of a complex idea, not by analysis, nor by abstract statement, but by a sudden perception of an objective relation. The complex idea is translated into a concrete equivalent. HERBERT READ (1983–1968), in *Forms of Rhetoric* (T. Kakonis and J. C. Wilcox), 1969.

There is no expedient to which man will not resort to avoid the real labor of thinking. JOSHUA REYNOLDS (1723–1792).

Partisanship is our great curse. We too readily assume that everything has two sides and it is our duty to be on one or the other. JAMES HARVEY ROBINSON (1863–1936), *The Mind in the Making,* 1921.

Few of us take the pains to study the origins of our cherished convictions. . . . We like to continue to believe what we have been accustomed to accept as true, and the resentment aroused when doubt is cast upon any of our assumptions leads us to seek every manner of excuse for clinging to them. JAMES HARVEY ROBINSON (1863–1936), *The Mind in the Making,* 1921.

The youthful heart is ready to believe what it wishes will happen. REGINA MARIE ROCHE (1764–1845), *Clermont,* 1798.

The more closed a system, the more is the acceptance of a particular belief assumed to depend on irrelevant internal arrives and/or particular arbitrary reinforcements from external authority. MILTON ROKEACH, *The Open and Closed Mind,* 1960.

First teach a child things as they really are; afterward you will teach him how they appear to us. He will then be able to compare popular ideas and truth and be able to rise above the vulgar crowd. . . . But if you begin to teach the opinions of other people before you teach how to judge their worth, . . . your pupil will adopt these opinions whatever you may do. JEAN-JACQUES ROUSSEAU (1712–1778), *Émile,* 1762.

Our experience is composed rather of illusions lost rather than of wisdom acquired. JOSEPH ROUX (1834–1905), *Meditations of a Parish Priest,* 1886.

Philosophy . . . is not a presumptuous effort to explain the mysteries of the world by means of any superhuman insight or extraordinary cunning, but has its origin and value in an attempt to give a reasonable account of our own personal attitude toward the more serious business of life. JOSIAH ROYCE (1855–1916), *The Spirit of Modern Philosophy,* 1892.

The most savage controversies are those about matters as to which there is no good evidence either way. BERTRAND RUSSELL (1872–1970), *Unpopular Essays,* 1950.

The essence of the liberal outlook lies not in what opinions are held, but in how they are held: instead of being held dogmatically, are they held tentatively, with a consciousness that new evidence may at any moment lead to their abandonment. BERTRAND RUSSELL (1872–1970), *Unpopular Essays,* 1950

Man is a credulous animal, and must believe something; in the absence of good grounds for belief, he will be satisfied with bad ones. BERTRAND RUSSELL (1872–1970), *Unpopular Essays,* 1950

The fact that an opinion has been widely held is no evidence that it is not utterly absurd; indeed, in view of the silliness of the majority of mankind, a widespread belief is more often likely to be foolish than sensible. BERTRAND RUSSELL (1872–1970), *Philosophical Papers,* 1903.

[Fear is] the main source of superstition, and one of the main sources of cruelty. To conquer fear is the beginning of wisdom. BERTRAND RUSSELL (1872–1970), *Outline of Intellectual Rubbish,* 1950.

The meaning of things lies not in the things themselves but in our attitudes toward things. ANTOINE de SAINT-EXUPÉRY (1900–1944), *The Wisdom of the Sands,* 1948.

Intelligence is quickness in seeing things as they are. GEORGE SANTAYANA (1863–1952), *Little Essays,* 1920.

When all beliefs are challenged together, the just and necessary ones have a chance to step forward and reestablish themselves alone. GEORGE SANTAYANA (1863–1952), *The Life of Reason,* 1905-06.

The same battle in the clouds will be known to the deaf only as lightening and to the blind only as thunder. GEORGE SANTAYANA (1863–1952).

Knowledge is recognition of something absent; it is a salutation, not an embrace. GEORGE SANTAYANA (1863–1952), *The Life of Reason,* 1905-06.

Theory helps us to bear our ignorance of facts. GEORGE SANTAYANA (1863–1952), *The Sense of Beauty,* 1896.

Wisdom comes by disillusionment. GEORGE SANTAYANA (1863–1952), *Reality in Common Sense.*

Every man takes the limits of his own field of vision for the limits of the world. ARTHUR SCHOPENHAUER (1788–1860), *Parerga and Paralipomena,* 1851.

Reason deserves to be called a prophet; for in showing us the consequence and effect of our actions in the present, does it not tell us what the future will be? ARTHUR SCHOPENHAUER (1788–1860), *Parerga and Paralipomena,* 1851.

Ridicule often checks what is absurd and fully as often smothers that which is noble. SIR WALTER SCOTT (1771–1832), *Quentin Durwood,* 1823.

Reason wishes that the judgment it gives be just; anger wishes that the judgment it has given seem to be just. SENECA (4 B.C.–65 A.D.), *On Anger.*

Who shrinks from knowledge of his calamities but aggravates his fear; troubles half seen do torture all the more. SENECA (4 B.C.–65 A.D.), *Agamemnon.*

This above all: to thine own self be true and it must follow, as the night the day, thou canst not be false to any man. WILLIAM SHAKESPEARE (1564–1616), *Hamlet,* 1600.

What a man believes may be ascertained, not from his creed, but from the assumptions on which he habitually acts. GEORGE BERNARD SHAW (1856–1950), *Man and Superman,* 1903.

What is the use of straining after an amiable view of things, when a cynical view is most likely to be the true one? GEORGE BERNARD SHAW (1856–1950).

The man who listens to reason is lost. Reason enslaves all whose minds are not strong enough to master her. GEORGE BERNARD SHAW (1856–1950), *Man and Superman,* 1903.

Reason respects the differences, and imagination the similitudes of things. PERCY BYSSHE SHELLEY (1792–1822), *A Defence of Poetry,* 1821.

The aim of ethics is to render scientific—i.e., true, and as far as possible systematic—the apparent cognitions that most men have of the rightness or reasonableness of conduct, whether the conduct be considered as right in itself, or as the means to some end conceived as ultimately reasonable. HENRY SIDGWICK (1838–1900), *The Methods of Ethics,* 1874.

The process of validating a factual proposition is quite distinct from the process of validating a value judgment. The former is validated by its agreement with the facts, the latter by human fiat. HERBERT SIMON, *Administrative Behavior,* 1957

Liberal education, then, must focus its main efforts on thinking about and examining our beliefs, studying them not as if they were alien objects, but rather from within, the beliefs as well as their study being seen as an integral part of the "serious play" of life in which we are involved. SOCRATES (470–399 B.C.).

It is notorious, that many positions are true in the abstract, which are utterly false when applied to particular cases and circumstances. WILLIAM SPENCE (1783–1860), *Tracts on Political Economy,* 1822.

There is a principle which is a bar against all information, which is a proof against all argument, and which cannot fail to keep a man in everlasting ignorance—that principle is condemnation before investigation. HERBERT SPENCER (1820–1903), *Social Statics,* 1850.

He alone is free who lives with free consent under the entire guidance of reason. BARUCH SPINOZA (1632–1677), *Tractatus Theologico-Politicus.*

I have striven not to laugh at human actions, not to weep at them, nor to hate them, but to understand them. BARUCH SPINOZA (1632–1677), *Tractatus Theologico-Politicus,* 1670.

It is the nature of an hypothesis, when once a man has conceived it, that it assimilates everything to itself as proper nourishment, and, from the first moment of your begetting it, it generally grows the stronger by everything you see, hear, read, or understand. LAURENCE STERNE (1713–1768), *Tristam Shandy.*

It is curious to observe the triumph of slight incidents over the mind: what incredible weight they have in forming and governing our opinions of both men and things. LAURENCE STERNE (1713–1768), *Tristam Shandy,* 1759.

If the determinist is right, reasoning can prove nothing: it is merely an ingenious method for providing us with apparently rational excuses for believing what in any case we cannot help believing. BURNETT H. STREETER (1874–1937), *Reality,* 1926.

The latter part of a wise man's life is taken up in curing the follies, prejudices, and false opinions that he contracted in the former. JONATHAN SWIFT (1667–1745), *Thoughts on Various Subjects,* 1706.

It is morally as bad not to care whether a thing is true or not, so long as it makes you feel good, as it is not to care how you got your money as long as you have got it. EDWIN WAY TEALE (1889–1980), *Circle of the Seasons,* 1953.

The reasons of Reason, unencumbered by moral consciousness, become, very soon, the reasons of interest, and then the reasons of State, and thence, in an uncontested progression, the rationalization of opportunism, brutality, and crime. E. P. THOMPSON, *The Poverty of Theory,* 1978.

To be a philosopher is not merely to have subtle thoughts, nor even to found a school, but so to love wisdom as to live according to its dictates, a life of simplicity, independence, magnanimity, and trust. HENRY DAVID THOREAU (1817–1862), *Walden,* 1854.

The character of human life, like the character of the human condition, like the character of all life, is "ambiguity": the inseperable mixture of good and evil, the true and false, the creative and destructive forces—both individual and social. PAUL TILLICH (1886–1965), *Time* magazine, May 17, 1963.

One of the most ordinary weaknesses of the human intellect is to seek to reconcile contrary principles, and to purchase peace at the expense of logic. ALEXIS de TOCQUEVILLE (1805–1859), *Democracy in America,* 1835–39.

The basis of fascism is blind belief and a contempt for reason. . . . Fascism exploits the fear of reason which lives secretly in the conscious and subconscious minds of many people. Reason means facing life and facts. ERNST TOLLER (1893–1939).

This is the great vice of academicism, that it is concerned with ideas rather than with thinking. LIONEL TRILLING (1905–1975), *The Liberal Imagination,* 1950.

The mind likes a strange idea as little as the body likes a strange protein and resists it with similar energy. It would not be too fanciful to say that a new idea is the most quickly acting antigen known to science . . . often . . . we shall find that we have begun to argue against a new idea even before it has been completely stated. WILLIAM TROTTER, *Collected Papers,* 1941.

It is wiser, I believe, to arrive at theory by way of evidence rather than the other way round. . . . It is more rewarding, in any case, to assemble the facts first and, in the process of arranging them in narrative form, to discover a theory or a historical generalization emerging on its own accord. BARBARA TUCHMAN (1912–1989), *Practicing History,* 1981.

We should be careful to get out of an experience only the wisdom that is in it—and stop there; lest we be like the cat that sits down on a hot stove lid. She will never sit down on a hot stove lid again—and that is well; but also she will never sit down on a cold one anymore. MARK TWAIN (1835–1910), *Following the Equator,* 1897.

Intellectuals resent the market because it makes people pay for economic value. Moral value is left out in the cold—and so are intellectuals, who are the producers of moral value, or moral approval and disapproval for public consumption. ERNEST van DEN HAAG, *Capitalism: Sources of Hostility,* 1979.

Imagination is more robust in proportion as reasoning power is weak. GIOVANNI BATTISTA VICO (1668–1744), *The New Science,* 1725–44.

Many are destined to reason wrongly; others, not to reason at all: and others to persecute those who do reason. VOLTAIRE (1694–1778), *Philosophical Dictionary,* 1764.

What is madness? To have erroneous perceptions and reason correctly from them. VOLTAIRE (1694–1778), *Philosophical Dictionary,* 1764.

There is nothing so unfortunate as to be a philosopher . . . and a reasoner, and to know what can and cannot be done. HORACE WALPOLE (1717–1797), 1777.

It ain't so much the things we don't know that gets us into trouble. It's the things we know that ain't so. ARTEMUS WARD (1834–1867).

Every scientific fulfillment raises new questions; it asks to be surpassed and outdated. MAX WEBER (1868–1920), *Methodology of the Social Sciences.*

The cause cannot necessitate the effect. If it did, the effect would exist when the cause did. What is normally termed a cause is only an antecedent condition. PAUL WEISS, in *Determination and Freedom* (Sidney Hook), 1958.

Reason is the wise man's guide, example the fool's. WELSH PROVERB.

We want the facts to fit the preconceptions. When they don't, it is easier to ignore the facts than to change the preconceptions. JESSAMYN WEST, *The Quaker Reader*, 1962.

Intelligence is quickness to apprehend as distinct from ability, which is capacity to act wisely on the thing apprehended. ALFRED NORTH WHITEHEAD (1861–1947), *Dialogues*, 1920.

A philosopher of imposing stature doesn't think in a vacuum. Even his most abstract ideas are, to some extent, conditioned by what is or is not known in the time when he lives. ALFRED NORTH WHITEHEAD (1861–1947), *Dialogues.*

A thing is not necessarily true because a man dies for it. OSCAR WILDE (1854–1900).

I can stand brute force, but brute reason is quite unbearable. There is something unfair about its use. It is hitting below the intellect. OSCAR WILDE (1854–1900), *The Picture of Dorian Gray*, 1891.

Reification . . . means any unwarranted extension of reality in the thing perceived or conceived. . . . Thus reification means the taking as real that which is only apparently real; the taking as objectively real that which is only subjectively real; the taking as factual, concrete, or perceptual that which is only conceptual; the taking as absolute that which is only relative, etc. JAMES W. WOODWARD, *Intellectual Realism and Culture Change*, 1935.

Skepticism

The first key to wisdom is this—constant and frequent questioning . . . for by doubting we are led to question and by questioning we arrive at the truth. PETER ABELARD (1099–1142), *Sic et non,* c. 1120.

Doubt is not below knowledge, but above it. ALAIN (1868–1951), *Librespropos,* 1908.

Philosophy means, first, doubt; and afterwards the consciousness of what knowledge means, the consciousness of uncertainty and of ignorance, the consciousness of limit, shade, degree, possibility. The ordinary man doubts nothing and suspects nothing. HENRI FRÉDÉRIC AMIEL (1821–1881), *Journal intime,* 1873–74.

Philosophy means the complete liberty of the mind, and therefore independence of all social, political, or religious prejudice. . . . It loves one thing only—truth. HENRI FRÉDÉRIC AMIEL (1821–1881), *Journal intime,* 1873–84.

A lively, disinterested, persistent loking for truth is extraordinarily rare. Action and faith enslave thought, both of them in order not to be troubled or inconvenienced by reflection, criticism or doubt. HENRY FRÉDÉRIC AMIEL (1821–1881), *Journal intime,* 1873–84.

I don't believe or disbelieve anything I don't understand. GERTRUDE ATHERTON (1857–1948), *Senator North,* 1900.

People everywhere enjoy believing things that they know are not true. It spares them the ordeal of thinking for themselves and taking responsibility for what they know. BROOKS ATKINSON (1894–1984), *Once around the Sun,* 1951.

Weary the path that does not challenge. Doubt is an incentive to truth and patient inquiry leadeth the way. HOSEA BALLOU (1771–1852).

Only reason can convince us of those three fundamental truths without a recognition of which there can be no effective liberty: that what we believe is not necessarily true; that what we like is not necessarily good; and that all questions are open. CLIVE BELL (1881–1964), *Civilization,* 1928.

In order to get the truth, conflicting arguments and expressions must be allowed. There can be no freedom without choice, no sound choice without knowledge. DAVID K. BERNINGHAUSEN, *Arrogance of the Censor,* 1982.

The crying need of today is to detach ourselves. And all you require is a sense of elegance; to regard the general situation with a modicum of skepticism. UGO BETTI (1892–1953), *The Fugitive,* 1953.

Cynic, n. A blackguard whose faulty vision sees things as they are, not as they ought to be. AMBROSE BIERCE (1842–1914), *Devil's Dictionary,* 1906.

A good writer of history is a guy who is suspicious. Suspicion marks the real difference between the man who wants to write honest history and the one who'd rather write a good story. JIM BISHOP (1907–1987), *New York Times,* February 5, 1955.

Every sentence I utter must be understood not as an affirmation, but as a question. NIELS BOHR (1885–1962), *New York Times Book Review,* 1957.

There is no absolute knowledge. And those who claim it, whether they are scientists or dogmatists, open the door to tragedy. All information is imperfect. We have to treat it with humility. J. BRONOWSKI (1908–1974), *The Ascent of Man,* 1973.

To believe only possibilities, is not faith, but mere philosophy. SIR THOMAS BROWNE (1605–1682), *Religio Medici,* 1642.

The mortalist enemy unto knowledge, and that which hath done the greatest execution unto truth, has been a peremptory adhesion unto authority, and especially our belief upon the dictates of antiquities. SIR THOMAS BROWNE (1605–1682), *Religio Medici,* 1642.

There is no such source of error as the pursuit of absolute truth. SAMUEL BUTLER (1835–1902), Notebooks, 1912.

We are not certain, we are never certain. If we were we could reach some conclusions, and we could, at least, make others take us seriously. ALBERT CAMUS (1913–1960), *The Fall,* 1956.

I grow daily to honor facts more and more, and theory less and less. THOMAS CARLYLE (1795–1881).

Skepticism means, not intellectual doubt alone, but moral doubt. THOMAS CARLYLE (1795–1881), Lecture, May 19, 1840.

It is assumed that the skeptic has no bias; whereas he has a very obvious bias in favor of skepticism. GILBERT KEITH CHESTERTON (1874–1936), *All Things Considered.*

[Intellectuals give in to] the noble temptation to see too much in everything. GILBERT KEITH CHESTERTON (1874–1936).

Materialists and madmen never have doubts. GILBERT KEITH CHESTERTON (1874–1936), *Orthodoxy.*

It is wrong always, everywhere, and for everyone, to believe anything upon insufficient evidence. W. K. CLIFFORD (1845–1879).

The business of the philosopher is well done if he succeeds in raising genuine doubt. MORRIS R. COHEN (1880–1947), *A Dreamer's Journey,* 1949.

Never be afraid to doubt, if only you have the disposition to believe, and doubt in order that you may end in believing the truth. SAMUEL TAYLOR COLERIDGE (1772–1834), *Aids to Reflection,* 1825.

[Freethinking is] the use of the understanding in endeavoring to find out the meaning of any proposition whatsoever, in considering the nature of the evidence for or against, and in judging of it according to the seeming force or weakness of the evidence. ANTHONY COLLINS (1676–1729).

Doubt is the vestibule which all must pass, before they enter into the temple of truth. CHARLES CALEB COLTON (1780–1832), *Lacon,* 1825.

Curiosity is free-wheeling intelligence. It endows the people who have it with a generosity in argument and a serenity in their own mode of life which springs from the cheerful willingness to let life take the forms it will. ALISTAIR COOKE, "The Art of Curiosity," *Vogue,* January 1953.

The ability to discriminate between that which is true and that which is false is one of the last attainments of the human mind. JAMES FENNIMORE COOPER (1789–1851), *The American Democrat,* 1838.

Suspicion is a thing very few people can entertain without letting the hypothesis turn, in their minds, into fact. DAVID CORT, *Social Astonishments,* 1963.

I have steadily endeavored to keep my mind free so as to give up any hypothesis, however much beloved, as soon as the facts are shown to be opposed to it. CHARLES DARWIN (1809–1882), *Life and Letters of Charles Darwin,* 1888.

The skeptic does not mean him who doubts, but him who investigates or researches, as opposed to him who asserts and thinks he has found. MIGUEL de UNAMUNO y JUGO (1864–1936), *Essays and Soliloquies,* 1924.

Nothing is easier than self-deceit. For what each man wishes, that he also believes to be true. DEMOSTHENES (385–322 B.C.).

Prudent minds have as a natural gift one safeguard which is the common possession of all, and this applies especially to the dealings of democracies with dictatorships. What is this safeguard? Skepticism. This you must preserve. DEMOSTHENES (385–322 B.C.).

If you would be a real seeker after truth, it is necessary that at least once in your life you doubt, as far as possible, all things. RENÉ DESCARTES (1596–1650), *Principles of Philosophy,* 1644.

To be genuinely thankful, we must be willing to sustain and protract that state of doubt which is the stimulus to thorough inquiry, so as not to accept an idea or make a positive assertion of belief, until justifying reasons have been found. JOHN DEWEY (1859–1952), *How We Think,* 1910.

What has not been examined impartially has not been well examined. Skepticism is therefore the first step toward truth. DENIS DIDEROT (1713–1784), *Pensées philosophiques,* 1746.

Doubt is an element of criticism, and the tendency of criticism is necessarily skeptical. BENJAMIN DISRAELI (1804–1881), 1864.

Who shall forbid a wise skepticism, seeing that there is no practical question on which anything more than an approximate solution can be had? RALPH WALDO EMERSON (1803–1882), *Representative Men,* 1850.

No facts are to me sacred; none are profane; I simply experiment, an endless seeker with no Past at my back. RALPH WALDO EMERSON (1803–1882), *Essays,* 1841.

Man's most valuable trait is a judicious sense of what not to believe. EURIPIDES (480–405 B.C.), *Helen,* 412 B.C.

The civilized man has a moral obligation to be skeptical, to demand the credentials of all statements that claim to be facts. BERGAN EVANS (1904–1978), *The Natural History of Nonsense,* 1946.

Freedom of speech and freedom of action [is meaningless] without freedom to think. And there is no freedom of thought without doubt. BERGEN EVANS (1904–1978), *The Natural History of Nonsense,* 1946.

We need tough-minded thinkers, gadflies, doubters. Doubt is an angel, not a devil; it assumes an order of truth. Only through the agony of doubt can we have the courage to be. MARSHALL W. FISHWICK, *Saturday Review,* December 21, 1963.

Stupidity consists in wanting to reach conclusions. We are a thread, and we want to know the whole cloth. GUSTAV FLAUBERT (1821–1880), Letters, 1850.

Increasingly constructive doubt is the sign of advancing civilization. JEROME D. FRANK (1889–1957), *Law and the Modern Man,* 1930.

The greatest and noblest pleasure which we have in this world is to discover new truths, and the next is to shake off old prejudices. FREDERICK the GREAT (1712–1786).

It cannot be demanded that we should prove everything, because that is impossible; but we can require that all propositions used without proof be expressly declared to be so. . . . GOTTLOB FREGE (1848–1925).

The quest for certainty blocks the search for meaning. Uncertainty is the very condition to impel man to unfold his powers. ERICH FROMM (1900–1980), *Man for Himself,* 1947.

On carelessly made or insufficient observations how many fine theories are built up which do not bear examination. ANDRÉ GIDE (1869–1951), Journals, August 5, 1931.

It is much easer to recognize error than to find truth; error is superficial and may be corrected; truth lies hidden in the depths. JOHANN WOLFGANG von GOETHE (1749–1832).

We know accurately only when we know little; with knowledge doubt enters. JOHANN WOLFGANG von GOETHE (1749–1832).

The deepest, the only theme of human history, compared to which all others are of subordinate importance, is the conflict of skepticism with faith. JOHANN WOLFGANG von GOETHE (1749–1832), *Wisdom and Experience.*

What probably distorts everything in life is that one is convinced one is speaking the truth because one says what one thinks. SACHA GUITRY (1885–1957), *Toutes Réflexions Faites,* 1949.

The tolerance of the skeptic . . . accepts the most diverse and indeed the most contradictory opinions, and keeps all his suspicions for the "dogmatist." JEAN GUITTON, *Difficulties of Believing,* 1948.

A society committed to the search for truth must give protection to, and set a high value upon, the independent and original mind, however angular, however rasping, however socially unpleasant it may be; for it is upon such minds, in large measure, that the effective search for truth depends. CARYL HASKINS, *New York Times,* December 9, 1963.

Every judgment teeters on the brink of error. To claim absolute knowledge is to become monstrous. Knowledge is an unending adventure at the edge of uncertainty. FRANK HERBERT, *Dune,* 1965.

He that knows nothing doubts nothing. GEORGE HERBERT (1593–1633), *Outlandish Proverbs,* 1640.

Intellectualism, though by no means confined to doubters, is often the sole piety of the skeptic. RICHARD HOFSTADTER (1916–1970), *Anti-Intellectualism in American Life,* 1963.

To have doubted one's own first principles, is the mark of a civilized man. OLIVER WENDELL HOLMES, JR. (1841–1935).

Rough work, iconoclasm, but the only way to get at truth. OLIVER WENDELL HOLMES, SR. (1809–1894).

The longing for certainty and repose is in every human mind. But certainty is generally an illusion and repose is not the destiny of man. OLIVER WENDELL HOLMES, SR. (1809–1894).

Life is a paradox. Every truth has its counterpart which contradicts it; and every philosopher supplies the logic for his own undoing. ELBERT HUBBARD (1856–1915), *The Notebook,* 1927.

Every great advance in natural knowledge has involved the absolute rejection of authority. THOMAS HENRY HUXLEY (1825–1895).

It is wrong for a man to say that he is certain of the objective truth of any proposition unless he can produce evidence which logically justifies that certainty. THOMAS HENRY HUXLEY (1825–1895), 1889.

I am too much of a skeptic to deny the possibility of anything. THOMAS HENRY HUXLEY (1825–1895), 1886.

What are the moral convictions most fondly held by barbarous and semi-barbarous people? They are the convictions that authority is the soundest basis of belief; that merit attaches to readiness to believe; that the doubting disposition is a bad one, and skepticism is a sin. THOMAS HENRY HUXLEY (1825–1895).

The improver of natural knowledge absolutely refused to acknowledge authority, as such. For him, skepticism is the highest of duties; blind faith the one unpardonable sin. THOMAS HENRY HUXLEY (1825–1895), *On the Advisableness of Improving Natural Knowledge,* 1866.

The deepest sin against the human mind is to believe things without evidence. THOMAS HENRY HUXLEY (1825–1895).

Doubt is the beginning, not the end, of wisdom. GEORGE ILES (1852–1942), *Jottings.*

Too much doubt is better than too much credulity. ROBERT G. INGERSOLL (1833–1899), "How to Reform Mankind."

History fades into fable; fact becomes clouded with doubt and controversy; the inscription molders from the tablet; the statue falls from the pedestal. Columns, arches, pyramids, what are they but heaps of sand; and their epitaths, but characters written in the dust. WASHINGTON IRVING (1783–1859), *The Sketch-Book,* 1820.

Man is fed with fables through life, and leaves it in the belief he knows something of what has been passing, when in truth he has known nothing but what has passed under his own eye. THOMAS JEFFERSON (1743–1826), U.S. President, Letter to Thomas Cooper, 1823.

There are those who feel an imperative need to believe, for whom the values of a belief are proportionate, not to its truth, but to its definiteness. Incapable of either admitting the existence of contrary judgments or of suspending their own, they supply the place of knowledge by turning other men's conjectures into dogmas. C. E. M. JOAD (1891–1953), *The Recovery of Belief,* 1952.

Every good historian, is almost by definition, a revisionist. He looks at the accepted view of a particular historic episode or period with a very critical eye. PAUL JOHNSON, *Insight,* May 5, 1986.

Curiosity is one of the permanent and certain characteristics of a vigorous intelligence. SAMUEL JOHNSON (1709–1784), *The Rambler,* 1750-52.

The word "belief" is a difficult thing for me. I don't believe. I must have a reason for a certain hypothesis. Either I know a thing, and then I know it—I don't need to believe it. CARL GUSTAV JUNG (1875–1961).

Mistakes are, after all, the foundations of truth, and if a man does not know what a thing is, it is at least an increase in knowledge if he knows what it is not. CARL GUSTAV JUNG (1875–1961).

Uncertainty is the worst of all evils until the moment when reality makes us regret uncertainty. ALPHONSE KARR (1808–1890), *L'Espirit d'A. Karr,* 1977.

The progress of science is strewn, like an ancient desert trail, with the bleached skeletons of discarded theories which once seemed to possess eternal life. ARTHUR KOESTLER (1905–1983), Address to the PEN Club, 1976.

The central theme of modern philosophy is skepticism. Given the intense confrontation between religion and science, it became an important weapon in the hands of philosophers and scientists, who wished to liberate themselves from the dead hand of authoritarian theology. PAUL KURTZ, *The Transcendental Temptation,* 1986.

No theory is ultimately confirmed decisively, since we may be mistaken and new data may be uncovered. A theory is only as good as the evidence adduced in its support; and this is often only comparative. PAUL KURTZ, *The Transcendental Temptation,* 1986.

Everyone believes very easily what he fears or desires. JEAN de LA FONTAINE (1621–1695), "The Wolf and the Fox," 1671.

People in general have no notion of the sort and amount of evidence often needed to prove the simplest fact. PETER MERE LATHAM (d. 1875), *Collected Works.*

The problem of belief, sometimes confused with that of knowledge, is nevertheless strongly distinct from it. To know and to believe are different things not having the same genesis. . . . A belief is an act of faith of unconscious origin which forces to admit as an entity an idea, an opinion, an explanation, a doctrine. Reason is foreign to its formation. By the time a belief tries to justify itself, it is already formed. GUSTAVE LE BON (1841–1931), *Opinions and Beliefs,* 1911.

It is so much easier to assume than to prove; it is so much less painful to believe than to doubt; there is such a charm in the repose of prejudice, when no discordant voice jars upon the harmony of belief. W. E. H. LECKY (1838–1903), *A History of Rationalism,* 1900.

To believe with certainty we must begin with doubting. STANISLAUS LESZCYNSKI (1677–1766), 1763.

Authority has every reason to fear the skeptic, for authority can rarely survive in the face of doubt. ROBERT LINDNER (1914–1956), *Must You Conform?,* 1956.

The tendency of the casual mind is to pick out or stumble upon a sample which supports or defies its prejudices, and then to make it representative of a whole class. WALTER LIPPMANN (1889–1974), *Public Opinion,* 1922.

One unerring mark of the love of truth is not entertaining any proposition with greater assurance than the proofs it is built upon will warrant. JOHN LOCKE (1632–1704), *An Essay concerning Human Understanding,* 1690.

Faith is the assent to any proposition not made out by the deduction of reason but upon the credit of the proposer. JOHN LOCKE (1632–1704), *An Essay concerning Human Understanding,* 1690.

The strength of our persuasions is no evidence at all of their own rectitude: crooked things may be as stiff and inflexible as straight and men may be as positive and preemptory in error as in truth. JOHN LOCKE (1632–1704), *An Essay concerning Human Understanding,* 1690.

A wise skepticism is the first attribute of a good critic. JAMES RUSSELL LOWELL (1819–1891), *Among My Books,* 1870.

Our duty is to believe that for which we have sufficient evidence, and to suspend our judgment when we have not. JOHN LUBBOCK (1803–1865).

All uncertainty is fruitful . . . so long as it is accompanied by the wish to understand. ANTONIO MACHADO (1875–1939), *Juan de Mairena,* 1943.

Men in general judge more for appearances than from reality. All men have eyes, but few men have the gift of penetration. NICOLO MACHIAVELLI (1469–1527), *The Prince,* 1513.

For the great majority of mankind are satisfied with appearance, as though they were realities, and are often more influenced by the things that seem than by those that are. NICCOLO MACHIAVELLI (1469–1527), *Discourses,* 1513–1517.

If truth is a value it is because it is true and not because it is brave to speak it. W. SOMERSET MAUGHAM (1874–1965), 1938.

The intensity of a conviction that a hypothesis is true has no bearing on whether it is true. PETER MEDAWAR, 1979.

Men become civilized, not in proportion to their willingness to believe but in proportion to their willingness to doubt. H. L. MENCKEN (1880–1956).

The curse of man, and cause of nearly of all his woes, is his stupendous capacity for believing the incredible. H. L. MENCKEN (1880–1956).

The most costly of all follies is to believe passionately in the palpably not true. H. L. MENCKEN (1880–1956), *A Mencken Chrestomathy,* 1949.

Moral certainty is always a sign of cultural inferiority. The more uncivilized the man, the surer he is that he knows precisely what is right and what is wrong. All human progress, even in morals, has been the work of men who have doubted the current moral values, not of men who have whooped them up and tried to inforce them. The truly civilized man is always skeptical and tolerant. H. L. MENCKEN (1880–1956), *Minority Report.*

The historian's first duties are sacrilege and the mocking of false gods. They are his indispensable instruments for establishing the truth. JULES MICHELET (1798–1874), *History of France,* 1833.

The fateful tendency of mankind to leave off thinking about a thing when it is no longer doubtful, is the cause of half their errors. A contemporary author has well spoken of "the deep slumber of a decided opinion." JOHN STUART MILL (1806–1873), *On Liberty,* 1859.

There is no such thing as absolute certainty, but there is assurance sufficient for the purposes of human life. JOHN STUART MILL (1806–1873), *On Liberty,* 1859.

A sound belief is always accompanied by a sane skepticism. It is only by disbelieving in some things that we can ever believe in other things. Faith does not mean credulity. SAMUEL H. MILLER, *The Great Realities,* 1955.

I see men ordinarily more eager to discover a reason for things than to find out whether things are so. MICHEL de MONTAIGNE (1533–1592), *Essays,* 1588.

Man prefers to believe what he prefers to be true. MICHEL de MONTAIGNE (1533–1592), *Essays.*

We should not investigate facts by the light of arguments, but arguments by the light of facts. MYSON, of Chen, 600 B.C.

The path of sound credence is through the thick forest of skepticism. GEORGE JEAN NATHAN (1882–1958), *Materia Critica,* 1924.

The desire for a strong faith is not the proof of a strong faith, rather the opposite. If one has it one may permit oneself the beautiful luxury of skepticism: one is secure enough, firm enough, fixed enough for it. FRIEDRICH NIETZSCHE (1844–1900), *Twilight of the Idols,* 1888.

Great intellects are skeptical. FRIEDRICH NIETZSCHE (1844–1900), *The Antichrist,* 1888.

Convictions are more dangerous enemies of truth than lies. FRIEDRICH NIETZSCHE (1844–1900), *Thus Spake Zarathustra,* 1883-92.

To become properly acquainted with a truth we must first have disbelieved it, and disputed against it. NOVALIS (1772–1801), Fragments, late 18th c.

There is nothing more effectual in showing us the weakness of any habitual fallacy or assumption than to hear it sympathetically through the ears, as it were, of a skeptic. MARGARET OLIPHANT (1828–1887), *Phoebe Junior,* 1876.

The greatest disorder of the mind is to let will direct belief. LOUIS PASTEUR (1822–1895).

Doubt is an uneasy and dissatisfied state from which we struggle to free ourselves and pass into the state of belief; while the latter is a calm and satisfactory state which we do not wish to avoid, or to change to a belief in anything else. CHARLES S. PEIRCE (1839–1914), *The Fixation of Belief,* 1877.

All the progress we have made in philosophy, that is, all that has been made since the Greeks, is the result of that methodical skepticism which is the element of human freedom. CHARLES S. PEIRCE (1839–1914), *Selected Writings*.

Doubt is the key to knowledge. PERSIAN PROVERB.

Doubt is intellectual self-opposition. It occurs when one's intuitive self and one's analytical self come into contradiction with each other. But doubt does not destroy one's power of intellectual performance, but rather strengthens and enhances it. FORREST H. PETERSON, *A Philosophy of Man and Society,* 1970.

To doubt everything or to believe everything are to equally convenient solutions: both dispense with the necessity for reflection. JULES HENRI POINCARÉ (1854–1912), *The Science of Hypothesis.*

It is not the possession of knowledge, of irrefutable truths, that constitutes the man of science, but the disinterested, incessant search for truth. SIR KARL POPPER, 1935.

It is only after doubt has come that intellectual belief arises. To entertain reasons for believing in the existence of a thing presupposes the possibility of its nonexistence. JAMES BISSET PRATT (1875–1944), *The Psychology of Religion and Belief,* 1907.

What a state of society is this in which freethinker is a term of abuse, and in which doubt is regarded as sin. W. WINWOOD READE, *The Martyrdom of Man,* 1972.

Facts have a cruel way of substituting themselves for fancies. There is nothing more remorseless, just as there is nothing more helpful, than truth. WILLIAM C. REDFIELD, Address, Case School, May 27, 1915.

Cynicism is a euphemism for realism. Seeing things as they really are, instead of the way we'd like them to be. HARRY RUBY.

Every man is encompassed by a cloud of comforting convictions which move with him like flies on a summer day. BERTRAND RUSSELL (1872–1970).

Dogmatism and skepticism are both, in a sense, absolute philosophies; one is certain of knowing, the other of not knowing. What philosophy should dissipate is certainty, whether of knowledge or of ignorance. BERTRAND RUSSELL (1872–1970), *Unpopular Essays,* 1950.

The fundamental cause of trouble in the world today is that the stupid are cocksure while the intelligent are full of doubt. BERTRAND RUSSELL (1872–1970).

It is undesirable to believe a proposition when there is no ground whatever for supposing it true. BERTRAND RUSSELL (1872–1970), *Skeptical Essays,* 1950.

All knowledge is in some degree doubtful, and we cannot say what degree of doubtfulness makes it cease to be knowledge, any more that we can say how much loss of hair makes a man bald. BERTRAND RUSSELL (1872–1979), *Human Knowledge: Its Growth and Limits,* 1948.

Skepticism is a discipline fit to purify the mind of prejudice and render it all the more apt, when the time comes, to believe and to act wisely. GEORGE SANTAYANA (1863–1952), *Skepticism and Animal Faith,* 1923.

When all beliefs are challenged together, the just and necessary ones have a chance to step forward and to reestablish themselves alone. GEORGE SANTAYANA (1863–1952), *The Life of Reason,* 1905.

The majority of thinkers agree that one of the important lessons of history is that in science there are no absolute guarantees. No matter how well founded a given belief may be, its truth cannot be established with ultimate certainty. GEORGE N. SCHLESINGER, *The Range of Epistemic Logic,* 1985.

The thesis of the ever-present possibility of error is called fallibilism. . . . The fallibilist may concede knowledge but not certainty. GEORGE N. SCHLESINGER, *The Range of Epistemic Logic,* 1985.

I always thought it better to allow myself to doubt before I decided, than to expose myself to the misery after I had decided, of doubting whether I had decided rightly and justly. JOHN SCOTT, LORD ELDON (1751–1838), in *Life of Lord Eldon* (Horis Twiss, ed.), 1844.

One pattern is a tendency toward intolerance of ambiguity. An individual may develop a propensity to perceive and evaluate things only as falling into definite categories, and be unable to distinguish nuances or intermediate grades. GEORGE SERBAN, M.D., *The Tyranny of Magical Thinking,* 1982.

Modest doubt is call'd the beacon of the wise. WILLIAM SHAKESPEARE (1564–1616), *Troilus and Cressida,* 1601-02.

The power of accurate observation is commonly called cynicism by those who have not got it. GEORGE BERNARD SHAW (1856–1950).

The fact that a believer is happier than a skeptic is no more to the point than a drunken man is happier than a sober one. GEORGE BERNARD SHAW (1856–1950).

It is not disbelief that is dangerous to our society, it is belief. GEORGE BERNARD SHAW (1856–1950), *Androcles and the Lion,* 1912.

Research is fundamentally a state of mind involving continual reexamination of doctrines and axioms upon which current thought and action are based. It is, therefore, critical of existing practices. THEOBALD SMITH, *American Journal of Medical Science,* vol. 178, 1929.

The authoritarian sets up some book, or man, or tradition to establish the truth. The freethinker sets up reason and private judgment to discover the truth. . . . It takes the highest courage to utter unpopular truths. HERBERT SPENCER (1820–1903), *Freedom and Its Fundamentals.*

Knowledge consists in understanding the evidence that establishes a fact, not in the belief that it is a fact. CHARLES T. SPRADLING, *Liberty and the Great Libertarians.*

A man should never be ashamed to own he has been in the wrong, which is saying, in other words, that he is wiser today than he was yesterday. JONATHAN SWIFT (1667–1745), 1711

You can prove almost anything with the evidence of a small enough segment of time. How often, in any search for truth, the answer of the minute is positive, the answer of the hour qualified, and the answers of the year contradictory. EDWIN WAY TEALE (1889–1980), *Circle of the Seasons,* 1953.

There lives more faith in honest doubt, believe me, than in half the creeds. ALFRED, LORD TENNYSON (1809–1892), *In Memoriam,* 1850.

No way of thinking or doing, however ancient, can be trusted without proof. What everybody echoes or in silence passes by as true today may turn out to be falsehood tomorrow, mere smoke of opinion. . . . HENRY DAVID THOREAU (1817–1862), *Walden,* 1854.

As a rule people fear truth. Each truth we discover in nature or social life destroys the crutches on which we used to lean. ERNST TOLLER (1893–1939).

Freethinkers are those who are willing to use their minds without prejudice and without fearing to understand things that clash with their own customs, privileges, or beliefs. This state of mind is not common, but it is essential for right thinking; where it is absent, discussion is apt to become worse than useless. LEO TOLSTOY (1828–1910), *War and Peace,* 1862.

Disinterested intellectual curiosity is the blood of real civilization. G. M. TREVELYAN (1876–1962), *English Social History,* 1942.

Ever insurgent let me be, / Make me more daring than devout; / From sleek contentment keep me free, / And fill me with a buoyant doubt. LOUIS UNTERMEYER (1885–1977).

That which has been believed by everyone, always and everywhere, has every chance of being false. PAUL VALÉRY (1871–1945), *Tel quel I,* 1943.

The unexamined idea, to paraphrase Socrates, is not worth having; and a society whose ideas are never explored for possible error may eventually find its foundations insecure. MARK van DOREN (1894–1973), *Man's Right to Knowledge,* 1954.

The outcome of any serious research can only be to make two questions grow where only one grew before. THORSTEN VEBLEN (1857–1929), *The Place of Science in Modern Civilization.*

Clearly it is not reason that has failed. What has failed—as it has always failed—is the attempt to achieve certainty, to reach an absolute, to find the course of human events to a final end. . . . It is not reason that has promised to eliminate risk in human undertakings; it is the emotional needs of men. ALLEN WHEELIS, *The Quest for Identity,* 1958.

[Intolerance of ambiguity] can be defined as an inability to recognize that a situation is ambiguous, that is, that the situation cannot yet be put clearly and confidently into a single familiar category, and consequently an inability to suspend judgment while examining the available evidence more carefully. RALPH K. WHITE, *Nobody Wanted War,* 1970.

There are no whole truths; all truths are half-truths. It is trying to treat them as whole truths that plays the devil. ALFRED NORTH WHITEHEAD (1861–1947), *Dialogues,* 1954.

State Socialism, Marxism-Leninism

The Christian opium makes the people passive, the Communist opium incites them to revolt. RAYMOND ARON (1905–1983), *The Great Debate*, 1965.

In Marxist eschatology, the proletariat is in the role of the collective savior. The expressions used by the young Marx leave one in no doubt as to the Judaeo-Christian origins of the myth of the class elected through suffering for the redemption of humanity. RAYMOND ARON (1905–1983), *The Opium of the Intellectuals*, 1957.

The left was born and took shape in opposition—the child of an idea. It denounced a social order which, like all things human, was indeed imperfect. . . . The left represented, not liberty against authority, or the people against the privileged few, but one power against another, one privileged class against another. RAYMOND ARON (1905–1983), *The Opium of the Intellectuals*, 1957.

I detest communism, because it is the negation of liberty. . . . I am not a communist because communism concentrates and absorbs all the powers of society into the state. MIKHAIL BAKUNIN (1814–1876), *God and the State*, 1882.

The expressions "learned socialist," "scientific socialism," et., which continuously appear in the speeches and writings of the followers of . . . Marx, prove that the pseudo-People's State will be nothing but a despotic control of the populace by a new and not at all numerous aristocracy of real and pseudo-scientists. The "uneducated" people will be totally relieved of the cares of administration, and will be treated as a regimented herd. A beautiful liberation, indeed! MIKHAEL BAKUNIN (1814–1876), *Critique of the Marxist Theory of the State*.

As a religion, Marxism is a secularized form of the idea of predestination. NICHOLAS BERDYAEV, *The Realm of Spirit and the Realm of Caesar*, 1952.

Socialism purports to do away with the inequalities and the savage competition of capitalist class societies. Even in its mildest forms, however, socialism creates new inequalities and new forms of competition. These inequalities are not the result of "class struggle" but of the hierarchical order of bureaucracy. The competition is in endless maneuvering for position within the bureaucratic hierarchies . . . stratification comes to be dominated by political rather than economic criteria. PETER L. BERGER, *Pyramids of Sacrifice: Political Ethics and Social Change*, 1974.

A basic contradiction of most of the existing socialist systems is precisely this political fact—the contradiction of a dictatorship that defines itself as a democracy. Marxist legitimations of this fact have largely involved a gigantic debasement of language. PETER L. BERGER, *Pyramids of Sacrifice: Political Ethics and Social Change,* 1974.

The strongly redistributionist state must become ever more intrusive, and the final trade-off may be between equality and liberty. PETER L. BERGER, *The Capitalist Revolution,* 1986.

In a society where everything is nationalized and is the property of the state, anybody can be expropriated and subject to export. . . . In Germany the phrase for chattel slaves or indentured servants was *Leibeigenen,* for the bodies belonged to their owners; now we have the new concept of *Geisteigene,* for minds and spirits are also part of the new social property relations. When a bureaucracy considers itself to be the owner of literature, then it has the absolute personal right not only to cultivate its own garden but also to remove ruthlessly such weeds as it deems harmful. FRANÇOIS BONDY, *Encounter,* April 1981.

Communists are bound together by no secret oath. The tie that binds them across the frontiers of nations, across barriers of language and differences of class and education, in defiance of religion, morality, truth, law, honor, the weakness of the body and the irresolutions of the mind, even unto death, is the simple conviction: It is necessary to change the world. Their power, whose nature baffles the rest of the world, because in a large measure the rest of the world has lost that power, is the power to hold convictions and act upon them. WHITTAKER CHAMBERS (1901–1961), *Witness,* 1952.

Both capitalism and communism rest on the same idea: a centralization of wealth which destroys private property. GILBERT KEITH CHESTERTON (1874–1936), *The End of the Armistice,* 1936.

One of the attractions of communism is that . . . the will and conscience are reposed in a depository of granite solidity under a guardianship that resolves all ethical and moral problems. MARQUIS W. CHILDS and DOUGLAS CATER, *Ethics in a Business Society,* 1954.

Of all tyrannies in history the Bolshevik tyranny is the worst, the most destructive, the most degrading. WINSTON CHURCHILL (1874–1965), Speech, 1919.

No socialist system can be established without a political police. WINSTON CHURCHILL (1874–1965), BBC Radio Speech, June 4, 1945.

Reactionary, n. One who opposes the party line, or Soviet or Communist policies for whatever reason; in general, any anti-Communist. ROY COLBY, *A Communese-English Dictionary,* 1972.

Self-Determination, n. The decision of a people, usually as a result of Soviet or Communist coercion, to establish a Soviet-oriented or Communist-oriented government. ROY COLBY, *A Communese-English Dictionary,* 1972.

Warmonger, n. Anyone who favors retaliation or defense against Soviet or Communist provocation, threats or aggression. ROY COLBY, *A Communese-English Dictionary,* 1972.

Every type of power besides being a means is at the same time an end— at least for those who aspire to it. Power is almost exclusively an end in communism, because it is both the source and the guarantee of all privileges. MILOVAN DJILAS, *The New Class,* 1957.

Contemporary communism is that type of totalitarianism which consists of three basic factors for controlling the people. The first is power; the second, ownership; the third, ideology. They are monopolized by the one and only political party. MILOVAN DJILAS, *The New Class,* 1957.

What is a communist? One who hath yearnings for equal division of unequal earnings. Idler or bungler, or both, he is willing, to fork out his copper and pocket your shilling. EBENEZER ELLIOTT (1781–1849), *Poetical Works,* 1840.

With the formation of the local committees [Committees for the Defense of the Revolution], the last refuge for the apolitical citizen or guilty anti-revolutionary has been turned down, the last set of excuses stripped away. . . . Nonparticipation has become . . . tantamount to failure to want to participate, which, in revolutionary Cuba, is a serious failure indeed. RICHARD FAGEN, *The Transformation of Political Culture in Cuba,* 1969.

The commonest weakness of left-wing radicalism, as we have seen, has been its disposition to assume that the destruction of an existing system of society in its entirety will necessarily be followed by something better. LOUIS J. HALLE, *The Ideological Imagination,* 1972.

Having awoken from their dogmatic slumber, the new philosophers are discovering the truth in a strikingly simple thought. The connection between the Gulag and Marx is obvious. It is not an accident which can be explained by bureaucracy, Stalinist deviation or Lenin's errors. Rather it is a direct and ineluctable logical consequence of Marxist princples. The classless society is not a messianic vision, but rather another name for terror. MONIQUE HIRSCHHORN, *Stanford French Review,* vol. 2, 1978.

The prospective member of a Communist party commits himself or herself to an intense and demanding set of activities and duties comparable, for some members at least, to that accepted by religious orders. ERIC J. HOBSBAWM, *Primitive Rebels,* 1958.

Totalitarianism is the possession of reality by a political idea—the idea of a socialist kingdom of heaven on earth, the redemption of humanity by political force. . . . It provides the meaning of a radical life. It is the solution that makes everything possible; it is the end that justifies the regrettable means. DAVID HOROWITZ, in *Political Passages* (John H. Bunzel, ed.), 1988.

Socialism is an earnest effort to get Nature to change the rules for the benefit of those who are tired of the game. ELBERT HUBBARD (1856–1915).

He [Karl Marx] is the apostle of class hatred, the founder of a semi-religion, which resembles some religions in its cruelty, fanaticism, and irrationality. WILLIAM RALPH INGE (1860–1954), *Assessments and Anticipation.*

The rule of the party knows no legal opposition, only opponents who must be "liquidated" because they are either ill-natured, owing to their origin or native character, or ill-disposed. Hence, the terrorism—which as a form of government maintains the fiction of the existence of dangerous enemies under various names, used to disparage the actual opposition of the basic human will to freedom: counterrevolutionaries, fascists, capitalists, nationalists, imperialists. KARL JASPERS (1883–1963), *The Future of Mankind,* 1961.

Far from being a classless society, Communism is governed by an elite as steadfast in its determination to maintain its perogatives as any oligarchy known to history. ROBERT F. KENNEDY (1925–1968), *The Pursuit of Justice,* 1964.

Marxian socialism must always remain a portent to the historians of Opinion— how a doctrine so illogical and so dull can have exercized so powerful and enduring an influence over the minds of men, and, through them, the events of history. JOHN MAYNARD KEYNES (1883–1946), *The End of Laissez-Faire,* 1926.

Leninism is a combination of two things which Europeans have kept for some centuries in different compartments of the soul—religion and business. JOHN MAYNARD KEYNES (1883–1946), *Essays in Persuasion,* 1933.

The party denied the free will of the individual—and at the same time it exacted its willing self-sacrifice. It denied his capacity to choose between two alternatives—and at the same time it demanded that he should always choose the right one. It denied his power to choose between good and evil—and at the same time is spoke accusingly of guilt and treachery. ARTHUR KOESTLER (1905–1983), *Darkness at Noon,* 1941.

Among the noble qualities of the Soviet citizen is class hatred. It is a sage and profound feeling of organic hatred toward the enemy—toward all the filthy, abominable remnants of the old world. KOMSOMOLSKAYA PRAVDA, quoted in *Time* magazine, October 7, 1935.

Communism and fascism are so much alike that most people are unable to observe any real differences between them. There is a general awareness that they have different names, fly different flags, and use abusive language toward each other. . . . [I]n both cases the means of production are in reality under the control of an unchallengeable dictatorship wielding unlimited power. KENNETH K. KROGH, *Saturday Review,* December 3, 1960.

The lack of well-grounded convictions, the absence of belief in truth create a dangerous hunger. And since nature abhors a vacuum, the absolutes of totalitarian systems find ready-made acolytes. ERIK von KUEHNELT-LEDDIHN, *Leftism Revisited,* 1990.

Socialism will bring in an efflorescence of morality, civilization, and science such as has never before been seen in the history of the world. FERDINAND LASALLE (1825–1864), *Worker's Program,* 1862.

Thanks to its promise of regeneration, thanks to the hope it flashes before all the disinherited of life, socialism is becoming a belief of a religious character rather than a doctrine. GUSTAVE LE BON (1841–1931), *The Psychology of Socialism,* 1898.

It is necessary . . . to resort to all sorts of stratagems, maneuvers and illegal methods, to evasion and subterfuges in order to penetrate the trade unions, to remain in them, and to carry on Communist work in them at all costs. V. I. LENIN (1870–1924), *Left-Wing Communism: An Infantile Disorder,* 1920.

The guillotine only terrorized, it only broke down active resistance. But this is not enough for us. . . . We have to break down passive resistance which doubtlessly is the most harmful and dangerous one. V. I. LENIN (1870–1924), in *The Guillotine at Work* (G. P. Maximoff).

Ideological talk and phrase mongering about political liberties should be disposed with; all that is just mere chatter and phrase mongering. We should get away from those phrases. V. I. LENIN (1870–1924), in *The Guillotine at Work* (G. P. Maximoff).

We do not have time to play at "oppositions" at "conferences." We will keep our political opponents . . . whether open or disguised as "nonparty," in prison. V. I. LENIN (1870–1924), *Selected Works,* 1937.

The nearer we come to the full military suppression of the bourgeoisie, the more dangerous becomes to us the high flood of petty-bourgeois anarchism. And the struggle against these elements cannot be waged with propaganda and agitation alone. . . . The struggle must also be waged by applying force and compulsion. V. I. LENIN (1870–1924), in *The Guillotine at Work* (G. P. Maximoff).

This network of agents will form the skeleton of the organization we need, namely, one that is sufficiently large to embrace the whole country; sufficiently tried and tempered unswervingly to carry out its own work under all circumstances, at all "turns" and in unexpected contingencies; sufficiently flexible to be able to avoid open battle against the overwhelming and concentrated forces of the enemy, and yet able to take advantage of the clumsiness of the enemy and attack him at a time and place where he least expects attack. V. I. LENIN (1870–1924), *Where to Begin,* 1901.

So long as the state exists there is no freedom. When there is freedom there will be no state. V. I. LENIN (1870–1924), *The State and Revolution,* 1917.

The state belongs to the sphere of coercion. It would be madness to renounce coercion, particularly in the epoch of the dictatorship of the proletariat. Here "administering" the administrator's approach is essential. V. I. LENIN (1870–1924), *Trade Unions, the Current Situation, and Mistakes of Trotsky and Bukharin,* 1921.

According to its form a strong revolutionary organization may also be described as a conspirative organization, because the French word *conspirative* means in Russian conspiracy, and we must have the utmost conspiracy for an organization of that kind. Secrecy as such is a necessary condition for such an organization that all the other conditions . . . must be surbordinated to it. V. I. LENIN (1870–1924), *What Is to Be Done?*, 1901–02.

The Communist parties must create a new type of periodical press for mass distribution among the workers; first, legal publications, which must learn, without calling themselves communist, and without announcing their affiliation with the party, to utilize every scrap of legality. V. I. LENIN (1870–1924), *Selected Works*, 1938.

Dictatorship is power based directly upon force and unrestricted by any laws. The revolutionary dictatorship of the proletariat is power won and maintained by the violence of the proletariat against the bourgeoisie, power that is unrestricted by any laws. V. I. LENIN (1870–1924), *Proletarian Revolution and the Renegade Kautsky*, 1918.

A democratic peace can be concluded only by proletarian governments after they have overthrown the rule of the bourgeoisie and begun to expropriate it. V. I. LENIN (1870–1924), *Collected Works*, vol. 23, 1917.

It is our duty as Communists to master all forms of struggle, to learn how to supplement with maximum rapidity one form with another, to substitute one for another, and to adapt our tactics to every change that is called forth by something other than our class, or our efforts. V. I. LENIN (1870–1924), *Left-Wing Communism: An Infantile Disorder*, 1920.

We must be able to agree to any sacrifice, and even, if need be, to resort to all sorts of tricks, slyness, illegal methods, evasion and concealment of truth. . . . V. I. LENIN (1870–1924), *Collected Works*, vol. 31, 1917.

Whoever expects that socialism will be achieved without a social revolution and the dictatorship of the proletariat is not a socialist. Dictatorship is power based on violence. V. I. LENIN (1870–1924), *The Disarmament Slogan*, 1916.

While at one time pacifists were single-mindedly devoted to the principles of nonviolence and reconciliation, today most pacifist groups defend the moral legitimacy of armed struggle and guerrilla warfare, and they praise and support the Communist regimes emerging from such conflicts. GUENTER LEWY, *Peace and Revolution: The Moral Crisis of American Pacifism*, 1988.

Criticism is not a passion of the head, but the head of a passion. It is not a lancet, but a weapon. Its object is an enemy it wants not to refute but to destroy . . . [it] is no longer an end in itself but simply a means. Its essential pathos is indignation. Its essential task, denunciation. KARL MARX (1818–1883), *Critique of Hegel's Philosophy of Law*, 1843.

Communism of every type and stripe brings with it an ideological straitjacket. Thought control, brain-washing, censorship, imprisonment, exile, mental and physical torture are the indispensable weapons of Communist rule. Totalitarianism is soulless. GEORGE MEANY, 1957.

For the fully developed, well-trained Communist, there is no conceivable area of life, of action, even of speculation, in which the judicious use of Marxist-Leninist theory cannot quickly yield certainties and clarities which fit with precision into the well-ordered pattern of his total outlook. FRANK S. MEYER, *The Moulding of Communists,* 1961.

Communist theory is powerful not because it is true; most obviously it is not. It is powerful because it is believed. Each aspect may be intellectually weak enough on its own, but in the total theoretical structure each strengthens the other and a unified view is created. Theories which, standing on their own, would be ludicrous take on the seeming luminosity of truth. FRANK S. MEYER, *The Moulding of Communists,* 1961.

Who is the reactionary? Everyone who opposes the inevitable historical processes, i.e., the Politburo police. The thesis of the "sin of the reactionary" is argued very cleverly: every perception is "oriented," i.e., at the very moment of perceiving we introduce our ideas into the material of our observations; only he sees reality truly who evaluates it in terms of the interests of the class that is the lever of the future, i.e., the proletariat. CZESLAW MILOSZ, *The Captive Mind,* 1953.

They don't ask much of you. They only want you to hate the things you love and to love the things that you hate. BORIS PASTERNAK (1890–1960), *Life* magazine, June 13, 1960.

[The nihilist] who tries to live without any beliefs [is] starved of social responsibility. . . . Marxism offered them a future, bearing unbounded promise to humanity . . . it endowed those who accepted it with a feeling of overwhelming moral superiority. They acquired a sense of righteousness. . . . MICHAEL POLYANI, *The Logic of Liberty,* 1951.

Marxists have been taught to think in terms not of institutions but of classes. Classes, however, never rule any more than nations. The rulers have always been certain persons. And, whatever class they may once have belonged to, once they are rulers they belong to the ruling class. SIR KARL POPPER, *Theories of History,* 1959.

The most characteristic element [of Marxists] seemed to be the incessant stream of confirmations, of observations which "verified" the theories in question; and this point was constantly emphasized by their adherents. A Marxist could not open a newspaper without finding on every page confirming evidence for his interpretation of history; not only in the news, but also in its presentation—which revealed the class bias of the paper—and especially, of course, in what the paper did not say. SIR KARL POPPER, *Conjectures and Refutations,* 1974.

In communism, inequality springs from placing mediocrity on a level with excellence. PIERRE-JOSEPH PROUDHON (1809–1865), *What Is Property?,* 1840.

Communism is inequality, but not as property is. Property is the exploitation of the weak by the strong. Communism is the exploitation of the strong by the weak. PIERRE-JOSEPH PROUDHON (1809–1865), *What Is Property?*, 1840.

The distinctive feature of totalitarian systems, and communism most notably of all, is the elaborately constructed apparatus of control which is inevitably set in place after the seizure of power. . . . Among authoritarian regimes, there is nothing comparable to the calculation, creative thinking, and long-range planning that totalitarianism devotes to the most mundane details of controlling society. ARCH PUDDINGTON, *Failed Utopias: Methods of Coercion in Communist Regimes*, 1988.

Cryptopolitics is not overt and channeled through "political" institutions, but covert, masquerading as the faithful performance of assigned organizational roles. It involves . . . biased reporting of information relevant to the formation or vetting of policy, informant networks or cliques, the use of personal powers to reward friends and punish enemies, and bias in the execution of policy so as to facilitate or prejudice its success or to favor certain affected interests rather than others. T. H. RIGBY, *Stalinism: Essays in Historical Interpretation*, 1977.

The Communist theory of the dictatorship assumes that ultimate success in achieving the goal is certain—so certain as to justify a generation at least of poverty, slavery, hatred, spying, forced labor, extinction of independent thought, and refusal to cooperate in any way with the nations that have heretical governments. BERTRAND RUSSELL (1872–1970), *Saturday Review*, 1951.

Should I betray the proletariat to serve truth, or betray truth in the name of the proletariat? JEAN-PAUL SARTRE (1905–1980), *Time* magazine, July 18, 1955.

The religious quality of Marxism also explains a characeristic attitude of the orthodox Marxist toward opponents. To him, as to any believer in a faith, the opponent is not merely in error but in sin. Dissent is dissapproved of not only intellectually but also morally. JOSEPH A. SCHUMPETER (1883–1950), *Capitalism, Socialism and Democracy*, 1942.

There is little reason to believe that this socialism will mean the advent of the civilization of which orthodox socialists dream. It is much more likely to present fascist features. That would be a strange answer to Marx's prayer. But history sometimes indulges in jokes of questionable taste. JOSEPH A. SCHUMPETER (1883–1950), *Capitalism, Socialism and Democracy*, 1942.

The deepest point of opposition between Marxism and Christianity comes from the fact that both are finally religious. ROGER L. SHINN, *Christianity and the Problem of History*, 1953.

The party as an ideological-political organization depends completely and exclusively on persuasion of the masses; whereas the state depends on force as well as on persuasion. . . . The methods of persuasion . . . are gaining more and more ground in the life of Soviet society, and under Communism they will become the sole regulator of relations among people. G. SHITAREV, *Politicheskoe Samoobrazovanie* 9 (1960).

There can be no breathing space in ideological warfare. On the ideological front, we must and we shall fight not by passive resistance but by an active and unceasing attack on our enemies. This is in accordance with our traditions. Let the enemy consider us nasty people. From the mouth of the enemy this is praise. K. SIMONOV, *Pravda,* November 22, 1946.

I have spent my whole life under a Communist regime, and I will tell you that a society without any objective legal scale is a terrible one indeed. But a society with no other scale than the legal one is not quite worthy of man, either. ALEXANDR SOLZHENITSYN, Commencement Address, Harvard University, 1978

With the Communist intellectuals I was always confronted by the fact that they had made a calculation when they became Communists which had changed the whole reality for them into the crudest black and white. . . . The Revolution was the beginning and the end, the sum of all sums. Someday, somewhere, everything would add up to the happy total which was the Dictatorship of the Proletariat and a Communist society. This way of thinking canceled out all experiential objections. STEPHEN SPENDER, *The God That Failed,* 1949.

It is impossible policy of course to preach general political freedom: during the epoch of the dictatorship of the proletariat there can be no policy of universal freedom in our country, i.e., no freedom of speech, press, etc., for the bourgeoisie. Our domestic policy reduces itself to granting a maximum of freedom to the proletarian strata, in denying even a minimum of freedom to the remnants of the bourgeois class. JOSEPH STALIN (1879–1953), *Selected Works,* vol. 4.

Communism is the death of the soul. It is the organization of total conformity— in short—of tyranny—and is committed to making tyranny universal. ADLAI E. STEVENSON (1900–1965), Nomination Speech, 1952.

Lenin was the first to discover that capitalism "inevitably" caused war; and he discovered this only when the First World War was already being fought. Of course he was right. Since every great state was capitalist in 1914, capitalism obviously "caused" the First World War; but just as obviously it had "caused" the previous generation of peace. A. J. P. TAYLOR, *The Origins of the Second World War,* 1962.

Democracy and socialism have nothing in common but one word: equality. But notice the difference: while democracy seeks equality in liberty, socialism seeks equality in restraint and servitude. ALEXIS de TOCQUEVILLE (1805– 1859), Speech, September 12, 1848.

The old religion which communism has revived is the worship of collective human power. ARNOLD J. TOYNBEE (1889–1975), *New York Times Magazine,* December 26, 1954.

Patriotism to the Soviet State is a revolutionary duty, whereas patriotism to a bourgeois state is treachery. LEON TROTSKY (1879–1940), *Disputed Barricade* (MacLean).

The dictatorship of the Communist party is maintained by recourse to every form of violence. LEON TROTSKY (1879–1940), *Terrorism and Communism,* 1924.

The problem of revolution as of war consists in breaking the will of the foe, forcing him to capitulate and accept the conditions of the conqueror. . . . The question as to who is to rule . . . will be decided on either side, not by references to the paragraphs of the constitution, but by the employment of all forms of violence. . . . War, like revolution, is founded upon intimidation. LEON TROTSKY (1879–1940), *Terrorism and Communism,* 1924.

State socialism . . . may be described as the doctrine that all the affairs of men should be managed by the government regardless of individual choice. BENJAMIN R. TUCKER (1854–1939), *State Socialism and Anarchism,* 1899.

The teaching of history is given the task of forming in youth a Marxist-Leninist world view, deep ideological convictions, a clear, class-oriented approach to phenomena of social life, Soviet patriotism, loyalty to proletarian international-ism, devotion to the party's cause, the task of developing a Communist attitude toward work, a feeling of duty and discipline, and irreconcilability to bourgeois ideology. U.S./USSR Textbook Study Project: Interim Report, 1981, in *Failed Utopias* (Arch Puddington), 1988.

Communist parties distrust intellectuals because these have a life outside the party and a will of their own. Poor workers or peasants who rise to become cadres are readier to agree with whatever the party proposes. The regime can count on the new status groups it creates. . . . Idealism soon wears thin, but dependence on the new order for good living, privilege, and power is solid. ROBERT WESSON, *Politics: Individual and State,* 1988.

Tolerance, Intolerance, and Prejudice

A reader seldom peruses a book with pleasure until he knows whether the writer of it be a black man or a fair man, of a mild or choleric disposition, married or a bachelor. JOSEPH ADDISON (1672–1719), *The Spectator,* 1714.

We may observe the behavior of some of the most zealous for orthodoxy, who have often great friendships and intimacies with vicious immoral men, provided they do but agree with them in the same scheme of belief. JOSEPH ADDISON (1672–1719), *The Spectator,* 1714.

Dogma is the convictions of one man imposed authoritatively upon others. FELIX ADLER (1851–1933).

Obstinacy / standing alone is the weakest of all things / in one whose mind is not possessed by wisdom. AESCHYLUS (525–456 B.C.)

He has the courage of his conviction and the intolerance of his courage. He is opposed to the death penalty for murder, but he would willingly have anyone electrocuted who disagreed with him on the subject. THOMAS BAILY ALDRICH (1836–1907), *Ponkapog Papers,* 1903.

A prejudice is an unwillingness to examine fairly the evidence and reasoning in behalf of a person or thing which is the object of prejudice. It is a prejudgment caused by indoctrination, conditioning, or some prior experience of a singularly pleasant or unpleasant character. A prejudice has strong and deep emotional support. ROBERT W. ALLEN and LORNE GREENE, *The Propaganda Game,* 1966.

Prejudice may be defined as thinking ill of others without sufficient warrant. GORDON ALLPORT (1897–1967), *The Nature of Prejudice,* 1954.

Some men are just as sure of the truth of their opinions as are others of what they know. ARISTOTLE (384–322 B.C.), *Nicomachean Ethics.*

The most fatal illusion is the settled point of view. Since life is growth and motion, a fixed point of view kills anybody who has one. BROOKS ATKINSON, *Once around the Sun,* 1951.

We tolerate differences of opinion in people who are familiar to us. But differences of opinion in people we do not know sound like heresy or plots. BROOKS ATKINSON, *Once around the Sun,* 1951.

Tolerance of diversity is imperative, because without it, life would lose its savor. Progress in the arts, in the sciences, in the patterns of social adjustment springs from diversity and depends upon a tolerance of individual deviations from conventional ways and attitudes. ALAN BARTH, *The Loyalty of Free Men,* 1951.

Hatred can at times be a positively joyous emotion. SIMONE de BEAUVOIR (1908–1986), *The Prime of Life,* 1962.

Other people have a nationality. The Irish and Jews have a psychosis. BRENDAN BEHAN (1923–1964), *Richard's Cork Leg.*

Conformities are called for much more eagerly today than yesterday; loyalties are tested far more severely; sceptics, liberals, individuals with a taste for private life and their own inner standards of behavior, are objects of fear or derision and targets of persecution for either side, execrated or despised by all the embattled parties in the great ideological wars of our time. SIR ISAIAH BERLIN, *Political Ideas in the Twentieth Century,* 1950.

Intolerance is natural and logical for in every dissenting opinion lies an assumption of superior wisdom. AMBROSE BIERCE (1842–1914), *The Devil's Dictionary,* 1906.

Accuse, v. To affirm another's guilt or unworth, most commonly as a justification of ourselves for having wronged him. AMBROSE BIERCE (1842–1914), *The Devil's Dictionary,* 1906.

Bigot, n. One who is obstinately and zealously attached to an opinion that you do not entertain. AMBROSE BIERCE (1842–1914), *The Devil's Dictionary,* 1906.

Prejudice, n. A vagrant opinion without visible means of support. AMBROSE BIERCE (1824–1914), *The Devil's Dictionary,* 1906.

Prejudices, strong prejudices, are visions about the way things are. They are divinations of the order of the whole of things, and hence the road to a knowledge of that whole is by way of erroneous opinions about it. Error is indeed our enemy, but it alone points the way to the truth and therefore deserves our respectful treatment. The mind that has no prejudices at the outset is empty. ALAN BLOOM, *The Closing of the American Mind,* 1987.

There is nothing that dies so hard and rallies so often as intolerance. The vices and passions which it summons to its support are the most ruthless and the most persistent harbored in the human breast. WILLIAM E. BORAH (1865–1940), U.S. Senator, Speech, April 24, 1929.

The essence of a heretic, that is of someone who has a particular opinion, is that he clings to his own ideas. JACQUES BÉNIGNE BOSSUET (1627–1704), *Histoire de Variations.*

Absolutism in morals is a guarantee of objectionable morals in the same way as absolutism in government is a guarantee of objectionable government. ROBERT BRIFFAULT (1876–1948), 1931.

Prejudices, it is well known, are most difficult to eradicate from the heart whose soil has never been loosened or fertilized by education; they grow there, firm as weeds among stones. CHARLOTTE BRONTË (1816–1855), *Jane Eyre,* 1847.

Sometimes we call a man a fascist simply because we dislike him. HEYWOOD BROUN (1888–1939).

Dialogue can be a very dangerous pastime, for it may force us to give up some of our most cherished caricatures—and these die hard. ROBERT McAFEE BROWN, *An American Dialogue,* 1960.

No man can justly censure or condemn another, because indeed no man truly knows another. SIR THOMAS BROWNE (1605–1682), *Religio Medici,* 1642.

Moral rigidity cultivates a positive contempt for political orientation in that it grants a higher value to words and deeds the more uncompromisingly they conform to ideals and ignore reality. HANS BUCHHEIM, *Totalitarian Rule,* 1962.

If you can impress any man with an absorbing conviction of the supreme importance of some moral or religious doctrine; if you can make him believe that those who reject that doctrine are doomed to eternal perdition; if you then give that man power, and by means of his ignorance blind him to the ulterior consequences of his own act,—he will infallibly persecute those who deny his doctrine. HENRY THOMAS BUCKLE, (1821–1862), *History of Civilization in England,* 1861.

Toleration is good for all, or it is good for none. EDMUND BURKE (1729–1797), Speech, House of Commons, 1773.

Morality, thou deadly bane, / Thy tens o'thousands thou hast slain! / Vain is his hope whose stay and trust is, / In moral mercy, truth and justice! ROBERT BURNS (1756–1796), *To Gavin Hamilton,* 1786.

It is the uncompromisingness with which dogma is held and not in the dogma or want of dogma that the danger lies. SAMUEL BUTLER (1835–1902), *The Way of All Flesh,* 1903.

How many crimes are committed simply because their authors could not endure being wrong. ALBERT CAMUS (1913–1960), *The Fall,* 1956.

It is sometimes said that toleration should be refused to the intolerant. In practice this would destroy it. . . . The only remedy for dogmatism and lies is toleration and the greatest possible liberty of expression. JOYCE CARY (1888–1957), *Power in Men,* 1939.

Everyone, whether cardinal or scientist, who believes that his own truth is complete and final must become a dogmatist. . . . The more sincere his faith, the more he is bound to persecute, to save others from falling into error. JOYCE CARY (1888–1957), *Power in Men,* 1939.

In the last analysis, we see only what we are prepared to see, what we have been taught to see. We eliminate and ignore everything that is not part of our prejudices. JEAN MARTIN CHARCOT (1825–1893), *De l'expectation,* 1857.

The peak of tolerance is most readily achieved by those who are not burdened by convictions. ALEXANDER CHASE, *Perspectives,* 1966.

We have a dark feeling of resistance towards people we have never met, and a profound and manly dislike of authors we have never read. GILBERT KEITH CHESTERTON (1874–1936), *Robert Browning,* 1902.

It is not bigotry to be certain we are right; but it is bigotry to be unable to imagine how we might possibly be wrong. GILBERT KEITH CHESTERTON (1874–1936), *The Catholic Church and Conversion,* 1926.

A man may be sure enough of something to be burned for it or to make war on the world, and yet be no inch nearer to being a bigot. He is only a bigot if he cannot understand that his dogma is dogma, even if it is true. GILBERT KEITH CHESTERTON (1874–1936), *Lunacy and Letters.*

Dogmatism does not mean the absence of thought, but the end of thought. GILBERT KEITH CHESTERTON (1874–1936).

The modern world is filled with men who hold dogmas so strongly that they do not even know they are dogmas. GILBERT KEITH CHESTERTON (1874–1936), *Heretics,* 1905.

Of course there is no absolute definition of madness except the definition which we should each endorse that madness is the eccentric behavior of somebody else. GILBERT KEITH CHESTERTON (1874–1936), *Lunacy and Letters.*

The essence of religious persecution is this: that the man who happens to have material power in the State, either by wealth or by official position, should govern his fellow-citizens not according to their religion or philosophy, but according to his own. GILBERT KEITH CHESTERTON (1874–1936), *All Things Considered.*

The rabble estimate few things according to their real value, most things according to their prejudices. MARCUS TULLIUS CICERO (106–43 B.C.)

Tolerance implies a respect for another person, not because he is wrong or even because he is right, but because he is human. JOHN COGLEY, *Commonweal,* April 24, 1959.

Cruel persecution and intolerance are not accidents, but grow out of the very essense of religion, namely, its absolute claims. MORRIS R. COHEN (1880–1947), in *Religion Today* (A. L. Swift), 1933.

Persecution was at least a sign of personal interest. Tolerance is composed of nine parts apathy to one of brotherly love. FRANK MOORE COLBY (1865–1925), *The Colby Essays,* 1926.

Persecution is a very easy form of virtue. JOHN DUKE COLERIDGE (1820–1894), English jurist, *Reg. v. Ramsey,* 1883.

I have seen gross intolerance shown in support of toleration. SAMUEL TAYLOR COLERIDGE (1772–1834), *Biographia Literaria,* 1817.

In politics as in religion, it so happens that we have less charity for those who believe the half of our creed, than for those who deny the whole of it. CHARLES CALEB COLTON (1780–1832), *Lacon,* 1825.

It is not so difficult a task to plant new truths, as to root out old errors; for there is this paradox in men, they run after that which is new, but are prejudiced in favor of that which is old. CHARLES CALEB COLTON (1780–1832), *Lacon,* 1825.

Wars of opinion, as they have been the most destructive, are also the most disgraceful of conflicts, being appeals from right to might and from argument to artillery. CHARLES CALEB COLTON (1780–1832), *Lacon,* 1825.

We hate some persons because we do not know them; and we will not know them because we hate them. CHARLES CALEB COLTON (1780–1832), *Lacon,*. 1825.

Men in authority will always think that criticism of their policies is dangerous. They will always equate their policies with patriotism, and find criticism subversive. HENRY STEELE COMMAGER, *Freedom and Order,* 1966.

Everybody happy, WE-WE-WE? / And to hell with the chappy who doesn't agree. E. E. CUMMINGS (1894–1962).

Hate is the consequence of fear; we fear something before we hate it; a child who fears noises becomes a man who hates noise. CYRIL CONNOLLY (1903–1974), *The Unquiet Grave,* 1945.

As in political so in literary action a man wins friends for himself mostly by the passion of his prejudices and the consistent narrowness of his outlook. JOSEPH CONRAD (1857–1924), *A Personal Record,* 1912.

There are only two ways to be quite unprejudiced and impartial. One is to be completely ignorant. The other is to be completely indifferent. Bias and prejudice are attitudes to be kept in hand, not attitudes to be avoided. CHARLES P. CURTIS (1891–1959), *A Commonplace Book,* 1957.

Fear and simplistic explanations lead people to develop inflexible attitudes and beliefs. Carried to the extreme these attitudes become authoritarian thinking . . . characterized by extreme rigidity and a total dedication to the belief that there is one correct way of doing things while all others are wrong. RAY P. CUZZORT, *Using Social Thought,* 1989.

The most dangerous tendency of the modern world is the way in which bogus theories are given the force of dogma. JEAN DANIELOU, *The Lord of History,* 1958.

Moral indignation is in most cases 2 percent moral, 48 percent indignation and 50 percent envy. VITTORIO DE SICA (1901–1974), 1961.

Intellectually, religious emotions are not creative but conservative. They attach themselves readily to the current view of the world and consecrate it. JOHN DEWEY (1859–1952), 1909.

Human diversity makes tolerance more than a virtue; it makes it a requirement for survival. RENÉ DUBOS (1901–1982), *Celebrations of Life,* 1981.

Because enemies, whether demonstratably harmful or not, do help marshal political and psychological support for their adversaries, the choice or definition of who the enemy is reflects an anticipation of which choice of enemy will most potently create and mobilize allies. MURRAY EDELMAN, *Politics as Symbolic Action,* 1971.

The enemy themes that most surely and consistently evoke mass arousal and anger are those that make it hardest to take the enemy as a significant other: those that emphasize the respects in which he does not share our human traits and potentialities for empathy, for compassion, and for social attachments. The alien, the stranger, or the subhuman are the themes struck repeatedly. MURRAY EDELMAN, *Politics as Symbolic Action,* 1971.

Few people are capable of expressing with equanimity opinions which differ from the prejudices of their social environment. Most people are not even capable of forming such opinions. ALBERT EINSTEIN (1879–1955), *Ideas and Opinions,* 1954.

Emotionally healthy people tend to give other humans the right to be wrong. While disliking or abhorring others' behavior, they refuse to condemn them, as total persons, for performing their poor behavior. ALBERT ELLIS, *On The Barricades,* 1989.

Let me never fall into the vulgar mistake of dreaming that I am persecuted whenever I am contradicted. RALPH WALDO EMERSON (1803–1882), Journals, 1838.

You must pay for conformity. All goes well as long as you run with conformists. But you, who are honest men in other particulars, know that there is alive somewhere a man whose honesty reaches to this point also, that he shall not kneel to false gods, and, on the day when you meet him, you sink into the class of counterfeits. RALPH WALDO EMERSON (1803–1882), *English Traits,* 1856.

When will the churches learn that intolerance, personal or ecclesiastical, is an evidence of weakness: the confident can afford to be calm and kindly; only the fearful must defame and exclude. HARRY EMERSON FOSDICK (1878–1969), *Adventurous Religion,* 1926.

Being tolerant does not mean that I share another one's belief. But it does mean that I acknowledge another one's right right to believe, and obey, his own conscience. VICTOR FRANKL, *The Will to Meaning.*

[Counterfeit tolerance includes] the opportunism of one who seeks, or accepts, tolerance for himself, as a minority, but who would deny it to others if ever he should be in a position to grant it; . . . one who is tolerant of views other than his own because the points of difference are of little moment; . . . [and] that attitude connoted best by the word condescension. It affords, or allows, tolerance to the opponent not because it believes an opponent may be right but because he is harmless. CARL J. FRIEDRICH, *The New Belief in the Common Man,* 1942.

There are many who lust for the simple answers of doctrine or decree. They are on the left and right. They are not confined to a single part of society. They are the terrorists of the mind. A. BARTLETT GIAMATTI (1938–1989), Yale University, May 26, 1986.

The fierce and partial writers of the times, ascribing all virtue to themselves, and imputing all guilt to their adversaries, have painted the battle of the angels and daemons. EDWARD GIBBON (1737–1794), *Decline and Fall of the Roman Empire,* 1776–88.

If it's a despot you would dethrone, see first that his throne erected within you is destroyed. KAHLIL GIBRAN (1883–1931), 1923.

Rulers ought to employ a page to repeat to them every morning: "See that you do not torment anyone on account of his religious opinions, and that you do not extend the power of the sword to touch the conscience." JOSEPH GLANVILLE (1636–1680), *The Vanity of Dogmatizing,* 1661.

Ideological thinking, whether right or wrong, is normative thinking so sure of its own rightness as to be intolerant of dissent. LOUIS J. HALLE, *The Ideological Imagination,* 1972

It is almost impossible to convince people who are under the influence of ideological bigotry that those whom they regard as belonging to the enemy species are human. LOUIS J. HALLE, *The Ideological Imagination,* 1972.

It's possible to disagree with someone about the ethics of nonviolence without wanting to kick his face in. CHRISTOPHER HAMPTON, *The Philanthropist.*

Heretics have been hated from the beginning of recorded time; they have been ostracized, exiled, tortured, maimed and butchered; but it has generally proved impossible to smother them; and when it has not, the society that has succeeded has always declined. LEARNED HAND (1872–1961), Judge, U.S. Court of Appeals, Address, January 29, 1955.

The spirit of liberty is the spirit which is not too sure it is right. LEARNED HAND (1872–1961), Judge, U.S. Court of Appeals, Speech, 1944.

There is no prejudice so strong as that which arises from a fancied exemption from all prejudice. WILLIAM HAZLITT (1778–1830), *The Round Table,* 1817.

The pleasure of hating, like a poisonous mineral, eats into the heart of religion, and turns it to ranking spleen and bigotry; it makes patriotism an excuse for fire, pestilence, and famine into other lands: it leaves to virtue nothing but the spirit of censoriousness. WILLIAM HAZLITT (1778–1830), *The Plain Speaker,* 1826.

Intolerance is the "Do Not Touch" sign on something that cannot bear touching. We do not mind having our hair ruffled, but we will not tolerate any familiarity with the toupee which covers our baldness. ERIC HOFFER, *The Passionate State of Mind,* 1955.

Deep-seated preferences cannot be argued about—you cannot argue a man into liking a glass of beer—and there, when differences are sufficiently far-reaching, we try to kill the other man rather than let him have his way. But that is perfectly consistent with admitting that, so far as appears, his grounds are just as good as ours. OLIVER WENDELL HOLMES, JR. (1841–1935), *Collected Legal Papers,* 1921.

There is always a type of man who says he loves his fellow men, and expects to make a living at it. EDGAR WATSON HOWE (1853–1937), *Ventures in Common Sense,* 1919.

Dogma is a lie reiterated and authoritatively injected into the mind of one or more persons who believe that they believe what someone else believes. ELBERT G. HUBBARD (1856–1915), *The Notebook.*

Orthodoxy: That peculiar condition where the patient can neither eliminate an old idea nor absorb a new one. ELBERT G. HUBBARD (1856–1915), *The Notebook.*

If you can't answer a man's arguments all is not lost; you can still call him names. ELBERT G. HUBBARD (1856–1915), *The Notebook.*

The vast majority of human beings dislike and even actually dread all notions with which they are not familiar. Hence it comes about that at their first appearance innovators have . . . always been derided as fools and madmen. ALDOUS HUXLEY (1894–1963).

One of the great attractions of patriotism—it fulfills our worst wishes. In the person of our nation we are able, vicariously, to bully and to cheat. Bully and cheat, what's more, with a feeling that we are profoundly virtuous. ALDOUS HUXLEY (1894–1964), *Eyeless in Gaza,* 1928.

Tolerance is giving to every other human being every right that you claim for yourself. ROBERT G. INGERSOLL (1833–1899).

The moment a person forms a theory, his imagination sees in every object only the traits that favor that theory. THOMAS JEFFERSON (1743–1826), U.S. President, Letter to Charles Thompson, September 20, 1787.

It does me no injury for my neighbor to say there are twenty gods, or no God. It neither picks my pocket nor breaks my leg. THOMAS JEFFERSON (1743–1826), U.S. President, Letter to Benjamin Rush, April 21, 1803.

Opinions founded on prejudice are always sustained with the greatest violence. FRANCIS JEFFREY (1773–1850).

It is the people with secret attractions to various temptations, who busy themselves with removing those temptations from other people; really they are defending themselves under the pretext of defending others, because at heart they fear their own weakness. ERNEST JONES (1879–1958), *Papers on Psychoanalysis,* 1918.

Persecution, whenever it occurs, establishes only the power and cunning of the persecutor, not the truth and worth of his belief. H. M. KALLEN (1882–1974).

We scapegoat and create absolute enemies, not because we are intrinsically cruel, but because focusing our anger on an outside target, striking at strangers, brings our tribe or nation together and allows us to be a part of a close and loving in-group. SAM KEEN, *Faces of the Enemy,* 1986.

The highest result of education is tolerance. HELEN KELLER (1880–1968), *Optimism,* 1903.

Tolerance implies no lack of commitment to one's own beliefs. Rather it condemns the oppression or persecution of others. JOHN FITZGERALD KENNEDY (1917–1963), U.S. President, 1960.

If one permits an infidel to continue in his role as a corrupter of the earth, his moral suffering will be all the worse. If one kills the infidel, and this stops him from perpetrating his misdeeds, his death will be a blessing to him. For if he remains alive, he will become more and more corrupt. This is a surgical operation commanded by God the all powerful. AYATOLLAH KHOMEINI, Speech, December 12, 1983.

The tyrant dies and his rule is over, the martyr dies and his rule begins. SØREN KIERKEGAARD (1813–1855).

In their tendencies toward tolerance, open-mindedness, faith in people and lack of authoritarianism, self-actualizers do appear to possess psychic strengths which allow them to work well in situations marked by a diversity of viewpoints. JEANNE KNUTSON, *The Human Basis of the Polity,* 1972.

When ye encounter the unbelievers, strike off their heads, until ye have made a great slaughter among them. Verily, if God pleased, He could take vengeance on them without your assistance, but He commandeth you to fight His battles. KORAN, ca. 625.

Genuine liberals have always wanted freedom. But the quest for freedom is precisely what leads certain minds to conclude that every firm conviction, every strong affirmation will automatically result in intolerance. ERIK von KUEHNELT-LEDDIHN, *Leftism Revisited,* 1990.

To speak of tolerance as the essence of liberalism, which might or might not exist alongside democracy, implies a readiness to . . . put up with the presence, the propagation of views and ideas that we reject or oppose. Marshalling our charity, we would suppress our indignation and give our fellow men the opportunity for open dissent despite our disagreement. Tolerance is a real virtue because it entails self-control and an ascetic attitude. ERIK von KUEHNELT-LEDDIHN, *Leftism Revisited,* 1990.

There are some men who turn a deaf ear to reason and good advice, and wilfully go wrong for fear of being controlled. JEAN de LA BRUYÈRE (1645–1696), *Les Caractères,* 1688.

Profound ignorance makes a man dogmatic. The man who knows nothing thinks he is teaching others what he has just learned himself; the man who knows a great deal can't imagine that what he is saying is not common knowledge, and speaks indifferently. JEAN de LA BRUYÈRE (1645–1696), *Les Caractères,* 1688.

Even those who fancy themselves the most progressive will fight against other kinds of progress, for each of us is convinced that our way is the best way. LOUIS L'AMOUR (1908–1988), *The Lonely Men,* 1969.

There is no more certain sign of a narrow mind, of stupidity, and of arrogance, than to stand aloof from those who think differently from us. WALTER SAVAGE LANDOR (1775–1864), *Imaginary Conversations,* 1824–1853.

Stereotypes are the mind's shorthand for dealing with complexities. They have two aspects: they are much blunter than reality; they are shaped to fit a man's preferences or prejudgments. Thus two principles are involved: differentiation or its lack, and biased preferential perception. ROBERT E. LANE, *Political Ideology,* 1962.

When our hatred is too keen it puts us beneath those whom we hate. FRANÇOIS, DUC de LA ROCHFOUCAULD (1613–1689), *Maxims,* 1665.

Smallness of mind is the cause of stubbornness, and we do not credit readily what is beyond our view. FRANÇOIS, DUC de LA ROCHFOUCAULD (1613–1689), *Maxims,* 1665.

We credit scarcely any persons with good sense except those who are of our opinion. FRANÇOIS, DUC de LA ROCHFOUCAULD (1613–1689), *Maxims,* 1665.

Dogma is a defensive reaction against doubt in the mind of the theorist, but doubt of which he is unaware. HAROLD D. LASSWELL, *Psychopathology and Politics,* 1930.

One of the most constant general characteristics of beliefs is their intolerance. The stronger the belief, the greater its intolerance. Men dominated by a certitude cannot tolerate those who do not accept it. GUSTAVE LE BON (1841–1931), *Opinions and Beliefs,* 1911.

In one age the persecutor burned the heretic; in another, he crushed him with penal laws; in a third, he withheld from him places of emolument and dignity; in a fourth, he subjected him to excommunication of society. Each stage of advancing toleration marks a stage in the decline of the spirit of dogmatism and of the increase of the spirit of truth. W. E. H. LECKY (1838–1903), *A History of Rationalism,* 1900.

Undoubtedly a certain amount of truth, and hence a certain utility, lies at the bottom of religious intolerance. Our philosophers talk of it as if it could be reasoned away, but that it assuredly cannot be. GEORGE C. LICHTENBERG (1742–1799), *Reflections,* 1799.

Tolerance is the positive and cordial effort to understand another's beliefs, practices, and habits without necessarily sharing or accepting them. JOSHUA LIEBMAN (1907–1948).

When men are brought face to face with their opponents, forced to listen and learn and mend their ideas, they cease to be children and savages and begin to live like civilized men. Then only is freedom a reality, when men may voice their opinions because they must examine their opinions. WALTER LIPPMANN (1889–1974), *The Indispensable Opposition,* 1939.

The tendency of the casual mind is to pick out or stumble upon a sample which supports or defies its prejudices, and then to make it the representative of a whole class. WALTER LIPPMANN (1889–1974), *Public Opinion,* 1922.

New opinions are always suspected, and usually opposed, without any other reason but because they are not already common. JOHN LOCKE (1632–1704), *An Essay concerning Human Understanding,* 1690.

We judge ourselves by what we feel capable of doing, while others judge us by what we have already done. HENRY WADSWORTH LONGFELLOW (1807–1882).

The dark side of pseudo-speciation is that it makes us consider the members of the pseudo-specie other than our own as not human, as many primitive tribes are demonstrably doing, in whose language the word for their own particular tribe is synonymous with "Man." From their viewpoint it is not, strictly speaking, cannibalism if they eat fallen warriors of an enemy tribe. KONRAD LORENZ, *On Aggression,* 1967.

Folks never understand the folks they hate. JAMES RUSSELL LOWELL (1819–1891), *The Biglow Papers,* 1867.

Every sect clamors for toleration when it's down. THOMAS BABINGTON MACAULAY (1800–1859), *Sir John MacIntosh's History of the Revolution,* 1835.

We know of no spectacle so ridiculous as the British public in one of its periodical fits of morality. THOMAS BABINGTON MACAULAY (1800–1859), *On Moore's Life of Byron,* 1831.

Those wearing Tolerance for a label, / Call other views intolerable. PHYLLIS McGINLEY (1905–1978), 1954.

When blithe to argument I come, / Though armed with facts and merry; / May providence protect me from, / The fool as adversary. / Whose mind to him a kingdom is, / Where reason lacks dominion; / Who calls conviction prejudice, / And prejudice opinion. PHYLLIS McGINLEY (1905–1978), 1960.

Tolerance not only means tolerating, it also encompasses attempts to comprehend the origins of different views, persuasions, ideologies and very often also irrational interests and inclinations. . . . Tolerance requires understanding of human weakness, motives, irrationalism, failures, "bad days," unreasonable longing, pluses and minuses of mind, will, and character. MIECZYSLAW MANELI, *Freedom and Tolerance,* 1984.

Tolerance is a better guarantee of freedom than brotherly love; for a man may love his brother so much that he feels himself thereby appointed his brother's keeper. EVERETT DEAN MARTIN (1880–1941), *Liberty,* 1930.

I wonder how anyone can have the face to condemn others when he reflects upon his own thoughts. W. SOMERSET MAUGHAM (1874–1965), *The Summing Up,* 1938.

Like all weak men he laid an exaggerated stress on not changing one's mind. W. SOMERSET MAUGHAM (1874–1965), *Of Human Bondage,* 1915.

The scapegoat has always had the mysterious power of unleashing man's ferocious pleasure in torturing, corrupting, and befouling. FRANÇOIS MAURIAC (1885–1970), *Second Thoughts,* 1961.

The rise of the militant anti-cult movement in America marks a new chapter in the history of human bigotry . . . many of the people who traditionally sounded the first alarm at signs of social scapegoating now remain, at best, relatively silent. At worst, they have become active supporters not only of dangerous anti-cult (and ultimately, antireligion) legislation, but also of the political use of establishment psychiatry. J. GORDON MELTON and ROBERT L. MOORE, *The Cult Experience,* 1982.

Moral certainty is always a sign of cultural inferiority. The more uncivilized the man, the surer he is that he knows precisely what is right and what is wrong. All human progress, even in morals, has been the work of men who have doubted the current moral values, not of men who have whooped them up and tried to enforce them. H. L. MENCKEN (1880–1956), *Minority Report,* 1956.

Precisely because the tyranny of opinion is such as to make eccentricity a reproach, it is desirable, in order to break through that tyranny, that people should be eccentric. Eccentricity has always abounded when and where strength of character has abounded; and the amount of eccentricity in a society has generally been proportional to the amount of genius, mental vigor, and moral courage it contained. That so few dare to be eccentric marks the chief danger of the time. JOHN STUART MILL (1806–1873), *On Liberty,* 1859.

The despotism of custom is everywhere the standing hindrance to human advancement. . . . JOHN STUART MILL (1806–1873), *On Liberty,* 1859.

The principle itself of dogmatic religion, dogmatic morality, dogmatic philosophy, is what requires to be rooted out; not any particular manifestation of that principle. JOHN STUART MILL (1806–1973), *The Spirit of the Age.*

He who knows only his own side of the case, knows little of that. JOHN STUART MILL (1806–1873), *On Liberty,* 1859.

In the human mind one-sidedness has always been the rule, and many-sidedness the exception. Hence, even in revolutions of opinion, one part of the truth usually sets while the other rises. JOHN STUART MILL (1806–1873), *On Liberty,* 1859.

How strange it is to see with how much passion / People see things only in their own fashion. MOLIÈRE (1622–1673), *School for Wives,* 1662.

One should examine oneself for a very long time before thinking of condemning others. MOLIÈRE (1622–1673), *The Misanthrope.*

Obstinacy and dogmatism are the surest signs of stupidity. Is there anything more confident, resolute, disdainful, grave and serious as the ass? MICHEL de MONTAIGNE (1533–1592), *Essays,* 1588.

The thing in the world I am most afraid of is.fear, and with good reason; that passion alone, in the trouble of it, exceeding all other accidents. MICHEL de MONTAIGNE (1533–1592), *Essays,* 1588.

All universal judgments are treacherous and dangerous. MICHEL de MONTAIGNE (1533–1592), *Essays,* 1580.

Knowledge humanizes mankind, and reason inclines to mildness; but prejudices eradicate every tender disposition. CHARLES-LOUIS de SECONDAT, BARON de MONTESQUIEU (1689–1755), *Spirit of the Laws,* 1748.

History is full of religious wars; but, we must take care to observe, it was not the multiplicity of religions that produced these wars, it was the intolerating spirit which animated that one which thought she had the power of governing. CHARLES-LOUIS de SECONDAT, BARON de MONTESQUIEU (1689–1755), *Lettres persanes,* 1721.

If tolerance is tolerant of intolerance it fears being destroyed by intolerance. If it is intolerant of intolerance, then it destroys itself. ARTHUR E. MORGAN (1878–1975), *Antioch News,* Antioch College, January 1934.

Our opinions are less important than the spirit and temper with which they possess us, and even good opinions are worth very little unless we hold them in a broad, intelligent, and spacious way. JOHN MORLEY (1838–1923), *Critical Miscellanies,* 1871–1908.

Everyone is a prisoner of his own experiences. No one can eliminate prejudices— just recognize them. EDWARD R. MURROW (1908–1965), News Commentary, December 31, 1955.

Toleration of people who differ in convictions and habits requires a residual awareness of the complexity of truth and the possibility of opposing views having some light on one or the other facet of a many-sided truth. REINHOLD NIEBUHR (1892–1971), "Tolerance," in *Collier's Encyclopedia,* 1966.

The fact is that any commitment, religious, political or cultural, can lead to intolerance if there is not a certain degree of residual awareness of the possibility of error in the truth in which we believe, and of the possibility of truth in the error against which we contend. REINHOLD NIEBUHR (1892–1971), "Tolerance," in *Collier's Encyclopedia,* 1966.

Liberal institutions straightaway cease from being liberal the moment they are soundly established. Once this is attained no more grievous and more thorough enemies of freedom exist than liberal institutions. FRIEDRICH NIETZSCHE (1844–1900), 1888.

Mistrust those in whom the impulse to punish is strong. FRIEDRICH NIETZSCHE (1844–1900).

Equality feeds on itself as no other single social value does. It is not long before it becomes more than a value. It takes on the overtones of redemptiveness and becomes a religion rather than a secular idea. ROBERT NISBET, *Twilight of Authority,* 1981.

Hatred is a feeling which leads to the extinction of values. JOSÉ ORTEGA y GASSET (1883–1955), *Meditations on Quixote,* 1914.

The greater the ignorance the greater the dogmatism. SIR WILLIAM OSLER (1849–1919).

No man is prejudiced in favor of a thing knowing it to be wrong. He is attached to it on the belief of its being right. THOMAS PAINE (1737–1809), *The Rights of Man,* 1791.

Ponder well the maxim: Never do to other persons what would pain thyself. PANCHATANTRA, ca. 200 B.C.

If it be an evil to judge rashly or untruly any single man, how much a greater sin it is to condemn a whole people. WILLIAM PENN (1644–1718), *A Key Opening The Way,* 1693.

It is with narrow-souled people as with narrow-necked bottles: the less they have in them, the more noise they make in pouring it out. ALEXANDER POPE (1688–1744), *Thoughts on Various Subjects,* 1727.

An obstinate man does not hold opinions, but they hold him. ALEXANDER POPE (1688–1744), *Thoughts on Various Subjects,* 1727.

There is an almost universal tendency, perhaps an inborn tendency, to suspect the good faith of a man who holds opinions that differ from our own opinions, whether those opinions are religious or political. . . . This tendency has been for many centuries the source of religious intolerance and religious persecution. It obviously endangers the freedom and the objectivity of our discussion if we attack a person instead of attacking an opinion or, more precisely, a theory. SIR KARL POPPER, "The Importance of Critical Discussion," in *On the Barricades,* 1989.

What we need and what we want is to moralize politics, and not to politicize morals. SIR KARL POPPER, *The Open Society and Its Enemies,* 1945.

People who are themselves concealing certain potential may be agitated when someone else flaunts similar behaviors and desires. SNELL and GAIL J. PUTNEY, *The Adjusted American,* 1964.

The fanatic who refused to admit the existence of a feared facet of himself may eventually be confronted with undeniable evidence that he harbors the very attitudes or desires he has sought to eradicate in others. SNELL and GAIL J. PUTNEY, *The Adjusted American,* 1964.

Heresy hunters are intolerant not only of unorthodox ideas; worse than that, they are intolerant of ideas—of any ideas which are really alive and not empty cocoons. PHILIP LEE RALPH, *The Story of Our Civilization,* 1954.

In highbrow circles, ridiculing Jews is Nazism, ridiculing Blacks is racism, ridiculing feminists is sexism, but ridiculing Christians is freedom of speech. WILLIAM REEL, 1977.

Most of our so-called reasoning consists in finding arguments for going on believing as we already do. JAMES HARVEY ROBINSON, *The Mind in the Making,* 1921.

The relative openness or closedness of a mind cuts across specific content; that is, it is not restricted to any one particular ideology, or religion, or philosophy, or scientific viewpoint. MILTON ROKEACH, *The Open and Closed Mind,* 1960.

Knowledge—that is, education in its true sense—is our best protection against unreasoning prejudice and panic-making fear, whether engendered by special interests, illiberal minorities, or panic-stricken leaders. FRANKLIN D. ROOSEVELT (1882–1945), U.S. President, Speech, October 31, 1932.

The infliction of cruelty with a good conscience is a delight to moralists. BERTRAND RUSSELL (1872–1970).

The most savage controversies are those about matters as to which there is no good evidence either way. Persecution is used in theology, not in arithmatic. BERTRAND RUSSELL (1872–1970), *An Outline of Intellectual Rubbish.*

Dogma demands authority, rather than intelligent thought, as the source of opinion; it requires persecution of heretics and hostility to unbelievers; it asks of its disciples that they should inhibit natural kindness in favor of systematic hatred. BERTRAND RUSSELL (1872–1970).

The collection of prejudices which is called political philosophy is useful provided it is not called philosophy. BERTRAND RUSSELL (1872–1970), 1962.

Bigotry is a form of egoism, and to condemn egoism intolerantly is to share it. GEORGE SANTAYANA (1863–1952).

All loving souls welcome whatsoever they are ready to cope with; all else they ignore, or pronounce to be monstrous and wrong, or deny to be possible. GEORGE SANTAYANA (1863–1952), *Dialogues in Limbo,* 1925.

Men show no mercy and expect no mercy, when honor calls, or when they fight for their idols or their gods. FRIEDRICH von SCHILLER (1759–1805), *The Maid of Orleans,* 1801.

Those who rush around ladling out moral judgments quickly arrogate to themselves an alarming and repellent sense of their own moral infallibility. ARTHUR M. SCHLESINGER, JR. (1888–1965), *The Crisis of Confidence,* 1969.

In time we hate that which we often fear. WILLIAM SHAKESPEARE (1564–1616), *Anthony and Cleopatra,* 1606.

Heretics were often most bitterly persecuted for their least deviation from accepted belief. It was precisely their obstinacy about trifles that irritated the righteous to madness. Why can they not yield on so trifling a matter. LEO SHESTOV, *All Things Are Possible,* 1905.

In so far as men are tormented by anger, envy, or any passion emplying hatred, they are drawn asunder and made contrary one to another, and therefore are so much the more to be feared. . . . BARUCH SPINOZA (1632–1677), *Tractatus Theologico-politicus,* 1677.

It would be almost unbelievable, if history did not record the tragic fact that men have gone to war and cut each other's throat because they could not agree as to what was to become of them after their throats were cut. WALTER PARKER STACY (1884–1951), in *Humor of a Country Lawyer* (S. Ervin), 1983.

One's belief that one is sincere is not so dangerous as one's conviction that one is right. We all feel we are right; but we felt the same way twenty years ago and today we know we weren't right. IGOR STRAVINSKY (1882–1971), *Conversations with Igor Stravinsky,* 1959.

It is human to hate those whom we have injured. CORNELIUS TACITUS (55–117 A.D.), *Life of Agricola,* 98 A.D.

Bigotry tries to keep truth safe in its hand with the grip that kills it. RABINDRANATH TAGORE, *Fireflies,* 1928.

If a man does not keep pace with his companions, perhaps it is because he hears a different drummer. Let him step to the music he hears, however measured or far away. HENRY DAVID THOREAU (1817–1862), *Walden,* 1854.

We cannot bring ourselves to believe it possible that a foreigner should in any respect be wiser than ourselves. If any such point out to us our follies, we at once claim those follies as the special evidences of our wisdom. ANTHONY TROLLOPE (1815–1882), *Orley Farm,* 1862.

At the extreme, the process of stereotyping eventuates in dehumanization: the enemy is judged to be so inhumanly evil or contemptible that anything may be done to "it" without subjectively compromising one's own humanity and sense of morality. AUSTIN J. TURK, *Political Criminality,* 1982.

It is truer to say that martyrs make faith than that faith makes martyrs. MIGUEL de UNAMUNO y JUGO (1864–1936), *The Tragic Sense of Life,* 1921.

An attitude of permanent indignation signifies great mental poverty. Politics compels its votaries to take that line and you can see their minds grow more and more impoverished every day, from one burst of righteous anger to the next. PAUL VALÉRY (1871–1945), *Tel quel,* 1941–43.

Most people grow old within a small circle of ideas, which they have not discovered for themselves. There are perhaps less wrong-minded people than thoughtless. MARQUIS de LUC de VAUVENARGUES (1715–1747), *Reflections and Maxims,* 1746.

The fewer dogmas, the fewer disputes; and the fewer disputes, the fewer calamities: if this is not true I am much mistaken. VOLTAIRE (1694–1778), *A Treatise on Toleration.*

Could it be brought home to people that there is no absolute standard in morality, they would perhaps be somewhat more tolerant in their judgments, and more apt to listen to the voice of reason. EDWARD WESTERMARCK (1862–1939), *Origin and Development of Moral Ideas,* 1906–08.

What is morality in any given time or place? It is what the majority then and there happen to like and immorality is what they dislike. ALFRED NORTH WHITEHEAD (1861–1947).

I never came across anyone in whom the moral sense was dominant who was not heartless, cruel, vindictive, log-stupid and entirely lacking in the smallest sense of humanity. OSCAR WILDE (1854–1900), Letter, 1897.

Morality is simply the attitude we adopt toward people whom we personally dislike. OSCAR WILDE (1854–1900), *An Ideal Husband,* 1895.

Once lead this people into war and they'll forget there ever was such a thing as tolerance. WOODROW WILSON (1856–1925), U.S. President, in *Mr. Wilson's War* (John Dos Passos), 1963.

Tolerance is an admirable intellectual gift; but it is of little worth in politics. Politics is a war of causes, a joust of principles. WOODROW WILSON (1856–1924), U.S. President, *University of Virginia Magazine,* March 1880.

Totalitarianism, Collectivism, and State Power

History is not a web woven with innocent hands. Among all the causes which degrade and demoralize men, power is the most constant and most active. LORD ACTON (1843–1902), *Essays of Freedom and Power.*

Power tends to corrupt and absolute power corrupts absolutely. Great men are almost always bad men, even when they exercise influence and not authority: still more when you superadd the tendency or the certainty of corruption by authority. LORD ACTON (1843–1902), Letter, April 5, 1887.

Whenever a single definite object is made the supreme end of the State, be it the advantage of a class, the safety or the power of the country, the greatest happiness of the greatest number, or the support of any speculative idea, the State becomes for the time inevitably absolute. LORD ACTON (1843–1902), *The Home and Foreign Review,* July 1862.

I am more and more convinced that man is a dangerous creature, and that power, whether vested in many or a few, is ever grasping, and like the grave, cries, "Give, Give!" ABIGAIL ADAMS (1744–1818), Letter to John Adams, November 27, 1775.

The effect of power and publicity on all men is the aggravation of self, a sort of tumor that ends by killing the victim's sympathies. HENRY BROOKS ADAMS (1838–1918), *The Education of Henry Adams,* 1907.

Power when wielded by abnormal energy is the most serious of facts. HENRY BROOKS ADAMS (1828–1918), *The Education of Henry Adams,* 1907.

The fundamental article of my political creed is that despotism, or unlimited sovereignty, or absolute power, is the same in a majority of a popular assembly, an aristocratical council, an oligarchical junta, or a single emperor. JOHN ADAMS (1735–1826), U.S. President, Letter to Thomas Jefferson, November 13, 1815.

The jaws of power are always open to devour, and her arms are always stretching out, if possible, to destroy the freedom of thinking, speaking, and writing. JOHN ADAMS (1735–1826), U.S. President, 1765.

Nip the shoots of arbitrary power in the bud, is the only maxim which can ever preserve the liberties of the people. JOHN ADAMS (1735–1826), U.S. President, *Boston Gazette,* February 6, 1775.

It is weakness rather than wickedness which renders men unfit to be trusted with unlimited power. JOHN ADAMS (1735–1826), U.S. President, 1788.

A power of the individuals who compose legislatures, to fish up wealth from the people, by nets of their own weaving . . . will corrupt legislative, executive, and judicial public servants. JOHN ADAMS (1735–1826), U.S. President, 1811.

There is a sickness rooted and inherent in the nature of a tyranny: he that holds it does not trust his friends. AESCHYLUS (525–456 B.C.), *Prometheus Bound,* 478 B.C.

The possession of unlimited power will make a despot of almost any man. There is a possible Nero in the gentlest human creature that walks. THOMAS BAILEY ALDRICH (1836–1907), *Ponkapog Papers,* 1903.

When a government takes over a people's economic life it becomes absolute, and when it has become absolute it destroys the arts, the minds, the liberties and the meaning of the people it governs. MAXWELL ANDERSON (1888–1959), *The Guaranteed Life.*

All despotisms, under whatever name they masquerade, are efforts to freeze history, to stop change, to solidify the human spirit. CHARLES A. BEARD (1874–1948).

Make men large and strong, and tyranny will bankrupt itself in making shackles for them. HENRY WARD BEECHER (1813–1887), *Proverbs from Plymouth Pulpit,* 1887.

At its first inception all collectivist reform is necessarily deflected, and involves, in the place of what it had intended, a new thing: a society wherein the owners remain few and where the proletarian mass accept a security at the expense of servitude. HILAIRE BELLOC (1870–1953), *The Servile State,* 1912.

We thought, because we had power, we had wisdom. STEPHEN VINCENT BENET (1898–1943), *Litany for Dictatorships,* 1935.

Among the several cloudy appellatives which have been commonly as cloaks for misgovernment, there is none more conspicuous in this atmosphere of illusion than the word Order. JEREMY BENTHAM (1748–1832), *The Book of Fallacies,* 1824.

He who has his thumb on the purse has the power. OTTO von BISMARK (1815–1895), Speech, North German Reichstag, May 21, 1869.

Tyranny is every wanton and causeless restraint of the will of the subject, whether practiced by a monarch, a nobility or a popular assembly. SIR WILLIAM BLACKSTONE (1723–1780).

War is the health of the State. It automatically sets in motion throughout society these irresistible forces for uniformity, for passionate cooperation with the government in coercing into obedience the minority groups and individuals which lack the larger herd sense. RANDOLPH BOURNE (1886–1918), in *War and the Intellectuals,* 1964.

Authority without wisdom is like a heavy axe without an edge, fitter to bruise than to polish. ANNE BRADSTREET (1612–1672), *Meditations Divine and Moral,* 1670.

The totalitarian claim to sole control, which not only limits the individual in his free development but also forces him into the scheme of a planned world and thus overpowers him, contains in its essence an offer that corresponds to one of man's most deeply rooted yearnings: the desire for a closed intellectual system, based on simple suppositions, which explains all existence and offers the guarantee of being able to cope with fate. HANS BUCHHEIM, *Totalitarian Rule,* 1962.

Men can have validity only as building blocks or structural materials, raw material, "human materiel"; totalitarian rule cannot as a matter of principle acknowledge the citizen's personal autonomy, on which political liberty is based, but must render him available for whatever service seems desirable. It destroys the old social elements and social processes and sets new, artificial ones in motion. Groups that are considered harmful are expunged. HANS BUCHHEIM, *Totalitarian Rule,* 1962.

To them, the will, the wish, the liberty, the blood, the toil of individuals is nothing. Individuality is left out of their scheme of government. The state is all in all. EDMUND BURKE (1729–1797), *Second Letter of a Regicide Peace,* 1795-97.

Power gradually extirpates from the mind every humane and gentle virtue. EDMUND BURKE (1729–1797), *A Vindication of Natural Society,* 1756.

All oppressors attribute the frustration of their desires to the want of sufficient rigor. They they redouble the efforts of their impotent cruelty. EDMUND BURKE (1729–1797), *The Impeachment of Warren Hastings,* 1788.

Those who have been once intoxicated with power, and have derived any kind of emolument from it, even though but for one year, can never willingly abandon it. EDMUND BURKE (1729–1797).

The new aristocracy was made up for the most part of bureaucrats, scientists, technicians, trade union organizers, publicity experts, sociologists, teachers, journalists and professional politicians. As compared with their opposite numbers in past ages, they were less avaricious, less tempted by luxury, hungrier for pure power, and, above all, more conscious of what they were doing and more intent on crushing opposition. JAMES BURNHAM (1905–1987), *The Managerial Revolution,* 1941.

It is not merely political actions, in the narrower sense, that are involved; nearly every side of life, business and art and science and education and religion and recreation and morality are not merely influenced by but directly subjected to the totalitarian regime. JAMES BURNHAM (1905–1987), *The Managerial Revolution,* 1941.

Authority intoxicates, / And makes mere sots of magistrates; / The fumes of it invade the brain, / And make men giddy, proud and vain. SAMUEL BUTLER (1612–1680).

Power intoxicates men. When a man is intoxicated by alcohol, he can recover, but when intoxicated by power, he seldom recovers. JAMES F. BYRNES (1879–1972).

He who surpasses or subdues mankind must look down on the hate of those below. LORD BYRON (1788–1824).

Only the history of free peoples is worth our attention; the history of men under a despotism is merely a collection of anecdotes. NICOLAS-SEBASTIEN CHAMFORT (1741–1794).

Arbitrary power has seldom . . . been introduced in any country at once. It must be introduced by slow degrees, and as it were step by step. LORD CHESTERFIELD (1694–1773).

Despotism can be a development, often a late development and very often indeed the end of societies that have been highly democratic. A despotism may almost be defined as a tired democracy. GILBERT KEITH CHESTERTON (1874–1936), *The Everlasting Man,* 1925.

The arts of power and its minions are the same in all countries and in all ages. It marks its victim, denounces it, and excites the public odium and public hatred, to conceal its own abuses and encroachments. HENRY CLAY (1777–1852), Speech, March 14, 1834.

History has taught me that rulers are much the same in all ages, and under all forms of government; that they are as bad as they dare to be. SAMUEL TAYLOR COLERIDGE (1772–1834), Letter, 1798.

Power, like the diamond, dazzles the beholder, and also the wearer; it dignifies meanness; it magnifies littleness; to what is contemptible it gives authority; to what is low, exaltation. CHARLES CALEB COLTON (1780–1832).

The law, unfortunately, has always been retained on the side of power; laws have uniformly been enacted for the protection and perpetuation of power. THOMAS COOPER (1759–1839), *Liberty of the Press,* 1830.

In the field of politics, force and consent are correlative terms, and one does not exist without the other. In the most liberal State as in the most oppressive tyranny there is always a consent, and it is always forced, conditioned, changeable. BENEDETTO CROCE (1866–1952), *Elements of Politics,* 1925.

The main task of a free society is to civilize the struggle for power. Slavery of the acquiescent majority to the ruthless few is the hereditary state of mankind; freedom, a (rarely) acquired characteristic. R. H. S. CROSSMAN (1907–1974), *New Statesman & Nation,* April 21, 1951.

It is not power itself, but the legitimation of the lust for power, which corrupts absolutely. R. H. S. CROSSMAN (1907–1974), *New Statesman & Nation,* April 21, 1951.

Nazi Germany, at its peak . . . was a society in which force, ostracism, ridicule, occupational control, belief systems, spheres of intimates, the contract, and deception were applied with great energy. The result was one of the most efficient and effectively organized large-scale social systems in history. RAY P. CUZZORT, *Using Social Thought,* 1989.

Political terror is generally effective in making possible the attainment of immediate goals—the liquidation of real, potential, or imaginary rivals for power and authority; the elimination or isolation of those suspected of actually or potentially holding beliefs and attitudes at variance with the official ones. ALEXANDER DALLIN and GEORGE W. BRESLAUER, *Political Terror in Communist Systems,* 1970.

Whereas coercion is the most effective in securing short-term compliance, it is least effective in securing subjective commitment over long periods. Normative power, in contrast, is the most economical and thorough but also the most difficult to manipulate with discrimination. Coercion is most effective in deterring and punishing behavior; it is least effective in promoting voluntary cooperation with commitment. ALEXANDER DALLIN and GEORGE W. BRESLAUER, *Political Terror in Communist Systems,* 1970.

The instruments of authority are education and propaganda, force and violence, and economic measures and economic manipulation. Political leadership . . . in part depends upon skill in working with these instruments of authority. ALFRED de GRAZIA, *Politics and Government,* 1962.

Integration of government agencies and coordination of authority may be called the keystone principle of fascist administration. LAWRENCE DENNIS, *The Coming American Fascism,* 1936.

Any doctrine that . . . weakens personal responsibility for judgment and for action . . . helps create attitudes that welcome and support the totalitarian state. JOHN DEWEY (1859–1952).

Watch out for the fellow who talks about putting things in order! Putting things in order always means getting other people under your control. DENIS DIDEROT (1713–1784).

[Tyranny is] to compel men not to think as they do, to compel men to express thoughts that are not their own. MILOVAN DJILAS, *The New Class,* 1957.

Power concedes nothing without demand. It never did, and it never will. Find out just what people will submit to, and you have found out the exact amount of injustice and wrong which will be imposed upon them. The limits of tyrants are prescribed by the endurance of those whom they suppress. FREDERICK DOUGLASS (1817–1895).

All executive power—from the reign of ancient kinds to the rule of modern dictators—has the outward appearance of efficiency. WILLIAM O. DOUGLAS (1898–1980), U.S. Supreme Court Justice, *Youngstown Sheet & Tube* v. *Sawyer,* 1952.

Power is more satisfying to some than wealth. . . . Power is, indeed, a heady thing—whether it be a king, a president, a legislature, a court, or an administration agency that is concerned. WILLIAM O. DOUGLAS (1898–1980), U.S. Supreme Court Justice, *We the Judges,* 1956.

[During the French Revolution] the State exercised over the manufacturing industry the most unlimited and arbitrary jurisdiction. It disposed without scruple of the resources of manufacturers; it decided who would be allowed to work, what things it should be permitted to make, what materials should be employed, what processes followed, what forms should be given to productions. It was not enough to do well, to do better; it was necessary to do according to the rules. CHARLES DUNOYER, *The Passage to Liberty.*

The broadening of the state apparatus leads to an increase in the numbers or people making decisions in the name of the state. The circle of rulers, that is the number of people whom citizens must obey, is widened. The single tyrant with his few associates is replaced by a host of petty despots. MAURICE DUVERGER, *The Idea of Politics,* 1964.

Another and cruder motive undoubtedly swung many once refined liberals into the camp of the brutalitarian tyrants. That is an underlying irresistible wish to associate with power. MAX EASTMAN (1883–1969), *Reflections on the Failure of Socialism,* 1944.

The real guarantee of freedom is an equilibrium of social forces in conflict, not the triumph of any one force. In trying to build, or defend a free society, our first concern should be to make sure that no one gang or group—neither the proletariat, nor the capitalists, not the landowners, not the bankers, nor the army, nor the church, not the state itself—shall have unlimited power. MAX EASTMAN (1883–1969), *Reflections on the Failure of Socialism,* 1944.

Any power must be the enemy of mankind which enslaves the individual by terror and force, whether it arises under a fascist or Communist flag. All that is valuable in human society depends upon the opportunity for development according to the individual. ALBERT EINSTEIN (1879–1955), 1933.

Ignorant power comes in the end to the same thing as wicked power; it makes misery. GEORGE ELIOT (1819–1880), *Felix Holt, The Radical,* 1866.

Frequent elections by the people furnish the only protection under the Constitution against the abuse of acknowledged legislative power. STEPHEN J. FIELD (1816–1899), U.S. Supreme Court Justice, *Ex parte Newman.*

The great difference between the Communist state and the fascist state is that in the Communist state the government plans for the industries of the nation which it owns and in the fascist state the government plans for industries which are owned by private persons. JOHN T. FLYNN (1883–1964), *As We Go Marching,* 1944.

A government big enough to give you everything you want is a government big enough to take from you everything you have. GERALD R. FORD, U.S. President, 1976.

The power to do good is also the power to do harm; and those who control the power today may not tomorrow; and, more important, what one man regards as good, another may regard as harm. MILTON FRIEDMAN, *Capitalism and Freedom,* 1962.

The history of the totalitarian regimes is reflected in the evolution and perfection of the instruments of terror and more especially the police. CARL J. FRIEDRICH, *The Pathology of Politics,* 1972.

The lust for power is not rooted in strength but in weakness. ERICH FROMM (1900–1980), *Escape From Freedom,* 1941.

Power tends to confuse itself with virtue and a great nation is peculiarly susceptible to the idea that its power is a sign of God's favor. Once imbued with the idea of a mission, a great nation easily assumes that it has the means as well as the duty to do God's work. J. WILLIAM FULBRIGHT, Speech, U.S. Senate, April 21, 1966.

Passion, joined with power, produceth thunder and ruin. THOMAS FULLER (1654–1734), *Gnomologia,* 1732.

The state represents violence in a concentrated and organized form. The individual has a soul, but as the state is a soulless machine, it can never be weaned from violence to which it owes its very existence. MOHANDAS K. GANDHI (1869–1948).

The strongest bulwark of authority is uniformity; the least divergence from it is the greatest crime. EMMA GOLDMAN (1869–1940).

One of Oceania's greatest methods of personal disorientation is the dissolution of the family. Breaking the emotional ties between man and woman, parents and children, eliminates bonds that would detract from a person's absolute devotion to the state. DAVID GOODMAN, in *Nineteen Eighty-Four to 1984* (C. L. Kuppig, ed.), 1984.

There is no more contemptible poison than power over one's fellow men. MAXIM GORKY (1868–1936), *Novaya Zhism.*

Perhaps the greatest consolation of the oppressed is to consider themselves superior to their tyrants. JULIEN GREEN, *Adrienne Mesurat,* 1927.

In the general course of human nature, a power over a man's subsistence amounts to a power over his will. ALEXANDER HAMILTON (1757–1804), *The Federalist,* 1788.

The plea of necessity, that eternal argument of all conspirators. WILLIAM HENRY HARRISON (1773–1841), U.S. President, Letter to Simon Bolivar, September 27, 1829.

There is no justification for the belief that, so long as power is conferred by democratic procedure, it cannot be arbitrary; the contrast suggested by this statement is altogether false: it is not the source but the limitation of power which prevents it from being arbitrary. FRIEDRICH A. HAYEK, *The Road to Serfdom,* 1944.

Economic control is not merely control of a sector of human life which can be separated from the rest; it is the control of the means for all our ends. FRIEDRICH A. HAYEK, *The Road to Serfdom,* 1944.

The garb of religion is the best cloak for power. WILLIAM HAZLITT (1778–1830), 1819.

The love of fame is consistent with the steadiest attachment to principle and indeed strengthens and supports it; whereas the love of power, where this is the ruling passion, even requires the sacrifice of principle at every turn. WILLIAM HAZLITT (1778–1830), 1807.

When once you have plunged into the strife for power, it is the fear of those who are seeking for power over you that so easily persuades to all the great crimes. AUBERON HERBERT (1838–1906), *Westminister Gazette,* November 22, 1893.

Who shall count up the evil brood that is born from power—the pitiful fear, the madness, the despair, the overpowering craving for revenge, the treachery, the unmeasured cruelty?" AUBERON HERBERT 1838–1906), *Westminister Gazette,* November 22, 1893.

I do not blame those who wish to rule . . . but those who are overready to serve. HERMOCRATES (d. 407 B.C.), in *History of the Peloponnesian War* (Thucydides).

The possession of power over others is inherently destructive both to the possessor of the power and to those over whom it is exercised. GEORGE D. HERRON (1862–1925), in *The Cry for Justice* (Upton Sinclair, ed.), 1920.

No man ever ruled other men for their own good; no man was ever rightly the master of the minds and bodies of his brothers; no man ever ruled other men for anything except for their undoing and for his own brutalization. GEORGE D. HERRON (1862–1925), in *The Cry for Justice* (Upton Sinclair, ed.), 1920.

But in the forefront of military training . . . the boy must be transformed into a man; in this school he must not only learn to obey, but must thereby acquire a basis for commanding later. He must learn to be silent not only when he is justly blamed but must also learn, when necessary, to bear injustice in silence. ADOLPH HITLER (1889–1945), *Mein Kampf,* 1925–27.

By educating the young generation along the right lines, the People's State will have to see to it that a generation of mankind is formed which will be adequate to this supreme combat that will decide the destinies of the world. ADOLPH HITLER (1889–1945), *Mein Kampf,* 1925–27.

The efficiency of the truly national leader consists primarily in preventing the division of the attention of a people, and always in concentrating it on a single enemy. ADOLPH HITLER (1889–1945), *Mein Kampf,* 1925–27.

In the first place, I put for a general inclination of all mankind, a perpetual and restless desire of Power after Power, that ceaseth only in Death. THOMAS HOBBES (1588–1679), *Leviathan,* 1651.

For the nature of power is in this point, like to fame, increased as it proceeds; or like the motion of heavy bodies, which the further they go, make still the more haste. THOMAS HOBBES (1588–1679), *Leviathan,* 1651.

Our sense of power is more vivid when we break a man's spirit than when we win his heart. ERIC HOFFER (1902–1983), *The Passionate State of Mind,* 1954.

Totalitarianism spells simplification: an enormous reduction in the variety of aims, motives, interests, human types, and, above all, in the categories and units of power. ERIC HOFFER (1902–1983), *The Ordeal of Change,* 1964.

I doubt if the oppressed ever fight for freedom. They fight for pride and power— the power to oppress others. The oppressed want above all to imitate their oppressors; they want to retaliate. ERIC HOFFER (1903–1983), *The True Believer,* 1951.

It is when power is wedded to chronic fear that it becomes formidable. ERIC HOFFER (1902–1983), *The Passionate State of Mind,* 1954.

There are similarities between absolute power and absolute faith: a demand for absolute obedience, a readiness to attempt the impossible, a bias for simple solutions—to cut the knot rather than unravel it, the viewing of compromise as surrender. Both absolute power and absolute faith are instruments of dehumanization. ERIC HOFFER (1902–1983), *New York Times Magazine,* April 25, 1971.

The only prize much cared for by the powerful is power. The prize of the general is not a bigger tent, but command. OLIVER WENDELL HOLMES, JR. (1841–1935), *The Path of the Law,* 1896.

A totally socialized society has a high totalitarian potential. Therefore, in the light of history and psychology, we need to encourage plural forms of ownership, plural forms of association, so that one can survive if it becomes necessary to oppose the groups in power. SIDNEY HOOK (1902–1989), *Free Inquiry,* Summer 1985.

You cannot extend the mastery of the government over the daily working life of a people without at the same time making it the master of the people's souls and thoughts. HERBERT CLARK HOOVER (1874–1964), U.S. President, *American Individualism,* 1922.

Indignation does no good unless it is backed with a club of sufficient size to awe the opposition. EDGAR WATSON HOWE (1853–1937), *Ventures in Common Sense,* 1919.

All property is common property. The owner is bound by the people and the Reich to the responsible management of his goods. His legal position is only justified when he satisfies this responsibility to the community. ERNST RUDOLF HUBER, Constitutional Law of the Pan-German Reich, 1939.

As long as men worship the Ceasars and Napoleons, the Ceasars and Napoleons will duly rise and make them miserable. ALDOUS HUXLEY (1894–1963), *Ends and Means,* 1937.

It is a characteristic of totalitarian leaders that they see every social movement as having within it the seeds of its own destruction, and that they are ridden by fear that within their own movement and social organization there is such a potentially destructive foreign body which must be wholly and violently expunged. A. INKELES, in *Totalitarianism* (C. J. Friedrich), 1954.

Fascism conceives of the State as an absolute, in comparison with which all individuals or groups are relative. ENCYCLOPEDIA ITALIANA, "The Doctrine of Fascism," 1932.

That wars and rumors of wars are the great threats to political stability and to liberty needs no demonstration. Total war means total subjection of the individual to the state. ROBERT H. JACKSON (1892–1954), U.S. Supreme Court Justice, *The Supreme Court in the American System of Government,* 1955.

An honest man can feel no pleasure in the exercise of power over his fellow citizens. THOMAS JEFFERSON (1743–1826), 1813.

It is the old practice of despots to use a part of the people to keep the rest in order. THOMAS JEFFERSON (1743–1813), Letter, 1798.

Timid men . . . prefer the calm of despotism to the tempestuous sea of liberty. THOMAS JEFFERSON (1743–1813), Letter, January 1, 1797.

Power is always gradually stealing away from the many to the few, because the few are more vigilant and consistent. SAMUEL JOHNSON (1709–1784), *The Adventurer,* no. 45.

My opinion is, that power should always be distrusted, in whatever hands it is placed. SIR WILLIAM JONES (1746–1794), Letter, 1782.

Princes are more sensitive to any offense that tends to diminish their authority than to any service that tends to reinforce it. JOSEPH JOUBERT (1754–1824), *Pensées,* 1842.

The function of the true State is to impose the minimum restrictions and safeguard the maximum liberties of the people, and it never regards the person as a thing. IMMANUEL KANT (1724–1804).

Nobody can compel me to be happy in his own way. Paternalism is the greatest despotism. IMMANUEL KANT (1724–1804), in *Two Concepts of Liberty* (Isaiah Berlin).

The enjoyment of power inevitably corrupts the judgment of reason, and perverts its liberty. IMMANUEL KANT (1724–1804), *Perpetual Peace,* 1795.

The state is the servant of the citizen, and not his master. JOHN F. KENNEDY (1917–1963), U.S. President, State of the Union Address, 1962.

Where the state regulates, it stands ready to coerce. Extension of regulation and coercion into all spheres of society is the meaning of totalitarianism. Since regulation in social and cultural areas is uniquely difficult to enforce, it requires more police, more surveillance, more terror. This is the reason that totalitarian regimes are uniquely repressive. JEANE J. KIRKPATRICK, *Dictatorships and Double Standards,* 1982.

It must never be forgotten . . . that the liberties of the people are not so safe under the gracious manner of government as by the limitation of power. RICHARD HENRY LEE (1732–1794)

It was to guard against the encroachments of power, the insatiate ambition of wealth that this government was instituted, by the people themselves. WILLIAM LEGGETT (1801–1839), *New York Evening Post,* 1834.

The great question which, in all ages, has disturbed mankind, and brought on them the greatest part of their mischiefs, which has ruined cities, depopulated countries, and disordered the peace of the world, has been, not whether there be power in the world, nor whence it came, but who should have it. JOHN LOCKE (1632–1704), *First Treatise on Government,* 1690.

For he that thinks absolute power purifies men's blood, and corrects the baseness of human nature, need read but the history of this, or any age, to be convinced to the contrary. JOHN LOCKE (1632–1704), *An Essay concerning Human Understanding,* 1687.

This freedom from absolute, arbitrary power is so necessary to, and closely joined with, a man's preservation, that he cannot part with it but by what forfeits his preservation and life together. JOHN LOCKE (1632–1784), *An Essay concerning Human Understanding,* 1687.

Times change, and men's minds with them. Down the past, civilizations have exposed themselves in terms of power, of world power or of other-world power. No civilization has yet exposed itself in terms of love-of-man. JACK LONDON (1876–1916), *The Cry for Justice.*

He who is firmly seated in authority soon learns to think security, and not progress, the highest lesson of statecraft. JAMES RUSSELL LOWELL (1819–1891), *Among My Books,* 1870.

A *coup* consists of the infiltration of a small but critical segment of the state apparatus, which is then used to displace the government from its control of the remainder. EDWARD LUTTWAK, *Coup d'État,* 1968.

Since the general civilization of mankind, I believe there are more instances of the abridgement of the freedom of the people, by gradual and silent encroachments of those in power, than by violent and sudden ursurpations. JAMES MADISON (1751–1836), Virginia Convention, June 16, 1788.

The accumulation of all power, legislative, executive, and judiciary, in the same hands, whether of one, a few, or many, and whether hereditary, self-appointed, or elective, may justly be pronounced the very definition of tyranny. JAMES MADISON (1751–1836), *Federalist Papers* #47, February 1, 1788.

What a perversion of the normal order of things, to make power the primary and central object of the social system, and Liberty but its satellite. JAMES MADISON (1751–1836), *National Gazette,* December 20, 1792.

The essence of Government is power; and power, lodged as it must be in human hands, will ever be liable to abuse. JAMES MADISON (1751–1836), Speech, December 2, 1829.

On a candid examination of history, we shall find that turbulence, violence, and abuse of power, by the majority, have produced factions and commotions which, in republics, have, more frequently than any other cause, produced despotism. JAMES MADISON (1751–1836), Address, Virginia Convention, 1788.

Politics is always a struggle for power, disguise and modified by prudence, reason and moral pretext. WILLIAM HURRELL MALLOCK (1849–1923).

Terror has been effective historically only if the terrorizing groups are already in power. Groups trying to gain power have never been able to use terror effectively for any length of time. HERBERT MARCUSE (1898–1979), *Psychology Today,* 1971.

That the power to tax involves the power to destroy . . . is not to be denied. JOHN MARSHALL (1755–1835), U.S. Supreme Court Justice, *McCullough* v. *Maryland,* 1819.

Dictatorship, like other forms of absolutism, is the highest form of expression of political centralization. But socialist dictatorship, "the dictatorship of the proletariat," is absolute centralization; it denotes a totalitarian state which is not confined to the realm of the political but centralizes all industries, all human activity. Every sphere of life is subject to its control and regulation. G. P. MAXIMOFF (1893–1950), *The Guillotine at Work.*

Totalitarian centralization of the medical service, while introducing a progressive principle of free health care for all, has also made it possible to use medicine as a means of government control and political regulation. ZHORES MEDVEDEV, *A Question of Madness,* 1971.

Totalitarianism is man's escape from the fearful realities of life into the virtual womb of the leader. The individual's actions are directed from this womb— from the inner sanctum. The mystic center is in control of everything; man need no longer assume responsibility for his own life. The order and logic of the prenatal world reign. There is peace and silence, the peace of utter submission. JOOST A. MERLOO, *The Rape of the Mind,* 1956.

Since totalitarianism is essentially the social manifestation of a psychological phenomenon belonging to every personality, it can best be understood in terms of the human forces that create, foster, and perpetuate it. Totalitarianism appeals to the confused infant in all of us. [It] is a monolithic and absolute state in which doubt, confusion, and conflict are not permitted to be shown. JOOST A. MERLOO, *The Rape of the Mind,* 1956.

Authoritarianism . . . is a barrier that seems to apply across the board to all types of partisan political activity (and possibly all Community activity). . . . Authoritarians may be slow to implement any anti-democratic prejudices they may possess, insofar as they shun the means of political expression commonly employed in the United States. LESTER W. MILBRATH and WALTER W. KLEIN, *Acta Sociologica,* vol. 6, 1962.

Society . . . practices a social tyranny more formidable than many kinds of political repression . . . penetrating much more deeply into the details of life, and enslaving the soul itself. JOHN STUART MILL (1806–1873), *On Liberty,* 1859.

Where liberty cannot be hoped for, and power can, power becomes the grand object of human desire. . . . The love of power and the love of liberty are in eternal antagonism. Where there is least liberty, the passion for power is the most ardent and unscrupulous. JOHN STUART MILL (1807–1873), *On Liberty,* 1859.

Even despotism does not produce its worst effects, so long as individuality exists under it; and whatever crushes individuality is despotism, by whatever name it may be called, and whether it professes to be enforcing the will of God or the injunctions of men. JOHN STUART MILL (1807–1873), *On Liberty,* 1859.

The people who exercize the power are not always the same people over whom it is exercized. JOHN STUART MILL (1807–1873), *On Liberty,* 1859.

The pressure of an all-powerful totalitarian state creates an emotional tension in its citizens that determines their acts. When people are divided into "loyalists" and "criminals" a premium is placed on every type of conformist, coward, and hireling. CZESLAW MILOSZ, *The Captive Mind,* 1953.

Tyranny is always and everywhere the same, while freedom is always various. The well and truly enslaved are dependable; we know what they will say and think and do. The free are quirky. Tyrannies may be overt and violent or covert and insidious, but they all require the same thing, a subject population in which the power of thought is occluded and the power of deed brought low. RICHARD MITCHELL, *The Graves of Academe,* 1981.

But constant experience shows us that every man invested with power is apt to abuse it, and to carry his authority as far as it will go. Is it not strange, though true, to say that virtue itself is in need of limits? CHARLES-LOUIS de SECONDAT, BARON de MONTESQUIEU (1669–1755), *The Spirit of the Law,* 1748.

Fear is what is needed in a despotism. Virtue is not at all necessary, and honor would be dangerous. CHARLES-LOUIS de SECONDAT, BARON de MONTESQUIEU (1669–1755), *The Spirit of the Law,* 1748.

Somehow liberals have been unable to acquire from life what conservatives seem to be endowed with at birth: namely, a healthy skepticism of the powers of government agencies to do good. DANIEL PATRICK MOYNIHAN, *New York Post,* May 14, 1969

The fascist conception of the state is all-embracing; outside of it no human or spiritual values can exist, much less have value. Thus understood, fascism is totalitarian, and the fascist state—a synthesis and a unit exclusive of all values—interprets, develops, and potentiates the whole life of a people. BENITO MUSSOLINI (1883–1945), *Encyclopedia Italiana,* vol. 14 (1932).

The capital point of the fascist doctrine is the conception of the State, its essence, the work to be accomplished, its final aims. In the conception of fascism, the State is an absolute before which individuals and groups [are] relative. BENITO MUSSOLINI (1883–1945), *Encyclopedia Italiana,* vol. 14 (1932).

Fascism . . . is not only a lawgiver and the founder of institutions, but an educator and a promoter of the spiritual life. It aims to rebuild not the forms of human life, but its content, the man, the character, the faith. And for this end it exacts discipline and an authority which descends into and dominates the interior of the spirit without opposition. BENITO MUSSOLINI (1883–1945), *Encyclopedia Italiana,* vol. 14 (1932).

Anarchy is the stepping stone to absolute power. NAPOLEON BONAPARTE (1769–1821), *Maxims,* 1804–15.

There are men who desire power simply for the sake of the happiness it will bring: these belong chiefly to political parties. FRIEDRICH NIETZSCHE (1844–1900), *The Will to Power,* 1888.

Liberalism has for the most part lost its historic objective in its growing fascination with the uses of centralized power. Where freedom from power was for a long time the chief end of liberal thought, participation in and control of power have become the chief idols of the liberal mind in our time. ROBERT NISBET, *Twilight of Authority,* 1981.

The state claims and exercises the monopoly of crime. It forbids private murder, but itself organizes murder on a colossal scale. It punishes private theft, but itself lays unscrupulous hands on anything it wants, whether the property of citizen or of alien. ALBERT JAY NOCK (1872–1945), *Our Enemy, The State,* 1935.

Under the species of syndicalism and fascism there appears for the first time in Europe a type of man who does not want to give reasons or to be right, but simply shows himself resolved to impose his opinions. JOSÉ ORTEGA y GASSET (1883–1955), *Revolt of the Masses,* 1930.

Power worship blurs political judgment because it leads, almost unavoidably, to the belief that present trends will continue. Whoever is winning at the moment will always seem to be invincible. GEORGE ORWELL (1903–1950), *Shooting an Elephant and Other Essays,* 1950.

The . . . motive of many socialists . . . is simply a hypertrophied sense or order. The present state of affairs offends them not because it causes misery, still less because it makes freedom impossible, but because it is untidy; what they desire, basically, is to reduce the world to something resembling a chessboard. GEORGE ORWELL (1903–1950), *The Road to Wigan Pier,* 1937.

The most common characteristic of all police states is intimidation by surveillance. Citizens know they are being watched and overheard. Their mail is being examined. Their homes can be invaded. VANCE PACKARD, *The People Shapers,* 1977.

Unlimited power is apt to corrupt the minds of those who possess it. WILLIAM PITT, the Elder (1708–1778), Speech, 1770.

Necessity is the plea of every infringement of human freedom. It is the argument of tyrants; it is the creed of slaves. WILLIAM PITT, the Younger (1759–1806), Speech, 1783.

The measure of man is what he does with power. PITTACUS (650?–569? B.C.).

The people have always some champion whom they set over them and nurse into greatness. . . . This and no other is the root from which a tyrant springs; when he first appears he is a protector. PLATO (427–347 B.C.), *The Republic,* ca. 390 B.C.

Plato's moral code is strictly utilitarian; it is the code of collectivist or political utilitarianism. The criterion of morality is what is in the interest of the state. Morality is nothing but political hygiene. This is the collectivist, the tribal, the totalitarian theory of morality: Good is what is in the interest of my group; or my tribe; or my state. SIR KARL POPPER, *The Open Society and Its Enemies,* 1966.

The holistic planner overlooks the fact that it is easy to centralize power but impossible to centralize all that knowledge which is distributed over many individual minds, and whose centralization would be necessary for the wise wielding of centralized power. SIR KARL POPPER, *The Poverty of Historicism,* 1963.

To be governed is to be watched, inspected, spied upon, directed, legislated at, regulated, docketed, indoctrinated, preached at, controlled, assessed, weighed, censored, ordered about, by men who have neither the right, nor the knowledge, nor the virtue. PIERRE-JOSEPH PROUDHON (1809–1865), *General Idea of Revolution in the Nineteenth Century,* 1851.

All parties without exception, when they seek for power, are varieties of absolutism. PIERRE-JOSEPH PROUDHON (1809–1865), *Confessions of a Revolutionary,* 1849.

Did you really think that we want those laws to be observed? We want them broken. There's no way to rule innocent men. The only power the government has is the power to crack down on criminals. Well, when there aren't enough criminals one makes them. One declares so many things to be a crime that it becomes impossible for men to live without breaking laws. AYN RAND (1905–1982), *Atlas Shrugged,* 1957.

The frontier is vague, the transition easy between the status of a loyal opponent wielding a privilege built into democratic institutions and that of an adversary subverting those institutions. To totalitarianism, an opponent is by definition subversive; democracy treats subversives as mere opponents for fear of betraying its principles. JEAN-FRANÇOIS REVEL, *How Democracies Perish,* 1983

If you give me six sentences written by the most innocent of men, I will find something in them with which to hang him. CARDINAL RICHELIEU (1585–1642).

For liberalism, the individual is the end, and society the means. For fascism, society is the end, individuals the means, and its whole life consists in using individuals as instruments for its social ends. ALFREDO ROCCO (1875–1925), *The Political Doctrine of Fascism.*

Fascism . . . faces squarely the problem of the right of the State and of the duty of individuals. Individual rights are only recognized in so far as they are implied in the rights of the State. In this preeminence of duty we find the highest ethical value of fascism. ALFREDO ROCCO (1875–1925), *The Political Doctrine of Fascism.*

Power always acts destructively, for its possessors are ever striving to lace all phenomena of social life into a corset of their laws to give them a definite shape. RUDOLPH ROCKER (1873–1958), *Nationalism and Culture.*

The problem of power is really the fundamental problem of our time and will remain the basic problem of all future history. HERBERT ROSINSKI, *Power and Human Destiny,* 1965.

The most absolute authority is that which penetrates into a man's inmost being and concerns itself no less with his will than with his actions. JEAN-JACQUES ROUSSEAU (1712–1778), *The Social Contract,* 1762.

There is no subjugation so perfect as that which keeps the appearance of freedom, for in that way one captures volition itself. JEAN-JACQUES ROUSSEAU (1712–1778), *Émile,* 1762.

A totalitarian regime . . . can be defined as a state in which the potentialities for control over society by governmental authority are exploited to the limit of available modern techniques—where no significant effort is made to achieve the compromise between the sanctity of the individual and the exigencies of efficient communal life. WALT W. ROSTOW, *The Dynamics of Soviet Society,* 1952.

Those who have seized power, even for the noblest of motives, soon persuade themselves that there are good reasons for not relinquishing it. This is particularly likely to happen if they believe themselves to represent some immensely important cause. They will feel their opponents are ignorant and perverse; before long they will come to hate them. BERTRAND RUSSELL (1872–1970), *Saturday Review,* 1951.

[Power is the] ability to cause people to act as we wish when they would have acted otherwise but for the effects of our desires. BERTRAND RUSSELL (1872–1970), *The Prospects of Industrial Society,* 1931.

Next to enjoying ourselves, the next greatest pleasure consists in preventing others from enjoying themselves, or more generally, in the acquisition of power. BERTRAND RUSSELL (1872–1970), *Skeptical Essays,* 1928.

People often manifest a diseased desire to express their will. A theory is adopted, not because the facts force it upon them, but because its adoption shows their power. MARK RUTHERFORD (1831–1913), *More Pages from a Journal,* 1910.

To live without omnipotence existing somewhere is full of risk and frightening. The "fear of freedom" that many have talked of really is a fear deep within everyone's psyche that existence is not possible without omnipotence, that the full democratic life that puts an end to the dream of absolute power is itself merely a dream. ELI SAGAN, *The Dawn of Tyranny,* 1985.

True, it is evil that a single man should crush the herd, but see not there the worst form of slavery, which is when the herd crushes out the man. ANTOINE de SAINT-EXUPÉRY (1900–1944), *Citadelle.*

The individual cannot exist separate from his existence in the nation. In this way, there is essentially no such thing as an individual within fascist ideology. An individual is one small part of the nation. LYMAN T. SARGENT, *Contemporary Political Ideologies,* 1969

Power is so apt to be insolent, and Liberty to be saucy, that they are very seldom upon good terms. GEORGE SAVILE (1633–1695), *Political Thoughts and Reflections,* 1750.

The more pronounced the ideology of the political-social power, and the less possible the participation of ordinary men and social groups in the decision-making processes, then the easier it is to see that all crimes are of a political nature. In the heavily ideological political structure, the concept of criminal responsibility is spelled out more vividly, the ideological basis of all crime definitions is less concealed. STEPHEN SCHAFER, *The Political Criminal,* 1974.

Orwell knew that the Jacobins controlling a centralized economy are prepared, once they can claim the endorsement of the general will, to do anything in behalf of their conceptions of Reason and Virtue, and he knew that, just here, is the seedbed of the totalitarian state. NATHAN A. SCOTT, JR., in *George Orwell and Nineteen Eighty-Four,* 1985.

However many people a tyrant slaughters, he cannot kill his successor. LUCIUS ANNAEUS SENECA (4 B.C.–65 A.D.), *Epistles.*

To be feared is to fear: no one has been able to strike terror into others and at the same time enjoy peace of mind himself. LUCIUS ANNAEUS SENECA (4 B.C.–65 A.D.), *Epistles.*

You cannot have power for good without having power for evil too. Even mother's milk nourishes murderers as well as heroes. GEORGE BERNARD SHAW (1856–1950), *Major Barbara,* 1905.

Power, like a desolating pestilence, pollutes whate'er it touches; and obedience, bane of all genius, virtue, freedom, truth, makes slaves of men, and of the human frame, a mechanized automaton. PERCY BYSSHE SHELLEY (1792–1822), *Queen Mab,* 1813.

[Totalitarianism is] a system in which no disagreement on ends is allowed. The end justifies the means, which therefore range from persuasion to coercion, from compromise to terror. HANS SIMONS.

No man is fit to be trusted with power. Any man who has lived at all knows the follies and wickedness he's capable of. C. P. SNOW (1905–1980), *The Light and the Dark,* 1961.

When you have robbed a man of everything, he is no longer in your power. He is free again. ALEXANDR SOLZHENITSYN, *The First Circle,* 1969.

For while power in itself may have no more than a tendency to corrupt, absolute power, as Mill and Acton said, corrupts absolutely. It gives its holders a new importance, a new set of habits. Finding themselves worshipped by others, they soon come to worship themselves. Finding that they can do as they like, they indulge in actions that previously seemed so improbable of achievement as to be put beyond the realm of serious contemplation. This is why it is foolish to assume, as the theorists of "democratic" personality are too often inclined to do, that a man out of power will remain the same man when in power. DAVID SPITZ (1916–1979), *American Political Science Review,* vol. 52, 1958.

Power does not corrupt. Fear corrupts, perhaps the fear of a loss of power. JOHN STEINBECK (1902–1968), *The Short Reign of Pippin IV,* 1957.

The state calls its own violence law, but that of the individual crime. MAX STIRNER (1806–1856), *The Ego and His Own,* 1845.

The state always has the sole purpose to limit, tame, subordinate, the individual— to make him subject to some generality or order. MAX STIRNER (1806–1856), *The Ego and His Own,* 1845.

The principal impediment to personal independence and political freedom lies, not surprisingly, in human nature: specifically in the fact that man possesses a powerful passion to control others; that the most effective way to do so is by infantilizing them and pretending to care for them. THOMAS SZASZ, *The Untamed Tongue,* 1990.

The lust for power in dominating others, inflames the heart more than any other passion. CORNELIUS TACITUS (55–117 A.D.).

You cannot have a decent, popular government unless the majority exercise the self-restraint that men with great power ought to exercise. WILLIAM HOWARD TAFT (1857–1930), U.S. President, Speech, October 10, 1909.

[Power is the] capacity of an individual or group of individuals to modify the conduct of other individuals or groups. R. H. TAWNEY (1880–1962), *Equality,* 1931.

The foundations of power vary from age to age, with the interests which move men, and the aspects of life to which they attach a preponderant importance. It has had its source in religion, in military prowess and prestige, in the strength of professional organization, in the exclusive control of certain forms of knowledge and skill, such as those of the magician, the medicine man, and the lawyer. R. H. TAWNEY (1880–1962), *Equality,* 1931.

Every central power which follows its natural tendencies courts and encourages the principle of equality; for equality singularly facilitates, extends, and secures the influence of a central power. ALEXIS de TOCQUEVILLE (1805–1859), *Democracy in America,* 1835.

Every central government worships uniformity: uniformity relieves it from inquiry into an infinity of details, which must be attended to if rules have to be adapted to different men, instead of indiscriminately subjecting all men to the same rule. ALEXIS de TOCQUEVILLE (1805–1859), *Democracy in America,* 1835

The religious superstition consists in the belief that the sacrifices, often of human lives, made to the imaginary being are essential, and that men may and should be brought to that state of mind by all methods, not excluding violence. The political superstition consists in the belief that, besides the duties of man to man, there are more important duties to the imaginary being, Government, and that the sacrifices—often of human lives—made to these imaginary beings are also essential, and that men may and should be brought to that state of mind by all possible means, not excluding violence. LEO TOLSTOY (1828–1910), *The Slavery of Our Times.*

In order to obtain and hold power a man must love it. Thus the effort to get is not likely to be coupled with goodness, but with the opposite qualities of pride, craft and cruelty. LEO TOLSTOY (1828–1910).

If you want an efficient goverment why then go someplace where they have a dictatorship and you'll get it. HARRY S. TRUMAN (1884–1972), U.S. President, Lecture, Columbia University, April 28, 1959.

If power corrupts, weakness in the seat of power with its constant necessity of deals and bribes and compromising arrangements, corrupts even more. BARBARA TUCHMAN (1912–1989), *The March of Folly,* 1984.

The appetite for power is old and irrepressible in humankind, and in its action almost always destructive. BARBARA TUCHMAN (1912–1989), *The March of Folly,* 1984.

It has ever been the tendency of power to add to itself, to enlarge its sphere, to encroach beyond the limits set for it; and where the habit of resisting such encroachment is not fostered and the individual is not taught to be jealous of his rights, individuality gradually disappears and the government or State becomes the all in all. BENJAMIN R. TUCKER (1854–1939), *Instead of a Book,* 1893.

In most cases, when the lion, weary of obeying its master, has torn and devoured him, its nerves are pacified and it looks around for another master before whom to grovel. PAUL VALÉRY (1871–1945), *Reflections on the World Today,* 1931.

The tragedy of the police state is that it always regards all opposition as a crime, and there are no degrees. LORD VANSITTART (1881–1957), Speech, 1947.

Servitude debases men to the point where they end up liking it. MARQUIS de LUC de VAUVENARGUES (1715–1747), *Reflections and Maxims,* 1746.

It is forbidden to kill; therefore all murderers are punished unless they kill in large numbers and to the sound of trumpets. VOLTAIRE (1694–1778), *Philosophical Dictionary,* 1764.

The tyranny of the many would be when one body takes over the rights of the others, and then exercises its power to change the laws in its favor. . . . One despot always has a few good moments, but an assembly of despots never does. VOLTAIRE (1694–1778), *Philosophical Dictionary,* 1764.

A society in which people are already isolated and atomized, divided by suspicions and destructive rivalry, would support a system of terror better than a society without much chronic antagonism. EUGENE V. WALKER, *Terror and Resistance,* 1969.

Politicians are not people who seek power in order to implement policies they think necessary. They are people who seek policies in order to attain power. EVELYN WAUGH (1903–1966).

An unlimited power to tax involves, necessarily, the power to destroy. DANIEL WEBSTER (1782–1852), Oral argument, *McCullough* v. *Maryland,* U.S. Supreme Court, 1819.

All authority is quite degrading. It degrades those who exercise it, and degrades those over whom it is exercised. When it is violently, grossly, and cruelly used, it produces a good effect, by creating, or at any rate bringing out, the spirit of revolt and Individualism that is to kill it. When it is used with a certain amount of kindness, and accompanied by prizes and rewards, it is dreadfully demoralizing. OSCAR WILDE (1854–1900), *The Soul of Man under Socialism,* 1891.

It is from weakness that people reach for dictators and concentrated government power. Only the strong can be free. And only the productive can be strong. WENDELL L. WILKIE (1892–1944), *This Is Wendell Wilkie,* 1940.

If a nation wishes, it can have both free elections and slavery. GARY WILLS, *Nixon Agonistes,* 1972.

People will endure their tyrants for years, but they will tear their deliverers to pieces if a millennium is not created immediately. WOODROW WILSON (1856–1924), U.S. President, in *Mr. Wilson's War* (Dos Passos), 1963.

Power is more easily manifested in destroying than in creating. WILLIAM WORDSWORTH (1770–1850), *The Borderers,* 1796.

Utopianism, Idealism, and Reformist Zeal

Liberty, next to religion, has been the motive of good deeds and the common pretext of crime. LORD ACTON (1834–1902), Lecture, 1877.

Remember, democracy never lasts long. It soon wastes, exhausts, and murders itself. There never was a democracy that did not commit suicide. JOHN ADAMS (1735–1826), U.S. President, Letter, April 15, 1814.

It is easier to fight for one's principles than to live up to them. ALFRED ADLER (1870–1937).

In spite of laughing at them, the world would never get along without reformers. LOUISA MAY ALCOTT (1832–1888), *Little Women,* 1869.

It is part of the moral tragedy with which we are dealing that words like "democracy," "freedom," "rights," "justice," which have so often inspired heroism and have led men to give their lives for things which make life worthwhile, can also become a trap, the means of destroying the very things men desire to uphold. SIR NORMAN ANGELL (1874–1967), 1956.

The myth of the revolution serves as a refuge for utopian intellectuals; it becomes the mysterious, unpredictable intercessor between the real and the ideal. RAYMOND ARON (1905–1983), *The Great Debate,* 1965.

The humorous man recognizes that absolute purity, absolute justice, absolute logic and perfection are beyond human achievement and that men have been able to live happily for thousands of years in a state of genial frailty. BROOKS ATKINSON, *Once around the Sun,* 1951.

As for the philosophers, they make imaginary laws for imaginary commonwealths, and their discourses are as the stars, which give little light because they are so high. SIR FRANCIS BACON (1561–1626), *The Advancement of Learning,* 1605.

The most melancholy of human reflections perhaps, is that, on the whole, it is a question whether the benevolence of mankind does more harm than good. WALTER BAGEHOT (1826–1877), *Physics and Politics,* 1869.

Nothing is more unpleasant than a virtuous person with a mean mind. WALTER BAGEHOT (1826–1977).

Idealism is the despot of thought, just as politics is the despot of will. MIKHAIL BAKUNIN (1814–1876).

A devotion to humanity . . . is too easily equated with a devotion to a Cause, and Causes, as we know, are notoriously bloodthirsty. JAMES BALDWIN (1924–1987), *Notes of a Native Son,* 1955.

No one is more dangerous than he who imagines himself pure in heart: for his purity, by definition, is unassailable. JAMES BALDWIN (1924–1987), *Nobody Knows My Name,* 1961.

Equality may perhaps be a right, but no power in the world can ever turn it into a fact. HONORÉ de BALZAC (1799–1850), *La Duchesse de Langeais,* 1834.

She [Gudrun Ensslin] was idealistic, with an innate disgust of any kind of compromise. She longed for the absolute, for the perfect solution. JULIAN BECKER, *Hitler's Children: Story of the Baader-Meinhof Terrorist Gang,* 1977.

We may say that the successful reformers are those who are seeking not so much to "make people good" as to share an enthusiasm. CHARLES A. BENNETT, *Philosophical Study of Mysticism,* 1923.

Perhaps a new century is beginning, a century in which the intellectuals and the cultivated class will dream of the means of avoiding utopias and of returning to a non-utopian society, less "perfect" and more free. NIKOLAS BERDYAYEV (1874–1948).

From the utopians' own point of view, there are usually only the most implausible prescriptions on how to get from the deplorable status quo to the hoped-for utopia. Intellectual acumen is mostly exhibited in efforts to demolish the positions of ideological adversaries. In those efforts there is indeed a "critical" attitude which unfortunately rarely extends to one's own intellectual constructions, and even less to the political programs of one's ideological co-religionists. PETER L. BERGER, *Pyramids of Sacrifice,* 1974.

Ideal goals lead to endless frustration and exaggerate the hostilities that are no longer supposed to be present, all under the guise of creating "a new heaven and a new earth." JOSEPH H. BERKE, *The Tyranny of Malice,* 1988.

But to manipulate men, to propel them towards goals which you—the social reformers—see, but they may not, is to deny their human essence, to treat them as objects without wills of their own, and therefore to degrade them. SIR ISAIAH BERLIN, *Two Concepts of Liberty,* 1958.

He who would do good to another must do it in Minute Particulars. General good is the plea of the scoundrel, hypocrite, and flatterer; for art and science cannot exist but in minutely organized particulars. WILLIAM BLAKE (1757–1827).

Sacrificers are not the ones to pity. The ones to pity are those they sacrifice. ELIZABETH BOWEN (1899–1973), *The Death of the Heart,* 1938.

The spirit of reform is terrible in its excess. It is a matter of great judgment to stay it at a proper point. HUGH HENRY BRACKENRIDGE (1748–1816), *Modern Chivalry*, 1792–1815.

Whenever there are tremendous virtues it's a sure sign something's wrong. BERTOLT BRECHT (1898–1956), *Mother Courage and Her Children*, 1941.

Good intentions unaided by knowledge will perhaps produce more injury than benefit. CHARLES BROCKDEN BROWN (1771–1810), *Arthur Mervyn*, 1800.

This dream of absolute, universal equality is amazing, terrifying and inhuman. And the moment it captures people's minds, the result is mountains of corpses and rivers of blood, accompanied by attempts to straighten the stooped and shorten the tall. VLADIMIR BUKOVSKY, *To Build a Castle*, 1979.

The dearest ambition of a slave is not liberty but to have a slave of his own. SIR RICHARD BURTON (1821–1890).

The optimist proclaims we live in the best of all possible worlds; and the pessimist fears this is true. JAMES B. CABELL (1879–1959), *The Silver Stallion*, 1926.

The evil that is in the world almost always comes of ignorance, and good intentions may do as much harm as malevolence, if they lack understanding. ALBERT CAMUS (1913–1960), *The Plague*, 1947.

The slave begins by demanding justice and ends by wanting to wear a crown. He must dominate in turn. ALBERT CAMUS (1913–1960), *The Rebel*, 1951.

To be happy we must not be too concerned with others. ALBERT CAMUS (1913–1960), *The Fall*, 1956.

Politics and the fate of mankind are shaped by men without ideals and without greatness. Men who have greatness within them don't go in for politics. ALBERT CAMUS (1913–1960), *The Rebel*, 1951.

Every revolutionary ends up by becoming either an oppressor or a heretic. ALBERT CAMUS (1913–1960), *The Rebel*, 1951.

The smashers of language are looking for a new justice among words. It does not exist. Words are unequal and unjust. ELIAS CANETTI, *The Human Province*, 1978.

The utopian, fixing his eyes on the future, thinks in terms of creative spontaneity: the realist, rooted in the past, in terms of causality. E. H. CARR, *The Twenty Years Crisis, 1919–1939*, 1946.

The utopian sets up an ethical standard which purports to be independent of politics, and seeks to make politics conform to it. The realist cannot logically accept any standard of value save that of fact. E. H. CARR, *The Twenty Years Crisis, 1919–1939*, 1946.

One is not superior merely because one sees the world in an odious light. FRANÇOIS RENÉ, VICOMTE de CHATEAUBRIAND (1768–1848).

The weakness of all utopias is this, that they take the greatest difficulty of man and assume it to be overcome, and then give an elaborate account of overcoming the smaller ones. GILBERT KEITH CHESTERTON (1874–1936), *Heretics,* 1905

The sin and sorrow of despotism is not that it does not love men, but that it loves them too much and trusts them too little. GILBERT KEITH CHESTERTON (1874–1936), *Robert Browning,* 1914.

For the worst tyrant is not the man who rules by fear; the worst tyrant is he who rules by love and plays on it as on a harp. GILBERT KEITH CHESTERTON (1874–1936), *Robert Browning,* 1914.

Utopia always seems to me to mean regimentation rather than emancipation; repression rather than expansion. It is generally called a republic and it always is a monarchy . . . because it is really ruled by one man: the author of the book. His ideal world is always the world that he wants; and not the world that the world wants. GILBERT KEITH CHESTERTON (1874–1936), *Generally Speaking,* 1929.

Humanitarians of a material and dogmatic type, the philanthropists and the professional reformers go to look for humanity in remote places and in huge statistics. But humanitarians of the highest type, the great poets and philosophers, do not go to look for humanity at all. For them alone among all men the nearest drawing room is full of humanity, and even their own families are human. GILBERT KEITH CHESTERTON (1874–1936), *Robert Browning,* 1914.

That all men should be brothers is the dream of men who have no brothers. CHARLES CHINCHOLLES, 1800.

One of the besetting fallacies of reformers is the delusion that their plans will be carried out by people who think precisely as they do. JOHN MAURICE CLARK, *Guideposts in a Time of Change,* 1949.

Every reform, however necessary, will by weak minds be carried to an excess, that itself will need reforming. SAMUEL TAYLOR COLERIDGE (1772–1834), *Biographia Literaria,* 1817.

Far from being necessarily dysfunctional, a certain degree of conflict is an essential element in group formation and the persistence of group life. LEWIS A. COSER, *Functions of Social Conflict,* 1956.

All zeal for a reform, that gives offense; / To peace and charity, is mere pretense. WILLIAM COWPER (1731–1800), *Charity,* 1782.

No people do so much harm as those who go around doing good. MANDELL CREIGHTON (1843–1901).

One of the tragic illusions of Communist leaders is their hubris —the Promethean belief in their ability to reshape men and societies at will, coupled with faith in the unlimited perfectibility of man and society—an outlook reinforced by their dictatorial powers but seemingly unaffected by the irrepressible consequences of their own actions. . . . Nevertheless, at the mobilization stage Communist regimes come closer to this utopian prospect than any others. ALEXANDER DALLIN and GEORGE W. BRESLAUER, *Political Terror in Communist Regimes,* 1970.

It is the besetting sin of the idealist to sacrifice reality for his ideals; to reject life because it fails to come up to his ideal; and this vice is just as prevalent among religious idealists as secular ones. CHRISTOPHER DAWSON (1889–1970), *The Judgment of the Nations,* 1942.

Pare an idealist to the quick and you'll find a Nero. BENJAMIN DeCASSERES, *Fantasia Impromptu,* 1933.

[Communism represents] a necessity of sacrificing the idea of what is excellent for the individual to the ideal of what is excellent for the whole. THOMAS DeQUINCY (1785–1859).

The astonishing and least comprehensible thing about [man] is his range of vision; his gaze into the infinite distance; his lonely passion for ideas and ideals. W. MACNEILE DIXON (1866–1945), *The Human Situation,* 1937.

Absolute despotism equates itself with the belief in absolute human happiness—though it is an all-inclusive and universal tyranny. MILOVAN DJILAS, *The New Class,* 1957.

Every revolution, and even every war, creates illusions and is conducted in the name of unrealizable ideals. During the struggle the ideals seem real enough for the combatants; by the end they often cease to exist. MILOVAN DJILAS, *The New Class,* 1957.

Throughout history there have been no ideal ends which were attained with nonideal, inhumane means, just as there has been no free society which was built by slaves. Nothing so well reveals the reality and greatness of ends as the methods used to obtain them. MILOVAN DJILAS, *The New Class,* 1957.

The golden age is the most implausible of all dreams. But for it men have given up their life and strength; for the sake of it prophets have died and been slain; without it the people will not live and cannot die. FYODOR DOSTOEVSKY (1821–1881), *The Possessed,* 1870–72.

All utopias will come to pass only when we grow wings and all people are converted into angels. FYODOR DOSTOEVSKY (1821–1881), *The Diary of a Writer,* 1876–77, 1880–81.

A reformer is a man who thinks that men can be turned into angels by an election. FINLEY PETER DUNNE (1867–1936).

Utopias of equality are biologically doomed, and the best that the amiable philosopher can hope for is an approximate equality of legal justice and educational opportunity. A society in which all potential abilities are allowed to develop and function will have a survival advantage in the competition of groups. WILL DURANT (1885–1981) and ARIEL DURANT (1898–1981), *The Lessons of History,* 1968.

History smiles at all attempts to force its flow into theoretical patterns or logical grooves; it plays havoc with our generalizations, breaks all our rules; history is baroque. WILL DURANT (1885–1981) and ARIEL DURANT (1898–1981), *The Age of Reason Begins.*

And what if Marx had not been betrayed? He did not desire the terrible regimes that claim to follow his teachings. They probably would have filled him with horror. But what if they are not an excrescence, an aberration, a deviation of his doctrine? What if they reveal the implicit logic of his doctrine, pushed to its ultimate conclusion? MAURICE DUVERGER, *The Orange Trees of Lake Balaton,* 1980.

It is the irony of democracy that the responsibility for the survival of liberal democratic values depends on elites, not masses. THOMAS R. DYE and HARMON ZIEGLER, *The Irony of Democracy,* 1971.

Life is a battle; it is a battle without any final or assured victory, and these aspiring idealists lack the pluck to go down fighting it. Bereaved of other-worldly goals, they have been yearning for some home, some certainty, some Absolute on earth, if it is only the absolute parody of their dreams. MAX EASTMAN (1883–1969), *Reflections on the Failure of Socialism,* 1944.

An election is coming. Universal peace is declared, and the foxes have a sincere interest in prolonging the lives of the poultry. GEORGE ELIOT (1819–1880), *Felix Holt, The Radical,* 1866.

Emotionally healthy people are true to themselves and do not masochistically subjugate themselves to or unduly sacrifice themselves for others. They tend to put themselves first—realizing that, if they do not take care of themselves, no one else will—a few selected others second, and the rest of the world not too far behind. ALBERT ELLIS, *On the Barricades,* 1989.

It is easy to live for others; everybody does. I call on you to live for yourselves. RALPH WALDO EMERSON (1803–1882), Journals, 1845.

The louder he talked of his honor, the faster we counted our spoons. RALPH WALDO EMERSON (1803–1882), *The Conduct of Life,* 1860.

We are reformers in the spring and summer; in the autumn and winter we stand by the old; reformers in the morning, conservers at night. RALPH WALDO EMERSON (1803–1882), *The Conservative,* 1841.

The degeneration of liberal doctrine during this century has been rooted in the unwillingness of liberals to accept certain basic assumptions about the political nature of human society. Thus liberals have been extremely reluctant to assume that politics arises out of, and only out of, rationally irreconcilable conflicts of interest among people. G. LOWELL FIELD and JOHN HIGLEY, *Elitism,* 1980.

Liberalism's doctrinal degeneration has been closely related to the problem of discriminating between fact and value propositions that have been so central to this century's intellectual life. G. LOWELL FIELD and JOHN HIGLEY, *Elitism,* 1980.

There is no zeal blinder than that which is impaired with the love of justice against offenders. HENRY FIELDING (1707–1754), *Tom Jones,* 1749.

In one's absorption in an ideal, it is possible to imagine that one generation can be sacrificed for the sake of its descendents. LOUIS FISCHER (1896–1970), *The God That Failed,* 1949.

Sire, the desire for perfection is the worst disease that ever afflicted the human mind. JEAN-PIERRE-LOUIS, MARQUIS de FONTANES (1757–1821).

Positive ideals are becoming a curse, for they can seldom be achieved without someone being killed, maimed, or interned. E. M. FORSTER (1879–1970), 1939.

"For your own good" is a persuasive argument that will eventually make a man agree to his own destruction. JANET FRAME, *Faces in The Water,* 1982.

Those who have given themselves the most concern about the happiness of peoples have made their neighbors very miserable. ANATOLE FRANCE (1844–1924), *The Crime of Sylvester Bonnard,* 1881.

The Golden Age never was the present age. THOMAS FULLER (1608–1661), *Gnomologia,* 1732.

Idealism increases in direct proportion to one's distance from the problem. JOHN GALSWORTHY (1867–1933), *Maid in Waiting,* 1931.

You can't make a silk purse out of a sow's ear, and you can't change human nature from intelligent self-interest into pure idealism—not in this life. JOSEPH G. CANNON (1836–1926), *The Baltimore Sun,* March 4, 1923.

No hint of genuine charity ameliorates our vision of society, once sentimentalism has been laid side. What passes for cooperation turns out to be a mixture of opportunism and exploitation. Scratch an altruist and watch a hypocrite bleed. MICHAEL GHISELIN, *The Economy of Nature and the Evolution of Sex,* 1974.

The very act of sacrifice magnifies the one who sacrifices himself to the point where his sacrifice is much more costly to humanity than would have been the loss of those for whom he is sacrificing himself. But in his abnegation lies the secret of his grandeur. ANDRÉ GIDE (1869–1951), *Journals,* 1931.

The worse the society, the more law there will be. In Hell there will be nothing but law and due process will be meticulously observed. GRANT GILMORE, *New York Times,* February 23, 1977.

All the evil in the world is the fault of the self-styled pure in heart, a result of their eagerness to unearth secrets and expose them to the light of the sun. JEAN GIRAUDOUX (1882–1944), *Electra,* 1937.

Lawgivers or revolutionaries who promise equality and liberty at the same time are either utopian dreamers or charlatans. JOHANN WOLFGANG von GOETHE (1749–1832).

Opponents fancy they refute us when they repeat their own opinion and pay no attention to ours. JOHANN WOLFGANG von GOETHE (1749–1832), *Maxims and Reflections.*

Could we perfect human nature, we might also expect a perfect state of things. JOHANN WOLFGANG VON GOETHE (1749–1832), 1824.

The chimerical pursuit of perfection is always linked to some important deficiency, frequently the inability to love. BERNARD GRASSET, *The Paths of Writing.*

No human being can really understand another, and no one can arrange another's happiness. GRAHAM GREENE (1904–1991), *The Heart of the Matter,* 1948.

Among the masses, even in revolution, aristocracy must ever exist. Destroy it in the nobility, and it becomes centered in the rich and powerful Houses of Commons. Pull them down, and it still survives in the master and foreman in the workshop. FRANÇOIS PIERRE GUIZOT (1787–1874), *Recollections to Serve the History of My Time,* 1858-67.

The foundations of every ideology are false, in the sense that every ideology bases itself on some vision of the world that does not correspond to existential reality. LOUIS J. HALLE, *The Ideological Imagination,* 1972.

An idealist believes the short run doesn't count. A cynic believes that the long run doesn't matter. A realist believes that what is done or left undone in the short run determines the long run. SYDNEY J. HARRIS, *Reader's Digest,* May 1979.

Each of us has his own little private conviction of rightness and almost by definition, the Utopian condition of which we all dream is that in which all people finally see the error of their ways and agree with us. S. I. HAYAKAWA, *Where, When & Why: Social Studies in American Schools* (Mayer, ed.), 1963.

Man is the only animal that laughs and weeps; for he is the only animal that is struck with the difference between what things are, and what they ought to be. WILLIAM HAZLITT (1778–1830), Lectures, 1819.

Goodness without wisdom always accomplishes evil. ROBERT A. HEINLEIN (1907–1988), 1961.

Never appeal to a man's better nature. He may not have one. Invoking his self-interest gives you more leverage. ROBERT A. HEINLEIN (1907–1988), *Methuselah's Children,* 1958.

More misery has been created by reformers than by any other force in human history. Show me someone who says, "Something must be done!" and I will show you a head full of vicious intentions that have no other outlet. FRANK HERBERT, *Dune,* 1965.

Utopianism is probably a necessary social device for generating the superhuman efforts without which no major revolution is achieved. Utopianism can become such a social device because revolutionary movements and revolutions appear to prove that almost no change is beyond their reach. ERIC J. HOBSBAWM, *Primitive Rebels,* 1959.

Some of the worst tyrannies of our day genuinely are "vowed" to the service of mankind, yet can function only by pitting neighbor against neighbor. The all-seeing eye of a totalitarian regime is usually the watchful eye of the next-door neighbor. ERIC HOFFER (1902–1983), *The Ordeal of Change,* 1964.

There is sublime thieving in all giving. Someone gives us all he has and we are his. ERIC HOFFER (1902–1983), *The Passionate State of Mind,* 1954.

We cannot win the weak by sharing our wealth with them. They feel our generosity as oppression. ERIC HOFFER (1902–1983), *The Ordeal of Change,* 1964.

A low capacity for getting along with those near us often goes hand in hand with a high receptivity to the idea of the brotherhood of men. ERIC HOFFER (1902–1983), *The Ordeal of Change,* 1964.

Man is born a predestined idealist, for he is born to act. To act is to affirm the worth of an end, and to persist in affirming the worth of an end is to make an ideal. OLIVER WENDELL HOLMES, JR. (1841–1935), Speech, June 28, 1911.

Drive out nature with a pitchfork, and she will always come back. HORACE (65–8 B.C.), *Satires,* 25 B.C.

Every man is a reformer until reform tramps on his toes. EDGAR WATSON HOWE (1853–1937), *Country Town Sayings,* 1911.

There is always a type of man who says he loves his fellow men, and expects to make a living at it. EDGAR WATSON HOWE (1853–1937), *Ventures in Common Sense,* 1919.

I do not love my neighbor as myself, and apologize to no one. I treat my neighbor as fairly and politely as I hope to be treated, but there is no law in nature or common sense ordering me to go beyond that. EDGAR WATSON HOWE (1853–1937), *Success Easier Than Failure,* 1917.

That at the core of every idealist there reigns a demon of cruelty, a monster thirsty for blood—no one must admit this as a universal law, else Time, that suave imposter, could not go on with life. ELBERT HUBBARD (1856–1915), *The Philistine.*

[An anarchist is] one who maps and surveys the air and constructs dainty Utopias with the building-blocks quarried from his . . . credulity. ELBERT HUBBARD (1856–1915), *The Philistine.*

The ideal of a perfect and immortal commonwealth will always be found as chimerical as that of a perfect and immortal man. DAVID HUME (1711–1776), *History of England,* 1759–62.

Idealism is the noble toga that political gentlemen drape over their will to power. ALDOUS HUXLEY (1894–1963), *New York Herald Tribune,* November 25, 1963.

Only one more indispensible massacre of capitalists or Communists or fascists and there we are—there we are—in the Golden Future! ALDOUS HUXLEY (1894–1963), *Time Must Have a Stop,* 1944.

Don't use that foreign word "ideals" when you have that excellent native word "lies." HENRIK IBSEN (1828–1906), *The Wild Duck,* 1884.

Meekness is the mask of malice. ROBERT G. INGERSOLL (1833–1899), *Prose-Poems and Selections,* 1884.

Mere human beings cannot afford to be fanatical about anything. Not even about justice or loyalty. The fanatic for justice ends by murdering a million helpless people to clear a space for his law courts. If we are to survive on this planet there must be compromises. STORM JAMESON (1891–1986).

Be not too hasty to trust or admire the teachers of morality; they discourse like angels but live like men. SAMUEL JOHNSON (1709–1784), *Rasselas,* 1759.

As I know more of mankind I expect less of them, and am ready now to call a man a good man upon easier terms than I was formerly. SAMUEL JOHNSON (1709–1974), in *Boswell's Life of Johnson,* 1791.

The mind is never satisfied with the objects immediately before it, but is always breaking away from the present and losing itself in schemes of future felicity. The natural flights of the human mind are not from pleasure to pleasure, but from hope to hope. SAMUEL JOHNSON (1709–1784), *The Rambler,* March 24, 1750.

One should be suspicious of "love" as a political slogan. A government which purports to "love" its citizens invariably desires all the prerogatives of a lover: to share the loved one's thoughts and to keep him in bondage. ERIC JULBER, *Esquire* magazine, 1969.

Every form of addiction is bad, no matter whether the narcotic be alcohol or morphine or idealism. CARL GUSTAV JUNG (1875–1961), *Archetypes and the Collective Unconsciousness.*

Two things fill the mind with ever increasing admiration and awe, the oftener and the more steadily we reflect upon them: the starry heavens above and the moral law within. IMMANUEL KANT (1724–1804).

Fanatics have their dreams, wherewith they weave, / A paradise for a sect. JOHN KEATS (1795–1821).

The utopian's moral goals are invoked to justify his use of power. The utopian's (imagined) monopoly of morality justifies his demand for a monopoly of power. Totalitarianism is rooted in the variety of utopian political philosophy which seeks moral reform ends through political means. Totalitarians use power to remake men. JEANE J. KIRKPATRICK, *Dictatorships and Double Standards,* 1982.

The absence of utopianism in the Constitution, law, and traditional political culture has been . . . important in limiting expectations concerning what can be achieved by politics. The history of the last two centuries confirms what the framers of the Constitution understood: that the perfect is the enemy of the good, and the search for unalloyed virtue in public life leads to unalloyed terror. JEANE J. KIRKPATRICK, *Dictatorships and Double Standards,* 1982.

If we survey history and compare the lofty aims, in the name of which revolutions were started, and the sorry end to which they came, we see again and again how a polluted civilization pollutes its own revolutionary offspring. ARTHUR KOESTLER (1904–1983), *The God That Failed,* 1949.

Devotion to pure utopia, and revolt against a polluted society, are thus the two poles which provide the tension of all militant creeds. ARTHUR KOESTLER (1904–1983), *The God That Failed,* 1949.

The Revolutionary's Utopia, which in appearance represents a complete break with the past, is always modeled on some image of the Lost Paradise, of a legendary Golden Age. . . . All utopias are fed from the sources of mythology; the social engineer's blueprints are merely revised editions of the ancient text. ARTHUR KOESTLER (1904–1983), *The God That Failed,* 1949.

The reformer is equally apt to forget that hatred, even of the objectively hateful, does not produce the charity and justice on which a utopian society must be based. ARTHUR KOESTLER (1904–1983), *The God That Failed,* 1949.

We would often be ashamed of our finest actions if the world understood the motives that produced them. FRANÇOIS, DUC de LA ROCHEFOUCAULD (1613–1680), *Maxims,* 1665.

Humility is often only feigned submission which people use to render others submissive. It is a subterfuge of pride which lowers itself in order to rise. FRANÇOIS, DUC de LA ROCHEFOUCAULD (1613–1680), *Maxims,* 1665.

What appears to be generosity is often only ambition disguised, which despises small interests to pursue great ones. FRANÇOIS, DUC de LA ROCHEFOUCAULD (1613–1680), *Maxims,* 1665.

We often do good in order that we may do evil with impunity. FRANÇOIS, DUC de LA ROCHEFOUCAULD (1613–1680), *Maxims,* 1665.

Morality which is based on ideas, or on an ideal, is an unmitigated evil. D. H. LAWRENCE (1885–1930), *Fantasia of the Unconscious,* 1922.

We think that love and benevolence will cure anything. Whereas love and benevolence are our poison, poison to the giver, and still more poison to the receiver. D. H. LAWRENCE (1885–1930), *Fantasia of the Unconscious,* 1922.

Do not confuse your vested interests with ethics. Do not identify the enemies of your privilege with the enemies of humanity. MAX LERNER, *Actions and Passions,* 1949.

Young and free of all attachments to the past . . . a new generation . . . smitten with liberty, eager for glory, above all young. With the naive faith of youth, generous illusions, limitless hope, they flattered themselves that they could avoid the pitfalls of their fathers and seize the conquests of the revolution while repudiating its crimes. FRANÇOIS PIERRE LEROUX (1797–1871), *The Globe,* 1830.

One of the marks of a certain type of man is that he can't give up a thing without wanting everyone else to give it up. C. S. LEWIS (1898–1963), 1944.

Ideals are an imaginative understanding of that which is desirable in that which is possible. WALTER LIPPMANN (1889–1974), *A Preface to Morals,* 1929.

The harder they try to make earth into heaven, the more they make it into a hell. WALTER LIPPMANN (1889–1974), *The Public Philosophy,* 1955.

The radical error of the modern democratic gospel is that it promises, not the good life of this world, but the perfect life of heaven. WALTER LIPPMANN (1889–1974), *The Public Philosophy,* 1955.

There's nothing we read of in torture's inventions like a well-meaning dunce with the best of intentions. JAMES RUSSELL LOWELL (1819–1891), *A Fable for Critics,* 1848.

The devil loves nothing better than the intolerance of reformers. JAMES RUSSELL LOWELL (1819–1891).

I have long been convinced that institutions purely democratic must, sooner or later, destroy liberty, or civilization, or both. THOMAS BABINGTON McCAULAY (1800–1859), Letter, May 23, 1857.

[They] try frantically to order and stabilize the world so that no unmanageable, unexpected or unfamiliar dangers will ever appear. They hedge themselves about with all sorts of ceremonials, rules and formulas so that no new contingencies may appear. They are much like brain injured cases . . . who manage to maintain their equilibrium by avoiding everything unfamiliar and strange and by ordering their restricted world in such a neat, disciplined, orderly fashion that everything in the world can be counted on. ABRAHAM MASLOW, *Psychological Review,* 1943.

There is no explanation for evil. It must be looked upon as a necessary part of the order of the universe. To ignore it is childish, to bewail it senseless. W. SOMERSET MAUGHAM (1874–1965), *The Summing Up,* 1938.

The chief beginning of evil is goodness in excess. MENANDER (342–291 B.C.).

An idealist is one who, on noticing that a rose smells better than a cabbage, concludes that it would make better soup. H. L. MENCKEN (1880–1956), *Minority Report,* 1956.

It is not materialism that is the chief curse of the world, as pastors teach, but idealism. Men get into trouble by taking their visions and hallucinations too seriously. H. L. MENCKEN (1880–1956), *Minority Report,* 1956.

The urge to save humanity is almost always a false front for the urge to rule. H. L. MENCKEN (1880–1956).

A large part of altruism, even when it is perfectly honest, is grounded upon the fact that it is uncomfortable to have unhappy people about one. H. L. MENCKEN (1880–1956), *Prejudices: Fourth Series,* 1924.

It's among the intelligentsia . . . that we often find the glib compulsion to explain everything and to understand nothing. JOOST A. MERLOO, *The Rape of the Mind,* 1956.

The most awful tyranny is that of the proximate utopia where the last sins are currently being eliminated and where, tomorrow, there will be no sins because all the sinners have been wiped out. THOMAS R. MERTON (1915–1968), 1948.

The spirit of improvement is not always a spirit of liberty, for it may aim at forcing improvements on an unwilling people. JOHN STUART MILL (1806–1873), *On Liberty,* 1859.

I wasn't driven into medicine by a social conscience but by rampant curiosity. JONATHAN MILLER.

A reformer is one who insists on his conscience being your guide. MILLARD MILLER.

The man who is forever disturbed about the condition of humanity either has no problems of his own or has refused to face them. HENRY MILLER (1891–1980), *Sunday after the War,* 1944.

Perfect reason avoids all extremes, and requires that one be good, in moderation. MOLIÈRE (1622–1673), *The Misanthrope,* 1666.

We may describe utopian thought as a belief in an unspoiled beginning and attainable perfection. . . . [T]he utopian may be pessimistic about individual human nature, but optimistic about the ability of man's social nature, as embodied in society, to overcome the recalcitrance of the individual. To overcome individual resistance will mean force, but the utopian holds that, if the goal is goodness and perfection, then the use of force is justified. It is even justifiable to establish a special government of the elect as repositories of the doctrine of the perfect society. THOMAS MOLNAR, *Utopia: The Perennial Heresy,* 1967.

The utopian has certain philosophical presuppositions about the past of the human race, its nature and potentialities. He uses his assumptions toward constructing an imaginary community and world order. In other words, in speaking of the utopian mentality, we are in another world of special data systematically organized by a logic which is determined by a specified ideal. THOMAS MOLNAR, *Utopia: The Perennial Heresy,* 1967.

Utopians . . . consider individual freedom as the stumbling block on which the grandiose idea of mankind's totalization may flounder. THOMAS MOLNAR, *Utopia: The Perennial Heresy,* 1967.

Uniformity, therefore, is an essential built-in element of utopian existence, and it is no less important that this uniformity remain permanent. THOMAS MOLNAR, *Utopia: The Perennial Heresy,* 1967.

Many have come to grief in their attempt to establish a better state of things in place of what they have destroyed. MICHEL de MONTAIGNE (1533–1592), *Essays,* 1588.

Let us permit nature to have her way: she understands her business better than we do. MICHEL de MONTAIGNE (1533–1592), *Essays,* 1588.

The greatest horrors in our world, from the executions in Iran to the brutalities of the IRA, are committed by people who are totally sincere. JOHN MORTIMER, *The Observer,* August 5, 1979.

There is no snobbishness like that of professional egalitarians. MALCOLM MUGGERIDGE (1903–1990), *Chronicles of Wasted Time,* 1978.

Perfection does not exist. To understand it is the triumph of human intelligence; to desire to possess it is the most dangerous kind of madness. ALFRED de MUSSET (1810–1857).

Among those who dislike oppression are many who like to oppress. NAPOLEON BONAPARTE (1761–1821), 1815.

The religious interpretation of the world is essentially an insistence that the ideal is real and that the real can be understood only in the light of the ideal. REINHOLD NIEBUHR (1892–1971).

The visionary denies the truth to himself, the liar only to others. FRIEDRICH NIETZSCHE (1844–1900), *Miscellaneous Maxims and Opinions,* 1879.

The idealist in incorrigible: if he be thrown out of his Heaven, he makes himself a suitable ideal out of Hell. FRIEDRICH NIETZSCHE (1844–1900), *Miscellaneous Maxims and Opinions,* 1879.

Whoever fights monsters should see to it that in the process he does not become a monster. FRIEDRICH NIETZSCHE (1844–1900), *Beyond Good And Evil,* 1886.

What has caused greater suffering than the follies of the compassionate? FRIEDRICH NIETZSCHE (1844–1900).

The human capacity to bend ideals into dogmas is inexhaustible. More lives have been tortured, terrorized, shot, hanged, poisoned, imprisoned, and exiled in the name of one or another of the modern political dogmas of freedom, fraternity, equality, and justice than in all other centuries combined. ROBERT NISBET, *Columbia Journalism Review,* March/April 1982.

What gives the new despotism its peculiar effectiveness is indeed its liaison with humanitarianism, but beyond this fact is its capacity for entering into the smallest details of human life. ROBERT NISBET, *Twilight of Authority,* 1981.

Creeds like pacifism and anarchism, which seem on the surface to imply a complete renunciation of power, [discourage] rather than encourage this habit of mind. For if you have embraced a creed which appears to be free from the ordinary dirtiness of politics . . . the more you are in the right [and] everybody else should be bullied into thinking likewise. GEORGE ORWELL (1903–1950), *Nineteen Eighty-Four,* 1949.

Men never do evil so thoroughly and cheerfully as when they do it for conscience sake. BLAISE PASCAL (1623–1662), *Pensées,* 1670.

Man is neither an angel nor a brute, and the very attempt to raise him to the level of the former sinks him to that of the latter. BLAISE PASCAL (1623–1662), *Pensées,* 1670.

The humanitarian wishes to be a prime mover in the lives of others. He cannot admit either the divine or the natural order, by which men have the power to help themselves. The humanitarian puts himself in the place of God. ISABEL PATERSON, *The God of the Machine,* 1943.

A good end cannot sanctify evil means; nor must we ever do evil, that good may come of it. WILLIAM PENN (1644–1718), *Some Fruits of Solitude in Reflections and Maxims.*

The individual who commits violence in the name of peace is steady on the road to becoming that which he hates. LAURENCE J. PETER, *The Peter Program.*

I find the remark, " 'Tis distance lends enchantment to the view" is no less true of the political than of the natural world. FRANKLIN PIERCE (1804–1869), U.S. President, Letter, 1832.

In efforts to soar above our nature we invariably fall below it. Your reformist demigods are merely devils turned inside out. EDGAR ALLAN POE (1809–1849), *Marginalia,* 1849.

No generation must be sacrificed for the sake of future generations, for the sake of an ideal of happiness that may never be realized. SIR KARL POPPER, 1968.

We can never return to the alleged innocence and beauty of the closed society. Our dream of heaven cannot be realized on earth. Once we begin to rely on our reason, and to use our powers of criticism, once we feel the call of personal responsibilities, and, with it, the responsibility of helping to advance knowledge, we cannot return to tribal magic. SIR KARL POPPER, *The Open Society and Its Enemies,* 1966.

The utopian method must lead to a dangerous dogmatic attachment to a blueprint for which countless sacrifices have been made. Powerful interests must become linked up with the success of the experiment. All this does not contribute to the rationality, or to the scientific value, of the experiment. SIR KARL POPPER, *The Open Society and Its Enemies,* 1966.

Of all political ideals, that of making the people happy is perhaps the most dangerous one. It leads invariably to the attempt to impose our scale of "higher" values upon others, in order to make them realize what seems to us of the greatest importance for their happiness; in order, as it were, to save their souls. It leads to utopianism and romanticism. . . . But . . . the attempt to make heaven on earth invariably produces hell. It leads to intolerance. It leads to religious laws, and to the saving of souls through the inquisition. SIR KARL POPPER, *The Open Society and Its Enemies,* 1966.

Every major horror of history was committed in the name of an altruistic motive. AYN RAND (1905–1982), *The Fountainhead,* 1943.

Do not fool yourself by thinking that altruists are motivated by compassion for the suffering; they are motivated by hatred for the successful. AYN RAND (1905–1982), 1982.

Men are created different; they lose their social freedom and their individual autonomy in seeking to become like each other. DAVID RIESMAN, *The Lonely Crowd,* 1950.

Nobody does good to men with impunity. AUGUSTE RODIN (1840–1917).

Truth is the same for all of us, but every nation has its own lie, which it calls idealism. ROMAIN ROLLAND (1866–1944), *Jean-Christophe.*

There is nothing in the human condition that is pure, ideal or absolute! Death is perfectly absolute and a certainty, but once that is achieved the individual in question is no longer human. To any extent that our culture propels us in the direction of purity it pushes us either to unreality or to death or to both. THEODORE ISAAC RUBIN, *Compassion and Self-Hatred,* 1975.

Much that passes for idealism is disguised hatred or disguised love of power. BERTRAND RUSSELL (1872–1970), *Atlantic Monthly,* January 1952.

I discovered to my amazement that average men and women were delighted at the prospect of war. I had fondly imagined what most pacifists contended, that wars were forced upon a reluctant population by despotic and Machiavellian governments. BERTRAND RUSSELL (1872–1970), *Autobiography,* 1967–69.

The dignity of the individual demands that he not be reduced to vassalage by the largess of others. ANTOINE de SAINT-EXUPÉRY (1900–1944), *Flight to Arras,* 1942.

Revolutions are ambiguous things. Their success is generally proportionate to their power of adaptation and to the reabsorption within them of what they rebelled against. GEORGE SANTAYANA (1863–1952), *The Life of Reason,* 1905–06.

A thousand reforms have left the world as corrupt as ever, for each successful reform has founded a new institution, and this institution has bred its new and congenial abuses. GEORGE SANTAYANA (1863–1952), *The Life of Reason,* 1905–06.

Ideal society is a drama enacted exclusively within our imagination. GEORGE SANTAYANA (1863–1952), *The Life of Reason,* 1905–06.

The superiority of the distant over the present is only due to the mass and variety of the pleasures that can be suggested, compared with the poverty of those which can at any time be felt. GEORGE SANTAYANA (1863–1952), *Little Essays,* 1920.

Let us take men as they are, not as they ought to be. FRANZ SCHUBERT (1797–1828), Diary, June 16, 1816.

Market-like arrangements . . . reduce the need for compassion, patriotism, brotherly love, and cultural solidarity as motivating forces. Harnessing the "base" motive of material self-interest . . . is perhaps the most important social invention mankind has achieved. C. L. SCHULTZE, *Public Use of the Private Interest,* 1977.

The first thing a man will do for his ideals is lie. JOSEPH A. SCHUMPETER (1883–1950), *History of Economic Analysis,* 1954.

It is difficult to change nature. LUCIUS ANNAEUS SENECA (4 B.C.–65 A.D.), *On Anger.*

Intellectuals are prone to romanticize about the past, so that when one speaks of something dying out historically it means that the dead past was better. That is a peculiar blindness of much utopian thinking: since the past was better than the present, the future ought to restore the past. RICHARD SENNETT, *The Uses of Disorder: Personal Identity and City Life,* 1970.

When a man's vision of order, of a pure and painless life, has been defeated by a social world too complex to be disciplined, the man isn't defeated, only his belief in his omnipotence is. RICHARD SENNETT, *The Uses of Disorder: Personal Identity and City Life,* 1970.

We preoccupy ourselves so much with changing the lives of others not out of proclaimed sentiments of selfness human charity, but out of our selfish desire to validate our own identities. There is, of course, enormous ego gratification in the exercise of power over other people, but such satisfaction is rooted in our need to have others believe and behave as we do. BUTLER D. SHAFFER, *Calculated Chaos,* 1985.

Dreams are the children of an idle brain, / Begot of nothing but vain fantasy; / Which is as thin of substance as the air, / And more inconstant than the wind. WILLIAM SHAKESPEARE (1564–1616), *Romeo and Juliet,* 1596.

How hard it is to hide the sparks of nature. WILLIAM SHAKESPEARE (1564–1616), *Cymbeline,* 1609.

Self-sacrifice enables us to sacrifice other people without blushing. GEORGE BERNARD SHAW (1856–1950), *Man and Superman,* 1903.

When they come downstairs from their ivory towers, idealists are apt to walk straight into the gutter. LOGAN PEARSALL SMITH (1865–1946), *Afterthoughts*, 1931.

During the Terror, the men who spilt most blood were precisely those who had the greatest desire to let their equals enjoy the golden age they had dreamt of, and who had the most sympathy with human wretchedness: optimists, idealists, and sensitive men, the greater desire they had for universal happiness the more inexorable they showed themselves. GEORGES SOREL (1847–1922), *Reflections on Violence*, 1910.

Never let man imagine that he can pursue a good end by evil means. Any other issue is doubtful; the evil effect on himself is certain. ROBERT SOUTHEY (1774–1843).

Policies are judged by their consequences but crusades are judged by how good they make the crusaders feel. THOMAS SOWELL, *Compassion versus Guilt*, 1987.

Those who are believed to be most abject and humble are usually most ambitious and envious. BARUCH SPINOZA (1632–1677), *Ethics*, 1677.

A race of altruists is necessarily a race of slaves. MAX STIRNER (1806–1856), *The Ego and His Own*, 1845.

Those who set out to be their brother's keeper sometimes end up by becoming his jailer. Every emancipation has within it the seeds of a new slavery, and every truth can easily become a lie. I. F. STONE, 1969.

[L. A.] Coser also observes that social conflicts are most radical and merciless when the participants are idealistic and righteous. These participants deny personal motivation and insist they are fighting for the ideal of the group. This coincides with the righteous indignation noted in the paranoid, who will deny any personal motive but justify physical attack on his persecutors. DAVID W. SWANSON et al., *The Paranoid*, 1970.

The totalitarian democratic school . . . is based upon the assumption of a sole and exclusive truth in politics. It may be called political Messianism in the sense that it postulates a preordained, harmonious and perfect scheme of things, to which men are irresistibly driven and at which they are bound to arrive. J. L. TALMON, *The Rise of Totalitarian Democracy*, 1952.

If anything ail a man, so that he does not perform his functions, if he have a pain in his bowels even—for that is the seat of sympathy—he forthwith sets about reforming the world. HENRY DAVID THOREAU (1817–1862), *Walden*, 1854.

The impotence of utopia is the fact that its negative content of untruth and unfruitfulness leads inevitably to disillusionment. Those who suffer such disillusionment may become fanatics against their own past. This is especially true of those—the intelligentsia above all—who at some time in their life committed themselves to a utopia. . . . PAUL TILLICH (1886–1965), in *Utopians and Utopian Thought*, 1966.

Americans are so enamoured of equality that they would be equal in slavery than unequal in freedom. ALEXIS de TOCQUEVILLE (1805–1859), *Democracy in America*, 1835.

I sit on a man's back, choking him and making him carry me, and yet assure myself and others that I am very sorry for him and wish to ease his lot by all possible means—except by getting off his back. LEO TOLSTOY (1828–1910).

Nothing so needs reforming as other people's habits. MARK TWAIN (1835–1910), *Pudd'nhead Wilson*, 1894.

Reformers are people who bear a commission from no one, who as a rule, are least informed on the principles of government, but who insist on exercising the power of government to make their neighbors live the lives they desire to prescribe for them. OSCAR W. UNDERWOOD (1862–1929).

The best is the enemy of the good. VOLTAIRE (1694–1778), *Philosophical Dictionary*, 1764.

Tyrants have no consciences, and reformers no feeling; and the world suffers both by the plague and by the cure. HORACE WALPOLE (1717–1797), Letter, 1790.

One common feature of utopia is a class of voluntary nobility or nonhereditary aristocracy, like Plato's philosophers or Wells's samurai. Where these exist, power rests with them. All in all, utopia seems more inclined to distrust the masses than the classes. CHAD WALSH, *From Utopia to Nightmare*, 1962.

From the utopian viewpoint, the United States constitution is a singularly hardbitten and cautious document, for it breathes the spirit of skepticism about human altruism and incorporates a complex system of checks, balances and restrictions, so that everybody is holding the reins on everybody else. CHAD WALSH, *From Utopia to Nightmare*, 1962.

Modern ideologists normally tend . . . to define their goals in unrealistically optimistic terms . . . [and they have a habit of] thinking in oversimplified terms of we and they, of friend and enemy. This is, indeed, a natural corollary and symptom of their basic utopianism. Anyone who believes that his goals are absolutely and overwhelmingly in the public interest will suspect something sinister about the motives of those who reject his conclusions. FREDERICK M. WATKINS, *The Age of Ideology—Political Thought, 1750 to the Present*, 1964.

The transformation from at worst eccentric, otherworldly, impractical utopianism to cold, paranoid inhumanity often appears to take place from one day to another. . . . [T]he psychological and intellectual consequences of believing in an ideology can be of a demonic pitilessness, in comparison with which the deeds of a hardened criminal only look like regrettable impertinence. PAUL WATZLAWICK, *The Invented Reality*, 1984.

It is always with the best intentions that the worst work is done. OSCAR WILDE (1854–1900), *Intentions,* 1891.

The worse form of tyranny the world has ever known is the tyranny of the weak over the strong. It is the only tyranny that lasts. OSCAR WILDE (1854–1900).

Every political good carried to the extreme must be productive of evil. MARY WOLLSTONECRAFT (1759–1797), *The French Revolution,* 1794.

The ideal can lead to killing men for the glory of the Good in the expectation that the Good will be served and will appropriately bless the killer with a crown of glory. F. J. E. WOODBRIDGE, *An Essay on Nature,* 1940.

I believe in the brotherhood of man, all men, but I don't believe in brotherhood with anybody who doesn't want brotherhood with me. I believe in treating people right, but I'm not going to waste my time trying to treat somebody right who doesn't know how to return that treatment. MALCOLM X (1925–1965), Speech, December 12, 1964.

I am little concerned with beauty or perfection. I don't care for the great centuries. All I care about is life, struggle, intensity. I am at ease in my generation. ÉMILE ZOLA (1840–1902), *My Hates,* 1866.

Index of Names

Abel, Lionel, 38
Abelard, Peter, 265
Abelson, Herbert I., 210
Acton, Lord, 38, 105, 118, 148, 157, 305, 326
Adams, Abigail, 305
Adams, Brooks, 9, 60
Adams, Franklin P., 84
Adams, Henry Brooks, 84, 305
Adams, Ian, 105
Adams, John, 60, 84, 118, 201, 218, 239, 305, 326
Adams, John Quincy, 60, 201
Adams, Maude, 239
Adams, Samuel, 118
Addison, Joseph, 38, 157, 218, 288
Adler, Alfred, 185, 326
Adler, Felix, 288
Aeschylus, 24, 288, 306
Aesop, 239
Agar, Herbert, 38, 84
Agar, Sabastien, 60
Agnew, Spiro, 218
Aiken, Henry David, 105
Alain, 38, 265
Alcott, A. Bronson, 157
Alcott, Louisa May, 326
Aldrich, Thomas Baily, 288, 306
Alexander, Hamilton, 311
Alinsky, Saul, 201
Allen, Robert W., 140, 201, 288
Allen, Wayne, 105, 106
Allport, Gordon, 288
Alther, Lisa, 239
American Heritage Dictionary, 84
Ameringer, Oscar, 84
Amiel, Henri Frédéric, 38, 84, 157, 239, 265
Amis, Kingsley, 84
Anderson, Maxwell, 306

Andrieux, L., 148
Angell, Sir Norman, 218, 326
Annesley, James, 239
Anouilh, Jean, 201
Antisthenes, 24
Aquinas, Saint Thomas, 239
Ardry, Robert, 38
Arendt, Hannah, 24, 148, 185, 201
Aretino, Pietro, 38
Aristophanes, 38
Aristotle, 9, 24, 38, 39, 85, 148, 185, 239, 288
Arnall, Ellis G., 39
Arnauld, Antoine, 239
Arnold, Matthew, 157
Arnold, Thurman, 9
Aron, Raymond, 106, 158, 240, 278, 326
Aronson, Elliot, 179, 215
Arrianus, Flavius, 240
Ashmore, Harry S., 85
Asimov, Isaac, 240
Atgeld, John Peter, 60
Atherton, Gertrude, 39, 265
Atkinson, Brooks, 85, 218, 265, 288, 326
Augustine, Saint, 158
Austen, Jane, 240
Austin, J. L., 39
Ayer, A. J., 158
Aytoun, William E., 158
Azuela, Mariono, 148

Bacon, Sir Francis, 9, 24, 60, 158, 240, 326
Bagdikian, Ben, 60
Bagehot, Walter, 9, 39, 106, 140, 218, 326
Bailey, F. G., 201, 240
Bailey, F. Lee, 9
Baker, Russell, 24, 39
Bakunin, Mikhail A., 9, 39, 85, 118, 148, 158, 278, 327